GERMAN JEWRY
BETWEEN HOPE AND DESPAIR

—————— EDITED BY NILS ROEMER ——————

Series: Jews in Space and TIme

Library of Congress Cataloging-in-Publication Data :
The bibliographic data for this title is available from the Library of Congress.

ISBN 978-1-934843-87-1 (hardback); ISBN 979-8-897830-93-0 (paperback)
Book design by Olga Grabovsky
On the cover: Hermann Junker. Kol Nidre service in Metz, 1870.
Postcard

Published by Academic Studies Press in 2013. Paperback 2025
1007 Chestnut St., Newton, MA 02464, USA
press@academicstudiespress.com
www.academicstudiespress.com

CONTENTS

ACKNOWLEDGEMENT

Some chapters of this volume have previously appeared in print in the following publications:

- Steven Aschheim, "German Jews Beyond Bildung and Liberalism: The Radical Jewish Revival in the Weimar Republic," *Culture and Catastrophe: German and Jewish Confrontations with National Socialism and Other Crisis*. New York: New York University Press, 1996, 31-44. Reprinted with permission of New York University Press.

- Avraham Barkai, "Between Deutschtum and Judentum: Ideological Controversies within the Centralverein," Michael Brenner and Derek J. Penslar, ed., *In Search of Jewish Community: Jewish Identities in Germany and Austria, 1918-1933*. Bloomington: Indiana University Press, 1998, 74-9 Reprinted with permission of Indiana University Press.

- Delphine Bechtel, "Cultural Transfers Between Ostjuden und Westjuden: German-Jewish Intellectuals and Yiddish Culture, 1897-1930," *Yearbook of the Leo Baeck Institute* 42 (1997): 67-83. Reprinted with permission of Oxford University Press.

- David Brenner, *Kafka's Kitsch: Laughter, Tears, and Yiddish Theater in Pre-Weimar*. London and New York: Routledge, 2008, 1-3, 5-8, and 12-28. Reprinted with permission of Routledge.

- Michael Brenner, "Gemeinschaft and Gemeinde: The Ideological and Institutional Transformation of the Jewish Community," *The Renaissance of Jewish Culture in Weimar Germany*. Princeton: Princeton University Press, 1996, 36-65. Reprinted with permission of Princeton University Press.

- Willi Goetschel, "Inside and Outside the University: Philosophy as Way and Problem in Cohen, Buber, and Rosenzweig." *The Discipline of Philosophy and the Invention of Modern Jewish Thought*. New York: Fordham University Press, 2013, 58-82. Reprinted with permission of Fordham University Press.

- Marion A. Kaplan, "Redefining Judaism in Imperial Germany: Practices, Mentalities, and Community," *Jewish Social Studies* 9 (2002), 1-33. Reprinted with permission of Indiana University Press.

- George L. Mosse, *The Jews and the German War Experience, 1914-1918*, Leo Baeck Memorial Lecture 21. New York: Leo Baeck Institute, 1977. Reprinted with permission of the Leo Baeck Institute, New York.

- Peter Pulzer, "Jews and Nation Building in Germany, 1815-1918," *Yearbook of the Leo Baeck Institute* 41 (1996): 199-217. Reprinted with permission of Oxford University Press.

- Nils Roemer, "A Jewish *Heimat* on Borrowed Time," *German Cities – Jewish Memories: The Story of Worms*. Hanover: Brandeis University Press, 2010, 118-141. Reprinted with permission of Brandeis University Press.

For Cricket, Max, Wyatt, Jonas, and Jackson

INTRODUCTION

Nils Roemer

Historical documents reflecting the diverse history of German Jewry have survived in libraries and museums, research institutes, and archives around the world. Next to official papers of local, regional, and state agencies, the archives of German Jewry include records from Jewish organisations, publications by individuals, memoirs, autobiographies, poems, novels, paintings, and musical scores, to name just a few. Collecting, surveying, and interpreting these scattered records became a formidable task. In an effort to give voice to the complicated modern German Jewish experience, German Jewish studies emerged after the Holocaust as a new, international focus of research at the intersection of various already established academic disciplines. Historical, literary, religious, and philosophical studies converged in the making of this discipline.

After the Holocaust, Leo Baeck, the last president of the umbrella organisation that had united German Jewry from 1933 to 1938, served as president of the Council of Jews from Germany.[1] In 1950, Baeck appealed in London for efforts to ensure the survival of German Jewry's achievements in the various countries of immigration. At a preliminary meeting in London held in August 1955, a number of German Jewish scholars debated establishing a research institution dedicated to the study of German Jewry.[2] Following this and similar deliberations, the council established the Leo Baeck Institute with offices in Jerusalem,

---

[1]   Hermann Muller, "Aus der Gründungzeit des Council of Jews from Germany," in *Zwei Welten. Siegried Moses zum Fünfundsiebzigsten Geburtstag* (Tel Aviv: Bitaon, 1962, 184–199).

[2]   "Leo Baeck Institute," *AJR Information* 10 (July 1955), 1.

London, and New York in May 1955.[3] It would be the institute's task, Weltsch, the former editor of a German Zionist newspaper, argued, to "keep alive the memory of German Jewry, in particular in the form it took from the Emancipation until the collapse of the Weimar Republic."[4]

Several émigré historians who were less involved in the work of the Leo Baeck Institute, such as Peter Gay, Walter Laqueur, George Mosse, and Fritz Stern, also sought to come to terms with German history. In comparison to their peers in postwar Germany, who promoted a new social history, the German Jewish historians struck out a different approach and understanding of modern German history. Their distinct life experiences shaped their perspective on the traumatic events of the twentieth century. To varying degrees, these German Jewish historians, who produced some of the most influential interpretations of modern German history, eventually contributed a great deal to the study of the German Jewish experience. While they came to define the contours of German history, they eventually also profoundly shaped the understanding of German Jewish history, particularly in the English-speaking world.

The cultural historian of the Enlightenment, the fin de siècle, and the Weimar Republic, Peter Gay, who taught at Columbia and Yale Universities, wrote extensively on German Jewish intellectual history. His research on German Jews was part of a much larger study, in which he famously claimed that the German Jewish outsiders were the true insiders of Weimar culture.[5] In his autobiography, *My German Question: Growing Up in Nazi Berlin* (1998), he recalled his own upbringing and recounted the perplexities and ambiguities of the perception of the Nazi regime amongst German Jews.

George Mosse, who in a succession of books offered a novel interpretation of fascism, wrote extensively on German Jews. He published several articles in the journal and volumes of the Leo

---

3   Minutes of the meeting of the Council of Jews from Germany, Israel Section, May 31, 1955.
4   Minutes of a meeting organized by LBI London, October 16, 1955, *LBI Archives New York*, AR 6682, box 6, folder 1.
5   Peter Gay, *Weimar Culture: The Outsider as Insider* (New York: Harper and Row, 1970) and Peter Gay, *The Berlin-Jewish Spirit: A Dogma in Search of Some Doubts* (New York: Leo Baeck Institute, 1972).

Baeck Institute and gave a Memorial Lecture on Jews and the First World War, reprinted in the present volume. In 1998, in recognition of his valuable contributions, he received the Leo Baeck Medal of the Leo Baeck Institute, and in 2000, he published his memoirs.[6] In his autobiography, he stated that his *German Jews Beyond Judaism* (1985) "is certainly my most personal book, almost a confession of faith."[7] *German Jews Beyond Judaism* did not just elaborate on the unique way in which German Jews adopted the ideals of *Bildung* to create a unique German Jewish subculture, but sought to rehabilitate a form of Jewish identity that Mosse deemed worthy of not just remembrance but also inspiration.

Laqueur, who wrote the foreword to Mosse's autobiography, served for many years as the director of the Wiener Library, which by 1939 had been transferred from Amsterdam to London. The library collected and disseminated information about the unfolding Holocaust and became a centre of research on the Holocaust after World War II. Laqueur, who succeeded Wiener as the director of the library, also contributed to the work of the Leo Baeck Institute, whose London branch shared the same address as the Wiener Library. In 1979, Laqueur gave a memorial lecture at the Leo Baeck Institute titled "The First News of the Holocaust."[8]

In New York, Fritz Stern illuminated in his *The Politics of Cultural Despair* (1963) the forces aiding the rise of National Socialism in

---

[6] Mosse, published, for example, "The Image of the Jew in German Popular Culture: Felix Dahn and Gustav Freytag," *Leo Baeck Institute Year Book* 2 (1957), 218–227; "The Influence of the Völkisch Idea on German Jewry," in *Studies of the Leo Baeck Institute*, ed., Max Kreutzberger (New York: Frederik Unger, 1967), 81–115; "German Socialists and the Jewish Question in the Weimar Republic," *Leo Baeck Institute Year Book* 16 (1971), 123–151; "Deutsche Juden und der Liberalismus. Ein Rückblick," *Das deutsche Judentum und der Liberalismus - German Jewry and Liberalism* (London: Comdok-Verlagsabteilung, 1986), 173–191; "German Jews and Liberalism in Retrospect. Introduction to Year Book XXXII," *Leo Baeck Institute Year Book* 32 (1987), xiii-xxv.

[7] George L. Mosse, *Confronting History: A Memoir*, with a foreword by Walter Laqueur (Madison: University of Wisconsin Press, 2000), 184.

[8] Walter Laqueur, "The German Youth Movement and the 'Jewish Question': A Preliminary Survey," *Leo Baeck Institute YearBook* 6 (1961), 193–205; Walter Laqueur, *Generation Exodus, The Fate of Young Jewish Refugees from Nazi Germany* (Hanover: Brandeis University Press, 2000); Walter Laqueur, "First News of the Holocaust," *Leo Baeck Institute Memorial Lecture* 23 (1979).

Germany, and in *Gold and Iron* (1977) he focused on the contentious relationship between Jews and Germans through the prism of Gerson Bleichröder, the personal banker and friend of Otto von Bismarck. In his memoir and study, *Five Germanys I Have Known* (2006), he recalls his own life to trace the transformation of German history. Stern, who served as director of the Leo Baeck Institute in New York, gave a memorial lecture at the Institute in 1984, entitled "Germany 1933: Fifty Years Later."[9] Accepting the Leo Baeck Medal in 2005, he noted that "to have witnessed even as a child the descent in Germany from decency to barbarism gave the question 'how was it possible' an existential immediacy. So I did no more than what others of my generation did as well: wrestle with that question, try to reconstruct some parts of the past, perhaps intuit some lessons."[10]

To these émigré historians as well as to other supporters of the Leo Baeck Institute, the history of German Jewry formed an object of immense personal and intellectual interest. Personal memories of harassment, intimidation, exile, and murder led to attempts to chronicle and comprehend the dynamics of the modern German Jewish experience. Therefore, the period from the founding of the Kaiserreich to the end of the Weimar Republic initially received special attention.

Legal equality that had hitherto only existed in several German territories and often with limitations came to all German Jews in 1871 with the creation of the Reich. The new opportunities ushered in intensified urbanisation and migration and increased social upward mobility, which together quickly transformed the Jews of Germany during the Kaiserreich into a highly visible element of the educated and urban German middle class. Jews in Germany experienced not just a high degree of urbanisation but moved in great numbers in particular to the metropolitan center of Berlin. In 1860, Berlin had a Jewish population of 19,000. By 1925, the German capital had 173,000 Jewish residents.

---

9   Fritz Stern, "Germany 1933: Fifty Years Later," *Leo Baeck Institute Memorial Lecture* 27 (1984).

10   http://www.lbi.org/fritzstern.html. See also "'Historian of Fate': Fritz Stern on the History of German Jewry: An Appreciation," *Fritz Stern at 70* (German Historical Institute Occasional Paper No. 19; Washington, D.C., 1997), 33–42.

The urbanisation and centralisation aided the ongoing process of integrating into the German middle class. The Jewish inhabitants of Berlin, with full access to the school system and institutions of higher education, took advantage of the new opportunities. The educational profile of the Jewish families started to look decisively different from that of their non-Jewish peers. The average educational level was far higher than that of the majority Christian population. Around 1900, the proportion of Jewish pupils at high schools represented one-third (compared to only 5 percent in the rest of the population). In the German Reich's universities at the beginning of the twentieth century, around 10 percent of all German Jews studied toward a higher degree (compared to around 1 percent for the general population).[11]

Reflecting their high educational profile, Jews became disproportionately overrepresented in the middle class and in the liberal political culture. Jews' social and economic advances, technological progress, and scientific discoveries gave rise to a sense of optimism. German Jews initially shared the optimism that was most ingrained in the propertied and educated middle class of the German society. Yet German Jewish responses to the turning of the century indicated a profound change in the face of renewed antisemitism and increasing concerns about weakened Jewish identities. German Jewry looked to the future with concern and dismay and no longer had the idea of unmitigated progress in common with the German bourgeoisie. As one of the many articles of the time lamented, "Also the past century was not free of faults, and its biggest failure was that it did not keep its promise in old age that it had made in its youth; it destroyed in its old age that which it had erected in its youth."[12]

A revival of antisemitism spurred this critical assessment. The court chaplain, Adolf Stoecker, had agitated in the late 1870s against Jews, joined by the liberal and eminent historian Heinrich von Treitschke, who gave legitimacy to antisemitic voices in his annual review in the

---

11   For a succinct discussion of the success and its limits of German Jewry in a European comparative perspective, see Reinhard Rürup, "A Success Story and Its Limits: European Jewish Social History in the Nineteenth and Early Twentieth Centuries," *Jewish Social Studies* 11:1 (2004), 3–15.

12   J. Kohn, "Zur Jahrhundertwende," *AZJ* 64 (1900), 76–78, here 77.

Preussische Jahrbücher, declaring Jews a national misfortune. While Treitschke had the *reputation* of a liberal who rejected the theological and racial attacks upon the Jews, he constructed the image of an "international Jewry" that undermined the ideal of German unity.[13]

In the ensuing public debate after Treitschke's indictment of German Jews in the so-called *Berliner Antisemitismusstreit*, Jewish commentators like Moritz Lazarus seized on the model of regional diversity to forge a framework for the multiplicity of German traditions that allowed for the assertion of Jewish particularisms. To him, *Volk* was not an ethnically homogenous entity but an intellectual and cultural construction based on a common language. By renegotiating the concept of nationhood, Lazarus's defence, which was unanimously praised in the Jewish press, put forward a vision of German society that radically differed from the view held by many German liberals insofar as it promoted cultural diversity.[14]

This tacit reorientation that underlined Lazarus's idea of identity and culture provided a framework for a renewal of Jewish culture at a time when economic troubles alleviated the situation, and by the 1890s, the antisemitic party had failed to make significant inroads. Emperor Wilhelm II even demoted his chaplain. However, even without an electoral success, antisemitic opinions had saturated the German public. Despair and hope therefore coexisted and gave impetus to the creation of new cultural and religious institutions. The year Treitschke's article was published, the *Deutsch-Israelitische Gemeindebund* launched an initiative to alter the public's perception of Judaism. On Moses Mendelssohn's 150th birthday, the *Gemeindebund* called for the commemoration of the Jewish Enlightener. The 1879 celebration of Mendelssohn's 150th birthday apostrophised and memorialised the

---

[13]   Nils Roemer, *Between History and Faith: Rewriting the Past—Reshaping Jewish Cultures in Nineteenth-Century Germany* (Madison: Wisconsin University Press, 2005), 81–91.

[14]   Moritz Lazarus, *Was heißt national? Ein Vortrag von Prof. Dr. M. Lazarus, mit einem Vorwort von Isid. Levy* (Berlin: Philo Verlag, 1925), 46. On the importance of the concept of Stamm, see Till van Rahden, "'Germans of the Jewish Stamm': Visions of Community between Nationalism and Particularism, 1850 to 1933," in *German History from the Margins, 1800 to the Present*, ed., Neil Gregor, Nils Roemer, and Mark Roseman (Bloomington: Indiana University Press, 2006), 27–48.

Jewish Enlightener in tandem with Gotthold Friedrich Lessing to represent the German Jewish symbiosis. As the many contributions indicate, Mendelssohn became the prism through which German Jews illustrated, above all, their place within the German society.[15]

Notwithstanding the more narrow focus of the German Jewish past, the *Gemeindebund* called for the establishment of new Mendelssohn societies to "awaken and maintain an interest for Judaism and its noble ideas, and a feeling of unity and community ... among our younger generation."[16] Thus, the celebration of Mendelssohn that otherwise explicated Jews' affinity for Germany facilitated the recollection of the Jewish tradition in general. Following along similar lines, in 1885 the *Gemeindebund* also established the *Historische Commission* that became the first concerted effort to inscribe the history of the Jews into the annals of the German past. In following the model of *Monumenta Germaniae Historica*, the organisation published valuable sources of medieval Jewish history until it folded in 1892.[17] More successful and lasting was Eugen Täubler's creation of the *Gesamtarchiv der deutschen Juden* (Central Archive of the German Jews) in October 1905, with the support of the *Deutsch-Israelitische Gemeindebund*, the B'nai B'rith, and the financial assistance of several larger Jewish communities like Berlin, Frankfurt a. M., Breslau, and Hamburg.[18]

Between the creation of the Historische Commission and the founding of the Gesamtarchiv, the popularisation of Jewish history had reached a new level. The *Allgemeine Zeitung des Judenthums* proclaimed in 1893 that an association for Jewish history and literature was founded on almost a weekly basis.[19] Approximately 48

---

15   Willi Goetschel, "Lessing, Mendelssohn, Nathan: German-Jewish Myth-Building as an Act of Emancipation," *Lessing Yearbook* 32 (2000), 341–360; and Christhard Hoffmann, "Constructing Jewish Modernity: Mendelssohn Jubilee Celebrations within German Jewry, 1829–1929," in *Towards Normality? Acculturation and Modern German Jewry*, ed., Rainer Liedtke and David Rechter (Tübingen: Mohr Siebeck, 2003), 27–52.

16   "Leipzig" *AZJ* 43 (1879), 163–164, here 163.

17   Roemer, *Between History and Faith: Rewriting the Past—Reshaping Jewish Cultures in Nineteenth-Century Germany*, 95–96.

18   "Bericht über die Tätigkeit des Gesamtarchivs der deutschen Juden," *Mitteilungen des Gesamtarchivs der deutschen Juden* 3 (1911), 55–84.

19   "Berlin," *Der Gemeindebote. Beilage zur AZJ* 57 (December 1, 1893), 1.

local associations existed before the nationwide umbrella organisation was formally constituted in Hannover in 1893. By 1900, the Union of Associations for Jewish History and Literature in Germany had become one of the largest Jewish organisations in Germany, with 12,149 members in 131 local societies.[20]

Antisemitism was not the sole reason for the developing renaissance of Jewish culture. Yet a still widely accepted view amongst scholars attributes the eventual transformation of the erstwhile Viennese playwright and journalist Theodor Herzl into the founder and leader of the Zionist movement in large part to the revival of antisemitism. In 1897, Herzl published *The Jewish State* and formed and convened the First Zionist Congress in Basel. According to the adapted program, Zionism not only sought a "home for the Jewish people in Eretz-Israel secured under public law," but aimed at the "strengthening and fostering of Jewish national sentiment and national consciousness."[21]

The very location of the first Zionist congress indicated both a lack of support amongst the broader segments of the German Jewish communities and also antagonism. The so-called *Protestrabbiner* challenged Herzl's original intention of Munich as the place of the Congress on political, religious, and cultural grounds, believing that Zionism presented a threat to their political loyalty to the German State. Moreover, they contended that to create a Jewish state in Palestine contradicted the basic premise of Jewish messianic expectations.[22]

Regardless of the debates about national and cultural-religious definitions of Jews that divided the camps, the Zionist cultural ambitions easily meshed with the already ongoing revival of Jewish culture. Moreover, the political conflict between Zionists and their opponents was less pronounced within Germany, where the Zionists

---

[20] In 1903, 180 local associations existed with over 15,000 individual members. By 1914, the number had climbed to 230 associations. See "Hundert Literaturvereine," *AZJ* 62 (1898), 553–555; "Mittheilungen aus dem Verband der Vereine für jüdische Geschichte und Literatur in Deutschland," *JJLG* 2 (1899), 269–300, here 271 and 278.

[21] Paul Mendes-Flohr and Jehuda Reinharz, ed., *The Jews in the Modern World: A Documentary History* (New York: Oxford University Press, 1995), 540.

[22] The declaration by the *Protestrabbiner* is reprinted in Paul Mendes-Flohr and Jehuda Reinharz, ed., *The Jew in the Modern World*, 538–539.

in Cologne, for example, underscored in their declaration that Jewish patriotism and political loyalty to the German state were not at odds.[23] They intentionally downplayed the political aspect of their nationalist aspirations in favour of their cultural educational activities. The political goals amongst German Zionists remained less pronounced until the Zionist conference in Posen in 1912 and the ascendancy of a more radical generation of German Zionists.[24] Likewise, the democratic fraction within the Zionist movement staged a dramatic walkout of the Fifth Zionist Congress in December 1901.[25] Clashing with the major representatives of the political-diplomatic Zionist faction like Herzl and cultural Zionists Martin Buber, Berthold Feiwal, and Ephraim Lilien put forward Jewish cultural education as an instrumental element in the Zionist rebellion.

Numerically insignificant, Zionism proved more successful in promoting cultural renewal at a time when fin de siècle uncertainties and growing discontent took hold of a generation that was looking for alternative paths to the model of Western European modernisation and rationality. Max Nordau, in his famous *Degeneration*, declared that the age was affected by uncertainty, where all values and norms started to be dislodged from their previous places of common acceptance and gave way to an almost apocalyptic sense of the end of civilisation. Much of the malaise manifested itself particularly in debates about urban life at a time when Jews had moved in disproportionate numbers to the larger urban centres. At the beginning of the twentieth century, the Zionist and director of the Bureau for Jewish Statistics and Demography, Arthur Ruppin, and the Berlin dermatologist Felix Theilhaber, associated urban centres with decay, fragmentation, rampant assimilation, and intermarriage. For Theilhaber, large cities had a levelling and deadening

---

[23] "Thesen zur national-jüdischen Vereinigung Köln," in *Im Anfang der zionistischen Bewegung eine Dokumentation auf der Grundlage des Briefwechsels zwischen Theodor Herzl und Max Bodenheimer von 1896 bis 1905*, ed., Henriette Hannah Bodenheimer (Frankfurt a. M.: Europäische Verlags-Anstalt, 1965), 22–23.

[24] Michael A. Meyer, "Liberal Judaism and Zionism in Germany," in *Judaism Within Modernity: Essays on Jewish History and Religion* (Detroit: Wayne State University Press, 2001), 239–255 and Stephen M. Poppel, *Zionism in Germany, 1897–1933: The Shaping of a Jewish Identity*, 45–67.

[25] *Stenographisches Protokoll der Verhandlungen des V. Zionisten-Congresses in Basel, 26, 27, 28, 29, and 30 December 1901* (Vienna: Erez Israel, 1901), 389–402 and 418–429.

influence where economic life in particular threatened the observance of the Sabbath; the urban environment probed and challenged the vitality of Jewish culture.[26] This diagnosis was part of the Zionist critique of the Diaspora that had absorbed the major tenets of the anti-urban discourse of the fin de siècle.

Zionists like Adolf Friedemann and others compared and contrasted the faltering Jewish identities of Jewish life in urban centres with the culture of the Eastern European Jews, who he believed had maintained a deeper sense of *Gemeinschaft*.[27] Searching for alternative paths, the "renaissance of Jewish culture," coined in 1901 by the Jewish philosopher Buber, who was both a Western and Eastern European Jew, was thus partly spurred by a new enchantment with Eastern European Jewry.[28] Journals like *Ost und West*, which began appearing in 1901, and the more short-lived journal *Die Freistatt*, published by Mordechai Kaufmann from 1913 until 1915, aimed to forge a new unity between Western and Eastern European Jews. These periodicals made available to Western Jewry extensive information about the cultural, political, and economic problems of Eastern Jewry and their traditions, as argued by David Brenner.[29]

---

[26] Felix Theilhaber, *Der Untergang der deutschen Juden. Eine volkswirtschaftliche Studie*, 2nd ed. (Berlin: 1911), 67–68; Arthur Ruppin, *Die Juden in der Gegenwart: Eine sozialwissenschaftliche Studie* (Berlin: 1911), 154–179; and Steven M. Lowenstein, "Was Urbanization Harmful to Jewish Tradition and Identity in Germany," *Studies in Contemporary Jewry* 15 (1999), 80–106.

[27] Adolf Friedemann, *Wir und die Ostjuden* (Berlin: Julius Sittenfeld, 1916), 1; Noah Isenberg, *Between Redemption and Doom: The Strains of German-Jewish Modernism* (Lincoln: University of Nebraska Press, 1999), 91–92.

[28] Martin Buber, "Jüdische Wissenschaft," *Die Welt* 5: 41 (1901), 1–2, and 5: 43 (1901), 1–2. In general, see Steven E. Aschheim, *Brothers and Strangers: The East European Jew in German and German Jewish Consciousness, 1800–1923* (Madison: University of Wisconsin Press, 1982), 121–84; Jack Wertheimer, *Unwelcome Strangers: East European Jews in Imperial Germany* (New York: Oxford University Press, 1987); Shulamit Volkov, "The Dynamics of Dissimulation: Ostjuden and German Jews," in *The Jewish Response to German Culture*, ed., Jehuda Reinharz and Walter Schatzberg (Hanover, NH: Published for Clark University by University Press of New England, 1985), 195–211; Paul Mendes-Flohr, "Fin de Siècle Orientalism: The Ostjuden and the Aesthetics of Jewish Self-Affirmation," in *Divided Passions: Jewish Intellectuals and the Experience of Modernity* (Detroit: Wayne State University Press, 1991), 77–132; David A. Brenner, *Marketing Identities: The Invention of Jewish Ethnicity in Ost und West* (Detroit: Wayne State University Press,1998).

[29] David A. Brenner, *Marketing Identities*; and David N. Myers, "'Distant Relatives

The outbreak of the First World War halted cultural renewal, as many German Jews like other Germans enthusiastically greeted the outbreak of the war. Even intellectuals and Zionists like Buber initially responded with euphoric hopes. Wilhelm II's proclamation on August 4, 1914, of a truce in domestic, confessional, socials and political conflicts led many German Jews to believe that the war offered an opportunity to become more fully accepted in Germany society.[30] Yet already Mosse, in his lecture reprinted in this volume, singled out the limits of German Jews' euphoric response and jingoism. Unlike many of their German counterparts, Jews had not abandoned the ideals of the Enlightenment, he asserts. They even continued to hold to the universal ideals of Bildung when many German Gentiles favoured jingoistic nationalism in the form of *völkisch* exclusivism. While some might have seen this dedication to Bildung as a cause of the German Jews' unwillingness to comprehend the approaching disaster, Mosse, in his study of the First World War, singles out the German Jews' commitment to Bildung as saving them from embracing forms of jingoism. More recent studies have detailed German Jews' myriad initial reactions. These studies document the fact that German Jews often responded with criticism, a sense of responsibility, fear, and doubt to the outbreak of war even though defending the German fatherland was self-evident to many. When the fortune on the battlefield turned, the strategy of attrition wore on the army, and home front complaints about the prolongation of the war seized upon the idea that Jews had disproportionally benefited from the war. Addressing these issues, in 1916, the War Ministry conducted a census to determine the number of Jews serving at the front as compared with those at the rear. The result proved the opposite. By 1916, 3,000 Jews had died on the battlefield and more than 7,000 had been decorated. By 1918, 100,000 Jews had fought for Germany, and 12,000 had died in combat. Never released, the census had a devastating effect and laid the groundwork for the view blaming the Jews for the defeat of the German Army in the First

---

Happing onto the Same Inn': The Meeting of East and West as Literary Theme and Cultural Ideal," *Jewish Social Studies* 1 (1995), 75–100.

[30] Ulrich Sieg, *Jüdische Intellektuelle im Ersten Weltkrieg: Kriegserfahrungen, weltanschauliche Debatten und kulturelle Neuentwürfe* (Berlin: Akademie Verlag, 2001).

World War. In the end, as Mosse maintains in his Leo Baeck memorial lecture, the First World War had a lasting negative impact on German Jewish relations.

The First World War, however, was also, in the words of Ute Frevert, an important moment "in terms of foreign encounters." [31] During the war, many German-speaking Jews experienced Eastern European Jews as soldiers of the German Army in the East. The German Jewish philosopher Franz Rosenzweig recorded in his letters to his mother the profound impression Eastern European Jews made upon himself. He confessed that in Poland, he "felt something I rarely feel, pride in my race, in so much freshness and vivacity." He found in the Eastern European Jews an affirmation of his own identity. Even five-year-old Eastern European Jewish children live in the "context of three thousand years."[32]

Rosenzweig's newly found veneration still reverberated with the uncertainty that had brought him only a few years earlier close to conversion. In the same year, the German Jewish writer Arnold Zweig joined the press department of the German Army Supreme Command for the East and collaborated with the artist Hermann Struck on *The Face of Eastern European Jewry*, which appeared in 1919. Neatly divided into distinct units, the book portrays various types of Eastern European Jews and their institutions, religious services, work, politics, and family, culminating in an account of the Jewish youth. Following theories of environmental determinism, Zweig contrasted their endurance, authenticity, and spiritual vitality with Jews of the West, who had "traded part of our soul with Europe, giving up part of our Jewishness."[33] Critical of modern life and Jewish culture in the West, Zweig aimed to document Jews' indestructibility and their orientation toward purity, as he explained in a letter to Buber.[34]

[31] Ute Frevert, "Europeanizing German History," *GHI Bulletin* 36 (Spring, 2005), 9–24, here 13.

[32] Nahum Glatzer, *Franz Rosenzweig: His Life and Thought* (New York: Schocken, 1953), 77.

[33] Arnold Zweig, *The Face of East European Jewry: With Fifty-Two Drawings by Hermann Struck*, ed., and trans. Noah Isenberg (Berkeley: University of California Press, 2004), 1.

[34] See the letter to Martin Buber on May 13, 1918, in Martin Buber, *Briefwechsel aus sieben Jahrzehnten, 1897–1918*, ed., Grete Schaeder (Gerlingen: Lambert Schneider,

The war experience therefore partly strengthened the ongoing fascination with Eastern European Jews and came to reinvigorate Weimar Jewish culture, while the collapse of the political and social imperial order in Germany at the end of the War simultaneously renewed the sense of confidence paired with the proclamation of the Republic. The new progressive government, under the socialist Friedrich Ebert, flanked by political and economic weakness, created a culture marked by violent political clashes and hopes for renewal and regeneration. Writings from this period testify to a measure of hope, as well as a dissatisfaction and weariness with present-day Germany and the state of the Jewish communities.

The concurrence of hope and longing in contrast to crisis and despair makes it all the more challenging to interpret the historical sources. Moreover, for the many historians of this period, the history they investigated represented not simply a distant past but a time associated in their memories with their own lives. Thus, regardless of the focus or emphasis, the interpretation of the modern German Jewish experience remained shaped by the knowledge of the destruction of German Jewry.

With the publication of Raul Hilberg's *The Destruction of the European Jews* (1961), the initial scholarly and memorial work of the Leo Baeck Institute became a contested issue. Hilberg's book made the Holocaust an even more visible element shaping the interest in the German Jew's experience from 1871 to 1933. In his work, Hilberg famously described German Jewry as essentially passive in the face of mortal peril—indeed partly complicit in its own destruction, a reflection of a tradition of compliance that had traditionally served Jews well when they were threatened but inadequate in the new radical circumstances. This thesis was further reinforced in sections of Hannah Arendt's *Eichmann in Jerusalem: A Report on the Banality of Evil*, first appearing in 1961 as a series of articles in the *New Yorker* and in 1963 as a book.

The LBI therefore focused its efforts on the "year of decision," 1932, with publication of a massive volume of essays in 1966. [35] Informed by

---

1972), 1: 534. See also Zweig, *The Face of East European Jewry*, 25.
[35] Werner E. Mosse and Arnold Paucker, ed., *Entscheidungsjahr 1932: Zur Judenfrage in der Endphase der Weimarer Republik. Ein Sammelband* (Tübingen: Mohr Siebeck, 1965).

the ongoing debate over Hilberg and Arendt, the volume's central concern addressed the sources of German Jewry's historical catastrophe—what Werner Mosse, professor of European history at the University of East Anglia and long-time chairman of the London Leo Baeck Institute, termed a problem of "Jewish and German history."[36] Conjointly, the volume sought to correct the idea of German Jewish passivity in the face of Nazism. To this end, the volume included a detailed study of Jewish self-defence efforts by Arnold Paucker, the long-time director of the London LBI, its first sentence summarising the outcome of the evidence he presented: "German Jewry was not idle in engaging the threatening dangers that it faced in the last years of the Weimar Republic."[37]

Another milestone volume of the comprehensive history of German Jewry appeared in 1971, entitled *Deutsches Judentum in Krieg und Revolution*, and treating German Jewish political and cultural activity between 1916 and 1923.[38] The collection of essays aimed overall, as Werner Mosse explained in his introduction, to address the question posed in the earlier volume: that of the sources of German Jewry's catastrophe, now located in a "critical turning point of German history."[39] Mosse and Eva Reichmann's contributions depicted the crisis of the European bourgeoisie and chronicled the transformations in Jewish self-understanding during this period. Mosse focused on the disintegration of civil society, Reichmann on the Great War's impact, the encounter with Eastern European Jews, the Balfour Declaration, the myth of an international Jewish-Bolshevik conspiracy, and the general dashing of German Jewry's high expectations.[40]

In 1976, a new volume in the comprehensive history series appeared, likewise edited by Werner Mosse. Focusing now on the Wilhelminian period, the volume had contributions from British,

---

[36] Mosse and Arnold Paucker, ed., *Entscheidungsjahr 1932*, vii.
[37] Arnold Paucker, "Der Jüdische Abwehrkampf," ibid., 405–499, here 405.
[38] Werner E. Mosse, ed., *Deutsches Judentum in Krieg und Revolution. Juden im Wilhelminischen Deutschland, 1916–1923* (Tübingen: Mohr Siebeck, 1971).
[39] Ibid., vii.
[40] Werner E. Mosse, "Die Krise der europäischen Bourgeoisie und das deutsche Judentum," ibid., 1–26; Eva Reichmann, "Der Bewußtseinswandel der deutschen Juden," ibid., 511–612.

Israeli, American, and German researchers who in part traced the rise and the metamorphosis of sociopolitical antisemitism between 1890 and the Great War's outbreak while outlining the dramatic Jewish encounter with antisemitism and describing Jews' contribution to and participation in Germany's economy and culture. Robert Weltsch finally aimed to strike a balance between the increasingly divergent scholarly agendas; his essay contended that with the greater possibilities available to Jews in *Kaiserzeit* Germany came an unavoidable weakening of Jewish identity.[41]

The study of the period from 1871 to 1933 thus quickly became a conflicted issue that scholars in Germany, Israel, and America were intent on elucidating. Apart from the different interpretations, these various scholars also brought different interests and methods to the study of German Jewry. Others challenged the very concept of German Jews' integration. Gershom Scholem, who had already emigrated to Palestine during the 1920s, dismissed Arendt's view on German Jewry and refuted the notion of a German Jewish dialogue. To him, there had never existed an open society in which Jews and Germans met and exchanged as equals. The many Jewish luminaries in art, music, philosophy, literature, and many other fields were celebrated as Germans, while their Jewish identities were never accepted. In other words, the encounter was a one-sided relationship in which the German Jews were doing all of the listening and adapting. In his memoirs, Scholem recalled that non-Jews never visited his father, who considered himself integrated and accepted.[42] For Scholem, the process of emancipation in Germany had failed and all attempts by Jews to integrate into German society had been illusionary and predicated on them repudiating their Jewishness.[43]

This fulminating dismissal of German Jewish history increasingly turned the attention to cultural and religious self-understanding alongside the larger question about the politics of inclusion and exclusion. This volume seeks to capture some of these varied voices. Far from simply describing Jews' exclusion and marginalisation or

---

[41] Werner Mosse, ed., *Juden im Wilhelminischen Deutschland, 1890–1914*, 689–702.
[42] Gershom Scholem, *On Jews and Judaism in Crisis* (New York: Schocken, 1976), 5.
[43] Gershom Scholem, *Judaica 2* (Frankfurt a. M.: Suhrkamp, 1970), 7–11.

the allegedly unmitigated process of assimilation, the publication of the Leo Baeck Institute, together with other publications, provided the beginnings of an ever more complex and varied account that investigates the identity formation of German Jewry and Jews' integration and acceptance into the German middle class. Where historians of the Holocaust and antisemitism forged a narrative of marginalisation, hatred, and violence, these historians of German Jewry found relative moments of openness and acceptance that complicate any attempt to place the history of German Jewry solely into an accelerating history of harassment and intimidation, eventually culminating in the Holocaust. In the period from 1871 to 1933, hope grated against despair, exclusionary politics against social advancement, and assimilation against renewal.

In his more personal historical introspection, George Mosse summed up much of the research that had accumulated by the early 1980s in his *German Jews beyond Judaism* (1985) and argued that the high level of social success amongst German Jewry occasioned their assimilation to the point that their Jewish identity was essentially formed around the concept of *Bildung*. Mosse concluded that "*Bildung* ... was transformed into a kind of religion—the worship of the true, the good, and the beautiful."[44]

Instead of positing a process whereby Jews increasingly lost their own tradition and became Germans, historians argue today that the period from 1871 to 1933 saw the emergence of a particular Jewish culture that was also German. Marion Kaplan significantly augmented the emphasis on Bildung with a new gender perspective. In *The Making of the Jewish Middle Class* (1991), Kaplan establishes the social and political parameters for the move toward the urban centres and the middle class, while at the same time arguing that the gendered nature of this process bequeathed a new importance on women as the preservers of cultural and religious identity in the family. Particularly in Jewish middle-class families, women cultivated a domestic Judaism. More recently, she developed this line of investigation further by interpreting individuals

---

[44] George Mosse, *German Jews Beyond Judaism* (Bloomington: Indiana University Press, 1997), 11.

in their ambiguities. To Kaplan, they are not simply Germans or Jews but individuals affected by class, gender, and locality.[45]

Like Kaplan's, Till van Rahden's studies testify to the lasting influence of German social studies in terms of methods and sources. Yet he also significantly challenges the established wisdom of viewing German Jews during this period as a fairly homogenous group who, notwithstanding their internal class, religious, and political differences nevertheless formed a cohesive subgroup. To him, the German Jewish communities overlapped in certain ways with German society but barely exhibited the comprehensiveness of, for example, the Catholics in Germany. Rahden's interpretation identifies Jews neither as members of a self-contained milieu nor as an excluded minority, but places them simultaneously as part of Jewish, German Jewish, and German history.

Traditional middle-class orientation also did not exhaust Jews' cultural orientation. Jews were prominent in the circus industry, the Jargon theatres, and revue shows as producers and consumers. Building on this growing research, David Brenner's article takes the modernist writer Franz Kafka (1883–1924), who was fond of popular culture, especially the cinema, as his starting point. "Film," Brenner writes, "was able to tear him [Kafka] away from his desk, from the fever of literature, from writing as 'a form of prayer.'" Preferring the cinema and popular Yiddish theatre to "legitimate" drama, Kafka moved from Prague to Berlin in the final years of his life and embraced the diversion of the bustling metropolitan popular culture comprising books and magazines, performances, films, and musical recordings. Jewish joke books and Yiddish theatre performances became part of the traditional middle-class form of entertainment.

Even within the realms of what is often deemed high culture, noticeable changes occurred amongst German Jews who, due to their central social positions at the margins, had made them highly visible participants in the making of a liberal German culture. Yet the presence of the marginal Jews at the centre of modern thought, literature,

---

[45] See Marion Kaplan's essay, "Redefining Judaism in Imperial Germany: Practices, Mentalities, and Community," in this volume.

and science, and the convergence of multiple identities in the lives, for example, of Walter Benjamin, Sigmund Freud, Max Liebermann, or Albert Einstein, remains a vexing problem. Until 1933, around 30 percent of all Nobel Prizes awarded to German scientists honoured the work of German Jews. Peter Pulzer takes this insight further and argues that Jews were also disproportionately represented in politics. In particular, beginning with the period leading up to the failed revolutions of 1848–1849, Jews increasingly identified with political liberalism and the labour movement, and subsequently became disproportionately overrepresented in the making of the institutions of German national unity and German working-class organisations.

Steven Aschheim, who had studied with George Mosse, further accentuated this interpretation when he argued that Jews did not simply integrate or assimilate, but were co-constitutive to the culture they embraced.[46] This assumption also clearly underlines Elana Shapira's article in this volume. Jews disproportionately supported the creation and maintenance of the larger museums in Berlin. Between 1890 and 1933, no less than 80 percent of all donations for the larger Berlin museums came from members of the Jewish community.[47] In art and architecture, design and aesthetics became intertwined with politics and identity formation. New aesthetic sensibilities even permeated the realm of production. The employment of artful design sought to legitimise the new machines and factories as part of a cultured modernity. In Germany, Emil Rathenau not only founded the Allgemeine Elektrizitäts-Gesellschaft (AEG) but in 1905 also hired the Jewish architect Alfred Messel to devise the office building of the AEG on Friedrich-Carl-Ufer in Berlin. Messel, who was still working on the final extension of the Wertheim department store in Berlin's Leipziger Platz, gave the office a highly pragmatic appearance entirely liberated from decorative elements to reflect the modern and purposeful production of the AEG. The simple and pragmatic vision became even more clearly embodied in the AEG

---

[46] Steven E. Aschheim, "German History and German Jewry: Boundaries, Junctions and Interdependence," *Leo Baeck Institute YearBook* 43 (1998), 315–322.
[47] Cella-Margaretha Girardet, *Jüdische Mäzene für die Preussischen Museen: Eine Studie zum Mäzenatentum im Deutschen Kaiserreich und in der Weimarer Republik* (Egelsbach: Hansel-Hohenhausen, 1997).

Turbine factory by Peter Behrens in the Moabit district of Berlin in 1908. Rathenau's architects clearly believed that their designs would help to unite art and technology and thereby transform the industrial production that allegedly threatened civilisation.

The embrace of new modernist aesthetics included a subtle reorientation away from the ideals of the Enlightenment. Commitment to Bildung was not the only social and cultural fact of German Jewish life. To be sure, the relationship to the legacy of the Enlightenment continued to matter, but, for example, in the realms of ideas too, more varied modern European and German philosophies and Jewish traditions shaped the intellectual biographies of many German Jews. Many of the German Jewish philosophers were philosophers as well as teachers, exegetes, translators, and public intellectuals whose lives and works crossed disciplinary boundaries, argues Willi Goetschel. Hermann Cohen, Martin Buber, and Franz Rosenzweig critically engage within their works the universal politics of inclusion and exclusion. Their projects represent critical responses to the discourse of philosophy, exposing its secularised claims and the impact that had on the philosophical representation of the Jewish tradition.

Michael Brenner's *The Renaissance of Jewish Culture in Weimar Germany* aptly documents the unprecedented popularisation of Jewish culture in new often secular forms in music, literature, and the arts, as well as on both institutional and individual levels. The lament of many of the famed thinkers like Cohen, Buber, Rosenzweig, or Scholem about the diminished relevance of Jewish traditions to the life of the Jews in Weimar appears less an assessment of the reality than expression of a profound longing for a community—a community they sought to forge. Brenner explores the meaning and ideas attached to a community. He draws on the larger German debate on *Gemeinschaft* (community) in opposition to *Gesellschaft* (society) and illustrates how these ideas transformed the local Jewish communities from exclusively religious institutions into more secular community centres, as well as the vital role cultural initiatives played in them.

The importance of the meeting of East and West far beyond several illustrious individuals but for the larger German Jewish community has been acknowledged. Delphine Bechtel analysed this encounter in several of her publications as a two-directional process. Her article aptly illustrates the extent to which the transfer, for example, of Yiddish literature into the Weimar Renaissance of Jewish culture entailed a creative process of reworking many of the key texts to infuse Jewish culture.

The revival of Jewish culture in the Weimar Republic, however, was as much spurred by the encounter with Eastern European Jews as by a conscious recourse to the German Jewish past. During the Weimar Republic, when urbanisation had peaked, small-town communities that prided themselves on being remnants of the past were presented as the last vestiges of a vanished world, as my chapter on Worms argues. Local and regional histories offered reassurance as German Jews became infatuated with rural communities and their traditional piety. Remembering Worms and its Jewish history served to reassure Jews of their place within Germany even on the eve of its destruction, when in 1934 German Jewry commemorated the 900th anniversary of the synagogue.

Paradoxically, then, German Jewry emerged on the eve of the Holocaust as an immensely vibrant, creative, but also internally diverse community. Despite increasing pressure from the outside, internal Jewish conflicts did not decrease. The Weimar Republic, which had brought full emancipation and unprecedented levels of antisemitism, elicited intense ideological tensions within the community. The election campaigns of 1926 and 1930 for the leadership of the Jewish community of Berlin, home to one-third of all German Jews, generated sharp divisions. Yet the ideological differences also compelled a reorientation of Jewish self-understanding. The *Centralverein* (CV), which had been founded to unite German Jewry and to combat antisemitism, significantly altered its understanding. Whereas in the nineteenth century the lingering influence of the Enlightenment continued to define Jews in a religious manner, proponents of the CV now believed that the Jews formed a "community of fate." Beneath the surface of the ideological clashes with Zionism emerges a growing rapprochement between the two opposing camps, which ironically only increased the tensions between the two camps, as Barkai argues in his article included in this volume. These conflicts even carried into the initial period of the Nazi regime, when intensified harassment and persecution of German

Jews by members of the Nazi party and its accomplices became on January 30, 1933, a menacing reality. In the initial weeks of January, Hitler's coming into power continued to elude attention, escaping even the particular notice of the Jewish press.[48]

After the enabling act, this obviously shifted, but the duality of hope and despair continued to exist as some members of the Jewish community saw the encroaching intimidation and state-sanctioned restrictions on Jews and Jewish life also as an opportunity for renewal, or at least as an historical moment that required a defiant response. In his editorial in the *Jüdische Rundschau*, Weltsch wrote in response to the April 1, 1933, Nazi boycott of Jewish shops, "Wear it with pride, the yellow badge."[49]

Temporary relaxing of anti-Jewish measures between the Nuremburg laws of 1935 and the 1936 Olympics once again made some speculate as to whether the worst had already occurred. In 1935, war veterans, like Gay's uncle received a Cross of Honor, issued by Adolf Hitler.[50] These circumstances continued to curtail full despair, which, however, took hold of German Jewry in the aftermath of Kristallnacht. Levels of emigration reached new heights when financial resources had become strained and welcoming countries had become scarce.

---

[48] Moshe Zimmermann, "Wie viele Zufall darf Geschichte vertragen? Über politische Zeit- und Krisenwahrnehmung deutscher Juden im Januar 1933," in *Jüdische Geschichte als Allgemeine Geschichte: Festschrift für Dan Diner zum 60. Geburtstag*, ed. Raphael Gross and Yfaat Weiss (Göttingen: Vandenhoeck & Ruprecht, 2006), 288–302.

[49] Mendes-Flohr and Reinharz, *The Jew in the Modern World*, 640–641, and Jacob Boas, "German Jewry's Search for Renewal in the Hitler Era as Reflected in the Major Jewish Newspapers (1933–1938)," *Journal of Modern History* 53 (1981), 1001–1024.

[50] Peter Gay, *My German Question: Growing Up in Nazi Berlin* (New Haven: Yale University Press, 1998), 71.

CHAPTER I

JEWS AND NATION BUILDING IN GERMANY, 1815–1918

Peter Pulzer

Jews as participants in public politics are a modern phenomenon. We meet them in the last 200 years out of the 2,000 of the Diaspora, beginning with the Enlightenment and the French Revolution. In Europe, the timescale varies from one region to another. Jewish public figures emerged first in Western Europe, particularly France and Britain, a little later in Germany and Italy, in the Habsburg dominions not until 1848, and in Eastern Europe, including the Russian Empire, not until the second half of the nineteenth century. For most of the time, the majority of politically active Jews were content to operate within the political system of their societies, although this could also involve, especially in the first part of our period, a concern with securing or defending the civil rights of their co-religionists. Whether as conservatives, liberals, democrats, or socialists, they were concerned—either explicitly or implicitly—with reducing the gap between Jew and Gentile. From the end of the nineteenth century onwards, a second category became significant: Jewish nationalists, "separatists," or Zionists who were interested in reestablishing a distinct Jewish political identity. Since this essay examines the part played by Jews in the construction of a German nation state, I shall deal only with those whose political ideology was "integrationist" rather than "separatist." Since, moreover, this essay examines the realms of ideas and political activism, I shall concentrate on a few individuals who were particularly influential in public affairs rather than consider the overall political affiliations of the Jewish population.

Within this category, the individuals concerned fall into three broad subdivisions: monarchist or loyalist conservatives, liberal reformers, and democratic or revolutionary radicals. In the first category, the most important figure was the Protestant convert Friedrich Julius Stahl. Central to the question of Jews as German "nation builders," in the second category were those involved in crucial moments of German constitution making. Here, I shall concentrate on five men: for 1848, Gabriel Riesser; for the foundation of the empire, Ludwig Bamberger, Eduard Lasker, and Levin Goldschmidt; and for the Weimar Republic, Hugo Preuß. Further to the left, there are radical Democrats like Johann Jacoby; the two theoretical founding fathers of the German labour movement, Karl Marx and Ferdinand Lassalle; and the leaders of the various later trends of German Socialism, such as Eduard Bernstein, Hugo Haase, Rosa Luxemburg, and Paul Levi.

THE VORMÄRZ PERIOD

For much of the period before 1848, the majority of Jews in the German states were politically quiescent or apathetic. The small number of Jews who rose to eminence in banking and commerce valued their close connections with rulers and bureaucrats. Even when they embraced the values of the Enlightenment, as they increasingly did from the last third of the eighteenth century onwards, this remained consistent with support for absolutism. The expectations of improved or equal civic rights for the Jewish population rested on rulers, not peoples, and this strategy seemed justified by the partial emancipations granted—to cite the more important instances—in the Habsburg lands (1781–1782), Baden (1809), Frankfurt a. Main (1811), and Prussia (1812). Many of the policy objectives of the early advocates of Jewish civic equality, such as the separation of church and state or the freedom of enterprise (*Gewerbefreiheit*), as favoured by Moses Mendelssohn, for instance, were quite compatible with the maintenance of existing political institutions.

Two developments brought about a change in these attitudes. The first was the French Revolution, which associated the cause of civic rights with the overthrow of the existing order. The second was the reaction in Germany against French revolutionary ideas, which made the wars against Napoleon an ideological crusade, and the victory over Napoleon in 1815 a victory for anti-emancipatory forces. A new agenda therefore emerged, however gradually, one that identified Jewish emancipation with the cause of political liberalism and radicalism and therefore, by extension, with the cause of German national unification. This change came slowly. It was the work of two generations to awaken Jews from centuries of political indifference, even when the pressures in favour of greater activism were intensifying. Shortly after the anti-Jewish "Hep! Hep!" riots of 1819, Karl August Varnhagen von Ense, the husband of the celebrated literary hostess Rahel Levin Varnhagen, noted that Jews continued to be loyal to their rulers even though it was in their interest to embrace liberalism.[1] More than a decade later, Gabriel Riesser, who led the campaign for civic equality during the 1830s and 1840s, found it necessary to defend Jews as much against the charge of the most despicable servility ("schmählichste[r] Servilismus") as against that of ultra-liberal convictions ("ultraliberal[e] Gesinnung").[2]

The reputation or ultra-liberalism derived less from the general activities of the Jewish population than from the well-publicised radicalism of a few. Indeed, the most notable development amongst the Jews of Germany in the twenty or so years before the Revolutions of 1848 was the emergence of an oppositional intelligentsia of journalists, publishers, and literary figures, those "oriental chorus leaders of cosmopolitanism and hatred of Christianity" that disgusted Heinrich von Treitschke so much.[3] This intelligentsia was united in its adherence to an ideology of the rights of man, derived from the experience of the French Revolution, but it was divided on the question of the constitutional future of Germany. The most radical of its members identified the cause of Jewish emancipation with that of the German people as a whole and even of mankind. For Leopold Zunz, the Jewish

---

[1]   "Man räth den Juden, liberal zu sein; bisher sehen sie sich mehr noch als Angehörige der Machthaber an." Letter to Konrad Engelbert Oelsner, dated 3 September 1819, in Karl August Varnhagen von Ense, *Briefwechsel zwischen Varnhagen von Ense und Oelsner,* ed., L. Assing (Stuttgart: Kröner, 1865), vol. 1, 300.

[2]   Gabriel Riesser, "Bemerkungen zu den Verhandlungen der Badischen Ständeversammlung über die Emancipation dcr Juden im Jahre 1833," in *Gesammelte Schriften* (Frankfurt a. M.: Verlag der Riesser-Stiftung, 1867–1868), vol. 2, 665.

[3]   Heinrich von Treitschke, *Deutsche Geschichte im 19. Jahrhundert* (Leipzig: S. Hirzel, 1889), vol. 4, 434.

cause was coterminous with that of freedom in general.[4] Moses Hess noted of the *Rheinische Zeitung's* support for Jewish rights that it fought for, or against, everything on the basis of one principle.[5] For Heinrich Heine, the cause of the Jews was identical with that of the German people,[6] and Johann Jacoby asserted even more emphatically, "As I am both a Jew and a German at the same time, so the Jew in me cannot become free without the German, nor the German without the Jew."[7] Statements such as these were proclamations of utopian aspiration or political identity, of the kind that would recur again and again in the course of German-Jewish political life, but they gave no guidance to a preferred solution to the German question. For that, we have to turn to the more moderate Jewish liberals. Riesser, for instance, saw his German patriotism in much more concrete terms. "We want to belong to the German fatherland. We shall belong to it everywhere," he proclaimed in 1833, at the beginning of his career as the advocate of emancipation; by the eve of the 1848 Revolution, he saw German unity on the basis of "equality and free unity."[8]

THE REVOLUTION OF 1848–1849

With the outbreak of the Revolution, a new chapter opened in German-Jewish political activity. On the one hand, the question of emancipation now appeared on the immediate political agenda, and the inclusion of

---

4   Letter Philipp Ehrenberg, dated 15 June 1833, in *Leopold und Adelheid Zunz: An Account in Letters 1815–1885*, ed. in Nahum N. Glatzer (London: East & West Library, 1958), 68.
5   "Wir haben das schöne Gewissen, alles aus einem Prinzip zu er- und zu bekämpfen." Lener to Berthold Auerbach, dated 27 July 1842, in Moses Hess, *Briefwechsel*, ed., Edmund Silberner (The Hague: 's-Gravenhage, 1959), 98.
6   Heinrich Heine, "Ludwig Marcus. Spätere Note" (1854), in *Sämtliche Werke*, ed., Julius Zeitler (Leipzig: Tempel-Verlag, 1910), vol. 9, 191.
7   "Wie ich selbst Jude und Deutscher *zugleich* bin, so kann *in mir* Jude nicht frei werden ohne den Deutschen und der Deutsche nicht ohne den Juden..." Letter to Alexander Kuntzel, dated 12 May 1837, in Johann Jacoby, *Briefwechsel 1816–1849*, ed., Edmund Silberner (Hanover: Fackelträger Verlag, 1974), 56.
8   Gabriel Riesser, "Vertheidigung der bürgerlichen Gleichstellung der Juden gegen die Einwürfe des [Herrn] H. E. G. Paulus. Den Gesetzgebenden Versammlungen Deutschlands gewidmet," idem, *Gesammelte Schriften*, vol. , 183–184; "Ein Wort übcr die Zukunft Deutschlands," (1848), vol. 4, 392.

religious equality in the *Gesetz über die Grundrechte des deutschen Volkes*, adopted by the National Assembly in Frankfurt a. Main, politicised the German-Jewish population as no previous event had managed to do. It also provided German Jews with an interest in and an identification with liberal parliamentary politics that distinguished them from their non-Jewish fellow citizens. On the other hand, there was now a wider public political realm open to all. While the character of Jewish political participation could, in many cases, be explained by the previous experience of discrimination and exclusion, the participants themselves ceased to be preoccupied with purely Jewish concerns. Freedom in general, rather than Jewish freedoms in particular, was now the objective. For many Jewish publicists, this was a source of pride: the liberal journal *Der Orient* talked of the "Maceabaean heroic struggle of our brothers"[9] and saw the Revolution in messianic terms: "the Messiah is freedom, our fatherland is Germany."[10] The consequence of this was that the Jewish reputation for radicalism was reinforced.

Although numerous Jews were elected to local revolutionary councils, state parliaments, and the Frankfurt National Assembly, they were at their most conspicuous in the new journalism. Heinrich Bernhard Oppenheim edited *Reform*; Bernhard Wolff, the *National-Zeitung*; Aron Bernstein, the *Urwählerzeitung*; and Karl Weil, the *Konstitutionelle Zeitung* (all in Berlin). Ludwig Bamberger edited the *Mainzer Zeitung*; and Bernhard Friedmann, the *Neue Oder-Zeitung* of Breslau; journals directed by Jews in Vienna are too numerous to list. On the extreme left, the *Neue Rheinische Zeitung* (Cologne) of Karl Marx and *Das Volk* (Berlin) and *Die Verbrüderung* (Leipzig) of Stephan Born stand out. It was in 1848 that the term *Judenpresse* first emerged as a pejorative description for liberal or radical newspapers.

The reputation for radicalism was only partly deserved. By no means, were all politically active Jews revolutionary or even liberal; some favoured only very moderate reforms; others were conservative or counter-revolutionary. But one question that none of them could escape was "What was the shape of the new Germany to be?" The question was

---

9   "Makkabaisch-heldenmüthigen Kampf unserer Brüder," *Der Orient* (April 1, 1848), 105.
10   *Der Orient* (August 12, 1848), 257.

of least interest to those on the far left, who saw political revolution only as a means to an end, the end being social revolution. This was true above all of Marx's *Bund der Kommunisten* and the *Allgemeine deutsche Arbeiterverbrüderung* under the aegis of Born. They demanded popular sovereignty and a "united German republic," but only a minority amongst them combined their revolutionary zeal with German patriotism. Thus Marx's collaborator, Andreas Gottschalk, evoked "the unity of the great fatherland,"[11] and Jacoby, at this stage not yet a Socialist, proclaimed, "Deutschlands Einheit über alles" in pursuit of his (initially unsuccessful) candidature for the Frankfurt Assembly.[12] In general, however, those primarily associated with the workers' movement had different priorities from those who were active in the Frankfurt Assembly.

Even amongst those whose activities were primarily parliamentary, there was no agreement on the constitutional future of Germany. Those Jewish delegates elected from Austria—Moritz Hartmann and Ignaz Kuranda—favoured a *großdeutsch* solution, to include the German-speaking crown lands of the Habsburg monarchy. Others ranged from republicans to moderate constitutionalists. But as the options narrowed during the months of prolix debate, a majority formed in favour of a Prussian-led *kleindeutsch*, federal, constitutional monarchy. No one embodied this consensus more clearly than Riesser, who had become second vice president of the assembly. He was one of nine Jewish delegates, in addition to ten who were baptised; one of the baptised, Eduard Simson, was president of the assembly. As before 1848, Riesser saw no distinction between the cause of Jewish emancipation and that of German unity. It was his eloquence that ensured the adoption of unconditional religious equality almost unanimously as part of the *Grundrechte des deutschen Volkes:* "Do not think that it is possible to enact discriminatory laws ... without inflicting a pernicious fissure on the whole system of freedom," he warned the assembly.[13] It was once

---

11 Konrad Repgen, *Märzbewegung und Maiwahlen des Revolutionsjahres* 1818 im *Rheinland* (Bonn: L. Röhrscheid, 1955), 23.

12 Letter to Hermann Alexander Berlepsch, dated 26 May 1848, in Jacoby, *Briefwechsel*, 461.

13 *Stenographischer Bericht über die Verhandlungen der deutschen constituirenden Nationalversammlung zu Frankfurt am Main* (Frankfurt a. Main: 1819), vol. 3, 1757 (August 29, 1818). For the general background of these developments, see Reinhard

more Riesser's eloquence that defended the proposal to establish a Prussian-led German federal state,[14] and he joined the delegation, led by Simson, to offer the German crown to King Friederich William IV of Prussia. When Frederick William refused the crown and the Frankfurt Assembly was dispersed by Prussian bayonets, Riesser's vision and that of the majority of the assembly faded from the scene. The future shape of Germany was once more uncertain: centralisation or particularism, Austrian or Prussian predominance, monarchy or democracy remained unanswered questions. But in the end, the *kleindeutsch* solution favoured in Frankfurt triumphed, even if not by the means the delegates had anticipated, and the way was clear for the reconvergence of the claims of Jewish emancipation and German national unification that the events of 1848–1849 had adumbrated.

THE CREATION OF THE EMPIRE

The failure of the 1848–1849 Revolutions was followed by a decade of political quietism, in which the defeated forces reconsidered their strategies. The leaders of the revolutionary Left—both Jewish and non-Jewish—scattered into exile: Marx to London, Born to Switzerland, and Bamberger to Paris. Some, including Bamberger and Heinrich Bernhard Oppenheim, moved towards a more moderate liberal position. Perhaps more interestingly, the 1850s were the last period in which Conservatives of Jewish origin (mostly baptised) played a significant public role. The historian Siegfried Hirsch had been one of the founders of the *Kreuzzeitung* (*Neue Preußische Zeitung*), the main organ of Prussian Conservatism, which came into being in the year of the Revolution. More influential still was Friedrich Julius Stahl, like Hirsch a convert to Protestantism, who had emerged as the main defender of the monarchical order in response to the challenge of democratic radicalism[15] and, on the

---

Rürup, "The European Revolutions of 1848 and Jewish Emancipation," *Revolution and Evolution: 1848 in German-Jewish History*, ed., Werner E. Mosse, Arnold Paucker and Reinhard Rürup (Tübingen: J. C. B. Mohr, 1981), 1–53.

14 *Stenographischer Bericht*, op. cit., vol. 8, 5899–5911 (March 21, 1819).

15 Friedrich Julius Stahl, *Das monarchische Prinzip. Eine staatsrechtlich-politischen Abhandlung* (Heidelberg: Mohr, 1845).

very eve of the Revolution, at the time of the Prussian United Diet's debate on the *Gesetz über die Verhältnisse der Juden*, as the articulator of the doctrine of the Christian state. For Stahl, Jewish emancipation was objectionable precisely because it rested on the principles of the French Revolution: "The political equality of all human beings is not by itself a destruction of the Christian state, but it is a clouding of its principle and a danger to its existence." The existing Prussian legislation had the merit in his eyes of qualifying civic equality as a protection against the consequences of the doctrine of equality, "which *a priori* pays no attention to the institution ... of the Christian state."[16]

Even at this stage, there was no doubt little support amongst Jews for a political programme that explicitly refused to lift the existing discriminations against them. But one should not underestimate the degree of political indifference that continued amongst the Jewish population even during the turmoils of 1848–1849 nor the confusion caused by the revolutionary events that on the one hand promised legal equality but on the other posed a threat to order and property. Above all, many Orthodox Jews were suspicious of a liberalism that was closely associated with Reform Judaism and advocated a secularisation of life. "You know I am no Democrat," the founder-editor of the Orthodox *Der Israelit*, Markus Lehmann, told Moses Hess.[17]

With the reawakening of political life at the end of the 1850s, the distribution of party preferences also changed amongst Jews as amongst Gentiles. The death of Stahl in 1862 removed the last of the influential Conservative thinkers of Jewish descent, although some individual Jews continued to be hostile to the now dominant liberal temper of the times. Radicalism too was still under a cloud. What revived was a liberalism directed against the existing structure of the German Confederation and against the semi-absolutism of its constituent states but in favour of German national unity. The outward sign of this was the creation of the *Deutscher Nationalverein* in 1859 and of the *Deutsche Fortschrittspartei* in 1861, which were dedicated

---

[16] Friedrich Julius Stahl, *Der christliche Staat und sein Verhältnis zu Deismus und Judentums* (Berlin: Ludwig Dehmigke, 1847), esp. 34, 35, 56.

[17] Letter from Lehmann to Hess, dated 16 January 1863 in Hess, *Briefwechsel*, 424.

to the programme adopted by the Frankfurt Assembly: guaranteed civil liberties and a *kleindeutsch* nation state. A number of Jews were prominently associated with both organisations from the start: those in the *Nationalverein* included Riesser, Jacoby, Moritz Veit, and Leopold Sonnemann, the owner and later editor of the *Frankfurter Zeitung*. They were joined at a later stage by Bamberger and Oppenheim, who became the editors of its main organ, the *Deutsche Jahrbücher für Politik und Literatur*. What attracted secularised middle-class Jews and Gentiles to this programme was the combined promise of civil liberties and an end to particularism. The failure of the Frankfurt Assembly had not entirely discredited its ideals. The necessity of Prussian leadership was accepted but not that of an unreformed Prussia.

The test for the allegiance of the *Nationalverein's* supporters to these twin ideals came when German unity was achieved by the military victories of an unreformed Prussia. The majority of liberals, Jewish and Gentile, bowed before *vollendete Tatsachen* and, having formed themselves into the *Natianalliberale Partei*, embarked on building the new German state with, rather than against, Bismarck. The National Liberals' manifesto was largely drafted by Eduard Lasker, one of the constitutional experts on the Left wing of the Party. The defeat of Austria at the battle of Königgrätz in 1866 meant the end of the loosely structured Austrian-led German Confederation. "As Germans we have no cause to mourn it," the *Allgemeine Zeitung des Judenthums* wrote.[18] The leading Jewish paper welcomed not only the destruction of the old but the creation of the new: "The main thing is ... that the German Empire will henceforth have an external representation [and] a legislature on the most important political, juridical and economic areas," it wrote after the proclamation of the Empire at Versailles.[19]

The reforms of German institutions that needed to accompany the creation of the empire in 1871 gained support on two grounds. On the one hand, there were the practical necessities of harmonising any number of the legal and economic provisions inherited from the particularist past.

---

[18] "Was haben wir zu thun," *Allgemeine Zeitung des Judentums* (September 18, 1866), 595.
[19] "Das Deutsche Reich und die Juden," *Allgemeine Zeitung des Judentums* (January 17, 1871), 41, 42.

On the other, there was a strong ideological component: new institutions were to symbolise the fact that the German nation now had its own state. As Lasker put it: "When a magnificent event takes place that shakes our hearts and brings about the unexpected, there is a general opinion that from now on the old rules no longer apply."[20] The two topics on which the debate concentrated were the legal system and the currency question. In both of these, Jewish experts took a leading part.

A single legal code required a single legislature with clearly overriding powers, and this had been one of Lasker's dominant concerns. From the beginnings of the debate on a future German constitution in the parliament of the North German Confederation (the successor to the defunct *Deutscher Bund*), he had insisted that in contrast to the *Bund*, it must have its own legislature.[21] In company with his (non-Jewish) fellow National Liberal, Johannes Miquel, he introduced a motion demanding that only the Confederation should have competence over a new civil law. However, it was not until after the foundation of the Reich that a preparatory commission on a new civil code was established, presided over by Levin Goldschmidt, professor of commercial law at Heidelberg and a Justice of the Supreme Commercial Court (*Bundesoberhandelsgericht*). The commission owed its existence to the undersecretary in the *Reich* Office of Justice, Heinrich Friedberg, himself a convert from Judaism to Protestantism.

Goldschmidt had made no secret of his advocacy of a uniform code. A state without an appropriately comprehensive legal code would lack moral appeal: "The German nation desires a statute book of civil law, not a handful of codified individual laws." Anything else "would not be enough to satisfy the nation's need for community [*Gemeinschajtsbedürfniß*]."[22] But the failure to produce a unitary code

---

[20] *Die Zukunft des Deutschen Reiches. Rede des Reichstagsabgeordneten Dr. Eduard Lasker, gehalten* in *der gemeinnützigen Gesellschaft zu Leipzig am 18. Januar 1877* (Leipzig: Schloemp, 1877), 11.

[21] Wilhelm Cahn ed., *Aus Eduard Laskers Nachlaß. Fünfzehn Jahre parlarmentarische Geschichte* (Berlin: Reimer, 1902), 73–77, 161–162.

[22] Levin Goldschmidt, "Über Plan und Methode für die Aufstellung des Entwurfes eines deutschen bürgerlichen Gesetzbuches," *Vermischte Schriften*, ed., Hermann Veit Simon (Berlin: J. Guttentag, 1901), vol. 1, 520; "Die Nothwendigkeit eines deutschen Civilgesetzbuches," *Im neuren Reich* 2:1 (1872), 746.

would also be a surrender to particularism: "It is no accident that the irreconcilable enemies of the German *Reich* are to be found among the opponents of a German legislative institution."[23]

Similar arguments were used by Bamberger in his campaign on behalf of a single bank of issue and a gold-based single currency. Such measures certainly favoured the financial and industrial interests which supported National Liberalism and were the dominant force during the decade of unification. But like the civil code, they were also symbols of national integration. Even before the empire was a reality, Bamberger prophesied that a single currency would contribute "not only to the material interests, but to furthering the intellectual and moral position of our nation." Its enemies were those "who see salvation only in those things that prevent the unity of Germany."[24] On visiting Alsace after the initial Prussian victories in 1870, he remarked to Rudolf von Delbrück, the president of Bismarck's Chancellery, "Now we can also go ahead with the gold currency."[25]

The advocates of a strong German nation state, based on unified fiscal and legal institutions, had mixed success. Bamberger, thanks to his expertise and oratorical persistence, largely achieved what he wanted: a *Reichsbank* with a monopoly of issue and a *Reichsmark* backed with gold. Lasker and Goldschmidt were less successful. The debate on the legal code dragged on. When a code was finally adopted in 1894, the nation-building enthusiasm of the 1860s and 1870s had ebbed and the brief but fruitful convergence of Jewish and Gentile liberal politics was no more. Liberal dominance of both Reich and Prussia came to an end in 1878–1879, when Bismarck turned from free trade to protection. This policy switch split the National Liberal Party, and most of the Jews within it, particularly those on its Left wing like Lasker and Bamberger, seceded. It was clear to the secessionists that more than free trade was at stake: "The demands of the Liberal Party are much more comprehensive, they penetrate the whole of public life," Lasker wrote to Miquel, to justify the

---

23   Ibid., 788.
24   *Stenographische Berichte über die Verhandlungm des...Deutschen Zoll-Parlaments*, Berlin 1870, 186 (May 5, 1870).
25   "Nun machen wir auch die Goldwährung." See Karl Helfferich, "Ludwig Bamberger als Währungspolitiker," in *Ludwig Bamberger. Ausgewählte Reden und Aufsätze über Geld- und Bankwesen*, ed., Karl Helfferich (Berlin: J. Guttentag, 1900), 31.

parting of their ways.[26] The founder generation of the German Empire saw no inconsistency between their liberalism and their patriotism. And there is no reason to doubt Bamberger's sincerity when he said at Lasker's graveside in 1884, "It was a piece of German patriotic history and it was a piece of the best of German history that we carried to its grave today ... Not he, but the majority of the German nation spoke through his mouth for more than ten years."[27]

RETURN TO REFORM AND REVOLUTION

But Lasker and Bamberger, for all their contributions to the construction of the German Empire, at the end of their careers, also showed politically active German Jews the way back to a position that had been characteristic for them in the years before 1848: that of opposition. Much of this opposition was moderate. While it concentrated from time to time on the continuing discrimination against Jews in many sectors of public service, especially the judiciary, education, and the military, this was in general seen as a symptom of the inadequacies in the constitutional development of an increasingly urbanised and industrial Germany. The dissident liberals of the moderate left, with whom the Jewish middle class increasingly identified from the 1880s onwards, were neither subversive nor radical. They too thought of themselves as nation builders, but they defined the nation in constitutional, not merely ethnic or diplomatic, terms. They wanted a Germany of equality before the law, a Germany with fewer privileges and a less arbitrary executive. "I do not fight for the Jewish reserve lieutenant ... I fight against the injustice that occurs in Germany ... The injustice that occurs against German Jewry and in part against the German middle class is not the greatest, but it is also one," Walther Rathenau wrote.[28]

---

[26] Letter to Johannes Miquel, dated 1 August 1879, in Julius Heyderhoff and Paul Wentzke, ed., *Deutscher Liberalismus im Zeitalter Bismarcks. Eine politischer Briefsammlung* (Bonn: Schroeder, 1925–1926), vol. 2, 261.

[27] Ludwig Bamberger, *Eduard Lasker. Gedenkrede, gehalten am 28. Januar 1884* (Leipzig: F. A. Brockhaus, 1884), 9, 14.

[28] Walther Rathenau, "Staat und Judentum. Eine Polemik" (1911), *Gesammelte Schriften* (Berlin: Fischer, 1925), vol. 1, 206–207.

In contrast with the period of nation building, there is no outstanding group of individuals with whom this liberal reformism can be associated. In part, it was articulated by a number of Jewish-owned metropolitan newspapers, especially the *Berliner Tageblatt*, in part by the parties of the liberal left, which operated under a variety of names after the great split of 1879 and for which the majority of German Jews voted. The main lobbies created to fight prejudice and discrimination, the Gentile-led *Verein zur Abwehr des Antisemitismus* and the *Centralverein deutscher Staatsbürger jüdischen Glaubens*, were closely linked to these parties. More significantly, this reformism found a voice in the various lobbies that grew up to favour free trade and the manufacturing industry against the government's bias in favour of protectionism for "rye und iron." The most important of these were the *Handelsvertragverein* of 1900 and the *Hansabund für Gewerbe, Handel und Industrie* of 1909. Jews were prominent in the leadership of both and included the banker Max M. Warburg, Emil Rathenau of the *AEG*, and Wilhelm Herz, president of the Berlin Chamber of Commerce, who also became chairman of the *Handelsvertragsverein*. The first chairman of the *Hansabund* was the nephew of Gabriel Riesser, the banker and academic Jakob Riesser. Its advocacy of an open society with equal opportunities for all talents gave it a particular appeal to Jews: "We do not want to participate in it as Jews, but as German citizens of the Jewish faith," the *Allgemeine Zeitung des Judentums* wrote: "We do not want to carry on denominational disputes there, but to find justice."[29]

The reversion of Jewish political loyalties to oppositional liberalism made it easy for its opponents to denounce it as "*Judenliberalismus*" and its newspapers as "*Judenpresse*." Yet there was a grave, and no doubt deliberate, distortion in this: although the majority of Jews were left-liberals, the majority of left-liberals and all the leaders of the left-liberal parties were non-Jewish. In any case, the oppositional temper of all of these groups fluctuated. Many Jewish business leaders, even if they tended towards reform and the *Hansabund*, were prepared to give their names and money in support of naval and colonial programmes at any rate until such programmes threatened to involve Germany in war with Britain.

---

[29] "Neue Fronten," *Allgemeine Zeitung des Judentums* (August 20, 1909), 6.

A parallel development in the reversion to pre-1848 political patterns was the renewed presence of Jews in radical politics. The parallelism operated in two ways: Jews were prominent in the leadership and, above all, the publicity of the working-class movement but, in this respect, were atypical of the Jewish community as a whole. What drew so many Jews, not only in Germany but in Europe generally, to socialism of various kinds between the middle of the nineteenth and the middle of the twentieth centuries has evoked a number of sometimes contradictory explanations. Some scholars have tried to see it as a continuation of the Jewish prophetic tradition; others have emphasised a particular Jewish social ethic. But many of the Jewish Socialists were far removed from any traditional Jewish background, and it is not clear whether the social ethic of Judaism is any stronger or more favourable to collectivism in property than that of the other major religions. Neither of these propositions is therefore very convincing as a comprehensive explanation. Perhaps a more plausible explanation lies in the experience of exclusion from general society that most Jews in this period shared to a greater or lesser extent. This would be felt especially strongly by those who had, on the one hand, severed their links with traditional Judaism and, on the other, encountered the barriers maintained by their host society. Of course, not all Jews suffered this dual marginalisation to the same extent, but then not all Jews became Socialists and plenty of non-Jews did. Nevertheless, one can see why a utopia in which all existing distinctions of birth, status, and belief would be suspended should appeal disproportionately to emancipated, secularised, educated, but not entirely assimilated Jews.

Whatever the reasons, the German labour movement owed its ideologies, if not its organisation, mainly to Jews. Historical materialism, which promised the future to the politically conscious revolutionary proletariat, was the gift of Marx. Ferdinand Lassalle preached cooperative association in combination with the existing state, as well as the need for a class-based party. Their influential contemporaries included Born and Hess. All of them were conscious of being Jews but, with the exception of Hess in his later years, did not identify with Jewish causes or even pay much attention to them. However, the founders of the Social Democratic Party in 1869 were not Jews; Marx was by then permanently settled in distant London, and Lassalle was dead. Lassalle's heirs in the *Allgemeiner Deutscher Arbeiterverein*, who merged with the Social Democrats in 1875, were not Jews either and were, in many cases, antisemitically inclined. The 1860s and 1870s were, after all, the decades in which Germany's Jews harboured the greatest hopes of integration into a modern nation state. Jewish interest in Socialism revived only as these hopes were disappointed and as right-wing antisemitism reasserted itself.

Within the organisation of the Social Democratic Party (SPD), the two most important figures were Paul Singer and Hugo Haase. Singer entered the *Reichstag* at the height of Adolf Stoecker's antisemitic campaign. He rapidly became the leader of the Social Democratic delegation in the Berlin city council, floor leader of the SPD in the *Reichstag*, and, in 1890, co-chairman of the party, with August Bebel, until his death in 1911. Haase, a lawyer who gained fame for his defence of prosecuted party members and newspapers, succeeded Singer both as floor leader and as co-chairman. After Bebel's death in 1913, he became the senior functionary of the party. It was his painful duty to announce the SPD's support for war credits on August 4, 1914, a course to which he himself was profoundly opposed.[30] His war-time role will be considered in the following discussion.

Singer's and Haase's positions in the parliamentary structure of the SPD was atypical for Jews of the Socialist Left. Their principal contribution, and the one for which they are best remembered, lay in professional expertise and a penchant for theory. While most of the non-Jewish SPD politicians were of working-class or lower middle-class origin and therefore lacked formal educational qualifications, this did not apply to the Jews in the SPD. Of the twelve *Reichstag* deputies of Jewish origin elected in 1912, eleven were graduates; of the non-Jews, this was true only of eight out of ninety-eight. The journalism of the SPD would have been unthinkable without Jewish editors or writers. Outstanding examples are Kurt Eisner, who de facto ran

---

[30] For the general background, see Ernest Hamburger, *Juden im öffentlichen Leben Deutschlands. Regierungsmitglieder, Beamte und Parlamentarier in der monarchischen Zeit, 1848–1918* (Tübingen: J. C. B. Mohr, 1968), 399–521.

the party's main newspaper, *Vorwärts*, during Wilhelm Liebknecht's nominal editorship and later moved to the *Fränkische Tagespost* of Nuremberg and the *Müncher Post*; Bruno Schoenlank at the *Leipziger Volkszeitung*; Georg Gradnauer at the *Sächsische Arbeiterzeitung* (later renamed *Dresdner Volkszeitung*); Ernst Heilmann at the *Chemnitzer Volksstimme*; Simon Katzenstein at the *Mainzer Volkszeitung*; and Friedrich Stampfer's syndicated *Parteikorrespondenz*. In the more ambitious theoretical publications, we find first Eduard Bernstein and then Emanuel Wurm as Karl Kautsky's assistants at the *Neue Zeit*, Joseph Bloch as editor of the *Sozialistische Monatshefte*, and Heinrich Braun as founder of the *Neue Gesellschaft*. These publications and their editors spanned the whole range of the party's doctrinal pluralism, and this was also true of the protagonists in the theoretical disputes that altered the turn of the century. Those on the party's radical wing, who developed traditional Marxism to elaborate new theories of imperialism, were, with few exceptions, Jewish: Rosa Luxemburg, Rudolf Hilferding, and Alexander Israel Helphand ("Parvus"), to name only the most influential.[31] On the party's right, the most prominent theoretician was Bernstein, who urged the abandonment of all revolutionary rhetoric, which he regarded as counterproductive as well as irrelevant to the actual needs of the modern working class,[32] and Bloch, who in contrast to Bernstein's pacifist anti-imperialism, advocated support for German colonial expansion.

The "revisionists" Bernstein and his followers and "reformists" (mainly non-Jews like Eduard David and Georg von Vollmar but including Jews like Ludwig Frank) posed the greater theoretical challenge to party orthodoxy. But since they were closer to its practicalities, they were able to remain in its mainstream. In their disavowal of revolution and their agenda of completing the democratisation of Germany, they too were nation builders, although their time for active participation was not to come until the end of the First World War. The radicals' influence, on

---

[31] Rosa Luxemburg, *Die Akkumulation des Kapitals* (Berlin: Verlag für Literatur und Politik, 1913); Rudolf Hilferding, *Das Finanzkapital* (Vienna: Wiener Volksbuchandlung, 1910).

[32] Eduard Bernstein, *Die Vorraussetzungen des Sozialismus und die Aufgaben der Sozialdemokratie* (Stuttgart: J. H. W. Dietz, 1899).

the other hand, was to be even more long term. Until 1914, they were isolated and might have remained so but for the World War. They were marginalised not only by their ideology but by their origins. It was one of the curiosities of the SPD's dominance over the European Socialist movement that it was able to attract talent from across its borders, mainly from Russian Poland and Austria-Hungary. That is where it recruited its Jewish radicals—Luxemburg, Hilferding, and Parvus—as well as Braun and non-Jews like Kautsky. But to be Jewish, Eastern European, and revolutionary represented a triple jeopardy not only in German politics generally but also in the SPD.

WAR, REVOLUTION, AND REPUBLIC

The outbreak of the war temporarily submerged whatever impulses to reform and revolution there had been in the preceding years. Most Jews were patriots. Most Jews hoped that the civic truce (*Burgfrieden*) proclaimed by the government would complete the promised but undelivered integration into state and society.[33] The recruitment of such prominent Jewish business personalities as Walther Rathenau, Albert Ballin, and Carl Melchior into high administrative posts which they could not possibly have occupied in peacetime seemed an earnest of a new dispensation. The civic truce did not last for long; what had to many Germans seemed a war of defence became indisputably a war of conquest, and the social and economic cost of the war became increasingly disproportionate to any benefits that might once have been expected. The consequence of these developments is that the oppositional forces of the pre-war period re-formed.

For the SPD, the impact of the war was traumatic. Its vote in the *Reichstag* for the war credits undoubtedly reflected opinion within the party at the time. By 1916, not only had the old Left recovered its anti-imperialist radicalism, it also recruited former moderates to the anti-war cause. When the party split in 1917 and the antiwar

---

[33]   For a general discussion of this topic, see David Engel, "Patriotism as a Shield. The Liberal Jewish Defence against Antisemitism in Germany during the First World War," *Leo Baeck Institute YearBook* 31 (1986), 147–171.

faction formed itself into the Independent Social Democratic Party (*Unabhängige Sozialdemokratische Partei Deutschlands/USPD*), six of the remaining eleven Jewish Reichstags deputies joined it. More significantly, the USPD contained not only Haase, who as we have seen had had misgivings from the start, but also Bernstein. Indeed, it was Bernstein who drafted the group's original manifesto, *Das Gebot der Stunde*, in June 1916. What united otherwise antagonistic Jews was an outlook that favoured if not outright pacifism, at least international conciliation.

What applied to Jews of the Left applied equally to liberal and even conservatively inclined Jews, although we need to emphasise that doubts about the wisdom of Germany's policies were not restricted to Jews. Whereas Jewish names were featured prominently on the patriotic "Manifesto of the Ninety-Three"[34] in the autumn of 1914, such support for nationalist causes soon faded, the more so since the annexationist cause became increasingly identified with the anti-liberal and, in some cases, antisemitic right. The leadership of the campaign for a compromise peace was in the hands of such Gentile scholars as Hans Delbruck, Lujo Brentano, and Adolf von Harnack. But much of the organisation was in the hands of the archetypal representative of the "*Judenpresse*," Theodor Wolff, the editor-in-chief of the *Berliner Tageblatt*. The opposition of the Left and the Centre combined in the *Reichstag* on 19 July 1917 to pass a resolution in favour of a compromise peace. This merely gave the far right a further enemy: "Jewish Liberalism" and the "Jewish press" were now to be responsible for a "*Judenfriede*." The parties that voted for the peace resolution—the two Social Democratic parties, the Left-Liberals, and the Catholic *Zentrum*—could not affect the course of the war, but their coming together presaged the coalition that would take power after the defeat of Germany. Defeat meant the collapse of the old order, but no agreement on what was to succeed it. It meant the last attempt to build a German political nation before the Nazi takeover and the last occasion on which Jews were to take a prominent part in defining Germany's political options. They did so, for however brief a period, on an unprecedented scale.

---

34 See "Aufruf an die Kulturwelt," *Frankfurter Zeitung* (October 4, 1914).

The first step towards a new order came in the form of a parliamentary government headed by Prince Max von Baden. It contained no Jews, although the prince wanted the Hamburg banker Max Warburg to take on the finance portfolio. Warburg refused: "I know the Germans and know that they would never ever [*nie und nimmer*] accept a Jewish Minister of Finance."[35] This reluctance was, however, as it turned out, exceptional. The second step consisted of the formation of revolutionary soldiers' and workers' councils (*Arbeiter- und Soldatenräte*). Here too Jews were virtually absent from the leadership. They were, however, conspicuously present in the third phase, that of the provisional governments that took over from Max von Baden. The provisional government for the *Reich*, the six People's Commissars (*Rat der Volksbeauftragten*), included two Jews, Haase of the USPD and Otto Landsberg of the majority SPD. The new prime minister of Prussia was Paul Hirsch, and the new prime minister of Saxony was Gradnauer, both of the SPD. In Berlin and other cities, Jews were prominently involved in municipal takeovers.[36]

Although the form of these new governments was revolutionary, their substance was not. There were only two exceptions to this. The first took place on the inhospitable soil of Bavaria, where Kurt Eisner, now of the USPD, headed an administration dedicated to utopian reconstruction. His regime came to an end with his assassination in February 1919 and was succeeded, after a constitutional interlude, by two Soviet-style republics, the first anarchist in character and the second Communist. Eisner's government contained one Jew, Edgar Jaffe, as minister of finance, and the Communist republic was headed by the Russian-born Engen Leviné. But the regime most identified with "Jewish revolutionary terrorism" was the week-long first Soviet republic, headed by Gustav Landauer, Erich Mühsam, and Ernst Toller. The second exception was the group on the extreme left of the USPD, the *Spartakusbund*, which formed itself into the German Communist

---

[35] Max M. Warburg, *Aus meinen Aufzeichnungen* (New York :1952), 64.

[36] For an exhaustive analysis of Jewish participation in the political upheavals of 1918 and 1919, see Werner T. Angress, "Juden im politischen Leben der Revolutionszeit," in *Deutsches Judentum in Krieg und Revolution 1916–1923*, ed., Werner E. Mosse and Arnold Paucker (Tübingen: J. C. B. Mohr, 1971), 137–315.

Party. Its leadership consisted of the prewar radicals Rosa Luxemburg and Wilhelm Liebknecht's son, Karl; other Jews, besides Luxemburg, who were involved in its foundation were Paul Levi and Leo Jogiches. Following the ill-fated Berlin rising of January 1919, in the course of which Luxemburg and Liebknecht were murdered, the prospects of a violent overthrow of the existing order disappeared. Only *Spartakus/ KPD* and the left wing of the USPD were genuinely revolutionary. The rest of the USPD wanted to combine soldiers' and workers' councils with parliamentary government. The SPD, along with the non-Socialist parties of the centre, wanted a democratic republic.

If one were to ask what the many Jews of the Left who were catapulted into power in 1918 and 1919 achieved, one would have to give an ambivalent answer. The revolutionaries were defeated. The others averted chaos under difficult circumstances. They laid the basis for a democratic republic and in that capacity were state builders—achievements that should not be despised. But they changed neither society nor the economic system, objectives to which their party had been primarily committed. What emerged from the upheavals of 1918 and 1919 was a bourgeois-democratic republic. This brings us to the last of the great Jewish liberal nation builders that Germany produced, Hugo Preuß.

Preuß is frequently referred to as the father of the Weimar constitution, although the document that was adopted differed significantly from what he had proposed. He was a father only in the sense that he put forward a coherent agenda. In one respect, he was within the tradition of the nineteenth-century National Liberals and the 1848 Democrats in wanting a unified nation state: "In the creation of a new constitution for the *Reich* the idea that the traditional territorial division of Germany, based on the accidental dynastic structures of the existing member states, was not a viable basis for the new national state, gained strong support … ," he noted retrospectively. The old order was to be replaced by "the final inter-penetration of nationality and state in the form of a national democracy."[37] "The starting point of the

---

[37] "Der endlichen Durchdringung von Nationalität und Staat in Gestalt der nationalen Demokratie." See Hugo Preuß, *Um die Reichsverfassung von Weimar* (Berlin: R. Mosse, 1924), 24, 47.

new constitution ... is the self-government of the German people," he told the Weimar Constitutional Assembly.[38] Anything else, he feared, would perpetuate the hegemony of Prussia and the veto of Bavaria. More significant than his advocacy of state unitarism was his notion of social pluralism. Like Thomas Jefferson, he did not want to replace the despotism of the monarch with the despotism of an electoral majority. Even in his earliest writings, he delineated a notion close to Anglo-American ideas of political pluralism and modern theories of "civil society." The "constitutional state based on the rule of law [verfassungsmäßigr(e) Rechtsstaat]" that he envisaged presupposed "a plurality of centers of power [eine Mehrzahl von Machtzentren]" and the "coexistence of a plurality of organs of policy initiation." Nothing else would do justice to the "manifold and differentiated character of the conditions of life of the present day."[39] Above all, he was convinced that, contrary to widespread German assumptions, self-government required party government.[40]

The constitution of the Weimar Republic as finally adopted differed substantially from Preuß's draft. It survived for a mere fourteen years, less because of defects in the constitution than because, as he himself put it, "the best constitution is of no use if those called upon to implement it do so incorrectly or amateurishly."[41] Other constitutional theorists of Jewish origin defended or tried to develop the principles on which the Weimar Republic was based in different ways—Otto Kirchheimer, Ernst Fraenkel, and the Austrian Hans Kelsen, to mention only some. What they had in common was a search for permanently valid norms from which to derive appropriate institutions. It was this that Preuß's great antagonist, Carl Schmitt,

[38] *Verhandlungen der verfassungsgebenden deutschen Nationatversammlung* (Berlin: Norddeutsche Buchdruckerei und Verlagsanstalt, 1920), vol. 326, 285 (February 24, 1919). For a general discussion of Preuß's role, see Ernest Hamburger, "Hugo Preuß: Scholar and Statesman," *Leo Baeck Institute YearBook* 20 (1975), 179–206.

[39] Hugo Preuß, "Die Sozialdemokratie" und der Parlamentarismus," (1891), *Staat, Recht, und Freiheit. Aus 40 Jahren deutschern Politik* (Berlin: 1929); idem, *Reich und Länder. Bruchstücke eines Kommentares zur Verfassung des deutschen Reiches*, ed., Gerhard Anschütz (Berlin: Hermanns, 1928), 26, 48.

[40] Preuß, *Reich und Länder*, 45, 269.

[41] Preuß, *Um die Reichsverfassung*, 42.

found so objectionable. "Thinking on the basis of norms," he observed, suited "peoples ... that exist without soil, without state, without church, only in 'the law.'"[42]

CONCLUDING THOUGHTS

The number of Jews, or persons of Jewish ancestry, who helped to fashion the ideas and the institutions of German national unity and the German working-class organisation is remarkable, when one considers that Jews never amounted to more than 1 percent of the German population or, perhaps more relevantly, not more than 5 to 10 percent of the educated liberal bourgeoisie. The question remains whether there was anything distinctive about this contribution. In one sense, the answer must be no. Nothing was said or done by any of the Jews mentioned here that could not have been said or done by a non-Jew. But in another sense, the answer has to be yes—at least for Germany, for what needs explanation is their sheer number. I have already hinted at some hypotheses that have been advanced to explain the prominence of European Jews in the movements of the liberal and socialist left. Some observers have seen embedded in Jewish culture a prophetic eschatological element that leads either to utopian visions of reconstruction or, at the very least, to seeing the status quo in a critical light. Others claim to discern in the ethic of Judaism an exceptional degree of social concern and responsibility. Such propositions are difficult to verify or falsify and have at best the status of stimulating ideas. Nietzsche advanced such ideas with characteristic hyperbole but also with a kernel of truth:

> What Europe owes to the Jews?—Many things, good and bad, and above all one thing that is at once of the best and of the worst: the grand style in morality, the dreadfulness and majesty of infinite demands, infinite significances, the whole romanticism and sublimity of moral

---

42   "Völker ... die ohne Boden, ohne Staat, ohne Kirche, nur im 'Gesetz' existieren," see Carl Schmitt, *Über die drei Arten des rechtswissenschaftlichen Denkens* (Hamburg: Hanseatische Verl.ags-Anstalt 1934), 9.

questionabilities—and consequently precisely the most attractive, insidious and choicest part of those iridescences and seductions to life with whose afterglow the sky of our European culture, its evening sky, is now aflame—and perhaps burning itself up. We artists among the spectators and philosophers are—grateful to the Jews for this.[43]

These propositions would be more convincing if such characteristics could be observed in an equal distribution amongst the Jews of the developed world. But they clearly apply more strongly to Germany than, say, to Britain, France, or North America, and more strongly still to Austria-Hungary, Russia, and Eastern Europe. It seems safest, therefore, to see as an independent variable the degree of integration and assimilation that was available to the Jewish population in any one society. Where, as in the nineteenth-century Germany, this was developing but only imperfectly present, we can witness on the one hand a strong degree of participation in public politics; on the other, a predominant bias in favour of egalitarian ideals, of the rule of law, of equality before the law, and of mutual respect and reciprocity within a differentiated, advanced society.

---

[43] Friedrich Nietzsche, *Beyond Good and Evil*, trans. R. J. Hollingdale (Harmondsworth: Penguin, 1973), 160–161.

CHAPTER II

SITUATIONAL ETHNICITY VERSUS MILIEU IDENTITY: JEWS AND CATHOLICS IN IMPERIAL GERMANY[*]

Till van Rahden

How best to define the post-emancipation Jewish community in modern Germany is an open question. Are German Jews in the late nineteenth century best understood as a religious community, did they constitute a social milieu, were they an ethnic group, or is it even possible to describe German Jews as a unified group? What role did religion play in the formation of the community? How did German Jewry organise itself as a social-cultural community? A comparison with German Catholics, the social-moral milieu par excellence, should provide some answers to these questions.

Many historians maintain the view that German Jews formed a milieu. Occasionally, a colloquial or vague notion of the term is used to describe German Jewry, especially rural and traditional Jews.[1] More significantly, important works by Shulamit Volkov, David Sorkin, and Peter Pulzer draw on the analytical concept of the social-moral milieu as defined by the sociologist M. Rainer Lepsius to describe German Jewry.[2] If the term milieu is not a dominant concept, it is influential in

---

[*] The following essay is an extended version with fewer references of an essay first published in 1996. For more comprehensive references, see Till van Rahden, "Weder Milieu noch Konfession. Die situative Ethnizität der deutschen Juden im Kaiserreich in vergleichender Perspektive," in *Religion im Kaiserreich*, ed. Olaf Blaschke and Frank-Michael Kuhlemann (Gütersloh: Gütersloh Verlagshaus, 1996), 409–434.

[1] See, for example, Monika Richarz, "Einführung," in *Jüdisches Leben in Deutschland*, 4 vols., ed. Monika Richarz (Stuttgart: Deutsche Verlagsanstalt, 1979), 2: 10, 50; Jost Hermand, "Vorbemerkung," in *Geschichten aus dem Ghetto*, ed. Jost Hermand (Frankfurt a. M.: Jüdischer Verlag, 1990), 18; Jacob Katz, *Zwischen Messianismus und Zionismus* (Frankfurt a. M.: Jüdischer Verlag, 1993), 119.

[2] Peter Pulzer, "Politische Einstellung und politisches Engagement jüdischer Unternehmer," in *Jüdische Unternehmer in Deutschland im 19. und 20. Jahrhundert*, ed., Werner Mosse and Hans Pohl (Stuttgart: F. Steiner, 1992), 314; David Sorkin,

the historiography on German Jews. A survey of the general discussion
of the term and its reception in the historiography on modern Germany
raises doubts about its usefulness, however. When Lepsius introduced
the notion of a social-moral milieu in 1966, he did not mention Jews. For
him, there was a Catholic, a conservative, a liberal, and a socialist, but
not a Jewish, milieu. He does not even raise the question as to whether
German Jews constituted a social-moral milieu in Imperial Germany,
and this holds true for the general discussion of the concept to this day.[3]

Authors who use the term as a synonym for related concepts without
carefully differentiating between them reinforce skepticism about
whether the concept of a social-moral milieu is applicable to German
Jewry. For Sorkin, Jews constitute not merely a milieu but first of all a
"subculture"; for Pulzer, sometimes also an "ethnic group." In Volkov's
work, the terms *ethnic group* or *cultural system* appear along with milieu.[4]

In contrast, Lepsius argued for a circumscribed understanding of
the concept. The sociologist understood social-moral milieux as "social
entities generated by the simultaneity of several structural elements
such as religion, regional tradition, economic circumstance, cultural
orientation, or the class-specific composition of intermediary groups."[5]
Lepsius believed that the social-moral milieux were responsible for
the failure of the German political system caused by the demands of
political modernisation between 1870 and 1930. In this period, each
of the major political parties, he argued, was inextricably linked to
a distinct milieu. Many controversies were not simply understood

---

The Transformation of German Jewry 1780–1840 (New York: Oxford University Press,
1987); Shulamith Volkov, *Jüdisches Leben und Antisemitismus* (München: C H. Beck,
1990), 114, 170, and 178.
3   M. Rainer Lepsius, "Parteiensystem und Sozialstruktur. Zum Problem der
Demokratisierung der deutschen Gesellschaft," in *Deutsche Parteien vor 1918*, ed.,
Gerhard A. Ritter (Cologne: Kiepenheuer und Witsch, 1973), 56–80, and Heinrich
Best, ed., *Politik und Milieu* (St. Katharinen: Scripta Mercaturae Verlag, 1989); Karl
Rohe, *Wahlen und Wählertraditionen in Deutschland* (Frankfurt a. M. Suhrkamp, 1992);
and Gangolf Hübinger, "*Sozialmoralisches Milieu*: Ein Grundbegriff der deutschen
Geschichte"; *Soziale Konstellation und historische Perspektive: Festschrift M. Rainer Lepsius*,
ed., Steffen Sigmund (Wiesbaden: Verlag für Sozialwissenschaften, 2008), 207–227.
4   Sorkin, *Transformation*; Peter Pulzer, *Jews and the German State* (Oxford: Oxford
University Press, 1992), 108f; Pulzer, "Politische Einstellung," 314.
5   Lepsius, "Parteiensystem," 68.

as political conflicts but as cultural struggles instead. Public life was permeated not by political battle lines but by "symbolically dramatised moral boundaries" which delimited a milieu. This tight nexus of cultural disposition and political action had been especially close in the case of the Catholic milieu. Lepsius thus emphasised the sharp boundaries of milieux in general and the success of communities in controlling the lives of their members.[6]

In Lepsius's view, the social-moral milieu is best understood as a closed rather than an open group. The identity of "we-groups" (the social-moral milieu as well as other social formations like class, ethnic community, or nation can be subsumed under this heading) may ask for differing degrees of loyalty by their members. In closed groups, the demands of loyalty and the extent of social control can be far-reaching, even absolute, and preclude other loyalties. Membership in other groups, sometimes even contact to members of other groups, is punished. But the demands of loyalty may also be limited. In open groups they are only partial and associated with a notion of identity that coexists with other identities and their demands of loyalty. Open communities do allow membership in other organisations and contact with their members.[7] Against this background, this essay argues that German Jews never were a social-moral milieu that required exclusive loyalty of its members. Instead, it draws on the concept of the ethnic group derived from American scholarship on ethnicity to describe German Jews. Unlike Lepsius's concept of a milieu, the ethnic group encompasses closed as well as open forms of development.

The concept of ethnicity that has been put to fruitful use by historians of American, English, and French Jewry has only recently begun to be invoked in the study of German Jewry.[8] Since the 1960s,

---

6   Ibid., 77 and 69 and 68. See also Thomas Nipperdey, *Deutsche Geschichte 1866–1918* (München: C. H. Beck, 1990), 1:444.

7   Frederik Barth, "Introduction," in *Ethnic Groups and Boundaries. The Social Organisation of Cultural Difference*, ed., Frederik Barth (Bergen: Universitets Forlaget, 1969), 17f; George Devereux, "Ethnic Identity: Its Logical Foundations and Its Dysfunctions," in *Ethnic Identity*, 2nd ed., ed. George De Vos and Leo Romanucci-Ross (Chicago: University of Chicago Press, 1982), 66f.

8   Marion Berghahn, *German-Jewish Refugees in England* (London: St. Martin's Press, 1984), 9–46; Marion Kaplan, *The Making of the Jewish Middle Class* (Oxford: Oxford

American social scientists increasingly analysed ethnic groups and ethnic identities, that is, at a time when the reality of a multicultural society called into question the traditional self-image of American society as a homogenising "melting pot."[9] According to these scientists, an ethnic group distinguishes itself through the notion of common origin and a common culture. Like a modern nation, it is an "imagined order" (Max Weber) based on the "invention of tradition."[10] But unlike a nation, an ethnic community does not lay claim to a particular state. It distinguishes itself by the specific appropriation within a greater social community—as a rule, a nation—of the dominant culture. The ethnic community constitutes itself by combining elements of its own cultural tradition (or those it regards as such) with elements of the predominant culture and thus establishes something new. In the nineteenth century, German Jews did not revive an ancient, comprehensive Jewish identity but created something entirely novel, namely, a German-Jewish ethnicity.

Central to the imagined order of an ethnic group is the construction of boundaries. Ethnicity does not denote a fixed, immutable core of culture, tradition, and religion. Unlike barriers around a milieu, ethnic boundaries need not be rigidly formed but are often fluid. Ethnicity often structures the very social contacts that transgress cultural boundaries. Membership in an ethnic group does not exclude loyalty to other social

University Press, 1991), particularly vi and 64; Steven M. Lowenstein, "Jewish Residential Concentration in Post-Emancipation Germany," *The Leo Baeck Institute YearBook* 28 (1983), 471–495; Steven M. Lowenstein, ed., *The Mechanics of Change: Essays on the Social History of German Jewry* (Atlanta: Scholars Press, 1992), 153–82, here 174f; Pulzer, *Jews and the German State*, 8, 12 and 108f.

9   For an instructive survey, see Thomas H. Eriksen, *Ethnicity and Nationalism* (London: Pluto Press, 1993) and Marcus Banks, *Ethnicity: Anthropological Constructions* (London: Routledge, 1996).

10   I am following those who emphasise the constructed nature of ethnicity. See the classical interpretation by Barth, "Introduction," in *Ethnic Groups and Boundaries*, ed., Fredrik Barth (Boston: Little, Brown, 1969), 9–38; Werner Sollors, *Beyond Ethnicity* (New York: Oxford University Press, 1986); Werner Sollors, *The Invention of Ethnicity* (New York: Oxford University Press 1989), ix-xx; Werner Sollors, "Konstruktionsversuche nationaler und ethnischer Identität in der amerikanischen Literatur," in *Nationale und kulturelle Identität*, ed. Bernhard Giesen (Frankfurt a. M.: Suhrkamp, 1991), 537–69; Marion Berghahn, *German-Jewish Refugees: The Ambiguities of Assimilation* (New York: St. Martin's Press, 1983), 9–20.

formations like class, gender, religion, occupation, or nation. Therefore, the concept of "situational ethnicity" seems particularly helpful in the analysis of German Jewry. It highlights the high degree to which some bonds of belonging are tied to a concrete social situation.[11] If belonging to an ethnic group plays an important role in family life, the domestic realm, or in associational life, ethnic bonds might become less relevant in situations in which other loyalties predominate.

In light of such conceptual considerations, this essay aims to contrast the nature of community building among Jews and Catholics in Imperial Germany. A comparison of the situational ethnicity of Jews and the milieu identity of Catholics is facilitated by the fact that scholarship on Jews and on Catholics has often explored similar subject matters. This essay focuses on five areas in particular: the study of mentality and identity, associational life, journals and other forms of popular readings, schools, and, finally, the realm of politics.[12]

---

[11]   For a comprehensive survey, see Jonathan Okamura, "Situational Ethnicity," *Ethnic and Racial Studies* 4 (1981), 452–65; Don Handelman, "The Organization of Ethnicity," *Ethnic Groups* 1 (1977), 187–200, here 188f and 192f; Barth, "Introduction," 16; as well as the stimulating discussions of John Higham's concept of pluralistic integration and Peter Medding's reflection on segmented identities. John Higham, *Send These to Me* (Baltimore: Johns Hopkins University Press, 1984), 233–48; Peter Y. Medding, "Jewish Identity in Conversionary and Mixed Marriages," *American Jewish Yearbook* 92 (1992), 3–76, here 16–19.

[12]   The heterogeneous nature of the Catholic milieu has recently become more apparent and dismisses the view of a monolithically sealed minority, but when comparing Jews and Catholics, the Catholic milieu appears necessarily more homogeneous. Catholic identity and group formation was less open and more comprehensive than in the Jewish case. For a sense of the heterogeneity of the Catholics and the Zentrum, see David Blackbourn, *Marpingen: The Apparitions of Virgin Mary in the Bismarkian Germany* (New York: Knopf, 1993); Wilfried Loth, "Soziale Bewegungen im Katholizismus des Kaiserreichs," *Geschichte und Gesellschaft* 17 (1991), 279–310; Margaret L. Anderson, "Piety and Politics," *Journal of Modern History* 63 (1991), 681–716; Thomas Mergel, *Zwischen Klasse und Konfession. Katholisches Bürgertum im Rheinland im 19. Jahrhundert* (Göttingen: Vandenhoeck und Ruprecht, 1994). For the traditional view of the "intransigent" Catholicism with its "totalitarian demands," see Hans-Ulrich Wehler, *Das deutsche Kaiserreich 1871–1918*, 5th ed. (Göttingen: Vandenhoeck und Ruprecht, 1983), 83–85, 120–22.

* * *

The age of secularisation and modernisation fundamentally revolutionised existing Jewish mentalities and identities. During the nineteenth century, a radical shift occurred in the meaning of religion for Jewish life. Well into the eighteenth century, Jewish religion had permeated every aspect of a Jew's existence. "Absolute, presumably invariable" (as per Shulamit Volkov), Jewish religious laws and customs determined everyday life and celebrations, work and rest, and the life cycle. The local rabbi, whose comprehensive authority was based on his knowledge of the scriptures, guarded against violations of Jewish law.[13]

In Imperial Germany more than a century later, the situation had profoundly changed. German Jewry had split into the Reformed, Conservative, and Orthodox movements. After about 1850 a majority of Jews, nearly 80 percent in Imperial Germany, belonged to the Reform movement of liberal Jewry, and almost the entire leadership of large Jewish communities was in liberal hands.[14] The Reform movement argued for a new understanding of Judaism and promoted a historical understanding not only of Jewish law but also of the Bible. In opposition to notions of an immutable authority of Jewish law, Reform Jews asserted the importance of the individual believer. They reformulated exclusive traditional messianic hopes into a universalised concept of the world to come. The historical interpretation of an evolving Jewish tradition empowered Reformers to change or even abolish traditional religious rituals within and outside the synagogue without calling into question the Jewish religion as such.

---

[13] Shulamit Volkov, "Erfindung einer Tradition: Zur Entstehung des modernen Judentum in Deutschland," *Historische Zeitschrift*, 253 (1991), 603–629, here 605f; Jacob Katz, *Tradition and Crisis*, 2nd ed. (New York: New York University Press, 1993), Jacob Katz, *Exclusiveness and Tolerance*, 2nd ed. (New York: Behrman House, 1982).

[14] Mordechai Breuer, *Modernity Within Tradition: The Social History of Orthodox Jewry in Imperial Germany* (New York: Columbia University Press, 1992), 3–4 and 14–15; Michael Meyer, *Response to Modernity. A History of the Reform Movement in Judaism* (Oxford: Oxford University Press, 1988), 142, 183, 429; Thomas Rahe, "Religionsreform und jüdisches Selbstbewußtsein im deutschen Judentum des 19. Jahrhunderts," *Menora* 1 (1990), 89–121, here 93.

Even at its heyday in fin de siècle Germany, members of Orthodox synagogues constituted a small minority of no more than 10 to 20 percent of German Jews. Orthodox Jews too hoped to reconcile the Jewish religion with the claims of modernity. In contrast to reformed Judaism, however, they maintained that Jewish distinctiveness was not based in subjective belief but in observance of the law. Thus, religious law was viewed not as a contingent product of history but as timeless divine revelation, which had to be preserved and observed. Moreover, the division into Reformed, Conservative, and Orthodox Judaism was also reflected institutionally. Each movement established its own rabbinical seminary and rabbinical association to debate religious questions and created its own press agencies, and in Frankfurt am Main, for example, the Orthodox even formed their own congregation, the *Austrittsgemeinde*.[15] German Jewry had become pluralised (and to some extent polarised). What had ceased to exist was a homogeneous version of Judaism that might have served as an ideological basis for a milieu. Unity of theological doctrine and religious discipline and practice was lost once and for all, opening the way to incertitude, retreat, and possibly disengagement.

But Judaism had not merely become pluralistic; it had also rapidly lost significance. By the end of the nineteenth century, secularisation among German Jews had progressed more dramatically than among their Protestant and Catholic fellow citizens. A popular joke had an "enlightened" Jew declare "all ritual in our religion" to be disagreeable to him; of the Jewish holy days he "observed only the Grünfeld concert."[16] Some, like Sigmund Freud, regarded themselves as "godless Jews."[17] The Jewish attorney and Social Democratic politician from Munich, Philip Löwenfeld (1887–1963), recalled in his memoirs, written between 1940 and 1945, that he had been a "so-called dissident in religious matters"; if

---

15   For the religious modernization of German Jewry, see Meyer, *Response to Modernity*; Michael Meyer, "Recent Historiography on the Jewish Religion," *Leo Baeck Institute YearBook* 35 (1990), 3–16; Breuer, *Modernity Within Tradition*.

16   Alexander Moszkowski, *Der jüdische Witz und seine Philosophie* (Berlin: Dr. Eysler & Co., 1922), 51.

17   Letter by Sigmund Freud to Oskar Pfister, 1918 in *Sigmund Freud, Oskar Pfister: Briefe, 1909–1939* (Frankfurt a. M.: S. Fischer, 1963), 64.

asked, he defined himself not as a "German citizen of the Jewish faith" but as "a German Jew of non-Israelite belief."[18] However, in addition to the small, deeply religious minority, many secular Jews often held on to remnants of their faith. Jewish women particularly were known to preserve religious traditions in the home.[19] Nonetheless, the decline of religious observance continued: the number of visitors to synagogues remained low; most Jews attended them on high holidays only or lived as "synagogal mayflies" (Aryeh Maimon). Fewer and fewer Jews observed the dietary laws, and in domestic life Jewish and Christian traditions became entwined;[20] among middle-class and especially upper middle-class Jewish families Christian maids and nannies often raised younger children.[21] Jewish schoolchildren attended religion classes less frequently than their Protestant or Catholic classmates, or even took part in Christian religious instruction.[22] Finally, the proportion of Jewish graduates from secondary schools who decided to study theology was smaller than that of Protestants or Catholics.[23]

[18]   Philip Löwenfeld, "Memoiren," Richarz, ed., *Jüdisches Leben in Deutschland: 1918–1945*, 3:86.
[19]   Kaplan, *Making*, 64–83; Marion Kaplan, "Frauen und jüdische Geschichte im deutschen Kaiserreich," *L'Homme* 3 (1992), 67–70. Forms of German Jewish popular religiosity have barely been studied. See Meyer, "Recent Historiography," 16.
[20]   Arye Maimon, *Wanderungen und Wandlungen. Die Geschichte meines Lebens* (Trier: Arye Maimon-Institut für Geschichte der Juden, Universität Trier, 1998), 29. For the mixing of religious traditions, see the autobiographical sources like Adolf Heilberg (1858–1936), Memoiren im Leo Baeck Institut, New York, 12–14 and 34; Victor Klemperer, *Jugend um 1900* (Berlin: Siedler, 1989), 1:34, 115–20, 213, 247; Gershom Scholem, *Von Berlin nach Jerusalem*, 4th ed. (Frankfurt a. M.: Suhrkamp, 1993), 20 and 41. See also Meyer, *Response to Modernity*, 115, 182, 185, 204; Breuer, *Modernity Within Tradition*, 5 16f; Gary Cohen, "Jews in German Society. Prague, 1860–1914," *Central European History* 10 (1977), 28–54, here 39f; Jacob Toury, *Soziale und politische Geschichte der Juden in Deutschland 1847–1871* (Düsseldorf: Droste, 1977), 161, 298f; "Theilnahme jüdischer Kinder an der Christbescheerung," *Israelitische Wochenschrift* 15 (1884), 373f, and "Weihnachtsbäume und Chanukkageschenke," *Israelitische Wochenschrift* 23 (1892), 417.
[21]   In Breslau, in 1890, for example, only 2 percent of the domestic employees in Jewish households were Jewish, 53 percent were evangelical, and 45 percent were Catholic. In general, see Kaplan, *Making*, 37–39. The history of the influence of non-Jewish family members on the education of children has not been explored.
[22]   Breuer, *Modernity Within Tradition*, 92–103; Kaplan, *Making*, 253f and Rahe, "Religionsreform," 98.
[23]   Between 1870 and 1910, in Breslau, 30 percent of the Catholics and 8 percent of the Evangelicals but only 2 percent of the Jewish high school students were enrolled in

In the course of the nineteenth century, an increasing number of German Jews embraced the modern concepts of *Bildung* and history, instead of religion, as the foundation from which to build a sense of community. George L. Mosse and David Sorkin have highlighted the centrality of *Bildung*, that is, the concept of liberal education and self-formation, for secular Jewry. When the age of emancipation dawned in the early nineteenth century, Jews began to embrace neo-humanist notions of liberal education that aimed at the free development of the individual, invoked the ideal of the perfection of the self, and promised to transcend social status and religion. The idea of *Bildung* promised social and political emancipation to all who subscribed to it, and this principle made it especially appealing to German Jews. Cultural icons like Goethe, whom "Jews of every rank … worshipped passionately," (Arnold Zweig) and Lessing, whose *Nathan der Weise* became the "Magna Carta" (George L. Mosse) of German Jewry, came to embody a reverence of *Bildung* among Jews.[24] Theodor Fontane's pronouncement that Berlin Jews were the true bearers of "cosmopolitan refinement [*Weltbildung*]" pointed to the prominent role Jews played in the cultural life of large German cities. Jewish veneration of *Bildung* found expression not only in elite patronage of high culture but also in the emphasis placed on education in marriage announcements by a broad social stratum in the Jewish population.[25]

---

the study of theology. See *Jahresschulschriften der Breslauer höheren Schulen 1870–1910* (Pädagogisches Zentrum, Berlin).

[24] George L. Mosse, *German Jews Beyond Judaism* (Cincinnati: Hebrew Union College Press, 1985); George L. Mosse, "Das deutsch-jüdische Bildungsbürgertum," in *Bildungsbürgertum im 19. Jahrhundert II*, ed. Reinhart Koselleck (Stuttgart: Klett-Cotta, 1990), 168–80; Kaplan, *Frauen und jüdische Geschichte*, 60f; Volkov, *Jüdisches Leben*, 121–23; Bertha Badt-Strauss, "My World, and How It Crashed," *The Menorah Journal* (Spring 1951), 91, 94. For the period before 1840, see Sorkin, *Transformation*, 86–104, 172–77, and for the admiration of Goethe, see Wilfried Barner, *Von Rahel Varnhagen bis Friedrich Gundolf: Juden als deutsche Goethe-Verehrer* (Göttingen: Wallenstein Verlag, 1992).

[25] Theodor Fontane, "Adel und Judenthum in der Berliner Gesellschaft, Die Juden in unsrer Gesellschaft," *Jahrbuch der deutschen Schillergesellschaft* 30 (1986), 34, 37–39, 59–66; Werner Mosse, *The German-Jewish Economic Elite II* (Oxford: Oxford University Press, 1989), 297–330; Trude Maurer, "Partnersuche und Lebensplanung. Heiratsannoncen als Quelle für die Sozial- und Mentalitätsgeschichte der Juden in Deutschland," in *Juden in Deutschland*, ed. Peter Freimark (Hamburg: Christian, 1991), 351f.

Equally important for post-emancipation visions of community among Jews was an intense interest in Jewish history, which had become "the faith of the fallen Jews" (Yosef H. Yerushalmi) in the nineteenth century.[26] Memory had played a central role in Judaism prior to the turn toward history in the early nineteenth century, but it had been tied to the notion of a metahistorical myth. Interest in the temporality of the recollected, in historical development and change, and in *history* as a collective singular arose only in the early nineteenth century under the influence of historicism. The initial result was a scholarly interest in Jewish history. Heinrich Graetz's eleven-volume *History of the Jews* (*Geschichte der Juden von den ältesten Zeiten bis auf die Gegenwart*), completed in 1876, epitomised such attempts to reconstruct Jewish history. This same historical interest manifested itself in professional publications like the *Monatszeitschrift für die Geschichte und Wissenschaft des Judentums* (1851–1939), the *Zeitschrift für die Geschichte der Juden in Deutschland* (1887–1892), and publications on the local history of Jewish communities. Simultaneously with these scholarly concerns emerged a more general interest in the Jewish past. Jewish weeklies regularly published articles on Jewish history geared toward a less intellectual readership, and associations for Jewish history and literature mushroomed across central Europe. Graetz's historical work became the handbook of the educated Jewish bourgeoisie but was also read in secularised homes.[27]

---

[26] Yosef H. Yerushalmi, *Zakhor: Jewish History and Jewish Memory* (New York: Schocken, 1989), 86.

[27] Volkov, "Erfindung einer Tradition," 612–14; Ismar Schorsch, "The Emergence of Historical Consciousness in Modern Judaism," *Leo Baeck Institute YearBook* 28 (1983), 413–37; Yerushalmi, *Zakhor*, 77–103; Meyer, *Response to Modernity*, 76, 79. For the popular reception of Graetz, see Michael Meyer, "Jewish Scholarship and Jewish Identity," *Studies in Contemporary Jewry* 8 (1992), 188; Klemperer, *Jugend um 1900*, 1:67, 487; Franz Kafka, *Tagebücher 1910–1923* (Frankfurt: 1983), November 1, 1911, 98, and Nils Roemer, *Jewish Scholarship and Culture in Nineteenth-Century Germany: Between History and Faith* (Wisconsin: Wisconsin University Press, 2005). The popular ghetto novels are also part of this process of creation and popularization of historical traditions. On this, see Richard Cohen, "Nostalgia and 'Return to the Ghetto: A Cultural Phenomenon in Western and Central Europe," in *Assimilation and Community*, ed. Jonathan Frankel and Steven Zipperstein (Cambridge: Cambridge University Press, 1992), 130–55; Klemperer, *Jugend um 1900*, 1:542.

Although Jews of Imperial Germany rarely invoked a language of ethnic belonging explicitly and mostly defined themselves as "German citizens of the Jewish faith," many intellectuals used the terms *tribe* (*Stamm*) and *tribal consciousness* (*Stammesbewusstsein*). Such semantics expressed a specifically Jewish loyalty based on the notion of common descent. Jews aimed to fashion a vision of community similar to contemporary concepts of ethnicity. As early as 1869, the Viennese Rabbi Adolf Jellinek (1820–1893), who had been active in Leipzig during the 1840s and the 1850s and was widely read in Germany, claimed that Jews were one of the many tribes in the Habsburg monarchy and encouraged them to preserve their "tribal consciousness." "After an unprecedented persecution of 1,800 years," the *Allgemeine Zeitung des Judenthums* opined in 1870 that the "Jewish tribe" was "chosen to provide in this new age the touchstone for the power of both the freedom of conscience and equality in the modern state."[28] The Jewish philosopher and ethnologist Moritz Lazarus (1824–1903) also availed himself of these terms when he repudiated Heinrich von Treitschke's attacks on the Jews in the Berlin debate on anti-semitism of 1880. Rather than assimilating "unconditionally," as Treitschke had demanded, Lazarus maintained that German Jews "had the duty" to preserve both "the intellectual peculiarity they possessed as a tribe and the inherited virtue and wisdom they possessed as a religion." In 1887, even a self-confessed "German loyal to the Empire of the Jewish confession" exhorted German Jews in the *Israelitische Wochenschrift* to combat anti-semitism out of "reverence for his religion and his tribe." Nathan Samter, arguing in 1900 against prophecies of an impending destruction of the German Jews, wrote that the "holy tribe [of the Jews] would forever preserve its driving force [*Triebkraft*]." In an editorial a year later, the culturally Zionist publication *Ost und West* declared that it too saw itself as contributing to the preservation of "our tribe."[29]

---

28 "Die Reichen," *AZJ* 34 (1870), 569–572, here 570 and 572.

29 Adolf Jellinek, *Der jüdische Stamm. Ethnographische Studien* (Wien: Herzfeld & Bauer, 1869); Moritz Lazarus, "Was heißt national?" (Berlin: Dümmler, 1880); quoted after Julius H. Schoeps and Ludger Heid, ed., *Juden in Deutschland. Von der Aufklärung bis zur Gegenwart. Ein Lesebuch* (München: Beck, 1995), 167; "Noch eine Stimme über

Walther Rathenau used the term as well, even though—or maybe because—the industrialist and combative intellectual felt few religious ties to the Jewish community. "If I have always underscored, in ways that were offensive to the Prussian state, my formal religious affiliation ... I did not mean to express an attachment to Judaism ... but a political protest against the state's unconstitutional intolerance."[30] Rathenau self-confidently emphasised that he was a "German of the Jewish tribe" and as such a proud member of a multitude of tribes that constituted the German nation. "My people are the German people, my home is the German lands," he wrote in his call "To Germany's Youth" of 1918, "my religion the German faith, which stands above all confessions." But "nature," he continued, had "combined both sources of my old blood into a boiling contradiction: a yearning for the genuine, a propensity for the intellect."[31] At the end of the Weimar Republic, the vaguely Zionist *Jüdisches Lexikon* reviewed this semantic tradition and noted that "in the last decades," the concept of "tribal community (*Stammesgenossenschaft*) had become a much-used designation for the Jewish community or people." Unlike the concept of religious community, the encyclopaedia concluded that the term *tribe* emphasized the "aspect of common descent and history."[32]

The concept of the tribe appealed to German Jews because in general political speech it also stood for a form of particularity that

Lazarus' Broschüre," *Israelitische Wochenschrift* 18 (1887), 99; Nathan Samter, *Was thun? Ein Epilog zu den Judentaufen im 19. Jahrhundert* (Breslau: Schatzky, 1900), 44–45; "Ost und West," *Ost und West* 1 (1901), 1.

30   Walther Rathenau, "Apologie," *Gesammelte Schriften* (Berlin: Fischer, 1929), 6:442f, quoted after Helmuth F. Braun, "Höre, Israel! Antisemitismus und Assimilation," in *Die Extreme berühren sich. Walther Rathenau 1867–1922*, ed. Hans Wilderotter (Berlin: 1993), 320.

31   Walther Rathenau, "Apologie," *Gesammelte Schriften* (Berlin: Fischer, 1929), 6:442f and idem, "An Deutschlands Jugend," *Gesammelte Schriften* (Berlin: Fischer, 1929), 6:99; quoted after Helmuth F. Braun, "Höre, Israel! Antisemitismus und Assimilation," Hans Wilderotter ed., *Die Extreme berühren sich. Walther Rathenau 1867–1922* (Berlin: Argon Verlag, 1993), 320 and 323.

32   Max Joseph, "Stammesgemeinschaft," *Jüdisches Lexikon* (Berlin: Jüdischer Verlag, 1930), 4, 2:628f, and George L. Mosse, *Germans and Jews* (Detroit: Wayne State University Press, 1987), 107f; Steven Aschheim, *Brothers and Strangers: The East European Jew in German and German-Jewish Consciousness, 1800–1923* (Madison: University of Wisconsin Press, 1982), 97.

while not religiously based was nevertheless regarded as a legitimate expression of difference. The concept found its way into political discourse as early as during the emergence of modern German nationalism. In 1815, the historian Friedrich Christoph Dahlmann (1785–1860) wrote euphorically after Napoleon's defeat at Waterloo that the now recapitulated "German tribes … were united in the main, in their common claim to freedom." The nationalistic enthusiasm of the Napoleonic wars also echoed in Jacob Grimm's preface to his *Deutsche Grammatik* from 1819, where he argued that "the German people" was striving for "its national reunification without the dissolution of the states and tribes that have emerged in history."[33]

During the final third of the nineteenth century, even prominent non-Jewish intellectuals began to view Jews as one among many German tribes. Theodor Mommsen, for instance, argued in his acerbic rejoinder to Treitschke in 1880 that the "German nation [was] based on the cohesion and, in a certain sense, the amalgamation of different German tribes," of which the Jews were one "no less than the Saxons, Swabians, or Pommeranians." Rather than deny this "diversity," the public should "take delight in it." Walter Rathenau was perhaps referring to Mommsen's wording when he argued in 1916, in a letter to Wilhelm Schwaner, the leader of the reformist national education movement (*Volkserzieher-Bewegung*), that the German nation was not based on the idea of "race." "My people," he asserted, are "the Germans, nobody else." To Rathenau, the Jews were "a German tribe just like the Saxons, the Bavarians, or the Wendish."[34] Through the concept of tribe, then, the German public could imagine the national community both as a united people and as a plurality of tribes. Such a pluralistic understanding stood in contrast to an older school of thought that had conceptualised diversity as the coexistence of dynastic principalities under the auspices of the empire. The liberal, antidynastic conception of tribal diversity culminated in the preamble

---

[33] Dahlmann quoted after Christoph Dipper, "Freiheit," *Geschichtliche Grundbegriffe*, 506; Jacob Grimm, Deutsche Grammatik, Bd. 1, Göttingen 1819, xiv.

[34] Theodor Mommsen, "Auch ein Wort über unser Judentum," in *Der Berliner Antisemitismusstreit,* ed., Walter Boehlich (Frankfurt a. M.: Insel-Verlag, 1965), 210–225, here 212.

to the Weimar Constitution of 1919. Whereas the German princes had entered into an "eternal alliance" in the Imperial Constitution of 1871, the democratic constitution emphasised that "the German people, united in its tribes," had given itself "this constitution."[35]

While during the nineteenth century, Jewish identities became pluralised and secularised, the Catholic notions of community evolved in a different direction. With the reassertion of papal authority and leadership, religion shaped a wide-ranging cohesion. The *Syllabus Errorum* of 1864, with its antimodern and antiliberal thrust, the dogma of papal infallibility in 1870, the uncontested authority and successful hierarchal order of the Catholic clergy, as well as the marginalisation of the internal-Catholic opposition, are mere examples of a more comprehensive process. The Catholic Church increasingly tended to isolate itself in opposition to competing worldviews. Against scientific knowledge in general and the historical perception of religion in particular, and against freedom and plurality of opinion, it stood firmly for traditional popular piety and a dogmatic ultramontanism. Pious practice in the mass, devotions, and confession; saying one's Rosary; pilgrimages as well as papal, Marian, and Sacred Heart cults advanced a narrow Catholic view of itself and the world with far-reaching integrative force: between 60 and 90 percent of all nominal Catholics were actively involved in the life of the church.[36]

---

[35] Gerhard Anschütz, *Die Verfassung des Deutschen Reichs vom 11. August 1919*, 14th ed. (Berlin: Reclam, 1932), xii; vgl, auch ibid., 2.

[36] Nipperdey, *Deutsche Geschichte 1866–1918*, 1:428–68; Christoph Weber, "Ultramontanismus als katholischer Fundamentalismus," Wilfried Loth ed., *Deutscher Katholizismus im Umbruch zur Moderne* (Stuttgart: W. Kohlhammer, 1991), 20–45; Michael Ebertz, "Herrschaft in der Kirche. Hierarchie, Tradition und Charisma im 19. Jahrhundert," in *Zur Soziologie des Katholizismus*, ed. Karl Gabriel u. Franz-Xaver Kaufmann (Mainz: Matthias-Grünewald-Verlag, 1980), 89–111; Jonathan Sperber, *Popular Catholicism in Nineteenth Century History* (Princeton: Princeton University Press, 1984); Mergel, *Klasse*, 329f; Max Weber, *Wirtschaft und Gesellschaft*, 5th ed. (Tübingen: J. C. B. Mohr, 1980), 825.

* * *

The cohesiveness of Jewish life in fin de siècle Germany depended to a great extent on associational life. Like the entire long nineteenth century, the Imperial period in Germany was a club-happy era. German-Jewish club life, whose flowering coincided with the empire, was a variation of the general associational frenzy.[37] Around the turn of the century, approximately 5,000 Jewish associations existed in Germany, of which more than 75 percent had been founded only after 1850.[38] Among them were charitable, educational, athletic, and youth organisations, as well as political clubs and Jewish lodges. The largest was the *Centralverein deutscher Staatsbürger jüdischen Glaubens* (Central Association of German Citizens of Jewish Faith), established in 1893. By 1903 it already boasted more than 100,000 members, and by 1916 there were more than 200,000. Nearly one in three Jews belonged to this organisation, which proudly fought for Jewish equality. Equally successful was the Jewish Women's Federation, to which one in seven Jewish women belonged by 1914, when it had existed for barely ten years.[39] Many of these organisations displayed a close relationship between ethnic identity formation and associational life (*Vergesellschaftung*). In 1907 the Israelite Community Home, an important meeting place for Jewish communal life in Hamburg, referred

---

[37] Sorkin, *Transformation*, 107–23; Volkov, *Jüdisches Leben*, 126f; Jacob Thon, *Die jüdischen Gemeinden und Vereine in Deutschland* (Berlin: Verlag des Bureaus für Statistik der Juden, 1906); Toury, *Soziale und politische Geschichte*, 211–76; Aharon Bornstein, "The Role of Social Institutions as Inhibitors of Assimilation. Jewish Poor Relief System in Germany, 1875–1925," *Jewish Social Studies* 50 (1993), 201–222; *Das deutsche Judentum. Seine Parteien und seine Organisationen* (München: Verlag der Neuen Jüdischen Monatshefte, 1919); Gary Cohen, "Organisational Patterns of Urban Ethnic Groups," in *Ethnic Identity in Urban Europe*, ed. Max Engman (Dartmouth: European Science Foundation, 1992), 407–18.

[38] Sorkin, *Transformation*, 116.

[39] On the *Centralverein* see Ismar Schorsch, *Jewish Reactions to German Antisemitism, 1870–1914* (New York: New York University Press, 1972), 119, and Marjorie Lamberti, *Jewish Activism in Imperial Germany* (New Haven: Yale University Press, 1978). On the Jewish women's organization, see Kaplan, *Die jüdische Frauenbewegung in Deutschland 1904–1938* (Hamburg: Christian, 1981).

to itself as the "pillar of our tribal consciousness."[40] These associations and clubs were especially vigorous at the municipal rather than the national level. In turn-of-the-century Breslau, for example, there were more than 50 organisations for barely 20,000 Jewish citizens.[41] The city's largest Jewish association was the Israelite Hospital and Burial Society, which by 1910 counted 2,500 members. Here, members of all the Jewish religious movements came together to support various Jewish charities with membership fees and generous contributions. They subsidised not only the ongoing expenses of the city's Jewish hospital but, shortly after 1900, collected more than 2 million reichsmarks to finance, solely through contributions, the construction of one of Germany's largest and most modern Jewish hospitals.

But the commitment and exclusive coherence of Jewish clubs and societies should not be overrated. Many members of these organisations were also active in non-Jewish associations, as long as their non-Jewish fellow citizens did not exclude them. They participated in women's, rifle, and sports clubs and were members in art, veterans', colonial, and consumers' associations; some were active as Freemasons and others in professional and status organisations.[42] Breslau Jews like Sigismund

---

[40] *Jahresbericht des Israelitischen Gemeinschaftsheims 1907* quoted after Erika Hirsch, *Jüdisches Vereinsleben in Hamburg bis zum Ersten Weltkrieg. Jüdisches Selbstverständnis zwischen Antisemitismus und Assimilation* (Frankfurt a. M.: Lang, 1996), 139. On the *Israelitischen Gemeinschaftsheim*, see ibid., 98–100.

[41] *Statistisches Jahrbuch des Deutsch-Israelitischen Gemeindebundes* 12 (1897), 23–25; *Statistisches Jahrbuch deutscher Juden* (Berlin-Halensee: Bureau für Statistik der Juden,, 1905), 139–56. For the development of the Jewish population, see Leszek Ziatkowski, *Rozwoj Liczebny Ludnosci Zydowkiej We Wroclawiu W Latach 1742–1914*," *Sobótka* 46 (1991), 169–89.

[42] Volkov, *Jüdisches Leben*, 126f; Diethard Aschoff, "Von der Emanzipation zum Holocaust. Die jüdische Gemeinde im 19. u. 20. Jahrhundert," in *Geschichte der Stadt Münster*, ed. Franz Josef Jacobi (Münster: Aschendorff, 1993), 2:470f; Hansjoachim Henning, "Soziales Verhalten jüdischer Unternehmer in Frankfurt/M und Köln 1860–1933," in *Jüdische Unternehmer*, ed. Mosse and Pohl, 259f; Arno Herzig, "Zwischen Integration und Identität. Das Stadtjudentum Ostwestfalens in der Kaiserzeit," in *Unter Pickelhaube und Zylinder*, ed. Joachim Meynert (Bielefeld: 1991), 314–17; Helga Krohn, *Die Juden in Hamburg, 1848–1918* (Hamburg: Christian, 1970), 111–19, 197; Kaplan, "Sisterhood under Siege" 242f.; Paul Y. Mayer, "Equality - Egality. Jews and Sport in Germany," *Leo Baeck Institute YearBook* 25 (1980), 221–241, here 227f; Jacob Katz, *Jews and Freemasons in Europe 1723–1939* (Cambridge: Harvard University Press, 1970).

Asch, Wilhelm Salomon Freund, and Adolf Heilberg are representative. The physician and politician Asch (1825–1901) served for a long time on the board of directors of the Breslau Election Association of the Liberal People's Party as well as the Association against Impoverishment and Mendicancy. He was a member of the Humboldt Association for Popular Education besides being chairman of the Breslau Association of Physicians and leader of the Silesian Association for Patriotic Culture.[43] The attorney Wilhelm Salomon Freund (1831–1915) held membership in the Israelite Hospital and Burial Society, and was chairman of the Synagogue's Council of Representatives. At the same time he chaired the bar association and became a member of the Humboldt Association for Popular Education and of the Silesian Association for History and Antiquities. From 1871 to 1914 he was a member of the liberal party and after 1887 president of the city council. He served from 1876 to 1879 as a representative of the Progressive Party in the Prussian Diet and in the Reichstag from 1879 to 1881.[44] Finally, Adolf Heilberg (1858-1936), like Freund an attorney, not only actively supported the liberal electoral association of the Jewish community and the Israelite Hospital and Burial Society, but was also concurrently a leading political liberal in Breslau. He was on the board of the bar association as well as the German Society for Peace, and was a member of the Giant Mountains Association, as well as the Breslau section of the Alpine Association and the Breslau popular education movement.[45] Voices that cautioned against membership in such non-Jewish organisations, like those of some Orthodox rabbis in the case of Freemasonry, remained in

---

[43] On Asch, see Aron Heppner, *Jüdische Persönlichkeiten in und aus Breslau* (Breslau: Schatzky, 1931), 3; Mitgliederverzeichnis 1876/77 des Humbolt-Vereins Breslau in UB Wroclaw GSL Yv 608; NL Asch im Besitz von Frau Dagmar Nick, München.

[44] Heppner, *Jüdische Persönlichkeiten*, 12f; *Jüdisches Volksblatt* 17 (1911), 396; Ernest Hamburger, *Juden im öffentlichen Leben Deutschlands* (Tübingen: J. C. B. Mohr, 1968), 296–98; Mitgliederverzeichnis 1906 des Humboldt-Vereins Breslau in UB Wroclaw GSL Yv 608; "Mitglieder=Verzeichnis für 1901," *Zeitschrift des Vereins für Geschichte und Alterthum Schlesiens* 35 (1901), 392.

[45] On Adolf Heilberg see Till van Rahden, *Jews and Other Germans: Civil Society, Religious Diversity and Urban Politics in Breslau, 1860 to 1925* (Madison: The University of Wisconsin Press, 2008), especially 75–76 and 170–172.

the minority.[46] Many German Jews felt comfortable belonging to both Jewish and non-Jewish organisations because their ethnic identity was pluralistic, not thoroughly exclusive.

Moreover, unlike Catholics, Jews never managed to consolidate the wide range of associations in Imperial Germany into a national umbrella organisation that might have obliged different factions to coordinate their activities. In fact, attempts to create such an organisation failed. The *Deutsche Israelitische Gemeindebund* remained a loose federation of local Jewish communities that expressly eschewed discussions of religion, ritual, and politics. A proposal to establish a Jewish Diet (*Judentag*), modelled on the Catholic Diet (*Katholikentag*), or a Jewish Centre Party (*Zentrum*) foundered from the start. The conflicts between Orthodox and Reformed and, after the turn of the century, increasingly between Zionists and anti-Zionists could no more be overcome than the unwillingness of local organisations to relinquish their authority or the lack of interest, on the part of most German Jews, in a central organisation.[47]

Within the Catholic milieu too, clubs and associations formed an important support system. Catholicism in Imperial Germany was a Catholicism of associations and federations. There were countless societies for religious and ecclesiastical purposes, charitable organisations, professional and status associations, and trade and labour unions. In 1890, the nationwide People's Association for Catholic Germany emerged as the largest mass organisation next to Social Democracy. At the same time, there existed, with the annual *Katholikentag*, an umbrella organisation for Catholic associational life. These essentially denominational and religious organisations, often dominated by priests, formed a tight associational network that contributed to the coherence of the Catholic milieu.[48]

---

[46] "Geistlichkeit, Jüdische," *Internationales-Freimauerlexikon* (Wien: 1932), 584.

[47] Jacob Toury, "Organizational Problems of German Jewry. Steps Towards the Establishment of a Central Organization (1893–1920)," *Leo Baeck Institute YearBook* 13 (1968), 57–90; Jehuda Reinharz, *Fatherland or Promised Land* (Ann Arbor: University of Michigan Press, 1975), 200–205; Marjorie Lamberti, "From Coexistence to Conflict, Zionism and the Jewish Community in Germany, 1897–1914," *Leo Baeck Institute YearBook* 27 (1982), 53–86; Volkov, *Juden und Judentum*, 87f., 103f.

[48] Nipperdey, 1:439–442, 461–64; Olaf Blaschke, "Die Kolonialisierung der Laienwelt," in *Religion im Kaiserreich*, ed. Frank-Michael Kuhlmann (Gütersloh: Gütersloher

This web of Catholic associations demanded from its members an exclusive and far-reaching loyalty. Unlike German Jews, members of the Catholic milieu did not, as a matter of course, take an active part in non-Catholic associations. Unity and cohesion were expected. A Catholic's membership in a Freemason lodge led to expulsion from the church. Moreover, there was a sharp divide between Catholic and Social Democratic workers' unions; joint membership to the Mainz Bishop von Ketteler was out of the question. During the *Kulturkampf*, only someone who repudiated the non-Catholic Veterans' Association could join the Catholic Veterans' Association in Bonn. *The Catholic Teachers' Journal* insisted that its members leave the general Teachers' Association, which was committed to parity, in order to organise exclusively in a Catholic professional organisation. "Avoid the religious scoffers and doubters wherever you can," Kolping's paternalistic Journeymen's Association admonished its members in the 1870s.[49] The constant repetition of such demands, of course, raises the question of whether all Catholics felt obliged to observe them. But it is nevertheless evident that the Catholic milieu, through pointed "concentration and segregation" (Michael Ebertz), drew its boundaries more sharply than did German Jewry.[50]

* * *

The reading habits of German Jews also reflected the fact that they constituted a group that was at once open and closed. They supported a wide range of Jewish publications and popular literature but also read

---

Verlag-Haus, 1996), 129–31; Horstwalter Heitzer, *Der Volksverein für das katholische Deutschland im Kaiserreich 1890–1918* (Mainz: Matthias Grünewald-Verlag 1979); Peter Kall, *Katholische Frauenbewegung in Deutschland* (Paderborn: F. Schöningh, 1983).

[49] A. Bongartz, *Das katholisch-soziale Vereinswesen in Deutschland* (Würzburg: 1879), 59, quoted after Ebertz, *Herrschaft*, 102; *Die Katholische Lehrerzeitung* quoted after *Schlesische Schulzeitung* 21 (1892), 12f. See also *Schlesische Schulzeitung* 20 (1891), 287f and *Schlesische Zeitung* 119 (March 12, 1874), 1; and *Schlesische Schulzeitung* 123 (March 12, 1874), 4. For an interesting contemporary comparative perspective, see "Excommunication im Judenthum und im Katholicismus," *Israelischen Wochenschrift* 6 (1875), 266f. u. 273–75.

[50] Ebertz, *Herrschaft*, 101f; Nipperdey, 1:461f; and Mergel, *Klasse*, 402.

non-Jewish papers and participated in German cultural life at large. A multifaceted and broad landscape of Jewish weeklies, monthlies, and quarterlies served as a means of self-discovery, self-comprehension, and self-representation; as a defence against antisemitism; and simply as a source of information. After the mid–nineteenth century, the Jewish publication market increasingly expanded; the German Jewish press became the "rouser of Jewish consciousness."[51] There were the large Jewish weeklies with a circulation of about 3,000 and a national readership' the *Allgemeine Zeitung des Judenthums* (1837–1922), the journalistic flagship of the Reform Movement; the neo-orthodox *Israelit* (1860–1938); and the Orthodox *Jüdische Presse* (1870–1938). The *Israelitisches Familienblatt* (1889–1938), which cannot be assigned a particular Jewish religious or political orientation, was a commercial entertainment journal. With a print run of more than 12,000, it boasted the highest circulation. Furthermore, the large Jewish associations maintained their own press organs: the *Centralverein* published *Im deutschen Reich* (1895–1922) and the Zionists' *Israelitische Rundschau* (1895–1938, after 1902 *Jüdische Rundschau*). In 1911, this weekly proclaimed: "During the past years, the Jewish press has become as powerful a factor for the Jewish population as the non-Jewish press is to the general public."[52]

But the Jewish press fever should not obscure the fact that Jews regarded the liberal daily press as its primary source of information. Unlike the case of American Jews or German Catholics, there was not a single Jewish daily in Imperial Germany. If the *Germania*, the *Kölnische Volkszeitung?* or the *Schlesische Volkszeitung* were the "body and soul" of German Catholics, great liberal newspapers like the *Frankfurter Zeitung*, the *Berliner Tageblatt*, the *Vossische Zeitung*, or the *Gartenlaube*

---

51   Barbara Suchy, "Die jüdische Presse im Kaiserreich und in der Weimarer Republik," in *Juden als Träger bürgerlicher Kultur in Deutschland*, ed. Julius H. Schoeps (Stuttgart: Burg Verlag, 1989), 167–91; Jacob Toury, "Das Phänomen der jüdischen Presse in Deutschland," Quesher, Journalism Studies, Tel Aviv University, Sonderheft: Jüdische Zeitungen und Journalisten in Deutschland, Mai 1989:4–13; Breuer, *Modernity Within Tradition*, 166–173; David Brenner, *Marketing Identities: The Invention of Jewish Ethnicity in Ost and West* (Detroit: Wayne State University Press, 1998); Volkov, "Erfindung einer Tradition," 617–22; Krohn, *Juden in Hamburg*, 197.

52   *Jüdisches Volksblatt* 17 (1911), 311f and "Eine nüchternere Beurteilung des Erfolges der jüdischen Presse," *IW* 22 (1891), 49–51, 58–59, here 50.

were the equivalent for German Jews.[53] "By force of habit," Jews in Breslau read the liberal *Breslauer Zeitung*, the local *Jüdisches Volksblatt* commented in 1898.[54] The family of the Berlin rabbi Wilhelm Klemperer subscribed to "Tante Voss" and the *Berliner Tageblatt* as its main sources of information.[55] Local correspondents of Jewish weeklies generally gleaned their information from the liberal daily press. Even neo-orthodox Jews did not fear contact with non-Jewish journalism. When the *Israelit* railed against an "un-Jewish" press, it did not target the general daily papers but Jewish competitors of the Reform Movement.[56] German Jews regarded only anti-semitic writing as bad press.

The Catholic milieu, conversely, supported and thrived on a dense network of daily newspapers, and weekly and monthly journals, as well as polemical and devotional literature. The church hierarchy attempted to oversee these publications and declared it a sin to read any other papers.[57] The lecture of good, that is, Catholic, journals was meant to convey a shared worldview, while distance from the non-Catholic press aimed at keeping alternative interpretations far from the faithful. The *Catalogue of Suitable Books and Plays for Catholic Libraries* exclusively contained Catholic and apologetic literature. Ketteler oversaw "books and journals" for his clergy and strove to ferret out "every resonance of a more liberal spirit."[58] Priests tried to ascertain, openly or covertly, which papers lay Catholics were reading in order to protect them from anticlerical publications.

---

53   Suchy, *Die jüdische Presse*, 169; Volkov, *Jüdisches Leben*, 173.
54   *Jüdisches Volksblatt* 3 (1898), 404.
55   Klemperer, *Jugend um 1900*, 1:100.
56   Breuer, *Modernity Within Tradition*, 167–168. Steven Beller has calculated for Vienna that 50% of the death announcements in the important liberal *Neuen Freien Presse* came from Jews. Unfortuantely, there are no comparable studies for Germany. Steven Beller, *Vienna and the Jews, 1867–1938* (Cambridge: Cambridge University Press, 1989), 42.
57   Blaschke, *Kolonialisierung*, 118–129; M. Schmolke, "Katholisches Verlags, Bücherei und Zeitschriftenwesen," in *Katholizismus, Bildung und Wissenschaft im 19. und 20. Jahrhundert*, ed. Anton Rauscher (Paderborn: F. Schöningh, 1987), 93–117; Mergel, *Klasse*, 312f and 317; Langewiesche, "Volksbildung," 118f. For examples of the suppression of the ultramontane inner Catholic opposition, see Christoph Weber, *Kirchengeschichte*, Zensur, *Selbstzensur* (Cologne: Böhlau, 1984).
58   F. Vigener, *Ketteler. Ein deutsches Bischofsleben im 19. Jahrhundert* (München: R. Oldenbourg, 1924), 287. Compare "Verzeichnis geeigneter Bücher ..." with *Katholische Kolportage, nebst einem Verzeichnis geeigneter Schriften*, 2nd ed (Mönchengladbach: Zentralstelle des Volksvereins für das katholischer Deutschland, 1907).

* * *

The fact that German Jewry did not form a self-contained milieu but can be regarded as an open ethnic group manifested itself also in its attitude towards education. After 1850, the majority of Jewish pupils attended non-Jewish, often Christian schools; in Imperial Germany, nearly all did. A German-Jewish school system did exist, but for the educational experience of Jews, it was less significant than the regular system. Of all Jewish pupils in Prussia, only 20 percent frequented a Jewish school in 1886. By 1896, the number had fallen to a mere 14 percent; and by 1916, it stood at 16 percent.[59] Even in Hamburg, which along with Frankfurt boasted the largest Jewish school system, less than two out of five schoolchildren attended a Jewish school.[60] In Berlin, home to 14 percent of all German Jews by the turn of the century, less than one out of ten Jewish children went to a Jewish primary school in 1897, and less than one out of twelve in 1908.[61] In Breslau, after 1874, all Jewish students attended non-Jewish schools.[62]

Although most Jewish parents in Imperial Germany sent their children to non-Jewish schools, some demanded a Jewish school system similar to that of Protestants or Catholics. Interdenominational schools,

---

[59] Calculated on the basis of *Preußische Statistik* 101 (1889), 32f, 438f, 482 and 151 (1898), 217; 321 (1913), 52f, 280f and 342, Detlev K. Müller and Bernd Zymek ed., *Sozialgeschichte und Statistik des Schulsystems in den Staaten des Deutschen Reiches, 1800–1945* (Göttingen: Vandenhoeck & Ruprecht, 1987), 166f. u. 182f. See also Jakob Thon, *Der Anteil der Juden am Unterrichtswesen in Preußen* (Berlin: Bureau für Statistik der Juden, 1905), 28f, and Lamberti, *Jewish Activism*, 125f and 165f.

[60] Krohn, *Juden in Hamburg*, 185; Ursula Randt, "Zur Geschichte des jüdischen Schulwesen in Hamburg (ca. 1780 - 1942)," in *Die Juden in Hamburg 1590–1990*, ed. Arno Herzig (Hamburg: Christian, 1991), 113–30; Inge Schlotzhauer, *Das Philanthropin 1804–1942. Die Schule der Israelitischen Gemeinde in Frankfurt* (Frankfurt a. M.: W. Kramer, 1990).

[61] Jacob Segall, "Schulbesuch christlicher und jüdischer Kinder in Berlin 1897 bis 1906," *Zeitschrift für Demographie und Statistik der Juden* 5 (1909), 113–21.

[62] Only for Jewish girls did the community maintain a separate school, but the enrollment during the Kaiserreich stagnated at 140, which never represented more than 10% of the Jewish female students of Breslau. See Verwaltungsbericht des Magistrats der Königlichen Haupt- und Residenzstadt Breslau 1880/83, 118; dass., 1904/07, 236, and ibid., 1907/10, 232 and also Andreas Reinke, "Zwischen Tradition, Aufklärung und Assimilation. Die Königliche Wilhelmsschule in Breslau 1791–1848," *Zeitschrift für Religions- und Geistesgeschichte* 43 (1991), 183–214, here 211–214.

which Jewish parents tended to support in principle, had not been able to establish themselves as a viable alternative to the confessional model.[63] Jewish teachers had no hope of employment in these schools, and the denominational character of primary schools intensified Jewish children's awareness of their position as outsiders.[64] Thus, proponents of Jewish schools were disappointed, above all, by the discrimination against Jewish teachers and pupils inherent in educational politics. Even the Breslau *Jüdisches Volksblatt*, which generally advocated Jewish special interests, favoured a universal school system in principle, but "as a confessional character has been imposed on the Breslau schools, it behooves us to request that consequently the Jewish population too should be granted its right" to a Jewish primary school.[65] Yet few Breslau Jews shared even this cautious argumentation. The majority of the city council supported, in theory as well as practice, the interdenominational schools and firmly rejected a Jewish primary school on the grounds that it would constitute "a Ghetto school that the parents want to avoid."[66]

Catholics staunchly repudiated interdenominational and pluralistic education, criticised the supposedly secularised secondary schools, and fought for the confessional division of the entire system.[67] Schools, as an influential Catholic pronounced in 1881, must be fertilised and guided by the church.[68] Catholic critics regarded the nonconfessional school as a "reformatory supporting a completely inopportune anti-confessionalism

---

[63] Hellmut Becker and Gerhard Kluchert, *Die Bildung der Nation* (Stuttgart: Klett-Cotta, 1993), 32f.; Nipperdey, *Deutsche Geschichte 1866–1918*, 1:534–37.

[64] Hamburger, *Juden*, 53–63.

[65] *Jüdisches Volksblatt* 10 (1904), 337f. u. 347f. Die *Allgemeine Zeitung* argued in 1874, for example, that Jewish schools are to be maintained to protect Jewish teachers and students from the discrimination they encounter in Christian schools. See *Allgemeine Zeitung* 38 (1874), 153, and Lamberti, *Jewish Activism*, 139.

[66] Quoted after *Jüdisches Volksblatt* 16 (1910), 63; 48f, and 10 (1904), 337f, 347f, 381; Marjorie Lamberti, *State, Society, and the Elementary School in Imperial Germany* (New York: New York University Press, 1989), 164–171.

[67] Lamberti, *State, Society, and the Elementary School in Imperial Germany*, 40–87; Geoffrey G. Field, "Religion in the German Volksschule, 1890–1928," *Leo Baeck Institute YearBook* 25 (1980), 46, 50–52, 66; Pulzer, *Jews and the German State*, 113; Mergel, *Klasse*, 371–73.

[68] L. Kellner, "Erziehung," Wetzer und Welte's Kirchenlexikon, 2nd ed., 4 (1886), 870–81, here 881; Michael Klöcker, "Katholizismus und Bildungsbürgertum," Koselleck ed., *Bildungsbürgertum II*, 121f.

that fettered all true humanity and tolerance."[69] Particularly secondary schools were the object of parochial censure for their "bad, liberal, antireligious spirit."[70] The respected Catholic *Schlesische Volkszeitung* condemned the hiring of four Jewish primary school teachers in 1910 as "the battering ram that breaches the principle of Christian, denominational elementary schools" because Jews, after all, were "the born enemy of Christian education."[71] Catholic opinion abominated the attendance of parochial schools by Jewish pupils as an "intrusion into the education of Christian youth of the Jewish element that strives to infuse Christian children with its Jewish-modern, i.e. infidel, spirit."[72] Therefore, leaders of the milieu urged Catholic parents to enter as many students as possible into schools whose parochial character had to be preserved at all costs.

Throughout Imperial Germany, Catholicism succeeded in keeping nearly all Catholic schoolchildren in parochial institutions of learning. Around 90 percent of all Catholic children in Prussia attended a Catholic school in both 1886 and in 1911, and only 5 and 7 percent, respectively, went to a nondenominational school. In 1886, only 242 of 18,197 Catholic pupils in Cologne did not attend a parochial school; and in 1906, only 8 out of 47,975. Even in Berlin, where Catholics were a small minority, only 9 percent of Catholic children in 1886 and 5 percent in 1911 were exposed to the un-Catholic influence of a nonparochial school.[73] The field of secondary education was hardly different. In 1870s Breslau, four out of five Catholic students attended the city's only Catholic secondary school, Matthias-Gymnasium; and by 1900, three out of four did so, shunning the four other grammar schools.[74]

---

69 Paul Majunke, *Confessionell oder Confessionslos?* (Breslau: Görlich und Coch, 1869), 116.
70 F. Heiner, *Eine Lebensfrage der katholischen Kirche in Deutschland oder der herrschende Priestermangel* (Paderborn 1883), 31, quoted after Mergel, *Klasse*, 372.
71 Quoted afer *Jüdisches Volksblatt* 16 (1910), 335.
72 L. Friedlieb, "Die Verjudung der christlichen Jugend," *Der katholische Beobachter* 17 (1880), 122–32 and 196–205, here 122 and 132.
73 Caculated on the basis of *Preußische Statistik* 101 (1889), 32f; *Preußische Statistik* 231, 54f. For Cologne, see H. Silbergleit, *Preußens Städte* (Berlin 1908), 216–21; and Frank-Michael Kuhlemann, "Niedere Schulen," Chista Berg, ed., *Handbuch der deutschen Bildungsgeschichte* 4 (1991), 185.
74 Since 1897 only Catholics visited the Matthias-gymnasium. See *Verwaltungsberichten des Magistrats der Königlichen Haupt- und Residenzstadt Breslau*; Kazimierz Bobowski, *Die Geschichte des Schulwesens vom Elementaren und Höheren Grad in Breslau bis 1914*

* * *

Finally, German Jewry did not develop a political party—the hallmark so typical of a social milieu. It is a banal but important observation that there was no Jewish party comparable to the Catholic Centre Party. Although Jews participated more actively than other Germans in political life, they usually pursued not Jewish but general politics. To be sure, there was, without a doubt, a specific German-Jewish affinity to liberalism, a Jewish-liberal partnership. During the early phase of the empire, about nine out of ten Jewish voters supported a liberal party.[75] Later, four out of five Jewish votes were still cast for liberal, mostly left-liberal, parties in Wilhelminian Germany. Jewish backing of liberalism was not indicative of the existence of a symbolic boundary but simply reflected that German Jews, who belonged largely to the bourgeoisie, tended to vote for a bourgeois party unless it was openly or covertly antisemitic, like the Conservatives or some regional undercurrents in the Centre Party.[76]

Although most German Jews backed the liberal movement, the antisemitic stereotype of a liberalism contaminated by Jews (*"verjudet"*) should not deceive anyone: although Jews were overrepresented in liberalism, at no time and nowhere did they constitute a majority.[77] If liberalism had a subcultural confessional stamp, it was above all

---

(Wroclaw: Uniwersytet Wrocławski, 1992), 50f; *Festschrift zur 250jährigen Jubelfeier des Königlichen St. Matthias Gymnasiums zur Jahrhundertfeier 1811–1911* (Breslau: 1911).

[75] Toury, *Die politischen Orientierungen*, 138.

[76] On anti-semitism amongst conservatives, see James Retallack, "Anti-Semitism, Conservative Propaganda, and Regional Politics in Late 19th Century Germany," *German Studies Review* 11 (1988), 377–403; Helmut Berding, *Moderner Antisemitismus in Deutschland* (Frankfurt a. M.: Suhrkamp, 1988), 153. On anti-semitism among Zentrum party members, see Berding, *Moderner Antisemitismus*, 154; Pulzer, *Jews and the German State*, 141f; David Blackbourn, "Roman Catholics, the Centre Party and Anti-Semitism in Imperial Germany," in *Nationalist and Racialist Movements in Britain and Germany Before 1914*, ed. Paul Kennedy and Anthony Nicholls (London: Macmillan, 1981), 106–29.

[77] Dieter Langewiesche, *Liberalismus in Deutschland* (Frankfurt a.M.: Suhrkamp, 1988), 114, 125f. The protestant character commonly entailed also a denigrative view of the Jewish religion and culture. Dieter Langewiesche, "Liberalismus und Judenemanzipation im 19. Jahrhundert," in *Juden in Deutschland*, ed. Peter Freimark, 155–57; Schorsch, *Jewish Reactions to German Antisemitism*, 98f, 238f.

Protestant. Between 75 and 95 percent of all left-liberal members and between 88 and 97 percent of all National Liberal delegates to the Prussian Diet were Protestant; at times, there was not a single Jewish delegate in the liberal delegations.[78] Although three out of five Jewish voters supported left-liberal parties at the turn of the century, they made up less than one-tenth of all left-liberal voters.[79] Even in Breslau, where the proportion of Jewish citizens stood at 5 to 6 percent and where Jews represented a core group of urban liberalism, they nevertheless formed a minority within the liberal camp, albeit one of 20 to 40 percent.[80]

Finally, the Jewish-liberal partnership was anything but free of tensions. For German Jews, the often concealed yet sometimes overt support for anti-semitic candidates, especially by National Liberals, was a bitter experience. A widely circulated Jewish joke ridiculed a National Liberal as a "man who changes his convictions like his underwear once every quarter." In runoff elections, for example, in which a Social Democrat stood against an antisemitic candidate, Liberal parties repeatedly supported the antisemitic candidate, to the horror of many Jews. For some liberals, the fight against Social Democracy carried more importance than that against anti-semitism. After the 1907 election, a speaker of the *Centralverein* vented his disappointment: "The anti-semites have moved into the Reichstag largely on the coattails of leftist parties."[81] It could hardly be reassuring to Jewish voters that National Liberals cooperated with the notoriously anti-semitic Agrarian League (*Bund der Landwirte*) and were closely allied with the no less anti-Jewish Pan-German League.[82]

---

[78] Langewiesche, *Liberalismus*, 320f, and Pulzer, *Jews and the German State*, 122f.; Hamburger, *Juden*, 339.

[79] Pulzer, *Jews and the German State*, 146.

[80] Manfred Hettling, "Von der Hochburg zur Wagenburg. Liberalismus in Breslau von den 1860er Jahren bis 1918," in *Liberalismus und Region*, ed. Dieter Langewiesche and Lothar Gall (München: C. H. Beck, 1995), 253–76.

[81] Moszkowski, *Der jüdische Witz und seine Philosophie*, 120; J. Lewy, "Die letzten Reichstagswahlen," *Im deutschen Reich* 13 (1907), 141–47, here 143; Lamberti, *Jewish Activism*, 37, 46, 64–66, 180f.; *Jüdisches Volksblatt* 3 (1898), 205f; ibid. 12 (1906), 562 and 13 (1907), 65; *Die Laubhütte* 6 (1889), 15; *Allgemeine Zeitung des Judenthums* 49 (1885), 208; Hamburger, *Juden*, 154–155.

[82] Langewiesche, *Liberalismus*, 146 u. 157; Dan S. White, *The Splintered Party* (Cambridge: Harvard University Press, 1976), 135f, 144–46; Richard S. Levy, *Downfall*, 148, 181–183;

If a Jewish party thus existed only as an antisemitic fantasy, the Catholic movement had in the Centre Party a dedicated, organised political forum. This party attracted the great majority of Catholic voters, even though its proportion fell from close to 90 percent in the 1880s to about 55 percent in late Wilhelminian Germany.[83] In view of the social heterogeneity of the Catholic population, these were remarkable electoral successes. They were the result of the tight integration of the Centre Party into the Catholic milieu, of clubs and associations, of the press, of the Catholic social culture, and of the church. Before 1900, the Centre Party developed a "nearly unbelievable force of political mobilization," especially in the heartland of the Catholic milieu. The bonding power of that milieu successfully prevented Catholic voters from deciding against the Centre Party.[84]

* * *

A number of Jewish critics during the empire despaired of the damaging internal Jewish fragmentation and looked with envy at the Catholic milieu. They admired the solidarity and cohesion that had created Catholic associational life, the Centre Party, and the *Katholikentag*. In 1913, the Breslau *Jüdische Volkszeitung* noted: "We should regard the

---

Geoff Eley, "Anti-Semitism, Agrarian Mobilization, and the Crisis in the Conservative Party. Radicalism and Containment in the Foundation of the Agrarian League 1890–93," in *Between Reform, Reaction, and Resistance: Studies in the History of German Conservatism from 1789 to 1945*, ed. Larry E. Jones and James Retallack (Providence: Berg, 1993), 219–23; Anthony Kauders, *German Politics and the Jews* (Oxford: Oxford University Press, 1996), 37f. On the antisemitism amongst farmers and the *Alldeutschen*, see Hans-Jürgen Puhle, *Agrarische Interessenpolitik und preussischer Konservativismus im Wilhelminischen Reich (1893–1914)*, 2ed. (Bonn: Verlag Neue Gesellschaft, 1975), 112–140; Roger Chickering, *We Men Who Feel Most German: A Cultural Study of the Pan-German League 1886–1914* (Boston: Allen & Unwin, 1984), 236–245, 300; Chickering too documents the high percentage of liberals amongst the Alldeutschen and other nationalistic associations.

83   Rudolf Morsey, "Der politische Katholizismus 1890–1933," in *Der soziale und politische Katholizismus* (München: Olzog, 1981), 1:110–65, 126; Lepsius, *Parteiensystem*, 69.

84   Rohe, *Wahlen*, 54f, 73–83 u. 117; Wilfried Loth, *Katholiken im Kaiserreich* (Düsseldorf: Droste, 1984); Nipperdey, *Deutsche Geschichte 1866–1918*, 2:337–50; Margaret L. Anderson, "Voter, Junker, Landrat, Priest. The Old Authorities and the New Franchise in Imperial Germany," *American Historical Review* 98 (1993), 1448–74, here 1451f and 1464–67.

manifestations of the Catholic Kirchentag as an example." Catholics had provided the broad public with an illustration of "steadfast coherence," and Jews should be glad "if we could find in our ranks anything close to this harmony and convergence."[85] These critics clearly recognised the difference between the Catholic milieu and the Jewish community. But they were in a minority with their call for emulation of the Catholics. The majority of Jews did not want a Jewish social milieu.

Instead, during the second half of the nineteenth century, German Jewry created and preserved its peculiar character as an ethnic group while at the same time participating politically, culturally, and socially in the life of society at large. The coexistence of cohesion and openness in modern German Jewish community building and identity formation can best be characterised as situational ethnicity. The group's demand for loyalty was partial, limited to the internal coherence of a Jewish sphere, but by no means excluded other affiliations. In comparison, the loyalty that the social-moral Catholic milieu expected of its members was more comprehensive and embraced a wider range of activities. To overstate the point somewhat, we can say that Catholics in Imperial Germany embraced an ultramontane view of the world, avoided non-Catholic associational life, read only the Catholic press, sent their children to parochial schools and, finally, voted for the Centre Party. Most German Jews, in contrast, shared an enlightened concept of education as well as a positive understanding of Jewish tradition and history, took an active role in both Jewish and non-Jewish organisations, read the *Daily Liberal* as well as the Jewish weekly press, sent their offspring to non-Jewish schools, and voted for liberal parties. The idea of "symbolically dramatized moral boundaries" so characteristic for a social-moral milieu would have struck most German Jews as odd.

This is not to claim that late nineteenth-century attempts to strengthen the bonds of belonging among German Jews came to nothing. With the surge in Jewish associational life after 1880, new spaces developed within Jewish civility, and one does not do them justice by understanding them simply as a response to antisemitism.

---

[85] "Der Katholikentag," *Jüdische Volkzeitung* August 29, 1913, 1; Toury, "Organizational Problems," 58 and 63.

New associations like the Independent Order of B'nai B'rith, founded in 1882, or the Associations for Jewish History and Literature, encouraged Jews to reclaim their own history, define Jewishness not only religiously but ethnically, and strengthen Jewish self-consciousness.[86] With these new forms of Jewish sociability in mind, the *Allgemeine Zeitung des Judenthums* noted in 1903 that in recent years, "hundreds of associations" had been founded. The slogan "A little more detachment, more Judaism!" had not "in the last decade remained only in the religious arena." However, there was to be no talk of a new Jewish subculture. True, there was a return to Jewish traditions, but there was no withdrawal from civil society. Most Jews, the journal claimed, continued to be active in the broader associational life: "Whoever is familiar with their efforts to reach beyond the middle class through their educational and charitable endeavours and their numerous associated federations and associations," the journal wrote, "knows that there has been, for a long time, thank God, no talk of a nascent, self-imposed isolation among Jews."[87] A few years after Georg Simmel declared in 1908 that the "number of different circles ... to which an individual belongs" is "an indicator of culture" and that the "intersection of social circles" is a sign of the modern, the philosopher of religion Julius Guttmann claimed to see an "especially developed case" of "the intersection of different communal relationships" in the Jewish diaspora.[88] A separate German-Jewish subculture, comparable to the "all-encompassing unity" of the Catholic or socialist milieus, existed only in the fantasies of a small minority of Zionist visionaries.

───────

[86]   Jacob Borut, "Vereine für Jüdische Geschichte und Literatur at the End of the Nineteenth Century," *Year Book of the Leo Baeck Institute* 41 (1996), 89–114, as well as Till van Rahden, "'Germans of the Jewish Stamm': Visions of Community between Nationalism and Particularism, 1850 to 1933," in *German History from the Margins, 1800 to the Present*, ed., Mark Roseman, Nils Roemer, and Neil Gregor (Bloomington, IN: Indiana University Press, 2006), 27–48.

[87]   "Unsere Geselligkeit," *Allgemeine Zeitung des Judenthums* 67 (1903), 145–148 (this citation relating to Berlin).

[88]   Georg Simmel, "Die Kreuzung sozialer Kreise," in Georg Simmel, *Soziologie: Untersuchungen über die Formen der Vergesellschaftung* (Frankfurt: Suhrkamp, 1992; first published in 1908), 456–511, 464; Julius Guttmann, "Der Begriff der Nation in seiner Anwendung auf die Juden," *K.C.-Blätter: Monatsschrift der im Kartell-Convent vereinigten Korporationen* 4 (1914), 69–79 and 109–116; here 70 and 78.

The comparison of Jews and Catholics demonstrates the wide range of social-cultural group and identity development in the empire. From the perspective of German-Jewish history, German Catholicism represented a comparatively homogenous, religious, and antimodern milieu. German Jewry, on the other hand, formed not a milieu but a pluralistic entity marked by a situational ethnicity that displayed a positive attitude toward modernity.

CHAPTER III

REDEFINING JUDAISM IN IMPERIAL GERMANY: PRACTICES, MENTALITIES, AND COMMUNITY[1]

Marion Kaplan

In the course of emancipation in Central Europe, as some have argued, Jews plunged headlong into "assimilation," absorbing West European culture as they integrated into their nation states.[2] Judaism lost its hold, allegedly evolving or declining—depending on one's viewpoint—into a religious creed rather than an all-enveloping environment.

We may modify these assumptions by pointing to the rich variety of Judaisms that evolved in Imperial Germany. Using the perspective of a school of history known in Germany as *Alltagsgeschichte*,[3] the history of everyday life, we can focus on how changing structures (such as urbanisation) and cultural shifts affect subjective experiences. Alltagsgeschichte reveals the qualitative aspects of ordinary people's existence—their emotions, perceptions, and mentalities. It can illuminate the multiple ways in which individuals interpreted and refashioned their religious beliefs and behaviours.[4]

---

[1]   I would like to thank the Leo Baeck Institute (New York) and the Center for Scholars and Writers at the New York Public Library for supporting my research, and the German Women's History study group of New York, Lisa Grant, and Robin Judd for their careful reading of this article.

[2]   See my discussion of these terms in "Tradition and Transition: The Acculturation, Assimilation and Integration of Jews in Imperial Germany: A Gender Analysis," *Leo Baeck Institute Year Book* 27 (1982), 3–35.

[3]   *Alltagsgeschichte* connotes history from "below." In Britain, this grew from labor history with Marxist influence; and in the United States, from non-Marxist sociology and the New Left. Although I have not done so, Alltagsgeschichte also focuses on micro-historical studies; see, for example, David Sabean, *Property, Production, and Family in Neckarhausen 1700–1870* (Cambridge: Cambridge University Press, 1990), and his *Kinship in Neckarhausen 1700–1870* (Cambridge: Cambridge University Press, 1998).

[4]   See also Marion Kaplan, ed., *Jewish Everyday Life in Germany, 1618–1945* (Oxford: Oxford University Press, 2005).

Jewish religious life changed unevenly, incorporating a multiplicity of voices and practices in perpetual motion. Two major developments within Judaism, themselves products of their changing times, provided the setting within which Jews could choose how they wished to worship and how they wished to manage their religious lives outside the synagogue: the Reform Movement, which spanned the nineteenth century and attracted increasing numbers of German Jews,[5] and Modern Orthodoxy, which remained a "viable religious movement almost everywhere in Germany for most of the century."[6] Moreover, Jewish migration to urban centres shifted the setting of Jewish life away from small towns and villages, where tradition lasted longer. That generalisation notwithstanding, even village behaviour was unpredictable. A number of Reform communities in the 1840s had switched to Orthodox rabbis in the twentieth century.[7]

If, to some extent, the religious cohesiveness of small communities, or "milieu religiosity," gave way to an "individualistic religiosity,"[8] there was actually a complicated relationship between the two. Individuals created their own Judaism, interacting with their surroundings but not tyrannised by them, reflecting the role, ultimately, of personal choices. Indeed, individuals within the very same family set out in different directions. Gershom Scholem's father celebrated Christmas, and his uncle observed Hanukkah. Of the four brothers, Gershom chose Zionism, another became a communist and an atheist, another became a German nationalist who distanced himself from Jewish tradition, and the fourth became a member of the Democratic Club.[9] Preserving Jewish tradition was an intensely private decision.

---

5   Michael A. Meyer, *Response to Modernity: A History of the Reform Movement in Judaism* (New York: Oxford University Press, 1988).

6   Robert Liberles, *Religious Conflict in Social Context: The Resurgence of Orthodox Judaism in Frankfurt am Main, 1838–1877* (Westport: Greenwood Press, 1985), 13.

7   Steven Lowenstein, "The 1840's and the Creation of the German-Jewish Religious Reform Movement," in *Revolution and Evolution: 1848 in German-Jewish History*, ed., Werner Mosse, et al. (Tübingen: J. C. B. Mohr, 1981), 273.

8   Leo Baeck coined the term *Milieufrömmigkeit*, and Alfred Jospe used *Individualfrömmigkeit*. Alfred Jospe, "A Profession in Transition: The German Rabbinate, 1910–1939," *Leo Baeck Institute Year Book* 19 (1974), 51.

9   Gershom Scholem, *From Berlin to Jerusalem: Memories of My Youth*, trans. Harry Zohn (New York: Schocken, 1980), 29, 42–43. Similarly, the four daughters of judge and law professor Alfred Wieruszowski, whose own background included an Orthodox *kheyder*

How did individuals manifest this diversity? This article will attempt an answer by focusing on personal and spontaneous expressions of faith or heritage. It analyses milieus in which practice[10] continued or diminished, attempting to look at the attachments of individuals to their religion even as these attachments changed over the course of a person's lifetime. In so doing, we may shed light on the question of what constitutes modern religion.

RECASTING TRADITION

The nineteenth century witnessed the gradual privatisation of religion among most Germans, especially in the cities. Educated urbanites subscribed to a "secular religion," a *Bildungsreligion*, originating in the German Enlightenment attempt to interpret divine revelation on the basis of reason and on the notion of a personal, inner process of development.[11] Whereas "God was indeed 'dead' for the educated city-dweller of Protestant Germany,"[12] religion was not. Between 1870 and 1880, Protestant weekly churchgoing reached its lowest rates of the century,[13] but "each person made up his own religion,"

---

education, chose different paths: one became Protestant, another Catholic, another Jewish, and the last, atheist. Jenny Wieruszowski, diary, LBI.

[10] Arnold Eisen, *Rethinking Modern Judaism: Ritual, Commandment, Community* (Chicago: Chicago University Press, 1998). Eisen argues that what mattered in modern religion was not whether individuals believed in it, but whether they practiced it, even in a selective manner.

[11] Hermann Timm, "Bildungsreligion im deutschsprachigen Protestantismus—eine grundbegriffliche Perspektivierung," in *Bildungsbürgertum im 19. Jahrhundert*, vol. 2: Bildungsgüter und Bildungswissen, ed., Reinhard Koselleck (Stuttgart: Klett-Cotta, 1990), 57–89; Wolfgang Schieder, "Sozialgeschichte der Religion im 19. Jahrhundert. Bemerkungen zur Forschungslage," in *Religion und Gesellschaft im 19. Jahrhundert*, ed., Wolfgang Schieder (Stuttgart: Klett-Cotta, 1993).

[12] By World War I, the most devout section of the urban Protestant population was the lower middle class. Hugh McLeod, *Religion and the People of Western Europe, 1789–1989* (Oxford: Oxford University Press, 1997), 98–99, 101, 116.

[13] Churchgoing declined to 1–5 percent. Lucian Hölscher, "Secularization and Urbanization in the Nineteenth Century," in *European Religion in the Age of Great Cities, 1830–1930*, ed., Hugh McLeod (London: Taylor and Francis, 1995), 278. Hölscher writes that already by 1850, "the core of loyal church people in German cities made up less than 10 percent of nominal parishioners." And these years were also low points for Catholic practice (ibid., 281).

participating in life-cycle events, home rituals, and organisations with a religious character.[14]

Similarly, Judaism lost its spiritual power to regulate the lives of many, but the vast majority of Jews did not abandon Judaism. Indeed, Jews evinced a profound attachment to German Enlightenment traditions. However, they were also drawn by an equally powerful attraction: the desire to retain their Jewish identities. Juggling both, late-nineteenth-century Jews appropriated German bourgeois culture while maintaining elements of traditional religious beliefs, practices, family, and (increasingly voluntary) communal commitments.

Some, like their non-Jewish counterparts, adopted a Bildungsreligion, modernising or relinquishing some religious practices. They redefined "Judaism" and what it meant to be "Jewish." Combinations of faith and secularism—the "freethinker" who fasted on the high holidays and whose wife maintained the Sabbath[15]—were fairly typical among German Jews. In fact, the diversity of expressions characteristic of modern Judaism may have been born in Imperial Germany. Arnold Eisen has suggested that "Jews for the most part navigated their way through modernity's unfamiliar terrain much as we do today: via eclectic patterns of observance and varied, often individual, sets of meanings discovered in those patterns or associated with them."[16] This is an apt description of Jewish religious life in Imperial Germany.

Although it is impossible to gauge precisely the extent of religious practice among Jews, there are some general external guideposts. Whether someone maintained the laws of kashrut (dietary laws), attended synagogue regularly, and observed holidays indicated some degree of devotion. But every practice can be interpreted in multiple ways—theological, familial, communal, or simply traditional. Does maintenance of ritual indicate deep faith, or did those who practiced

---

14   McLeod, *Religion and the People*, 98. Protestants maintained high participation in rites of passage—baptism, marriage and burial—and preserved some home rituals such as grace or prayers at night. Hölscher, "Secularization and Urbanization," 281–82.

15   Andrea Hopp, *Jüdisches Bürgertum in Frankfurt am Main im 19. Jahrhundert* (Stuttgart: F. Steiner, 1997), 240.

16   Eisen, *Rethinking Modern Judaism*, 2.

rituals do so out of "consideration for their reputations and relatives ... fear or habit?"[17] Conversely, "a good deal of religious consciousness and sentiment can live on without necessarily finding expression in socially observable conduct."[18] Did "three-day Jews" (who frequented synagogues only on the high holidays), for example, lose all attachment to Judaism? To the synagogue as a place for spiritual expression? Or to spirituality as such?

Synagogue attendance (like church-going for Christians) expressed spirituality for some, habit for others, and, for many, a combination of both that also changed over time. As a child, Alex Bein attended a liberal Nuremberg synagogue regularly. Subsequently, his faith waned, but "I was always edified by the aesthetic of the room ... also ... the sermons ... with their eloquent connection between traditional learning and modern Bildung."[19] Bein wondered, though, whether the service had lacked "simple religiosity." More critically, Jakob Wassermann saw synagogue services as a "noisy routine of drill," complaining bitterly of "a gathering without devotion."[20]

Wassermann may have been right for some. Others eschewed regular services but continued to experience their devotion privately. The inward-looking nature of Bildung, contemporary Lutheranism's emphasis on morality above dogma, and Pietism's stress on the "inner self"[21] provided a context in which some Jews reduced their practice but maintained—maybe even increased—their faith. And to the extent that individualism began to replace community in all religions, faith may have replaced practice. Berthold Freudenthal (born 1873) provides a test case. Superficially, he appeared to lack devotion, attending his Frankfurt synagogue only on the high holidays.[22] His practice did not,

17   Jakob Wassermann memoir, in F. E. Menken, ed., *Stachel in der Seele: Jüdische Kindheit und Jugend* (Weinheim: Quadriga, 1986), 119.
18   Fritz Stern, "Comments on the Papers of Ismar Schorsch, Vernon Lidtke and Geoffrey Field," *Leo Baeck Institute Year Book* 25 (1980), 73.
19   Alex Bein (born 1903), *Hier kannst Du nicht jeden grüssen: Erinnerungen und Betrachtungen*, ed., Julius H. Schoeps (Hildesheim: Olms, 1996), 86.
20   Wassermann was born in 1873 in Fürth; Menken, ed., *Stachel*, 119.
21   F. W. Graf and H. M. Müller, eds., *Der deutsche Protestantismus um 1900* (Gütersloh: Chr. Kaiser, 1996).
22   Margarete Sallis-Freudenthal (born 1893; hereafter Sallis), memoir, LBI, 93.

however, correspond to a decline in beliefs, defined either as feelings or convictions. He prayed nightly and recorded an ongoing monologue to God in his diary, thanking God for a career promotion and praying for a German victory in World War I.[23]

Similarly, in the 1870s, Philippine Landau's family in Worms limited its observance to three days.[24] Like many Jews of her generation, she tended to use the Yom Kippur fast to gauge religiosity. Although Jews might be lax about *kashrut* or the Sabbath, they generally complied longer with the obligation to fast. The Landaus eventually gave it up but with ambivalence: their meals were "somewhat abridged," because "by every right we actually should have been fasting." Moreover, "an aura of sacredness and deep solemnity" still hovered over their house, and in the synagogue, "I was in an enchanted, better world, full of holiness.... I felt strangely purified and lifted up."[25] Performing or ignoring rituals allowed Jews to express "a variety of meanings—whether to [themselves], to fellow Jews, or to Gentiles."[26]

FAMILIES, GENDER, AND JUDAISM

Alongside the synagogue, Jewish leaders pointed to the family as crucial in fostering Judaism.[27] Families transmitted Judaism on a daily, personal basis: "What parents gave their children ... wasn't religiosity, nor knowledge, but their lived lives."[28] This meant that men and women passed on gendered traditions deeply embedded in Judaism: women focused on the home, while men "counted" in public expressions of religion.

The public and private, however, needed each other. The Sabbath and holidays required home and synagogue observances. A kosher home

---

[23]   Sallis, memoir, LBI, 55, 73–74.
[24]   Monika Richarz, ed., *Jüdisches Leben in Deutschland: Selbstzeugnisse zur Sozialgeschichte im Kaiserreich* (Stuttgart: DVA, 1979), 343.
[25]   Monika Richarz, ed., *Jewish Life in Germany: Memoirs from Three Centuries*, trans. Stella and Sidney Rosenfeld (Bloomington, IN: 1991), 249–51.
[26]   Eisen, *Rethinking*, 4.
[27]   Samson Raphael Hirsch, *Versuche über Jissroels Pflichten in der Zerstreuung* (Frankfurt a. M.: J. Kauffmann, 1909), 365.
[28]   Richarz, *Kaiserreich*, 178.

entailed the diligence of women and men. Food symbolised cultural continuities or breaks and set the tone of the household.[29] But kosher meals also required public arrangements consisting of (male) rabbis to resolve questions regarding food rituals, (male) butchers who could ritually slaughter meat,[30] and (mostly male) merchants whom one could trust to sell kosher foods. The public and private reinforced Jewish life.

When (male) synagogue attendance began to decline, Judaism, by default, shifted its focus (though not its theology) to revolve around women's domestic practice.[31] However, the home alone could not sustain Judaism. Curt Rosenberg, born in Berlin in 1876, learned little of his religion except the prayers his mother had taught him, without which he could not fall asleep. His grandmother prayed every morning, but this impressed him far less than the Christian prayers that started his school day and the Christian tunes "that I liked a lot and ... still know by heart."[32] Mothers who hoped to imbue their children with a religious spirit faced an uphill battle, one that many lost. The philosopher Edith Stein reported that her mother kept Jewish practices, much to the amusement of her siblings. The children negotiated for shorter seders with her, and she capitulated. Stein, who later became a Carmelite nun, was murdered by the Nazis as a Jew.[33]

Often the privatisation of religion coincided with its marginalisation because women's activities and beliefs did not carry as much respect as those of men. Moreover, when men lost interest in passing on the more formal aspects of Judaism (generally to their sons), children no longer understood its intellectual content and saw their mothers' practices as

---

[29] Werner Cahnmann suggested that "internally Jewish life was suspended between the emotional poles of prestige (*kavod*) and food (*achila*)" ("The Village Jew," *Leo Baeck Institute Year Book* 19 [1974], 118).

[30] In small towns, some kosher butchers posted hours during which they would ritually slaughter for anyone to see. "Schlachtstunden für Geflügel auf dem Synagogenhofe" (1897), Gesamtarchiv der deutschen Juden, Centrum Judaicum, Berlin (hereafter GDDJ), #65, A al 1, Nr. 55 [film 12, frame 275].

[31] Marion Kaplan, *The Making of the Jewish Middle Class: Women, Family and Identity in Imperial Germany* (New York: Oxford University Press, 1991), chap. 2.

[32] Richarz, *Kaiserreich*, 298–99 (written in 1947).

[33] Bettina Kratz-Ritter, Für "fromme Zionstöchter" und "gebildete Frauenzimmer" (Hildesheim: Olms, 1995), 94.

empty.[34] Piety became a "feminine" attribute and was devalued as such. Feminist leaders like Bertha Pappenheim understood this and encouraged women to educate themselves in Judaism (despite, as she noted, the texts' male perspectives). She hoped that women's piety combined with new knowledge would revitalise Judaism and enhance women's status.[35]

Differences between male and female observance notwithstanding, each succeeding generation practiced ever fewer rituals.[36] For example, when village boys found lodgings in nearby cities to study at the gymnasium, their parents tried to find them kosher pensions or send kosher food with them.[37] Nevertheless, many of the young gave up this practice.[38] Around 1905, an urban child found her provincial grandmother wearing a wig (an Orthodox requirement for married women), her otherwise-observant aunt with no hair covering at all,[39] and her small cousins dressed in naval outfits in imitation of the emperor's family.[40]

Orthodoxy too, despite its self-image as "bearer and guardian of the ancient Jewish faith and tradition," had evolved over time.[41] Also,

---

[34] Ibid.

[35] Ibid., 44.

[36] Andreas Gotzmann, *Jüdisches Recht im kulturellen Prozess: Die Wahrnehmung der Halacha im Deutschland des 19. Jahrhunderts* (Tübingen: M. Siebeck, 1997), 375–77; Kratz-Ritter, Frauenzimmer, 22. A far less common phenomenon was the turn to Orthodoxy of the children of liberal Jews. Hopp, *Jüdisches Bürgertum*, 243.

[37] Richarz, *Kaiserreich*, 200.

[38] Paul Friedhoff left his tiny village for an apprenticeship, carrying his kosher food. However, there were no kosher restaurants in his new town, and he preferred eating in the factory cafeteria with the other apprentices. Bernhard Kukatzki, … Das einzige Hotel in der ganzen Gegend das koscher geführt wurde: *Das Hotel Victoria in Rülzheim* (Schifferstadt: B. Kukatzki, 1994), 24.

[39] Wigs were considered more modern than the caps women had worn up to mid-century. As they were seen as too modern, some Orthodox families did not sanction wigs, but Rabbi Esriel Hildesheimer permitted them during the last quarter of the nineteenth century, at a point when many Orthodox women allowed their own hair to show. Mordechai Breuer, *Modernity Within Tradition: The Social History of Orthodox Jewry in Imperial Germany* (New York: Oxford University Press, 1992), 7.

[40] Richarz, Kaiserreich, 196, photo of Herz family in 1905. The wig replaced the hair cap by the mid–nineteenth century and fell into disuse generally even among some Orthodox women by the twentieth century. Breuer, Modernity, 9, and Salomon Carlebach, *Ratgeber für das jüdische Haus: Ein Führer für Verlobung, Hochzeit und Eheleben* (Berlin: Hausfreund, 1918), 12.

[41] Breuer, *Modernity*, vii, 4–11.

membership in an Orthodox synagogue did not prove private loyalty to religious law: "Some people were more or less consistent in their attendance at public weekday prayer, others less so. Not everyone was equally punctilious in the choice of a future son-in-law." Moreover, the birth rate among Orthodox Jews declined, an indication that many were using birth control despite Orthodox teachings against it.[42] Nor did Orthodox East European immigrant Jews always perpetuate their ways.[43] One woman whose sisters all acceded to marriages arranged by their Orthodox father, a rabbi, broke from her family to become a communist. Gender and generation influenced religiosity, but location probably had equal or greater power.

LOCATION, LOCATION, LOCATION

Location—geographically and in one's own life cycle—played a significant role in an individual's connection to Judaism. In villages and small towns, everyday life and traditional Judaism complemented each other more easily than in cities. This period witnessed an extraordinarily rapid rate of Jewish urbanisation. In 1871, about 30 percent of Jews lived in big cities, but by 1910 almost 70 percent did. Jews who migrated to cities left the more stringent degrees of religious compliance behind them—or had already given them up. Often (but not always) those who achieved the most financial and social success absorbed urban secular culture fastest.[44]

---

[42]   Ibid., 4–5, 7.

[43]   Mischket Liebermann, *Aus dem Ghetto in die Welt: Autobiographie* (Berlin: Verlag der Nation, 1977), 6–8. See also *Die Welt*, June 10, 1904, 2–3, included in Nancy L. Green, ed., *Jewish Workers in the Modern Diaspora* (Berkeley: University of California Press, 1998), 53.

[44]   Hopp, *Jüdisches Bürgertum*, 239. However, some rural Orthodox Jews migrated to the cities to join viable Orthodox communities, and Orthodox circles also included the very wealthy. Nevertheless, even poor, Eastern immigrant Jews broke away from strict observance once they moved to cities. *Die Welt*, June 10, 1904, 2–3, included in Green, ed., *Jewish Workers*, 53. Immigrant Jews did not influence religious culture in German cities as they may have done in Vienna or Warsaw. Marsha Rosenblit, *The Jews of Vienna, 1867–1914: Assimilation and Identity* (Albany: State University Press of New York, 1983), 150–53, and W. Bartoszewski and A. Polonsky, eds., *The Jews in Warsaw* (New York: B. Blackwell, 1991).

The "sinking relevance of holidays and fasting days" resulted not only from the secularism and seductions of urban life but also from interest in such philosophers as Darwin, Haeckel, Spinoza, Schopenhauer, Nietzsche, and Hermann Cohen.[45] Margarete Sallis's parents no longer observed religious practices because "they were deeply influenced by the spirit of the times; they had read 'enlightened' books like Haeckel ... and the socialists, and their protest was not as such against Judaism but against religion in general."[46]

German Jewry supported about 1,855 synagogues in 1903.[47] These ranged from grand and conspicuous ones like the New Synagogue in Berlin,[48] the largest synagogue in the world upon its completion in 1866, to tiny, makeshift ones, in some cases two rooms above a stable where one could hear the mooing of the cows as congregants prayed.[49] Leadership, too, varied. In 1905, 1,101 cantors and only 217 rabbis officiated in Germany. The greatest number of rabbis, cantors, and religious teachers per capita could be found in Alsace-Lorraine, Württemberg, and Bavaria.[50]

---

[45] Hopp, *Jüdisches Bürgertum*, 244–47.

[46] Sallis, memoir, LBI, 3. A few families, including that of Sallis, took advantage of the "Austrittsgesetz of 1876" and left their religion without converting. See Peter Honigmann, *Die Austritte aus der Jüdischen Gemeinde Berlin, 1873–1941* (Frankfurt a. M.: P. Lang, 1988), 11–13.

[47] Of these, 1,089 synagogues were in Prussia, 200 fewer than in 1867. Jacob Thon, *Die jüdischen Gemeinden und Vereine in Deutschland. Veröffentlichungen des Bureaus für Statistik der Juden*, Heft 3 (Berlin: Verlag des Bureaus für Statistik der Jude, 1906), 6.

[48] Although I cannot discuss synagogue architecture, it too affected the daily lives of Jews aesthetically and politically as Christian neighbors took note of new buildings. For examples of the varieties and politics of architecture, see Harold Hammer-Schenk, *Synagogen in Deutschland*, vol. 1 (Hamburg: Christians, 1981); Annie Bardon, "Synagogen in Hessen um 1900," in *Neunhundert Jahre Geschichte der Juden in Hessen*, Christiane Heinemann, ed. (Wiesbaden: Kommission für die Geschichte der Juden in Hessen, 1983), 351–76; and Frank Ahland, "Probleme der Integration der Wittener Juden im Kaiserreich," in *Juden im Ruhrgebiet*, ed., Jan-Pieter Barbian, Michael Brocke, and Lüdger Heid (Essen: Klartext, 1999), 335–37.

[49] Richarz, *Kaiserreich*, 173–74.

[50] In many towns, the cantor or the teacher provided the only religious leadership. Miserably paid, cantors eked out a living on the side. In 1878, for example, the cantor of Hohenstein (E. Prussia) earned extra money by hand-copying the Torah and then running a lottery to select a winner (1878, GDDJ, 75A Br 9, #1383 [film 1383, frame 256]). See also Monika Richarz, "Jüdische Lehrer auf dem Lande im Kaiserreich," *Tel Aviver Jahrbuch für Deutsche Geschichte* 20 (1991), 181–194.

Similar to Protestants, urban Jews did not expand the number of their religious leaders proportionately to their growth in population. There were fewer leaders per capita, but urban Jews had easier access to them than rural Jews, if they cared to seek them out.[51]

Urban synagogues tried to reach out to cosmopolitan populations, attempting an "intensification and shortening" of the service.[52] Nevertheless, in Berlin, the congregation only filled the 3,000 seats of the New Synagogue on the high holidays.[53] In contrast, rural communities of between 100 and 300 people held daily services and Jews in larger towns frequented services weekly.[54] The small size of villages and towns meant that most Jews saw each other commemorate the Sabbath or holidays and may have felt social pressure to join in. Large cities, more anonymous, provided cover for those no longer interested.

Rural and small-town Judaism persisted as an organic part of the landscape. Jews observed the weekly and annual holidays openly, in full view of their non-Jewish neighbours, attesting to a comfort level rarely experienced before.[55] In towns such as Worms, Landau noticed

---

[51] Thon, *Die jüdischen Gemeinden*, 7. In some places, like Berlin, there were ten synagogues (about 1 for every 10,400 Jews), compared to a province like Mecklenburg-Schwerin, in which 18 synagogues served 98 Jews scattered throughout the province (ibid., 6–7). The urban ratio was similar to Protestant parishes, which served between 10,000 and 30,000 people. Hölscher, "Secularization," 278. In Berlin, the Protestant ratio was 1 minister to 9,593 parishioners in 1893. McLeod, ed., *European Religion in the Age of Great Cities*, 16.

[52] *Allgemeine Zeitung des Judentums*, Oct. 14, 1904, 497–98, quoted by Chaim Schatzker, *Jüdische Jugend im zweiten Kaiserreich* (Frankfurt a. M.: P. Lang, 1988), 160. Some of these synagogues championed sermons in German and offered youth services (GDDJ, #695, Jugendgottesdienst in Breslau [frame 381]). Some encouraged singing, including choirs with male and female voices, the latter anathema to Orthodox doctrine and sensibilities. Thon, *Die jüdischen Gemeinden*, 5, 14–17.

[53] Michael A. Meyer, "Gemeinschaft within Gemeinde: Religious Ferment in Weimar Liberal Judaism," *in Search of Jewish Community: Jewish Identities in Germany and Austria, 1918–1933*, ed., Michael Brenner and Derek Penslar (Bloomington: Indiana University Press, 1998), 16.

[54] Thon, *Die jüdischen Gemeinden*, 10–14. In contrast to the United States today, 100 Jewish people could be a thriving community, and communities as small as 30 or 40 individuals were viable. Steven M. Lowenstein, "Decline and Survival of Rural Jewish Communities," in Brenner and Penslar, ed., *Search of Jewish Community*, 224 (using the research of Jacob Borut in Hebrew in Oded Heilbronner, ed., *Yehudei Weimar: Hevrah be-mashber ha- moderniyut, 1918–1933* [Jerusalem: Y. L. Magnes, 1994]).

[55] As late as the mid-1850s, synagogues had not faced the street, nor were they allowed on main thoroughfares.

festively dressed Jews outside the synagogue "simply taking a break from worship and spending some time in the open air."[56] During Purim, the most public festival, the Jews of Gailingen, the largest Jewish rural community in Baden, held parades dressed in their holiday costumes.[57] Village Jews also celebrated Sukkot publicly, building a *sukkah* near their homes and eating meals there, in full public view.[58]

Life-cycle rituals concerning birth, coming-of-age ceremonies, marriage, or death appeared to have an even more tenacious hold than holidays. At the intersection of family and life cycle, they appealed to pious and secular Jews alike. In villages, "usages that had a family connotation, continued to be strictly upheld."[59] In cities, too, Jews tended to follow life-cycle conventions, if not always the letter of the law. The birth of a boy meant that his family celebrated the Brit Milah, his circumcision, as a religious initiation.[60] The birth of a girl brought far less excitement and almost no communal ritual.[61]

---

[56] Richarz, *Kaiserreich*, 250. This can be seen in photos as well: Bein, *Hier kannst Du nicht jeden grüssen*, 55.

[57] Jews made up 28 percent of the population in 1918, down from over 50 percent in 1858. Regina Schmid, *Verlorene Heimat: Gailingen, ein Dorf und seine jüdische Gemeinde in der Weimarer Zeit*, Schriftenreihe des Arbeitskreises für Regionalgeschichte Konstanz (Constance: Arbeitskreis für Regionalgeschichte, 1988), 17, 57–60 (including photos of 1910 parade), 99.

[58] Despite occasional negative reactions by Gentile villagers, most Jews continued to build these structures at least until the end of World War I. Elfie Labsch-Benz, *Die jüdische Gemeinde Nonnenweier* (Freiburg im Breisgau: Landeszentrale für politische Bildung Baden-Württemberg, 1981), 93–94; Utz Jeggle, *Judendörfer in Württemberg* (Tübingen: Tübinger Vereinigung für Volkskunde, 1969), 264.

[59] Werner Cahnmann, "Village and Small-Town Jews in Germany: A Typological Study," *Leo Baeck Institute Year Book* 19 (1974), 119.

[60] A few Jews even went so far as to object to circumcision. They criticized this ritual for what they saw as modern, hygienic reasons. The sucking of blood by the *mohel*, or *metsitsa*, had been forbidden by many German state governments by the 1880s. Breuer, *Modernity*, 258–59. Others, embarrassed, believed circumcision to be a primitive vestige of their ancient religion. Some refused circumcision while still insisting on membership in the Jewish community. W. Gunther Plaut, ed., *The Rise of Reform Judaism* (New York: World Union for Progressive Judaism, 1963), 206–11. See Robin Judd, "Cutting Identities: German Jewish Bodies, Rituals and Citizenship" (Ph.D. diss., University of Michigan, 2000).

[61] In some areas, a naming celebration, Holekrasch, took place. Kaplan, *Making of the Jewish Middle Class*, 80.

Namings connected families to previous generations and to religious traditions as parents passed on the Hebrew names of their ancestors to their newborns. Namings also confronted Jews directly with the vexed issue of tradition versus acculturation as families began to pass on secular first names—or "Germanised" old Jewish names. Sometimes only a first letter remained as a reminder of the person after whom the child had been named.[62] Jewish parents (like non-Jews) "were quicker to release their female descendants from the constraint of traditions of names."[63] Jews preferred boys' names such as Moritz, Adolf, or Hermann to those of their own or their parents' generation, such as Isidor, Abraham, or Moses. Urban and professional Jews, especially, were extremely sensitive to an "antisemitism through polemics against names."[64] The more humble Jewish population followed at a distance, but follow they did. In a Hessian village in the 1880s, the local Jewish teacher who also ran the synagogue services insisted that newborns be given modern names, like Isidor instead of Itzig. The latter would "only bring the child ridicule."[65]

The male coming-of-age ceremony, the bar mitzvah, was de rigueur even among "three-day Jews." Another chance to reaffirm family and community, it was celebrated in both country and city. At thirteen, the age of religious responsibility, the boy prayed in front of the congregation during the Sabbath services and attained religious manhood. Of course, boys did not always understand the meaning of their bar mitzvah, and city boys appear more removed from its significance than their country cousins. In Breslau, in 1897, Adolf Riesenfeld underwent hasty tutoring and later wrote: "I rapidly read off the incomprehensible Hebrew words without getting stuck, and then ... at home ... gifts were showered upon me."[66]

Marriages not only marked important life-cycle events but also merged families and communities. Hence, the interest in arranging "appropriate"

---

[62] Hopp, *Jüdisches Bürgertum*, 269.

[63] Dietz Bering, *The Stigma of Names: Antisemitism in German Daily Life, 1812–1933*, trans. Neville Plaice (Cambridge: Cambridge University Press, 1992), 69.

[64] Name changes (in adulthood) were more frequent in urban circles. Bering, *The Stigma*, 118.

[65] Richarz, *Jewish Life*, 212.

[66] Adolf Riesenfeld, diary, LBI, entry of Dec. 7, 1916.

unions and the joy in intrafaith marriages, which would ensure Jewish continuity. In the countryside, marriage partners rarely came from the same town. Thus, celebrations, even in tiny villages, tended to be large and cosmopolitan by rural standards. In Baden, for example, in 1896–1897, two wedding invitation lists from the village of Kippenheim show visitors from the "outside," including Karlsruhe, Erfurt, and Paris.[67] Urban weddings tended to be more elaborate, more extravagant, and less kosher.[68]

Funerals offered occasions for Jews to come together to fulfil religious precepts as well as to show familial and communal solidarity. Death occurred at home with doctors increasingly in attendance,[69] but nurses and—most often—relatives provided sick care.[70] When Lily Pincus's father lay dying in 1916, a cousin travelled to Berlin to help nurse him. His three children attended him regularly, sometimes reading him stories.[71] In villages, the (male or female) Hevrah Kadishah (Holy Burial Society) took over the death watch and the religious rites, including cleaning, guarding, and dressing the body. The practice continued well into the twentieth century, although some communities had hired undertakers earlier.[72] Urban Jews, too, could elect to have professionals intervene rather than burial societies. Death brought even secular urban families back to traditional rituals. When Alice Salomon's father died (1886), they hired a rabbi who led the funeral procession of horse-drawn coaches.[73]

[67] Ulrich Baumann, *Zerstörte Nachbarschaften: Christen und Juden in badischen Landgemeinden, 1862–1940* (Hamburg: Dölling und Galitz, 2000), 73. See also Labsch-Benz, *Nonnenweier*, 102.

[68] Of course, some villagers no longer observed kashrut either. On the village of Lemgo (in Lippe), see Steven Lowenstein, "Jüdisches religiöses Leben in deutschen Dörfern. Regionale Unterschiede im 19. und frühen 20. Jahrhundert," in *Jüdisches Leben auf dem Lande: Studien zur deutsch-jüdischen Geschichte*, ed., Monika Richarz and Reinhard Rürup (Tübingen: Mohr Siebeck, 1997), 225–26.

[69] By 1900, between 65 and 75 percent of Germans had been attended by a doctor upon their deaths. Faure, "Der Arzt," in *Der Mensch des 19. Jahrhunderts*, ed., Ute Frevert and Heinz-Gerhard Haupt (Frankfurt a.M.: Deutscher Verlag, 1999), 101.

[70] Sallis's mother moved in with Sallis's cancer-stricken grandmother until she died in 1912. Sallis, memoir, LBI, 17.

[71] Lily Pincus, *Verloren-gewonnen: Mein Weg von Berlin nach London* (Stuttgart: Deutsche-Verlags Anstalt, 1980), 32.

[72] GDDJ, Nr. 1425, Synagogen-Gemeinde zu Bromberg [frames 9–10].

[73] Alice Salomon, *Charakter ist Schicksal: Lebenserinnerungen* (Weinheim: Beltz, 1983), 25–26; on traditional Jewish death rituals in families, see also Pincus, *Verloren*, 33.

The Jewish calendar and Jewish laws did not fare as well as life-cycle rituals, although Jews adhered to these traditions more carefully in rural than in urban areas. A Jewish villager insisted, "No one doubted that every village Jew kept a kosher home,"[74] and kosher butchers could count on regular customers.[75] These observations notwithstanding, it would be a mistake to assume uniform devotion.

We can find a multiplicity of customs among villages.[76] Small, isolated villages differed markedly. In parts of Bavaria and Hesse, village Jews strictly observed the Sabbath, kosher laws, and the ritual bath, whereas in parts of rural Westphalia and the Rhineland Jews were less rigorous, keeping mainly the high holidays and rites of passage.[77] Hugo Mandelbaum's community of 18 Jewish families in Geroda (Lower Franconia) observed the Sabbath. When he attended middle school a short way from home in rural Buttenhausen (Württemberg), a community of 40 Jewish families, he found only two still observing the Sabbath. There, the Jewish horse dealers paraded their newly purchased horses through town on Saturdays.[78]

Even within the same small community, observance showed great diversity. All Jews prayed together since they could only support one synagogue, yet religious demarcations existed. Sometimes these were in the form of *sehr fromm* (very religious or very observant), *nicht besonders fromm* (not especially religious), and *nicht so kosher* (a bit lax),[79] or *sehr fromm*, *fromm*, and *liberal*. The last term connoted adherence to Reform Judaism.[80]

---

74 Kukatzki, *Das einzige Hotel*, 19.
75 Ibid.
76 Lowenstein, "Jüdisches religiöses Leben."
77 Steven M. Lowenstein, "Decline" and "Religious Life," in *German-Jewish History in Modern Times*, vol. 3, ed. Michael Meyer (New York: Columbia University Press, 1997), 104–5. For religious splits in Westphalia, see Isi Kahn, "Streiflichter aus der Geschichte der Juden Westfalens," in *Aus Geschichte und Leben der Juden in Westfalen*, ed., Hans Chanoch Meyer (Frankfurt a.M.: Ner-Tamid Verlag, 1962), 64–65.
78 Hugo Mandelbaum, *Jewish Life in the Village Communities of Southern Germany* (New York: Feldheim, 1985), 28, 88, 93 (between 1906 and 1910).
79 Labsch-Benz, *Nonnenweier*, 120–22.
80 The term "Reform Judaism" generally meant the tiny, atypical Berlin Reformgemeinde. Meyer, *Response to Modernity*, chap. 5; Lowenstein, "Religious Life," 103.

What did this multiplicity of behaviours look like in daily practice? It appears that Jews gave up ritual purity first. By the turn of the century, the *mikvah*, or ritual bath, had fallen into general disuse. Only 55 percent of communities maintained one at all,[81] and except for the Orthodox prayer book, women's prayer books no longer mentioned it.[82] Food rituals and Sabbath observance lasted longer, but Jews treated them with great individuality. One man (born in 1889 in Bavaria) who considered his home "religious" noted that his parents kept kosher and did not work on the Sabbath, but other families interpreted "work" far more strictly.[83]

In the cities, many of the divisions already visible among rural Jews intensified. Most communities split between Orthodox and liberal Jews (the adherents of Reform), not to mention a growing number of secular Jews.[84] Although the Prussian law of 1876 made secession from the synagogal community possible without loss of membership in the Jewish religion, giving Orthodoxy new legal and political powers, only about 15 percent of German Jews could still be considered Orthodox by 1900.

REDEFINING JUDAISM

Measured in lagging synagogue attendance or in rising rates of intermarriage or conversion, "Judaism" as a practice declined, especially in the cities. Values and beliefs, however, cannot be measured as easily. Urban Jews, in particular, turned Judaism into a form of "ethnic encounter"—ceremonies formerly attached almost entirely to religious practice evolved into family occasions and community events.[85]

---

81 Thon, *Die jüdischen Gemeinden*, 17–18. For an example of a half-built mikvah the community could not afford to complete, see Request from Jutroschin (Posen) in 1892 in GDDJ, Nr. 695 [frame 418].

82 Kratz-Ritter, *Frauenzimmer*, 148–49, 152–53.

83 Richarz, *Kaiserreich*, 199.

84 Liberles, *Religious Conflict in Social Context*, 13; Meyer, *Response to Modernity*, chap. 5; Lowenstein, "Religious Life," 103.

85 Phyllis Albert, "L'Intégration et la persistence de l'ethnicité chez les Juifs dans la France moderne," in *Histoire politique des Juifs de France: Entre universalisme et particularisme*, ed., Pierre Birnbaum (Paris: Presses de la Fondation nationale des sciences politiques, 1990).

FAMILY (AND FOOD)

For urban, increasingly secular Jews, the family provided a crucial location for Jewish observance, a central form of religious activity, and, indeed, a replacement for it. Similar to many Christian families in which "[t]he family honored Christian holidays as a way of celebrating itself,"[86] many Jews experienced the Sabbath and holidays as familial celebrations, often around the table. In the 1880s, a Berlin woman recalled "a strict commandment of family togetherness" for Friday night dinners.[87] Other families gathered on Friday evenings without any rituals at all, but the two elements—family meals and religion/ethnicity—cannot be disentangled. Even when Jews reduced the holidays they celebrated, they attempted to commemorate the major holidays with a family reunion and a traditional meal, a form of "gastronomic Judaism."[88] As Jews minimised religious content, these holidays provided a way of reaffirming the family and its group heritage. The family became a cornerstone of a more secular version of Judaism,[89] what George Mosse called the "embourgeoisement of Jewish piety."[90]

The extended family and the older generations also served as bridges to traditional Judaism. Rural relatives provided traditional models and meals for urban visitors. A child from Hamburg participated with rural cousins in Sabbath rituals that she had never seen practiced at home.[91] In the 1890s, a boy in Munich noted that his grandfather preferred an allegedly more kosher restaurant than did his parents.[92] Families held celebrations

---

86   Michelle Perrot and Anne Martin-Fugier, "The Actors," in *A History of Private Life: From the Fires of Revolution to the Great War*, ed., Michelle Perrot (London: Belknap, 1990), 286.
87   Johanna Meyer Loevinson, memoir, LBI, 23.
88   Joëlle Bahloul, "Foodways in Contemporary Jewish Communities: Research Directions," *Jewish Folklore and Ethnology Review* 9, no. 1 (1987), 2.
89   Kaplan, *Making of the Jewish Middle Class*, 75–77.
90   George Mosse, "The Secularization of Jewish Theology," in *Masses and Man: Nationalist and Fascist Perceptions of Reality*, ed., George Mosse (New York: H. Fertig, 1980), 258.
91   Ruth von Bialy interview, Hamburg, 1997. A child from Breslau similarly visited relatives in Posen and learned about the Sukkot holiday. Hirschberg, (long) memoir, LBI, 3. Similarly, see Sallis, memoir, LBI, 2–3.
92   Richarz, *Kaiserreich*, 311.

in kosher restaurants or hotels so that the entire family—those who observed *kashrut* and those who did not—could gather.[93]

Although most urban Jews no longer observed *kashrut*,[94] they maintained food traditions to appease older generations, to ease their own consciences, or from habit. Gender too played a role, with women insisting on maintaining kosher kitchens longer than their husbands or children.[95] Contemporaries approached these complicated and symbolic compromises—some of which may baffle us—with a sense of humour or irony. Most commonly, children of religious Jews maintained a kosher kitchen so that their parents would agree to eat in their homes.[96] But this could bring its own strange twists. In Breslau, for example, the Hirschberg family kept a kosher kitchen out of respect for the grandmother, a pious woman whose religiosity amused her husband. Heeding the stricture to separate milk and meat, however, did not discourage the rest of the family from eating pork on separate plates.[97]

Similarly, traditional Jewish recipes might include nonkosher ingredients. Around 1900, one of Victor Klemperer's friends took great pride in cooking the traditional Sabbath casserole. She had learned to prepare the meal as the daughter of the Jewish teacher in Hildesheim. When Klemperer asked her for the recipe, she replied, "This is the ritual way of making it ... and that is how I ate it in my parents' home ... but I, myself, always add a ham bone to it."[98]

A sense of ambivalence pervades these stories: the legitimacy of some observance lingered among Jews as they remodelled the

---

93   Hopp, *Jüdisches Bürgertum*, 214.

94   The extent of nonadherence to kashrut can be seen in some rabbis' suggestions to religion teachers to bypass this issue in order to avoid a crisis of conscience (Gewissenskonflikt) in the children. *Allgemeine Zeitung des Judentums*, May 1, 1908, p. 205, quoted by Schatzker, *Jüdische Jugend*, 124.

95   Kaplan, *Making of the Jewish Middle Class*, chap. 2.

96   Gershom Scholem, "On the Social Psychology of Jews in Germany," in *Jews and Germans from 1860 to 1933: The Problematic Symbiosis*, ed., David Bronson (Heidelberg: Winter, 1979), 12.

97   Hirschberg, (short) memoir, LBI, 2. See also Michael Zimmermann and Claudia Konieczek, eds., *Jüdisches Leben in Essen 1800–1933* (Essen: Klartext, 1993), 33.

98   Victor Klemperer, *Curriculum Vitae: Jugend um 1900*, 2 vols. (Berlin: Rütten und Loening, 1989), 1:154.

practice.[99] In fact, did fewer requisites perhaps help to keep the legitimacy intact?[100] Even secular, intermarried Jews occasionally observed Jewish food customs in their daily lives, especially around holidays when the extended family gathered.[101] Some intermarried Jewish women still cooked traditional holiday meals, and a number of mixed families celebrated all the important Jewish holidays alongside Easter and Christmas. The son of one such union noted that "[we] celebrated the Jewish holidays by eating," and another assumed that the Easter bunny was Jewish because the eggs he found in his garden had been protected by shreds of the same paper in which his matzos were normally wrapped.[102] Foods as "ethnic emblems"[103] provide clues as to changing norms, but more important than the food itself was the site of celebration, the family.

BILDUNG AND COMMUNITY

Urban Jews appropriated not only family but also Bildung as a cornerstone of their Judaism. An entrée into middle-class respectability, Bildung—education and cultivation—became a secular version of religion. For many Jews, it became "synonymous with their Jewishness."[104] Bildung allowed Jews to merge Jewish traditions of learning with secular appreciation of German language, literature, and etiquette. Mosse concluded that "Bildung ... was transformed into a kind of religion—the worship of the true, the good, and the beautiful."[105] Increasingly, love of literature, music, and theatre replaced purely Jewish learning. In his will, Adolf Fröhlich, born in 1872, recommended Goethe's autobiography, *Truth and Poetry*, and his novel, *Wilhelm*

---

[99] On ambivalence and tension, see Gotzmann, *Jüdisches Recht*, 359–79.

[100] My thanks to Robin Judd for this insight.

[101] Kirstin Meiring, *Die Christlich-Jüdische Mischehe in Deutschland, 1840–1933* (Hamburg: Chritians, 1998), 130–35.

[102] Ibid., 132–34.

[103] Bahloul, "Foodways," 2.

[104] George L. Mosse, *German Jews Beyond Judaism* (Bloomington: Indiana University Press, 1985), 4. See also David Sorkin, *The Transformaton of German Jewry* (New York, 1987).

[105] Mosse, *German Jews*, 4.

Meister's Apprenticeship, to his children.[106] Orthodox families, too, embraced German culture. Sabbath meals followed traditional ritual, but occasionally there might also be a reading from a German book, and "[t]he bookshelves of many Orthodox Jewish homes were likely to hold incomparably more German books—Schiller and Goethe were particular favorites—than books in Hebrew."[107]

The diary of Helene Eyck, a Berlin mother of six, offers a glimpse into the inner world of someone for whom Bildung and piety were intertwined. The family belonged to a synagogue in Berlin, but the essence of Eyck's spirituality can be seen in her diary entry of May 1895. She prayed that Lilli, her adorable two-year-old, remain loving and sweet. Instead of a Hebrew benediction in transliteration or in German translation, she wrote: "It seems as though I must lay then, My hand upon thy brow, Praying that God may preserve thee, As pure and fair as now."[108] Her words came from Heine's "Thou Art So Like a Flower," a poem Eyck had probably memorised at school or knew from musical compositions by, among others, Franz Liszt or Robert Schumann.

Eyck exemplified some of the typical incongruities of Jews in the process of secularisation. Just as casually as she mentioned one of her children eating ham, she wrote about cooking "ritually prepared fish" for Friday evenings,[109] considering Friday a "half holiday."[110] Although she never mentioned attending synagogue, she continually referred to a very personal God. She taught each of her children to pray in a meaningful manner, admonishing them when they simply droned on: "That's not how one prays to our dear God."[111] She also wanted her sons to begin Hebrew lessons when they were four and five. Since her husband opposed this idea, she justified it as an act of deference toward

---

[106] Wiltrud Fröhlich, "Adolf Fröhlich, Kommerzienrat (1872–1946)," *Jüdische Lebensgeschichten aus der Pfalz. Arbeitskreis für neuere jüdische Geschichte in der Pfalz* (Speyer: Evangelischer Presseverlag, 1995), 164–65.

[107] Contemporary authors were also popular. Breuer, *Modernity*, 11, also 46, 83, 150.

[108] Eyck, diary, LBI, 64. Heine, "Du bist wie eine Blume," published 1825. Translator unknown from song by George Whitefield Chadwick, op. 11, no. 3, cited on http://www.recmusic.org/lieder/h/heine/du.wie.blume.html.

[109] Eyck, diary, LBI, 4, 6, 14, 45, 56, 64, and 84.

[110] Ibid., 45.

[111] Ibid., 19.

his parents.[112] The boys eventually did learn Hebrew, and the second son proved committed enough to Judaism and to his family to say the mourner's prayer daily for months after his grandfather's death.[113] Her apparent interest in their Jewish knowledge notwithstanding, Eyck cast her sons' bar mitzvahs as family festivities.[114] In Eyck, a religion of Bildung blended with family meals on the Sabbath and the importance of Hebrew (for her sons). Feelings, convictions, and allegiances lingered long after ritual had waned: "the blandly generic term secular Jew gives no indication of the richly nuanced variety within the species."[115]

Jewish local, regional, national, and international voluntary organisations reinforced and extended the impact of family and Bildung on Jewish identity.[116] Jewish organisational life experienced a revitalisation, coinciding with an era of explosive associational growth in late-nineteenth-century Germany. Jews formed cultural, political, and self-defence associations. By the turn of the century, 12 national organisations stretched across Germany, and 312 major Jewish associations, not including myriad local ones, flourished there.[117] The *Centralverein Deutscher Staatsbürger Jüdischen Glaubens* (founded 1893), the major Jewish defence organisation, attracting over 100,000 Jews, stressed not only its "Germanness" but also became "intensely preoccupied with strengthening the sense of Jewish identity."[118] Moreover, the small Zionist movement found adherents among young German Jews and East European immigrants.[119] When counting national, regional, and local groups, approximately 5,000 Jewish clubs thrived in Germany, with tens of thousands of members. They offered conviviality as well as the opportunity to pursue Jewish interests.

---

[112]   Ibid., 10.

[113]   Ibid., 10, and F. Eyck introduction to Eyck diary, 8.

[114]   Ibid., 47 (1890) and 53 (1891).

[115]   Yosef H. Yerushalmi, *Freud's Moses: Judaism Terminable and Interminable* (New Haven: Yale University Press, 1991), 9.

[116]   Rainer Liedtke, *Jewish Welfare in Hamburg and Manchester* (Oxford: Oxford University Press, 1998).

[117]   Thon, *Die jüdischen Gemeinden*, 58, 59.

[118]   Ismar Schorsch, *Jewish Reactions to German Anti-Semitism, 1870–1914* (New York: Columbia University Press, 1972), 119, 147.

[119]   Zionism reached about 10,000 German Jews before World War I.

On a grassroots level, Jews embraced the mitzvah, or commandment, of charity. In the 1880s and 1890s, this included very personal ministrations as well as institution-building. In the town of Allenstein (East Prussia), the women's group, founded in 1879, intended to help other Jewish women "who through no fault of their own" had fallen into poverty.[120] In cities too, care could be very personal. In Stettin, Max Daniel's father brought poor members of the synagogue home for dinner every Friday night and, with the help of other Jews, bought a four-story shelter for Jews fleeing the Russian pogroms. Seven women volunteered to cook for the refugees.[121]

Even in small, relatively isolated communities, Jews conceived of themselves as part of a supralocal community. In Allenstein, for example, the local Jewish community received entreaties from poorer communities and individuals in the region.[122] These calls for help presumed that Jews would demonstrate solidarity.[123] Cries for assistance came from afar as well. In 1877, the international *Alliance Israélite Universelle* sent an appeal to Jewish communities to help Ottoman Jews affected by the third Russo-Turkish war (1877–1878).[124] In 1881, local communities responded to the pogroms in Russia.[125] In 1889, a committee of Berlin Jews requested money for Ottoman Jews dying of cholera in Baghdad.[126] Palestine, too, belonged to the extended community: in 1889, German Jews sent

---

120   Aussteuerverein, 1903, GDDJ, Nr. 26 A, Al 1, Nr. 16. [film 26–40, frame 23]. *Statut des Frauen-Vereins zur Unterstützung hilfsbedürftiger Israeliten weiblichen Geschlechts zu Allenstein. 1879*. GDDJ, #60, A Al 1, Nr. 50 [film 12, frame 9].

121   Richarz, *Kaiserreich*, 216–18.

122   On families: GDDJ, 75 A Al 1 [film 26, frame 50] (from town of Rhein near Osterode Ostpr., 1889); *Deutsch-Israelitische Darlehnskasse für Frauen und Jungfrauen* (1875), *GDDJ*, A Al 1, Nr. 14 [film 7, frame 20].

123   *GDDJ*, A Al 1, Nr. 14 [film 7, frame 103] from Flatow, W. Prussia, 1876. For another example [End Page 28] of fundraising for synagogue renovation, see request from Landeck W. Pr, Aug. 7, 1889, in *GDDJ*, A Al 1, Nr. 17, Allenstein [film 26, frame 62].

124   *GDDJ*, A Al 1, Nr. 14 [film 7, frame 140].

125   Ibid., frame 279.

126   The small community of Allenstein succeeded in collecting over 20 marks, at the rate of 1 mark or 50 pfennige per person for this cause (*GDDJ*, 75 A Al 1 #26, Nr. 16 [film 26, frame 152–53]).

money for matzos to needy Jews in Jerusalem.[127] They acknowledged responsibility—religious and social—for a far-reaching community of Jews.

For some individuals, Jewish associations fulfilled a religious precept. For others, associational life provided the community they no longer sought from the synagogue alone. Such activity "became their principal mode of Jewish identification."[128] In the 1880s, Paul Mühsam's father regularly attended Jewish community meetings, "but he never went to services."[129] Similar to Christians, who manifested their (non-churchgoing) allegiance to Christianity by participating in a wide range of charitable organisations "pursued in a Christian spirit,"[130] Jewish private charities provided a voluntary forum in which to express loyalty to the faith and the community. They created structures that held Jews together. Recognising this, one observer wrote: "The more women and men … participate in organisational life, the more people remain interested in Jewish matters, [the more] their joy in belonging, [the more] their feelings of solidarity are strengthened."[131]

A lively Jewish press and charitable institutions also provided group cohesion and demonstrated concern for Judaism. Even before the establishment of most national organisations, Jews developed a wide array of newspapers. These papers never replaced the local or national German press, but they revealed an interest in Jewish communal, cultural, and religious affairs. Over 30 newspapers and

---

127 *GDDJ*, Beuthen, Nr. 695: Matzoh [frame 372] and cemetery [frame 377]. Charity had its limits, however. German Jews felt themselves beleaguered by itinerant beggars, a phenomenon that leaders deridingly labeled the "Schnorrer-Unwesen" (sponger-nuisance). "Mitteilung!" *GDDJ*, #62, A Al 1, Nr. 52 [film 12, frame 73].

128 Steven M. Lowenstein, "The Community," in Meyer, ed., *German-Jewish History in Modern Times*, 144.

129 Richarz, *Jewish Life*, 255.

130 For Protestants, see Hölscher, "Secularization and Urbanization," 282; for Catholics, see Josef Mooser, "Katholische Volksreligion, Klerus und Bürgertum in der zweiten Hälfte des 19. Jahrhunderts. Thesen," in Schieder, ed., *Religion und Gesellschaft*, 150–52.

131 Kaplan, *Making of the Jewish Middle Class*, 195. See also Sabine Knappe, "Jüdische Frauenorganisationen in Hamburg zwischen Assimilation, jüdischer Identität und weiblicher Emanzipation während des Kaiserreichs" (Master's thesis, University of Hamburg, 1991), 194.

newsletters enlivened Jewish reading and included family and youth, Orthodox and Liberal, teachers' and gymnasts', and bibliographical and literary periodicals.[132]

TEMPTATIONS AND BREAKS:
THE NANNY AND THE CHRISTMAS TREE

Family, Bildung, and community helped recast and reinforce modern Judaism in its religious and secular variants, but a Christian world, its symbols and holidays, surrounded and penetrated the Jewish milieu. Jewish children learned Christian stories and songs in public school, and Jewish adults had to close their shops on the Christian day of rest. Many experienced firsthand contact with Christian belief and practice through Christian nannies and household help.[133]

Children grasped that their nannies favoured Christianity. Jakob Wassermann's nanny hugged him and said, "You have a Christian heart!"

---

[132] The paper with the largest circulation could be found in Berlin, where between 40,000 and 50,000 Jews received the *Gemeindeblatt der Jüdischen Gemeinde zu Berlin*. Barbara Suchy, "Die jüdische Presse im Kaiserreich und in der Weimarer Republik," in *Juden als Träger bürgerlicher Kultur in Deutschland*, ed., Julius Schoeps (Stuttgart: Burg-Verlag, 1989), 181. Among the most famous weeklies were the *Allgemeine Zeitung des Judentums*, founded in 1837, which represented the liberal majority of German Jews, and the Hamburger Israelitisches Familienblatt, "a gemütliche, middle-brow journal written for the average petit-bourgeois family ... to edify, educate and comfort." Herbert A. Strauss, "The Jewish Press in Germany, 1918–1939," in *The Jewish Press That Was*, ed. Aryeh Bar (Tel Aviv: World Federation of Jewish Journalists, 1980), 323. Founded in 1898, the *Familienblatt* attempted to remain above religious divisions. The Orthodox press included, among others, the *Israelit*, founded in 1860 (the only paper to appear twice weekly between 1883 and 1905), and the Berlin *Jüdische Presse*. The former imparted religious instruction to its readers, distinguishing between strict and lax observance, and sometimes taking "the place of actual Torah study for unschooled readers," whereas the latter, like other Jewish papers, tended to look at issues of broad concern. Breuer, *Modernity*, 171–72. Led by the Centralverein organ, *Im deutschen Reich*, most Jewish journals insisted on Jewish rights and assailed the antisemitic waves of the 1880s and 1890s. Only the Zionist press, which grew in the prewar years, underemphasized German events "with almost studied neglect," looking toward Palestine and Jewish lives abroad. Strauss, "Press," 331.

[133] There were simply too few Jewish domestics to go around, and even rabbis hired Christian help. Richarz, *Jewish Life*, 176. Christian helpers frequently learned Jewish routines and rituals in order to practice them with the children. Kratz-Ritter, *Frauenzimmer*, 89.

At the same moment that he felt her love, this compliment frightened him because it demeaned his Jewishness.[134] Some household helpers openly indicted Judaism. Kurt Blumenfeld recalled the Catholic maid telling him that she went to confession because of her sin—serving Jews. When he asked why that was a sin, she responded, "The Jews crucified Christ!"[135] Nannies could also terrify children with Christian folktales.[136]

Domestics often familiarised their charges with Christianity.[137] When the daughter of a rabbi begged to be brought to church just once, her caretaker complied. The girl "spoke to God, like I did in the temple, and I was certain that he heard me exactly [as clearly] here as there."[138] Another child compared boring visits to her grandfather's synagogue with her nanny's "mysterious" church services.[139] Sometimes Jewish children learned Christian bedtime prayers without realising the origin of the rhymes. Usually words about Christ had been changed to more neutral ones about heaven.[140]

Christian household helpers also introduced children to Christmas. As Christmas became the central German bourgeois family celebration, replete with gifts and with its original religious meaning diminished,[141] the Christmas tree made its entrée into a number of Jewish homes. Memoirs illustrate some families that eschewed a tree but exchanged presents on Christmas,[142] some who had a Christmas tree "for the help" but still celebrated Hanukkah,[143] and others who celebrated Christmas with a tree and gifts but without Christ.

———————

[134]   Menken, ed., Stachel, 122.
[135]   Kurt Blumenfeld, *Erlebte Judenfrage* (Stuttgart: Deutsche Verlagsanstalt, 1962), 27. He was born in 1884 in Insterburg, East Prussia.
[136]   Riesenfeld, diary, LBI, 1916. He was born in 1884 in a small town in Upper Silesia.
[137]   Kratz-Ritter, *Frauenzimmer*, 87.
[138]   Ibid., 89.
[139]   Malka Schmuckler, *Gast im eigenen Land: Emigration und Rückkehr einer deutschen Jüdin* (Cologne: Verlag Wissenschaft und Politik, 1983), 6.
[140]   Klemperer, *Curriculum Vitae*, 1:34.
[141]   The tree's popularity among Germans increased after the wars of 1870–1871 and then spread "like wildfire." Ingeborg Weber-Kellermann, *Die deutsche Familie: Versuch einer Sozialgeschichte*, 4th ed. (Frankfurt a. M.: Suhrkamp, 1978), 226, 223–43. For Europe, see Perrot and Martin-Fugier, "The Actors," 286, 289–91.
[142]   Richarz, *Jewish Life*, 257.
[143]   Interview with Lee Ziegler, whose family had a tree "for the servants." New York, 1995.

Jews who displayed trees did not always make the transition easily. Some families resisted for a time and then bought them "for the servants," and only later admitted to their own pleasure. Moreover, Jewish families revealed a variety of attitudes toward these trees, reflected, for example, on a linguistic level. Most referred to the Christmas tree as the "tree with lights" (Lichterbaum) or the Christmas tree (Weihnachtsbaum) rather than the "Christ tree" (Christbaum).[144] Theodor Herzl, the father of Zionism, did not care what label he used for his tree: "As far as I'm concerned they can call it the Hanukkah tree."[145]

Jews (like many secular Christians) stripped the tree of Christian symbolism, some pointing to ancient festivals, others to the winter solstice. In the 1880s, a Frankfurt Jewish woman decorated the room with mistletoe and "heathen and pre-Christian" palm and pine branches. She did not allow standard Christmas decorations.[146] Most Jews with trees, however, conflated their tree with Germanness. Toni Ehrlich (1880s) celebrated a "German holiday," a "northern winter festival," seeing the tree as a hallmark of Germanness.[147] Gershom Scholem's family (1900–1910) also joined in a "German folk festival" as Germans.[148]

Memoirs identify consideration for Christian personnel as the reason—or rationalisation—for the tree.[149] Scholem recalled the "big distribution of presents for servants, relatives and friends"

---

[144] Hopp, *Jüdisches Bürgertum*, 178–79. There were also regional differences: Northern Germans tended to use Weihnachtsbaum, whereas other regions referred to the Tannenbaum and Christbaum as well. Jacob and Wilhelm Grimm, *Deutsches Wörterbuch* (Leipzig, 1960), vol. 14, sec. I, part I, 717. Similarly, the *Weihnachtsmann* dispensed gifts in northern Germany and the Christkind in the south. Weber-Kellermann, *Die deutsche Familie*, 228.

[145] Monika Richarz, "Der jüdische Weihnachtsbaum—Familie und Säkularisierung im deutschen Judentum des 19. Jahrhunderts," in *Geschichte und Emanzipation: Festschrift für Reinhard Rürup*, ed., Michael Grüttner, Rüdiger Hachtmann, and Heinz-Gerhard Haupt (Frankfurt a. M.: Campus, 1999), 285, 287.

[146] Hopp, *Jüdisches Bürgertum*, 179.

[147] Ehrlich, memoir, LBI, 9.

[148] Scholem, *From Berlin to Jerusalem*, 28. In Frankfurt, Siegfried Sommer, an Oberlandesgerichtsrat, and his wife hesitated to set up a tree until World War I when he also construed the tree as a symbol of belonging to the German people. Hopp, *Jüdisches Bürgertum*, 179.

[149] Hopp, *Jüdisches Bürgertum*, 178.

and an aunt who played "Silent Night, Holy Night" for the "cook and servant girl."[150] In Speyer (1890s), Margarete Sallis's parents commemorated all Jewish life-cycle rituals, a secularised Sabbath dinner with the extended family, and Passover with matzos and bread but also celebrated Christmas—including a tree and gifts—with the Christian help.[151]

Some, however, saw servants as a pretext. Julius Posener recalled his Berlin Christmases:

> Even if parents followed the common bourgeois-Jewish excuse that they did it for the servants, they couldn't have entirely believed this. Does the master of the house climb around on a ladder for the better part of Christmas Eve morning ... to decorate a Christmas tree that reaches to the ceiling only for the servants?[152]

Posener's point is partially correct, but it understates the importance of servants. Servants were like family in many cases. Some ate with the family, most received birthday presents, still others were included in the children's prayers, and some remained loyal to "their" families during the Nazi years.[153] Despite increasing turnover among servants and, hence, increasing emotional distance, it was possible that the "master of the house" would decorate a tree "for the servants"—especially if it would simultaneously please his children and spouse.

It is instructive to analyse the self-understanding of "Christmas tree Jews." Some were rather removed from religious practice. Walter Benjamin (born 1892), whose parents infrequently sent him to high holiday services, recalled his eager anticipation of the tree and gifts as a Christian prayer flowed through his mind.[154] Another family whose observance consisted of spending Passover with Orthodox grandparents regarded Christmas

---

150 Scholem, *From Berlin to Jerusalem*, 28.
151 Margarete Sallis-Freudenthal, *Ich habe mein Land gefunden: Autobiographischer Rückblick* (Frankfurt a.M.: 1977), 12.
152 Richarz, "Weihnachtsbaum," 284.
153 Jeggle, *Judendörfer*, 224–25.
154 "Alle Jahre wieder / kommt das Christuskind / auf die Erde nieder / wo wir Menschen sind." Walter Benjamin, *Berliner Kindheit um Neunzehnhundert* (Frankfurt a. M.: Suhrkamp, 2000), 32, 103.

as a major family holiday.[155] Yet more observant families too enjoyed the tree. Nora Rosenthal's father, who said prayers after every meal, set up their first tree in their Frankfurt home in 1900.[156] In 1880s Baden, Otto Baer-Oppenheimer characterised himself as a "good Jew" who attended synagogue twice daily for a year after his mother's death. He experienced his first Christmas tree introduced by the French housekeeper who had been hired to care for him. He found the "Christ tree" in the woman's room "beautiful," recalling it 50 years later. He and his brother lingered around the tree, but his father did not join them.[157] Even some Orthodox families permitted a tree for the servants.[158]

Conversely, eschewing a tree did not automatically correspond to profound religiosity. Many a "three-day" Jew rejected the tree. Born in 1898, one woman described her tree-less childhood in a family of "three-day Jews" (including her envy of Jews who had trees).[159] For most Jews, Judaism became a mélange of rituals to be observed or neglected, but the Christmas tree remained taboo.

Even when they rejected trees, German Jews remembered Christmas. They focused on pageants at school and in the local environment.[160] Jewish children in a small town in Württemberg in the early 1890s attended the Sisters of Mercy school. There, the nuns assured them that they did not have to pray along or cross themselves, although the Jewish children would have liked to do so! The Jewish children dressed as angels in the Christmas pageant, and their mothers attended the event. These parents, whose own Judaism was deep-seated, did not fear that their "Jewish angels" would be negatively influenced by the Christian milieu.[161] Similarly, in Bavaria, Jewish children in a Catholic day-care centre enjoyed receiving candies from St. Nicholas and participating in the Christmas

[155]   Eleanor E. Alexander (born ca. 1908), "Stories of My Life," memoir, LBI, 11. By the time of the Weimar Republic, Naomi Lacqueur believed that most middle-class Jews celebrated both Christmas and Hanukkah. Lacqueur, *A Memoir, 1920–1995* (Frankfurt, 1996), 10–11.
[156]   Rosenthal, memoirs, LBI, 6–7.
[157]   For Baden, Otto Baer-Oppenheimer, archives, LBI, 23.
[158]   Breuer, *Modernity*, 313.
[159]   Hirschberg, (short) memoir, LBI, 2.
[160]   Richarz, "Weihnachtsbaum," 283; Benjamin, *Berliner Kindheit um Neunzehnhundert*, 103; Alice Ottenheimer, memoirs, LBI, 4.
[161]   Richarz, *Kaiserreich*, 175–76.

play. The nuns carefully chose roles, like that of King David, for the Jewish children, intending not to offend the Jewish parents.[162] In Breslau, Toni Ehrlich found the "many pine trees with their forest-like scent in the snow covered streets" alluring. She characterised the Christmas market (Kindelmarkt)—whose booths "glittered and gleamed like a fairytale land," offering countless, colourfully frosted gingerbread men, children's toys, and multicoloured decorations—as equally enticing.[163]

Christmas trees as symbols are far more powerful than their numbers—or meanings—in Jewish homes warranted.[164] Jews who celebrated Christmas generally came from circumscribed, secular, urban, bourgeois circles, like those of Berlin West. That newspaper articles and sermons condemned the "Jewish Christmas tree" indicated their own anxiety or politics more than the tree's widespread use.[165] Memoirs also tend to skew the picture. A disproportionately high number of memoirs were written by precisely the urban bourgeoisie most likely to have observed Christmas. And these memoirs stress similarities between the Jewish and non-Jewish bourgeoisie, a group for which Christmas had evolved into the all-encompassing German family event. Moreover, meanings, as has been noted, varied. The majority of Jews lived amid Christians and Christian symbols, acknowledging—and even enjoying—them without giving up Judaism. The nanny and the Christmas tree were rarely the cause of a final break with Judaism.

CONVERSION AND INTERMARRIAGE

Instances of conversion in the Imperial era were closely related to waves of antisemitism. Some baptisms of Jewish children by parents who remained Jewish, for example, accompanied the rise of antisemitism

---

[162] Ibid., 194–95. Of course, not all Jewish children joined in Christian entertainment. Some refused parts offered them in the Christmas play in their Protestant or Catholic school without further repercussions. Menken, ed., *Stachel*, 140.
[163] Ehrlich, memoir, LBI, 9; Meyer-Loevinson, memoir, LBI, 41.
[164] Easter egg hunts or the exchange of *matzos* for Easter eggs seem widespread as well but did not raise the same controversy. In the tiny village of Hochberg am Neckar, "Baskets filled with sugar bunnies, candies and Easter eggs ... were hidden in the garden," for Alice Ottenheimer (born 1893) to discover. Memoirs, LBI, 4.
[165] Richarz, *Kaiserreich*, 367, 401.

in the 1880s.[166] These parents intended to make their children's lives easier.[167] Also, some professions, like academic medicine, put great pressure on members to convert if they hoped to achieve higher status positions,[168] and some Jewish men in these fields yielded. Urbanisation, too, led to increased formal withdrawals from the Jewish community[169] and conversion. Berlin Jews converted at a much higher rate than any others: between 1875 and 1888, for example, 890 of 1,901 conversions (to Protestantism) in Prussia occurred in Berlin.[170] In Imperial Germany about 23,000 Jews converted overall.[171]

Urbanisation also led to increased intermarriage. In 1875, with the introduction of civil marriage, the German Empire legalised marriage between Jews and other Germans. Given the small size of the Jewish community in total—as well as intra-ethnic affinities and antisemitism— intermarriage rates remained relatively low. However, the rate of intermarriage rose rapidly in the pre-war years and, in 1909, the *Centralverein* declared apostasy a bigger threat than antisemitism.[172] During the war, intermarriage rates soared, especially in several large cities. In Hamburg, the rate reached 25 percent of all Jewish marriages by 1910 and 49 percent in 1915; in Berlin, the rate was 18 percent of all Jewish marriages in 1910 and 33 percent in 1915. Breslau, too, showed an increase in intermarriages, from 11 percent of all Jewish marriages in 1890 to 39 percent in 1920. During the war, the rate there rose to 53 percent. Similarly, in Königsberg the intermarriage rate rose from 7

---

[166] The numbers should not be exaggerated: for example, the largest number of conversions took place in 1888, among which, there were only 39 baptisms of children. Between 1885 and 1888 (inclusive), there were 114 baptisms of children. *Allgemeine Zeitung des Judentums*, May 11, 1894, 218–19.

[167] Inadvertently, they may have added to their children's confusion. Ludwig Haas (born 1875) noted, "You have to have a strong character in order not to suffer from the fact that your parents belonged to a different community from your own." Schatzker, *Jüdische Jugend*, 150–51.

[168] Honigmann, *Die Austritte*, 109.

[169] After the Law of Secession of 1876 in Honigmann, *Die Austritte*.

[170] *Allgemeine Zeitung des Judentums*, May 11, 1894, 218.

[171] This is out of a population of 512,000 increasing to 615,000 Jews and does not include baptisms shortly after birth. Richarz, *Kaiserreich*, 16.

[172] Jacob Boas, "German Jewry's Search for Renewal in the Hitler Era," *Journal of Modern History* 53, no. 1 (Mar. 1981), 1003.

percent of all Jewish marriages in 1885 to 35 percent in 1914 and hit a high point of 47 percent during the first year of the war.[173]

Jewish men led the way in intermarriage and conversion.[174] In 1901–1902, for example, 1 in 12 (8.3 percent) Jewish grooms and 1 in 14 (7 percent) Jewish brides married out.[175] These percentages jumped during the war to 24 and 17 percent, respectively. Women were a quarter of all converts between 1873 and 1906. Their share grew to 40 percent by 1912, as more women entered the workforce and there faced antisemitism and the resulting temptation to convert.[176]

Most Jews disdained conversion.[177] Even secular families that evinced no close connection to the Jewish religion saw conversion as a form of dishonour and desertion.[178] Indeed, even Jews who eagerly sought social integration with non-Jews expressed disappointment or indignation when other Jews converted: one simply did not "abandon a besieged fortress" even if one no longer believed in its tenets. It was a matter of character, not faith.[179]

Those who did convert usually saw it as the final step to "becoming" German or a tribute to German nationalism.[180] In an age of "creeping" secularisation for German Protestants, too, Jews who left the faith saw themselves as very distant from religion of any sort and intent on Germanising. Sallis's uncle converted after his marriage to a Protestant woman "because one was convinced of the need to blend into the majority."[181] Fritz Haber converted in 1892 at the age of 24,

---

[173] Till van Rahden, *Juden und andere Breslauer: Die Beziehungen zwischen Juden, Protestanten und Katholiken in einer deutschen Grossstadt von 1860 bis 1925* (Göttingen: Vandenhoeck & Ruprecht, 1999).

[174] This was also the case with regard to resignations from the Jewish community: between 1873 and 1918, 68 percent of those who left the Jewish community were male and 32 percent were female. Honigmann, *Die Austritte*, 134.

[175] Arthur Ruppin, *Die Juden der Gegenwart* (Berlin, 1904), 81.

[176] Much like men, women hoped to enhance their job prospects, but female converts came from the lowest income categories. Kaplan, *Making of the Jewish Middle Class*, 82.

[177] Sallis, memoir, LBI, 18, 50.

[178] Hopp, *Jüdisches Bürgertum*, 295.

[179] Richarz, *Jewish Life*, 236.

[180] Schieder, "Sozialgeschichte der Religion," 18.

[181] Sallis, memoir, LBI, 16. His was not a religious conversion, since he always bragged that he had been in a church only twice.

thereafter adopting German nationalism as his religion. Quite typically, he continued to associate with friends who were Jewish or of Jewish descent, and non-Jews often disparaged him for his Jewish origins.[182] Indeed, converts were often still seen as Jews by non-Jews.[183] When two converted Jews in the senate of Heidelberg University were absent on the day of a meeting, the president, a Protestant theologian, remarked sarcastically, "I notice, to my regret, our Jewish co-Christians [*jüdische Mitchristen*] are not here today."[184] It was nearly impossible to "escape" being Jewish in one generation in Imperial Germany.

Victor Klemperer's complicated conversions offer a glimpse into the motives and feelings of a convert. When one of his brothers converted, Victor saw it as a "blending into Germanness"[185] but objected when another brother tried to convince him to do the same in 1903. An atheist, he argued: "But it is a change of faith and I don't believe in Christian dogma." Finally, he agreed "that we are and wish to be Germans and ... that Christianity belongs to Germanness."[186] More mundane reasons for converting concerned his brothers. The university career to which he aspired—and for which they were paying—required such a step.

The actual conversion involved a pastor who proposed several hours of religion lessons but relented when Victor's brother said they had no time. Klemperer stood before the pastor, a small table between them with a bowl of water on it. He had to affirm with a yes and a handshake that he would remain true to the church: "He reached for my hand and I managed to get out a halfway audible 'yes.'"[187] Then the pastor touched Klemperer's forehead with the water, agreed to accept him into the church, and handed him his conversion certificate. Klemperer paid 14

---

[182] Fritz Stern, *Einstein's German World* (Princeton: Princeton University Press, 1999), 74.
[183] Earlier in the nineteenth century, Heine noted directly after his conversion that "I am now hated by Christian and Jew... No sooner have I been christened than I am cried down as a Jew." Letter of Jan. 9, 1826, in Gustav Karpeles, ed., *Heinrich Heine's Life Told in His Own Words*, trans. Arthur Dexter (New York: H. Holt, 1893), 145.
[184] Hugo Marx, *Werdegang eines jüdischen Staatsanwalt und Richters in Baden, 1892–1933* (Villingen: Neckar-Verlag, 1965), 25.
[185] Klemperer, *Curriculum Vitae*, 1:106.
[186] Ibid., 350.
[187] Ibid., 351.

marks, 75 pfennige. He reflected: "The whole event was repugnant to me, but not at all tragic."[188]

Afterward, Klemperer experienced doubts for having buckled to his brothers. He privately "un-converted" by signing "mosaic" on his official wedding certificate in 1906 upon marrying his Protestant wife.[189] At that moment, he saw his conversion as "pure careerism ... as mindless imitation of my brothers."[190] Finally, in 1912, he conceded that his career depended on his conversion and, once again, converted.[191]

Unlike conversions, intermarriages often had romantic beginnings. Couples fell in love, confronted parents who faced the marriage either reluctantly or with intense opposition, and overcame these obstacles to achieve a happy ending—or at least a happy beginning.[192]

Conversion and intermarriage could cause permanent divisions, especially in religious families. To avoid just such a split, Adolf Fröhlich, for example, courted his Protestant girlfriend for eight years, marrying in 1912, exactly one year—the official Jewish mourning period—after his last parent died.[193] In another instance, a disagreement between a man and his sister regarding his possible conversion led to a list he wrote for her perusal: "A Refutation of the Reasons that Lisi offers against my Conversion to Christianity."[194] Then he waited ten years until he took the final step. Johanna Harris's father, who taught in the Jewish primary school and conducted synagogue services in their village, refused to see his sons or their families after they intermarried.[195]

---

[188] Ibid., 352.

[189] Ibid., 405.

[190] Ibid.

[191] Ibid., 2:15–16. Career enhancement as a result of "Germanness"—as symbolized in Christianity and German names—can be seen in Bering, *The Stigma*, 228–36.

[192] Statistics indicate that divorce was slightly higher among intermarriages than among marriages within the same religion. Ruppin, *Die Juden der Gegenwart*, 246. Of course, people who decide to marry against convention may also be more inclined to divorce rather than to remain in an unhappy marriage.

[193] Fröhlich, "Adolf Fröhlich," 162–65.

[194] The conversion occurred during the early Imperial years, and the convert was Viktor Steiner. Benigna Schönhagen, "'Ja es ist ein weiter Weg von der Judenschule bis hierher ...' Kilian von Steiner und Laupheim," *Spuren* 42 (April 1998), 9.

[195] Richarz, *Kaiserreich*, 165. See also Eleanor Alexander, "Stories of My Life," memoir, LBI, 11. Her grandfather never spoke to two sons again after they intermarried.

Often, children of these marriages grew up as Christians, another form of distancing from the grandparents and the ultimate form of distancing from Judaism.[196]

Generally, however, angry relatives were asked to forgive the "culprit" and did so. When Martin Freudenthal, a gifted musician and lawyer, converted in 1908, his mother, an observant Jew, wrote to her irate relatives that "we have lived as Jews, have observed all the holidays, and have felt like Jews." But, she reminded them, "We have to ... learn to accept reality and we don't change things with our pain." She admitted that her son's decision hurt her but believed he hoped to make his and his children's lives easier. He had discussed his thoughts with his parents some years earlier, "and as little as we agreed with him—we did not have the right to forbid it."[197] His brother, too, hoped that the rest of the family "who had banished him because of his conversion" would forgive Martin, especially after he had earned the Iron Cross in the war.[198] When Philip Löwenfeld decided to marry a non-Jew around 1912, his grandfather swore he would kill himself, but "he did not jump out of the window. He overcame his negative feelings."[199]

Those family members who made rapid peace with the converts or intermarriages had generally moved away from strict religious observance themselves.[200] When Georg Klemperer decided to intermarry and convert, his father, a rabbi (but considered a deist by his son Victor), accepted the conversion with a sigh, and his mother, too, countenanced it without complaint. She only hesitated to call her

---

[196] About 25–35 percent of the children of marriages between Jews and Christians grew up Jewish. Meiring, Die *Christliche-Jüdische Mischehe*, 104–5. For Breslau, Till van Rahden's careful analysis shows that between 1890 and 1910, about 30–35 percent of offspring were nominally Jewish. Up to half of the offspring of Jewish fathers remained Jewish as of 1890, although these figures dropped in the following years. Van Rahden, *Juden und andere Breslauer*, 171–72.

[197] Sallis, memoir, LBI, 88.

[198] Ibid., 73.

[199] Richarz, *Kaiserreich*, 320–21.

[200] Honigmann argues that the Jews who left the Jewish community were more assimilated—in his definition, had taken on different values—than those who remained. Die Austritte, 69. Hence, family members who had become more acculturated could accept such a decision more easily than those who remained more traditional.

new daughter-in-law by her "all too Christian name" Maria, preferring Marie or the diminutive Mariechen.[201] Sometimes, however, a lack of religiosity did not predict acceptance of either intermarriage or conversion. Scholem's father, for example, who purposely ignored Jewish rituals, "declined ... to have any further contact" with the son who intermarried.[202]

Conversions and intermarriages formed a transitional stage. Those involved in them generally departed from official Judaism but remained influenced by their upbringing and an informal Jewish community. They did not abandon Jewish familial and friendship networks, nor were they abandoned in return.

CONCLUSION

At the turn of the twentieth century, the Orthodox *Der Israelit* praised the previous century as one that had seen such extraordinary progress for Jews that the few "prejudices and shortcomings" that still existed paled in contrast. It worried only that the progress of Jews (*Judenheit*) had come at the expense of Judaism (*Judentum*)—that Jews were no longer as observant as they had once been.[203]

By the late nineteenth century, Jewish religious behaviour spanned a vast spectrum. For many, the family evolved from a site for domestic religious practices to a surrogate for religion itself,[204] providing the most intimate link to Jewish values and traditions. In addition, Jewish organisations conveyed Jewish ideals, creating strong communal bonds, even across national borders. And Jewish adherence to a *Bildungsreligion* provided a secular frame in which Jewish traditions lived on.

Most Jews practiced an individualistic religiosity, influenced by their family, location, community, or nation—and even by their own

---

201 Klemperer, Curriculum Vitae, 1:106.
202 Scholem, *From Berlin to Jerusalem*, 31.
203 *Der Israelit*, Feb. 4, 1901, 219–20.
204 This was also a Christian phenomenon. Hugh McLeod, "Weibliche Frömmingkeit—Männlicher Unglaube? Religion und Kirchen im bürgerlichen 19. Jahrhundert," in *Bürgerinnen und Bürger: Geschlechterverhältnisse im 19. Jahrhundert*, ed., Ute Frevert (Göttingen: Vandenhoeck und Ruprecht, 1988), 123–156.

life cycles. They found a comfort zone somewhere between tradition and Bildung, between conformity to hallowed customs and openness to new forms of Jewish life. Judaism was no longer what one did in a synagogue or at home but the myriad private and public ways in which one connected to tradition, family, and community. Older beliefs blended with Bildung, behaviour focused on the family, and belonging meant a voluntary Jewish community. Thus, Jews expanded and revised "Judaism," their beliefs, behaviours, and belonging, transforming old traditions into modern Jewish practice.

CHAPTER IV

KAFKA'S KITSCH: LAUGHTER, TEARS, AND YIDDISH THEATRE IN PREWAR WEIMAR BERLIN

David A. Brenner

Even though Franz Kafka (1883–1924) is better known as a modernist writer of the highest calibre, he was also fond of popular culture, especially the cinema. While many artists and intellectuals seemed almost to fear the new medium, Kafka was virtually obsessed with it.[1] In time, going to the movies became *the* escapist activity for this notably ascetic writer. Film was able to tear him away from his desk, from the fever of literature, from writing as "a form of prayer."[2] Kafka even incorporated the newer media into his fiction. Preferring the cinema and popular Yiddish theatre to the "legitimate" drama, Kafka moved from Prague to Berlin in the final years of his life, referring to the latter's "easy life, great opportunities [and] *pleasurable diversions*."[3]

More typically, German-Jewish writers such as Kafka are viewed through a post-Holocaust lens, lending them an aura of tragic nobility. Indeed, even the tone of scholarly discussion about German Jewry has been rarely free of polemics. In the most infamous instance, Gershom Scholem diagnosed the "German-Jewish dialogue" as a one-way monologue spoken (if not "shouted") *by* Jews *at* non-Jews in Germany. Yet what Scholem portrayed as a nearly masochistic fantasy of "German-Jewish symbiosis" has been characterised by many others as the essential progressive project of modernity and/or a core paradigm of secularisation in the West. As Amos Elon concludes in the most recent historical survey of Jewish Germans, "For long periods, they had cause

---

1   Hanns Zischler, *Kafka geht ins Kino* (Hamburg: Rowohlt, 1996).
2   Franz Kafka, *Zur Frage der Gesetze und andere Schriften aus dem Nachlaß*, ed., H-G. Koch (Frankfurt a.M.: Fischer, 1994), 171.
3   Kafka to Max Brod, 5 November 1923, Franz Kafka, *Briefe: 1902–1924*, ed., Max Brod (Frankfurt a.M.: Fischer, 1975), 464; my emphasis.

to believe in their ultimate integration, as did most Jews elsewhere in Western Europe, in the United States, and even in czarist Russia. It was touch and go almost to the end."[4] If in the post-Holocaust era, we can acknowledge that the catastrophe was unpredictably uncertain, then the "assimilationist self-hatred" attributed to Jewish Germans can be exposed as a discourse and instrument of ideology.

In less particularist studies of popular culture, resistance to acculturation is conceived not as triumphant or even as liberating but simply as a recognition that hegemony was rarely total. To Raymond Williams, the founder of the "Birmingham School" of Cultural Studies, there was always struggle and contestation even when the dominant culture proved victorious. In contrast to the total dominion implicit in the (overdetermined) ideological concepts of *base* and *superstructure*, Williams conceived of alternative and oppositional cultures as challenging the hegemony of any single culture. According to Stuart Hall, William's *de facto* successor, popular culture "is one of the sites where this struggle for and against a culture of the powerful is engaged: it is also the stake to be won or lost in the struggle ... the arena of consent and resistance."[5] Then Hall adds, in an *aperçu* rarely noted, "That is why 'popular culture' matters. Otherwise, to tell you the truth, I don't give a damn about it."[6]

Mass-mediated culture for German-Jewish audiences was already in Kafka's day "middlebrow" culture, consisting of books, concerts, and theatre as well as the emerging media of film, the sound recording, and the magazine. Just as for other Westerners, a middle-class popular culture provided the material out of which German-Jewish identities were forged—identities articulated not only in terms of ethnicity but also class, gender, and nationality. The images and stories most often cited or "performed" by Jewish Germans shaped their view of the world and their deepest values, what they considered "good"

---

4   Amos Elon, *The Pity of It All: A History of the Jews of Germany, 1743–1933* (New York: Metropolitan/Henry Holt, 2002), 12.

5   Stuart Hall, "Notes on Deconstructing the Popular," quoted in R. Butsch, *The Making of American Audiences: From Stage to Television, 1750–1990* (New York: Cambridge University Press, 2000), 284–85.

6   Ibid.

or "bad," "familiar" or "alien." These media—themselves mediated through language and other signifying practices—supplied Jewish Germans with the symbols, myths, and other resources through which their identities were formed. By instructing them how to conform to dominant systems of norms, values, and institutions, the middle-class media were constitutive and hence unavoidable for German-Jewish culture-makers.

Living an identity that was *hyphenated* or *hybridised* (before those terms became fashionable), Jews in the German cultural sphere had at their disposal a corpus of texts and discourses that informed, indeed *per*formed their Jewish identities. No longer availing themselves exclusively of canonical texts (such as the Bible, the Talmud, or the Midrash) or of folk traditions, they began in the nineteenth century to mediate their identities by way of novels, films, and the theatre—in short, by way of an emergent *popular culture*. This culture became the highly complex site of their identity formation, as it had become for other Central and Western Europeans of the epoch.

For the nineteenth century was a turning point in the history of how culture was produced, consumed, and otherwise disseminated. This turning point preceded the "homogenisation" of audiences allegedly perpetrated by *mass culture*, a term associated with "mass production." Thus, the Anglo-American concepts of "popular culture" and "mass culture"—though not as pejorative as the German term *Kitsch* (or the Yiddish *shund*)—suggest a negative judgment about a work's artistic merit and, by extension, its audience. Within the fields of German and Jewish Cultural Studies, mass culture is often still interpreted in the shadow of Theodor W. Adorno and Max Horkheimer. Their *Dialectic of Enlightenment* (completed in 1944, published in 1947) linked all forms of popular culture, from jazz and movies to detective fiction, to a near-monolithic "culture industry."[7] In the conclusion to their famous essay, one reads that "[t]he triumph of advertising in the culture industry is that consumers feel compelled to buy and use its products even though

---

[7] Theodor W. Adorno and Max Horkheimer, *Dialektik der Aufklärung: Philosophische Fragmente* (Amsterdam: Querido, 1947). The 1944 edition appeared in mimeograph and was circulated only to a handful of associates.

they see through them."[8] What is presented here as paradoxical emerged from two thinkers of German-Jewish background who rendered the dominant genres of popular entertainment part of a sinister yet (oddly) transparent campaign of diversion, manipulation, and "reification."[9]

To postwar American Germanists, many of them newly exiled Jewish Germans, this ideology of mass culture had a distinct appeal in the immediate aftermath of horrors committed in the name of Germany.[10] Some of them, not unlike Adorno and Horkheimer, seemed nostalgic after Auschwitz for an ideology of *Bildung* ("education"). Yet a new generation of historians, including Anson Rabinbach and Steven Aschheim, has since revised the notion that *Bildung* was some sort of timeless transcendent, especially for German Jews.[11] Nor were the disasters of National Socialism and the Holocaust inevitable, even if the nineteenth-century invention of a distinctively national German culture seems in hindsight to hint at its twentieth-century excesses.[12]

---

[8] Theodor W. Adorno and Max Horkheimer, "The Culture Industry: Enlightenment as Mass Deception," *Dialectic of the Enlightenment* (New York: Herder and Herder, 1972), 167.

[9] See, for instance, Peter U. Hohendahl, *Building a National Literature, The Case of Germany 1830–1870* (Ithaca: Cornell University Press, 1989), 309–11.

[10] Similar deficits can be found in the work of postwar Judaics scholars, some of whom were also newly (or previously) exiled Jewish Germans. Indeed, the field of Jewish Studies continues to be focused on intellectual and political history at the expense of the history of mass culture, studies of which have been almost entirely limited to post-1945 America. The work of Stephen Whitfield (see, for instance, his *In Search of American Jewish Culture*; Hanover, NH: University Press of New England, 1999) is the exception which proves this rule.

[11] This interpretation of *Bildung* ("cultivation" or "formation") is most often associated with George Mosse; see George Mosse, *German Jews* Beyond *Judaism* (Cincinnati: Hebrew Union College Press, 1985). Works by the revisionists include Anson Rabinbach, "Between Enlightenment and Apocalypse: Benjamin, Bloch and Modern German Jewish Messianism," *New German Critique* 34 (1985), 78–124, and Steven E. Aschheim, "German Jews beyond *Bildung* and Liberalism: The Radical Jewish Revival in the Weimar Republic," in *The German-Jewish Dialogue Reconsidered: A Symposium in Honor of George L. Mosse*, ed. Klaus L. Berghahn (New York: Peter Lang, 1996), 125–40. Cf. as well Jacques Derrida's problematic essay, "Force of Law: The 'Mystical' Foundation of Authority," originally published in *Cardozo Law Review* 11 (July/August 1990); 919–1045.

[12] Adorno himself later warned against precisely such pessimistic stocktaking: "Those who make a plea to preserve a radically guilty and shabby culture set themselves up as co-conspirators, while those who deny themselves this culture promote the very barbarity that culture has revealed itself to be"; Theodor W. Adorno, *Negative Dialektik. Jargon der Eigentlichkeit*, ed., Rolf Tiedemann (Frankfurt a.M., Suhrkamp, 1996), 360; my translation.

While Adorno and Horkheimer's chapter on "The Culture Industry" ostensibly ended without hope of liberation from "mass deception," its unpublished conclusion remained faithful to the possibilities of the Enlightenment for autonomous subjectivity: "It depends on human beings themselves whether they will ... awaken from a nightmare that only threatens to become actual as long as they believe in it."[13] To be sure, these two philosophers were so highly acculturated that their identities were scarcely informed by what I refer to as *German-Jewish popular culture*.[14] But theirs was a kind of secondary reaction-formation, a possible response (among many) to perceived deficits in nineteenth-century German and German-Jewish culture. Indeed, when analysed more closely, popular culture may always have been the necessary basis for what is termed "high culture." As suggested above, many intellectuals in the modernist movement (prior to Dada and Surrealism at least) displayed a supercilious, alarmist view of mass democracy, perceiving culture and art to be constantly endangered by the "lowbrow."[15]

---

[13] Adorno, "The Schema of Mass Culture, " in Theodor W. Adorno, *The Culture Industry: Selected Essays in Mass Culture*, ed. J. M. Bernstein (London: Routledge, 1991), 83. James Schmidt highlights the importance of the announced sequel to *Dialectic of Enlightenment*: "The unwritten *Rettung der Aufklärung* [Rescue of Enlightenment] would awaken the enlightenment from its nightmare, restore it to consciousness, and set it back on its path"; James Schmidt, "Language, Mythology, and Enlightenment: Historical Notes on Horkheimer and Adorno's *Dialectic of Enlightenment*," *Social Research* 65:4 (Winter 1998), 835. In addition, see Geoffrey Hartman, *The Fateful Question of Culture* (New York: Columbia University Press, 1997), 123.

[14] Adorno and Horkheimer were not atypical. For it was often the most highly acculturated German Jews who managed to become American academics. This fact is not surprising if one considers that "[o]nly eighteen percent of gainfully employed refugees arriving near World War II were professionals, and many of these were doctors and lawyers rather than intellectuals"; Steven M. Lowenstein, *Frankfurt on the Hudson: The German-Jewish Community of Washington Heights, 1933–1983* (Detroit: Wayne State University Press, 1989), 23.

[15] John Carey, *The Intellectuals and the Masses: Pride and Prejudice Among The Literary Intelligentsia, 1880–1939* (Boston: Faber and Faber, 1992). By the same token, then, one can argue that "high culture" is essentially a mass or middlebrow culture legitimated for (and usually *by*) social elites. See also Lawrence Levine, *Highbrow/Lowbrow: The Emergence of Cultural Hierarchy in America* (Cambridge, MA: Harvard University Press, 1990). The relationship between the middlebrow and postmodernism is delineated by (Jewish American) critic Leslie Fiedler in his seminal essay, "Cross

In a contrary tendency, Raymond Williams and other practitioners of British (or Birmingham School) Cultural Studies have at times tended to *overlook* popular culture's "dark side," just as the remaining disciples of Adorno and Horkheimer omit its heritage of dissent. But one need not make an absolute choice between ideology critique on the one hand and Williams on the other.[16] The industrialisation of culture and communication, highly advanced, though it most assuredly is, has itself not been fully realised as prophesied by Adorno and Horkheimer. This is not only valid for present-day America or Germany but was also true in the nascent days of the German-Jewish "culture industry" in the late nineteenth century. In ways not foreseen by the early "Frankfurt School," the expansion and diversification of the culture industry has opened up spaces in the public sphere where a non-manipulative, even critical employment of the means of cultural communication has become possible. Culture, in short, has become a site for critical resistance (or "negativity," in Adorno's terminology) as well as for ideological manipulation.[17]

The same holds for *ethnic* culture as a site of potential resistance or autonomous performance. Until recently, German Jewry was known less for its ethnic experiences and more for its valuable "contributions" to modern German and modern Judaic (high) cultures. Nonetheless, it also participated in the invention of one of the first middle class and minority cultures in the modern West. Yet taking a cursory glance at the last 50 years of scholarship, one might conclude that most German-speaking Jews in pre-Holocaust Europe preferred philosophy to popular culture, lyric poetry to ladies' journals, the Jewish youth

---

the Border—Close the Gap," *Playboy* (December 1969), 151, 230, 252–254, 256–258. Fiedler had already declared in the 1950s that contemporary American literature was a Jewish *and* middle-class affair, associating Saul Bellow with "highbrow" literature, J. D. Salinger with "upper middlebrow," Irwin Shaw with "middle middlebrow" and Herman Wouk with "lower middlebrow."

16 Brent O. Peterson, personal communication, April 3, 1997; see also Brent O. Peterson, *History, Fiction and Germany: Writing the Nineteenth-Century Nation* (Detroit: Wayne State University Press, 2005).

17 Adorno often preferred what might be termed *lose-lose*" dialectics; on this, see Russell A. Berman, "Cultural Studies and the Canon: Some Thoughts on Stefan George," in *Profession 1999* (New York: Modern Language Association of America, 1999), 173–74.

movement to joke books, and Schnitzler and Mahler to comic theatre and cabaret. Long after becoming a Zionist and the preeminent scholar of Jewish mysticism, Gershom (born *Gerhard*) Scholem was still embarrassed that his parents owned "Jewish joke-books."[18] Other evidence, though, suggests that Scholem's coreligionists in Germany and Austria did not universally eschew popular Jewish culture. The idea that German Jews were lacking in humour and averse to pleasure still abides in the stereotype of the *yekke* (or *Jecke*, i.e., "German Jew"). And according to other pundits, any Jew in Germany must have been bent on "assimilation"—or worse, apostasy.

Yet most Jewish Germans, even the non-observant or non-Zionist, were familiar with things Jewish. One goal of studying how they created and consumed *German Jewish* popular culture is to learn how this culture *constituted* their sentiments and values. In what follows, I examine the reception of East European Jewish culture by Kafka's German-Jewish contemporaries. In particular, this chapter considers Yiddish theatre as performed in Germany around 1900. When Kafka proposed to his (then) fiancée that she catch a performance of his friend Jitzchak Löwy's Yiddish dramatic troupe in the Jewish immigrant neighbourhood of Berlin (the *Scheunenviertel* or "barn quarter"), he again proved himself less of a snob than we might expect. His warning to Felice Bauer (1887–1960) that the theatre in question might seem "shabby" could easily have been misunderstood. But Kafka was by that point of his life a fan of Yiddish theatre, who rarely attended "legitimate theatre" thereafter. Prior to the Weimar era "Jewish renaissance," Kafka was veritably obsessed with Eastern Jewish culture. In contrast to the mainstream German drama and its depiction of Jews, Yiddish theatre in pre-Weimar Germany was ironic and bittersweet, a mixture of laughter with tears.

---

18 Even though Scholem rarely missed an opportunity to expose what he viewed as the "indignities, illusions, and contortions" of German-Jewish assimilation, he confessed to Adorno in June 1939 that "the strangest and most alluring thing is the fact that the most original products of Jewish thinking are, as it were, products of assimilation"; quoted in Steven E. Aschheim, "The Metaphysical Psychologist: On the Life and Letters of Gershom Scholem," *Journal of Modern History* 76 (2004), 915 and 928–929.

I

Observers of German Jewry have long used metaphors such as "symbiosis" to diagnose the status of modern Jewish identity in the German cultural sphere. Particularly since the Third Reich and the Holocaust, they have tended to be critical of the idea of "symbiosis." The notion that an individual could be, at one and the same time, "German" and "Jewish" was anathema in the wake of Nazi Germany. A good deal of post-1945 historiography laments those Jews living in Germany before World War II as "assimilationist," "self-hating," or just plain delusional.[19]

In particular, some historians censure German-Jewish attitudes and behaviour toward other Jews, especially those from Eastern Europe (referred to as "Eastern Jews" or *Ostjuden* in this chapter).[20] Steven Aschheim's *Brothers and Strangers* (1982) represents one in a chorus of voices seeking to rescue the *Ostjude* from supposed German-Jewish domination. Aschheim demonstrates that German Jews, like their non-Jewish compatriots, adopted negative attitudes toward East European Jewry. He documents wide-scale production of negative stereotypes of *Ostjuden* by Jews and non-Jews. Yet, while duly noting that the idealisation of *Ostjuden* took on cultic proportions after Martin Buber's earliest rehabilitations of the Hasidic tale, Aschheim's narrative and that of more strident critics of Western Jewry seemed to suggest that all attempts to reconcile Eastern and Western Jewish cultures were doomed from the start.[21]

---

[19] This thesis is recapitulated in recent work as well; see Alon Elon, *The Pity of It All*. On the terms "acculturation" and "assimilation," see David Sorkin, "Emancipation and Assimilation—Two Concepts and Their Application to German-Jewish History," *Year Book of the Leo Baeck Institute* 35 (1990), 27–33; Milton M. Gordon, *Assimilation in American Life: The Role of Race, Religion and National Origins* (New York: Oxford University Press, 1964).

[20] "Western Jewish" and "Eastern Jewish" refer to cultures and cultural tendencies, for what is "Eastern Jewish" and what is "Western Jewish" cannot always be demarcated geographically. On the history of the term *Ostjude* to refer to East European Jews, see Steven E. Aschheim, *Brothers and Strangers: The East European Jew in German and German Jewish Consciousness, 1800–1923* (Madison: University of Wisconsin Press, 1982), 257, fn. 1, and Trude Maurer, *Ostjuden in Deutschland 1918–1933* (Hamburg: Hans Christians, 1986), 12–13. Aschheim and Maurer maintain that the term did not achieve popular currency until 1910.

[21] On the "revenge of the *Ostjuden*," see Jack Wertheimer, "The German-Jewish Experience: Toward a Useable Past," *American Jewish Archives* 40 (November 1988), 422.

Now it is legitimate to ask whether the contempt of Western Jews for Eastern Jews might be categorised as "Jewish antisemitism." And certainly antisemitic attacks on Eastern Jews made German Jews look and feel under attack. According to the thesis of Jewish self-hatred, Western Jews hated not only their Eastern brethren but also—as a result of psychological projection—the Eastern Jew within themselves.[22] The assumption is that German Jews felt threatened by the prospect of "hordes" of Jewish aliens pouring across the eastern border. Even though Jewish migration to Germany never exceeded a few hundred per year until 1918 and even though the new Jewish immigrants were statistically insignificant in comparison to the host populations—the total number of *Ostjuden* who settled in Germany never exceeded 100,000—their presence was immediately noticed by some government officials and most political opportunists. On this basis, Aschheim and others have argued that worried Jewish communities feared an antisemitic backlash and tried to keep the numbers of immigrants down or less visible.

Another set of historians, in the meantime, has presented evidence that the Jews in Germany responded proactively to the challenge posed by antisemitic attacks on Jews from the East. To be sure, some German Jews blamed Eastern Jews for antisemitism, pinpointing them as a source of shame or embarrassment. And the established Jews of the West may well have avoided contact with immigrant "Russians" and "Galicians," even treating them with condescension. But, writes one historian, the Jewish middle classes in Germany "also displayed compassion for the suffering of their coreligionists…. [T]hey provided various types of support—legal aid, political support, and care for the needy…. [F]rom the evidence at our disposal, it appears that their actions on behalf of the immigrants were incompatible with hatred."[23] The point is not that Jews were incapable of mutual animosity. Centuries of "divide and conquer" practiced upon Jews, in both the East and the

---

22   Sander L. Gilman, *Jewish Self-Hatred: Anti-Semitism and the Hidden Language of the Jews* (Baltimore: Johns Hopkins University Press, 1986), 1–5.

23   Jack Wertheimer, *Unwelcome Strangers: East European Jews in Imperial Germany* (New York: Oxford University Press, 1987), 149.

West, had certainly left their mark. Nonetheless, the extent of their interactions and their cultural similarities suggest that a relationship existed, if not always a symbiotic one.

II

As studies of popular Berlin theatre, including Yiddish-language theatre, are few and far between, scholars must rely on evidence of reception such as that found in the Jewish and non-Jewish press.[24] *Ost und West* is an ideal source for evaluating this reception when considered not only as a textual apparatus extending over twenty years but also as a public relations enterprise promoting specific images of Jewishness to specific Jewish audiences.

Even though *Ost und West* (Berlin, 1901-1923), an illustrated Jewish monthly, succeeded in creating a public sphere for "pan-Jewry" (*Gesamtjudentum*), it was confronted with challenges. East European Jews had been perceived negatively by many Western Jews and non-Jews since the Enlightenment. Since the late eighteenth century, an elite of intellectuals and policy makers had called upon *Ostjuden* to become less Jewish. It was hoped instead that they would "regenerate" themselves into a group more like "the Germans," "the French," and so on. The *Ostjuden* were increasingly caricatured in a number of media and genres, from literature and the arts to the sciences. This trend was more widespread than ever when *Ost und West* began publication in 1901. At the same time, the journal sought to "re-educate" Jews in Western Europe who knew little about Eastern Jewry.

This task was well suited for Leo Winz (1876?–1952), the transplanted Ukrainian Jew and public relations man responsible for the magazine.[25] Winz was a veteran "image maker" who had served

---

24   See Heidelore Riss, *Ansätze zu einer Geschichte des jüdischen Theaters in Berlin 1889–1936* (Frankfurt: Peter Lang, 2000), 68.

25   Winz arrived in Berlin from Russia in the early 1890s. Unlike many other Eastern Jewish students at the Friedrich-Wilhelm-Universität, he concentrated in the humanities. On the Eastern Jewish student milieu in the Prussian capital at the turn of the century, see Inka Bertz, "Politischer Zionismus und Jüdische Renaissance in Berlin vor 1914," in *Jüdische Geschichte in Berlin. Essays und Studien*, ed. Reinhard Rürup(Berlin: Edition Hentrich, 1995), 149–54.

between 1906 and 1908 as the head of public relations for the oldest major German advertising firm, Haasenstein & Vogler. To date, there is no biography of Winz or of his main associates at *Ost und West*.[26] Besides owning and investing in a range of businesses, Winz was also, between 1927 and 1934, the publisher of the largest Jewish newspaper in Germany, the *Gemeindeblatt der jüdischen Gemeinde zu Berlin* (The Communal News of the Jewish Federation of Berlin).

Judging by its wide circulation, *Ost und West* was a success. According to Winz's and independent estimates, the journal had anywhere from 16,000 to 23,000 subscribers in the period between 1906 and 1914. These figures in turn can be multiplied by a factor of three (or more) to allow for the magazine's circulation within cafés, reading rooms, and libraries. Hence, *Ost und West* reached at least 10 percent of the 625,000 Jews in Germany at its height. After the *Israelitisches Familienblatt* (Israelite Family Journal), published in Hamburg between 1898 and 1938, it was the best-selling German-Jewish publication of the epoch, proving there was a potential market in Germany for the magazine and its version of East European Jewish culture.[27]

To promote an ethnic Jewish identity, Winz published a rich variety of materials. In its first three years, *Ost und West* was best known for images that portrayed Eastern Jewry positively. The journal thus differed visibly from competing German-Jewish publications in boldly asserting its Jewishness. As soon as the reader picked up an issue, he or she knew that the stories, essays, artwork, and photographs were provided chiefly by Jews, about Jews, and for Jews.[28] The very first issue (January 1901) featured an essay entitled "Jüdische Renaissance" by Martin Buber, a review of Robert Jaffé's *Ahasver* (1900) by Samuel Lublinski, a story by Isaac Leib Peretz in German translation, drawings by Ephraim Moses

---

26   For an introduction to Winz and *Ost und West*, see David Brenner, *Marketing Identities: The Invention of Jewish Ethnicity in Ost* und West (Detroit: Wayne State University Press, 1998).

27   Wertheimer may be correct in claiming that Eastern Jews formed few public or political organizations, instead preferring synagogue associations and *Gemeinde* activities. At the same time, he may be too categorical when denying that the foreigners created cultural institutions of their own; see Wertheimer, *Unwelcome Strangers*, 179–80.

28   I would argue that reception of a text ultimately renders it "Jewish," more so than its producers or framework of production.

Lilien, and an article on the Hebrew language by Simon Bernfeld. In this and later issues, European Jewry was presented as having a proud ethnic heritage and diverse cultural traditions. Yet it was not enough to "repackage" the Eastern Jew, who remained dirty, poor, and superstitious in the minds of some Westerners. Rather, *Ostjuden* were to be subtly rehabilitated using the criteria of Western culture and aesthetics.

Such tensions are central in *Ost und West*'s first article glorifying the Yiddish language, in March 1901. Here Fabius Schach, a close associate of Winz, shows a willingness to reevaluate the term *Yiddish*. While parodying the Western Yiddish dialect (or "Judeo-German") of Jewish horse and cattle dealers in Bavaria and Württemberg, Schach contends that the standard (Eastern) Yiddish language is more than a pidgin or creole.[29] Significantly, it meets the criteria of established (i.e., Western) languages and literatures: it is "organised," "grammatical," with a "strong periodical culture" and a literary output "more Realist than Romantic" in its style.[30]

Two months later, Schach again employs positive stereotyping to address the nature and the history of the Yiddish theatre: "The Jew has a fighting nature: he speaks and thinks dramatically.... No people can speak so characteristically with eyes and fingers."[31] Yet Schach then labels Abraham Goldfaden (1840–1908) and other early Yiddish dramatists as purveyors of "low" culture. As if aware that he may be going too far in the opposite direction, he quickly issues an apologia:

> You cannot judge a people which is belated in its aesthetic education by the standards of [Gotthold Ephraim] Lessing's *Hamburg Dramaturgy*.... We need theater for Russian Jews so that they may become culturally and aesthetically healthy.... What is simple, beautiful and natural has not been understood by the Russian Jew. He has been raised for generations on *pilpul*, and he has been entertained by the "sport" of Talmud in lieu of flowers and sunlight. The soul of the Russian Jew is sick, perhaps even more sick than his body.[32]

---

29 Fabius Schach, "Der deutsch-jüdische Jargon," *Ost und West* (March 1901) col. 179–90.

30 Despite his praise of (Eastern) Yiddish, Schach valorizes a set of theses that are questionable according to the present state of research on Yiddish.

31 Fabius Schach, "Das jüdische Theater, sein Wesen und seine Geschichte," *Ost und West* (May 1901) col. 351–52. All translations from the German are my own.

32 Fabius Schach, "Das jüdische Theater," *Ost und West*, col. 351, 356, 357–58. Schach and

Such a Zionist approach to Eastern Jewish culture, ultimately derived from Max Nordau's *Degeneration* (1892), was by no means grounded in Ashkenazic folk tradition. In line with the presuppositions of modern Western scholarship being produced by Jews and non-Jews, certain cultural forms and genres were to be accorded more respect. Language and legend, first valorised by Johann Gottfried von Herder (1744–1803), ranked highest, followed by poetry, sculpture, and painting. The essay rounded out this hierarchy of forms. Close to the bottom, in contrast, was nonclassical drama, including the popular theatrical entertainments of East European Jews.

In line with its target audience, the typical ordering of genres in a given issue of *Ost und West* favoured Western rather than Eastern Jewish readers. Even if many of the artists featured in the journal hailed from the East, they were repackaged for the Western Jewish reader. The only truly Eastern Jewish products in *Ost und West* were fiction, folklore, and the press summary, all of which appeared in German translation. The writers published most regularly—Peretz, Sholem Asch (1880–1957), Sholem Aleichem (1859–1916), and David Pinski (1872–1959)—were well known for their sensitivity to West European trends. In fact, most of the Eastern Jewish *belles-lettres* that appeared in *Ost und West* were decidedly humoristic and posed little or no obstacle to being understood by German-Jewish audiences.

The humoristic similarly dominated ethnic Jewish entertainment in fin de siècle Berlin. The following characterisation of Yiddish theatre, penned by the British-based, Rumanian-born, Jewish scholar Moses Gaster, was typical for the era: "It shows us our defects, which we have like all men, but not with a tendency to strike at our own immorality with ... ill will, but with only an ironic spirit that does not wound us as we are wounded by representations on other stages where the Jew plays a degrading role."[33] For Gaster and other Jewish commentators, irony

---

other leading writers of *Ost und West* hoped to persuade middle-class (especially female) Western Jews to identify positively with Eastern Jews depicted as downtrodden (and male); see Brenner, *Marketing Identities*.

[33]   Quoted in Israil Bercovici, *O sută de ani de teatru evreiesc în România* (One hundred years of Jewish theater in Romania), 2nd rev. ed. (Bucharest: Editura Integral, 1998), 79. Online. Available at http://en.wikipedia.org/wiki/Yiddish_theatre (accessed July

was the essential factor in nineteenth-century Eastern Jewish drama.

This also corresponded to developments in nineteenth-century Yiddish fiction, specifically a movement from the satire of Mendele Moykher-Sforim (and other *maskilim*) to the post-pogrom irony of Sholem Aleichem. Yiddish theatre in fin de siècle Germany was similarly ironic. Jewish comedy, in particular, was capable of a good measure of self-irony. Early vaudeville in the United States also "poked fun at ethnic stereotypes—usually (but not always) their own."[34] This was a trend that was also taken up by the American Yiddish theatre. Interwoven with affection vis-à-vis the *shtetl*, though, Yiddish performance could call up previously repressed "strong emotions."[35] Kafka analysed this concern in his "Speech on the Yiddish Language," a diagnosis which gets repeated in the history of Jewish encounters with reinvented traditions.[36] German-based Yiddish performances at times evinced reactions of shame, rendering them a "nostalgic domain reserved for our collective intimacy."[37] Or in Kafka's turn of phrase, Western Jews around 1900 "understood" more Yiddish than they could comfortably admit.[38]

III

In his diaries, Kafka also recorded the spectacle of watching *Alone At Last* (1913, directed by Max Mack), a film starring the German-Jewish stage actors the Herrnfeld Brothers as one of his most moving cinematic experiences.[39] Most scholarly assessments of *fin de siècle* Jewish theatre

---

15, 2006); emphasis added.

[34] Jules Chametzky, "The Golden Age of the Broadway Song," in *Jewish American Literature: A Norton Anthology*, eds. Jules Chametzky, John Felstiner, Hilene Flanzbaum and Kathryn Hellerstein (New York: Norton, 2001), 963.

[35] Such was the diagnosis by a reader of the *Jüdische Rundschau* as to why "Zionists" were not attending the Yiddish theater around 1921 (cited without footnote reference in Maurer, *Ostjuden in Deutschland*, 738).

[36] For an instructive summary of Kafka's Yiddish song evening, see Reiner Stach, *Kafka. Die Jahre der Entscheidungen* (Frankfurt a.M.: S. Fischer, 2002), 57–65.

[37] Albert Memmi, *Portrait of a Jew*; cited in Kun, *Audiotopia*, 72.

[38] Franz Kafka, ["Einleitungsvortrag über Jargon"], in *Nachgelassene Schriften und Fragmente I*, ed. Malcolm Pasley (Frankfurt a.M.: Fischer, 1993), 188–193. The text is based on notes taken by Elsa Taussig.

[39] On this and other films which Kafka saw, see Zischler, *Kafka geht ins Kino*.

in Berlin have also focused on the Herrnfeld Theatre, established by Anton and David Herrnfeld in the final decade of the nineteenth century. The Herrnfeld brothers ultimately developed a performance style so unique that the phrase "Herrnfeld Theatre" became a stock expression. The Herrnfelds become *the* standard for comparison when one attempts to gauge what was "too Jewish" in performance culture of the period. Whenever popular theatre ventured into "too Jewish" territory in Imperial Berlin, it was likely that the Herrnfelds were involved.

As a result, the self-irony of the Herrnfeld style was frequently misunderstood by critics, Jewish and non-Jewish alike. Jewish ones in particular discerned a "lack of aesthetic quality" in Herrnfeld performances. More direct criticisms were directed at the brothers' slapstick comedy and use of *Mauscheln* (speaking German with a Yiddish accent) as sufficient evidence of an antisemitic propensity, as though fearing that any caricature would confirm antisemitic prejudices.[40] Although "the brothers' brand of comedy was based primarily on stereotyped figures that ... were received as self-caricatures taken from everyday Jewish life," the overproportionately Jewish audiences did not laugh *at* the Herrnfelds as much as *with* them. In turn, the Herrnfelds did not just parody Yiddish-inflected German but also Viennese dialect, the Berlin idiom, and so forth.

Suspicion of the Herrnfelds ultimately revealed as much about the alleging party as about the actual performance. But by the 1920s at the latest, a major change was underway. Critics began to reassess the Herrnfelds. The positive spin brought together both the liberal Jewish *C.V.-Zeitung* (the Anti-Defamation League publication of its day) and its Zionist rival, the *Jüdische Rundschau*. In time, reviewers for both organs came to acknowledge that it was unfair to accuse the Herrnfelds of "self-hatred," particularly when compared to the rise of aggressively antisemitic discourse in mid-1920s Germany. Thus, the

---

[40] The Herrnfeld's slapstick clowning may be more than merely comparable with Ernst Lubitsch's earliest comedies, such as *Schuhpalast Pinkus* (1916). This comic cinema was not the unique creation of Lubitsch (as is often assumed) since the Herrnfelds also directed films in the same epoch, many of them now lost; Peter Sprengel, *Populäres jüdisches Theater in Berlin von 1877 bis 1933* (Berlin: Haude & Spener, 1997), 97.

theatre critic of the *Jüdische Rundschau* wrote: "I can't help it, and I may render myself a run-of-the-mill admirer of kitsch, a Jewish one, mainly for *Jewish* kitsch. But it [the Herrnfeld Theatre] is great stuff."[41]

In this sense, Schach's critical prejudices toward Yiddish theatre in 1901 proved to have been trendsetting for *Ost und West*, where an uncritical acceptance of Eastern Jewish culture gradually took a back seat to Western Jewish middlebrow sensibilities. The magazine's drive to publish "legitimate" Jewish culture also applied to its status as a medium. Not to be perceived as a "low," cheap amusement, the magazine pretended to carry only high art and high culture. But from its inception, there were cracks and fissures in *Ost und West*'s project to make Yiddish "respectable."[42] In the same pages where there is a general bias against theatre for the masses, the magazine gives voice to the diverse nature of the Eastern Jewish dramatic culture offered in turn-of-the-century Berlin.

In the August 1901 issue, a few months after Schach's fulminations, the audience at an evening of Yiddish theatre is specifically described as "uniformly Jewish" and "serious." Although they "laugh hard" at the comic Yiddish shtick being performed, they somehow manage to remain "classy" and "sophisticated."[43] So who are these "uniformly Jewish" yet—paradoxically—"restrained" theatregoers?[44] The author of the article elides the details. Extratextual evidence suggests that this audience consisted largely of immigrant Eastern Jews at a performance in the *Scheunenviertel*. Located just north of the Alexanderplatz, this impoverished quarter had a bad reputation because its underprivileged inhabitants were not only working class or unemployed but also at times had to resort to criminal activity. One of the best known descriptions of the *Scheunenviertel*, albeit of Weimar Republic vintage, can be found in Alfred Döblin's novel *Berlin Alexanderplatz* (1929). The sociocultural locus of Yiddish theatre in Germany could therefore be

---

41   A. Hellmann, "Stall Levy mit *y*—Lustspiel von Anton Herrnfeld. Herrnfeldtheater im Intimen Theater, Bülowstrasse," *Jüdische Rundschau* 23 December 1925, quoted in Riss, *Ansätze zu einer Geschichte*, 35–36.

42   On "respectability," see George Mosse, *Nationalism and Sexuality: Middle-Class Morality and Sexual Norms in Modern Europe* (New York: H. Fertig, 1985).

43   I. Abrahamsohn, "Sternensöhne," *Ost und West* (August 1901) col. 619–622.

44   Ibid.

found in the same streetscape as one of Europe's highest densities of cinemas and carnivals. For Jews living there, peddling and petty trade were among the most common sources of (legal) income.

Clearly, there were already at least two distinct Jewish theatregoing publics in turn-of-the-century Berlin. In the same August 1901 article of *Ost und West*, Winz and his co-workers were rendering Yiddish performance reputable for Western Jews, not for the East European Jews who had formed the original audiences for Yiddish theatre in Berlin since the earliest documented performance of 1883. Yet if one wishes to consider those forms of theatre exclusively for Jews in the German cultural sphere, one is compelled to look at popular Yiddish theatre. Yiddish theatre in this period was consciously lowbrow, closer to show business than high art. In fact, its earliest manifestations in late nineteenth-century Eastern Europe were entertainment oriented, encompassing operetta, musical comedy, and revue. Only after the encounter with Western theatre practice did this melodramatic "kitsch" yield to modernist influences, such as Naturalist and Expressionist drama, the emblematic example being S. Ansky's *The Dybbuk* (1919).

Music, song, and dance thus figured prominently in early Yiddish performances. In particular, travelling troupes copied Goldfaden's successful formula of mixing musical vaudeville with light comedy. Even though Yiddish theatre since its beginnings involved *varieté* or revue, melodramatic "good kitsch" was imported from the West European stage in order to round out the repertoire. With time, educators and intellectuals called for a serious, "educational" Jewish theatre, one that went beyond "making people laugh or cry."[45] Still, that "good" kitsch remained popular, even with Goldfaden, who himself had at first concurred with the reformers. Near the end of his career, he explained: "Laugh heartily if I amuse you with my jokes, while I, watching you, feel my heart crying. Then brothers, I'll give you a drama, a tragedy drawn from life, and you shall also cry – while my heart shall be glad."[46]

---

45 Moses Schwarzfeld, 1877, quoted in Bercovici, *Teatru evreiesc în România*, 71–72. Online. Available at http://en.wikipedia.org/wiki/Yiddish_theatre (accessed July 15, 2006).

46 A. Goldfaden, quoted in Bercovici, *Teatru evreiesc în România*, 68. Online. Available at http://en.wikipedia.org/wiki/Yiddish_theatre (accessed July 15, 2006).

Critics of Yiddish theatre, however, continued to be concerned that working-class spectators be "educated" and not just "entertained."[47] Theatre reform in this era predictably paralleled developments in the nascent medium of cinema. The middle classes in Germany, like Kafka and others in the West, were lured by the spectacle of the silver screen. By 1910 or so, the larger project of acquiring respectability for the movies was complete, in both Europe and the United States. Even though many in Germany initially feared or rejected film as "low culture," studios and producers set about to make the medium respectable. Through well-appointed movie houses and middlebrow films, the new industry successfully attracted bourgeois viewers.[48]

At its zenith between the late nineteenth century and World War II, the Yiddish theatre was very much an international theatre. That *Berlin* Yiddish theatre dates back to the year 1883 is no coincidence. Yiddish performances in Russia were banned that year, in the aftermath of the assassination of Tsar Alexander II in 1881 and the imposition of the May Laws of 1882, effectively shifting the locus of Yiddish theatre toward Western Europe and the United States. Many Yiddish theatregoers therefore sought out lighter fare. In Berlin, such kitsch was not always characterised as "bad," nor was it performed poorly. Some actor/producers, such as Jacob Adler (1855–1926), performed the newly emerging classics of the "higher" Yiddish theatrical repertoire, but Boris and Bessie Thomashefsky (1868?–1939; 1873–1962) succeeded in reading their New York audiences right. In rehabilitating the popular kitsch style, they made a significant profit off *shund* ("trash") theatre. Many today still associate this style, often sentimental and larger-than-life, with the Yiddish stage.[49]

---

47 Bercovici, *Teatru evreiesc în România*, 82–83. Online. Available at http://en.wikipedia.org/wiki/Yiddish_theatre (accessed July 15, 2006).

48 The film industry functioned as "a Trojan horse that smuggled nonbourgeois and antibourgeois values and modes of representation into the minds and hearts of the middle classes"; Peter Jelavich, "'Am I Allowed to Amuse Myself Here?' The German Bourgeoisie Confronts Early Film," in *Germany at the Fin de Siècle: Culture, Politics, and Ideas*, ed. Suzanne Marchand and David Lindenfeld (Baton Rouge: Louisiana University Press, 2004), 249.

49 The founder of German cabaret, Ernst von Wolzogen (1855–1934), wrote in 1911 that the best comedies he had seen in the U.S. were in one of New York City's Yiddish theaters; see Ernst von Wolzogen, "Das jüdische Theater in Amerika," *Selbstwehr*

Shifting from weepy melodrama to wild Purim play, *shund* became a term of the trade. And the struggle between *shund* and *kunst* ("art") played itself out across the international Yiddish scene. The popular *Jüdische Bühne* (Jewish Theatre) in Vienna, for example, was an entertainment venue "which knew its audience and its desires well."[50] Its fare consisted mainly of operetta and melodrama, not unlike the offerings in Prague to which Kafka was exposed. The productions were thus closer to vaudeville, that is, brief comic *shticks* interrupted by short musical interludes and often based on hastily composed texts. As elsewhere, a movement developed in Vienna to reform the Jewish stage.[51] In Berlin, less populated by *Ostjuden*, the situation was not very different. At first, there was Quarg's Theatre, also known as Quarg's Vaudeville, as well as Puhlmann's Varieté and the main competitor of the Herrnfelds, the Folies Caprice. Although their names and locations differed, each featured revue theatre. The one-act plays, songs, comedy, and similar attractions made it relatively easy for travelling troupes from Eastern Europe to guest from time to time.

The origins of the Herrnfeld Theatre also lay in such varieté, although not exclusively of the Yiddish type. Instead, as mentioned already, the recipe for the Herrnfelds' remarkable success was a self-reflexive deployment of Jewish stereotypes. According to Berlin theatre historian Peter Sprengel, the Herrnfelds did not set out to ridicule or scorn things Jewish. Rather, they depicted Jewishness from a Jewish perspective, that is, "with self-irony." The Herrnfelds practiced a form of "ethnic comedy" (*Ethno-Komik*), which emerged out of a "tension between caricature and realism."[52] The stereotypes

---

(Prague) vol 5, number 42 (27 October 1911), n.p.; cited also in *The Nation* (4 April 1912), n.p.

[50] Brigitte Dalinger, *Verloschene Sterne. Geschichte des jüdischen Theaters in Wien* (Vienna: Picus Verlag, 1998), 54.

[51] One such theater, called the "Freie Jüdische Volksbühne," was founded officially in 1919; see Peter Marx, "Im Schatten der Theatergeschichte? Ein Überblick zur Forschung zum jüdischen Theater im deutschsprachigen Raum," *IASL Online. Eine elektronische Zeitschrift für literatur- und kulturwissenschaftliche Rezensionen und Foren* (March 27, 2001). Online. Available at http:iasl.uni-muenchen.de (accessed July 15, 2006).

[52] Sprengel, *Populäres jüdisches Theater*, 71–73; translation by author.

that the Herrnfelds manipulated not surprisingly became a matter of concern for those struggling against antisemitism. They feared that the Herrnfelds' performances could and would be instrumentalised by anti-Jewish forces.[53]

Among others, the film director Ernst Lubitsch—the son of Russian Jewish immigrants who settled in the *Scheunenviertel*—was influenced by the Herrnfeld style. Not surprisingly, his early slapstick film comedies such as *Der Stolz der Firma* (The Pride of the Company, 1914) and *Schuhpalast Pinkus* (Shoe Palace Pinkus, 1916) were not popular with those Jewish critics who worried such films only provided more fodder for antisemites.[54] Alternatively, his self-ironic performances as Siegmund Lachmann and Sally Pinkus in those films might be read "as a modern and self-confident approach to Jewish tradition, one that uses strategies and conventions considered to be 'Jewish humor,'" and in which "Lubitsch is poking fun at himself rather than at others."[55]

Other theatre historians come to similar conclusions on the matters of kitsch and Jewish stereotyping. Peter Jelavich, the historian of Berlin and Munich cabaret, contends that the more he examines the Herrnfeld productions and other forms of popular theatre in Berlin that were sympathetic to Jews, the more he sees

> a pattern of placing stereotypes of Jews ... with other stereotyped minorities in Germany, e.g. Saxons, Bavarians, Bohemians, and Berliners. By adding Jews to that German "ethnic" mix on a popular comic stage, the Herrnfelds were trying to pass the somewhat condescending, but ultimately feel-good attitudes generated toward Saxons, Bavarians, etc. in such works onto Jews as well.[56]

In diagnosing this subgenre as kitsch, Jelavich maintains that "it was kitsch that generated good vibes, and that contributed to a popular

---

53 Sprengel, *Populäres jüdisches Theater*, 92.
54 "The Herrnfeld Theater and Ernst Lubitsch." Online. Available at http://www.filmportal.de/df/e0/ArtikelEF9DE528041CD872E03053D50B3775B0.html (accessed January 15, 2011).
55 Ibid.
56 Peter Jelavich, personal communication, 2003. The use of dialect in popular America nsong is associated with Jewish composer (and son of a cantor) Irving Berlin.

image (though hardly a reality) of Jewish ethnicity." This kind of ethnic comedy, multiply mediated as it was, might be paralleled today in variety shows on television such as *Saturday Night Live*.[57]

IV

Historians of Western Europe and America have begun in recent years to probe the intersections of elite and popular culture after 1900. From the written word to visual art and the cinema, a war of taste was being waged. The drive to make "low" culture respectable was no less apparent in making Yiddish respectable. In fact, the *Kunst/Schund* distinction in German and German-Jewish milieu was precisely paralleled in the *kunst/shund* debates taking place in Yiddish-speaking environs.

The rhetorical attacks on Yiddish popular theatre involved the social realities of its not particularly *justes milieux*.[58] Until the rise of avant-garde drama after World War I, forever linked with S. Ansky (1863–1920) and the Vilna Troupe, the audience and appeal of Yiddish theatre were overwhelmingly lower or working class. Winz (of *Ost und West*) was no doubt aware that the backers of the veritable Yiddish "Broadway" in Warsaw were often from the underworld, not unlike Yekl Shapshavitsh, the protagonist of Asch's *God of Vengeance*, who is a brothel-keeper. The insistent denial of Jewish historiography, particularly since the Holocaus of the existence of this theatre *demimonde* is equalled only by its denial of a Jewish criminal world in European history, which Gershom Scholem (1897–1982), in addition to his research on Jewish mysticism, considered a necessary pursuit.[59]

---

[57] Another reason why the "good" Jewish kitsch of the Herrnfelds (and later Ernst Lubitsch) attracted attention as "too Jewish" was the lack of a larger audience of Eastern Jews for Yiddish theater in Berlin. The situation in Vienna reveals a similar trajectory in the decades between 1880 and 1930. The early Yiddish ensembles did not only run afoul of the Viennese municipal authorities but also the Viennese "Israelite Community," which feared anti-semitic riots on the basis of Yiddish-only performance; Dalinger, *Verloschene Sterne*, 44–45.

[58] Michael C. Steinlauf, "Fear of Purim: Y. L. Peretz and the Canonization of Yiddish Theater," *Jewish Social Studies* 1:3 (Spring 1995), 44–65, here 51.

[59] See Gershom Scholem in *"—Und alles ist Kabbala": Gershom Scholem im Gespräch mit Jörg Drews* (Munich: dtv, 1980).

Kafka himself knew "Yekl Shapshavitshes" having become acquainted with Yiddish theatre in a tawdry Prague nightclub run by a brothel-keeper. Winz too was familiar with these inhabitants of the "low" milieu and rumoured to be associated with them.[60] It is in just such a framework that *Ost und West* was continually inventing ways to make Yiddish reputable. In addition to the venues in Berlin's *Scheunenviertel* that actually performed in Yiddish, avant-garde Yiddish drama registered its first triumph in German translation in the 1907 performance of Sholem Asch's *God of Vengeance* at Max Reinhardt's *Kammerspiele*, arguably the most prestigious theatrical venue in turn-of-the-century Berlin.[61]

On linguistic grounds alone, it would have been difficult for Western Jews to appreciate Yiddish-language drama. The case of Kafka is the exception that proves the rule.[62] But even those few bohemians willing to acquaint themselves with actual Yiddish performances, ten years prior to Kafka's fateful meeting with Jitzchak Löwy (1887–1942), were unlikely to have attended them. For theatre in Berlin's *Scheunenviertel* was a highly regulated practice. So regulated that there were in all likelihood fewer than five performances per year until 1908. In fact, over seventy censors' copies have survived of plays by Goldfaden, Jacob Gordin (1853–1909), Joseph Lateiner (1853–1935), Sigmund Feinmann, and others. As theatre historian Sprengel concludes:

---

60 On Winz's other business ventures, both dubious and legitimate, see D. Brenner, *Marketing Identities*, and Winz's Papers, Central Zionist Archives, Jerusalem.

61 Marline Otte has recently examined *Jargon* theatres in Wilhelmine Berlin as spaces that allowed for an unexpected blurring of Jewish-Gentile relations. Otte argues that *Jargon* theatre, such as the Herrnfelds, did not emerge from authentic Yiddish entertainment, but that it employed Jewish themes and accents "to consciously play on cultural differences, not religious or racial ones, which should place them into the trajectory of German *Volkstheater*"; Marline Otte, "A World of Their Own? Bourgeois Encounters in Berlin's *Jargon* Theaters, 1890–1920," in *Germany at the Fin de Siècle: Culture, Politics, and Ideas*, ed. Suzanne Marchand and David Lindenfeld (Baton Rouge: Louisana State University Press, 2004), 254. See also Marline Otte, "Eine Welt für sich? Bürger im Jargontheater von 1890 bis 1920,"in *Juden, Bürger, Deutsche: Zur Geschichte von Vielfalt und Differenz, 1800–1933*, ed. Andreas Gotzmann, Rainer Liedtke, and Till van Rahden (Tübingen: Mohr, 2001), 121–146.

62 Cf. Kafka's comment that his fellow Jews in Prague knew "more Yiddish" than they thought; Kafka, ["Einleitungsvortrag über Jargon"], *Nachgelassene Schriften und Fragmente I*, 188–193.

The strict interpretation of individual statutes in the theater code by the authorized censors actually worked to block, in part to ban, a Jewish theater praxis whose authentic forms—vagabond theater, hybrids of musical and spoken theater, etc.—existed in an obvious tension with the binding regulations for theater performance in Prussia. And it is not unusual for one to get the impression that this objectively given conflict was exploited and exacerbated by the responsible officials with a certain subjective gratification.[63]

This understanding is borne out in censors' reports that Sprengel and others have uncovered in the archives of the Berlin police. Brief disdainful descriptions abound, ranging from "burlesque," "pornographic," and "corrupting" to "slapstick," "pedestrian," and "moronic." To be sure, all these epithets have a measure of truth: Berlin Yiddish theatre *was* kitsch and was performed in infamous circumstances.

The situation of Eastern Jewish actors in Germany was at best precarious, as was that of other non-citizens in Imperial Germany. Foreign performers not in possession of a permit or authorised to perform in public ran the risk of being deported. In addition, the earliest examples of Yiddish theatre in Germany were viewed by the authorities as a threat, not only to the tax base but also to the "social order."[64] The broad administrative powers granted to German civic officials did not have to be used, however. And yet Alexander Granach (1890–1941), the Galician Jewish immigrant who became a featured actor in Max Reinhardt's theatre, spoke for many Eastern Jews in the *Scheunenviertel* when he praised the revolutionary tendencies of early Yiddish drama: "He [the playwright Gordin] was for the poor and against the rich. For the whores and against the fine ladies. For the orphans and the bastards and against those who'd achieved wedded security. He was also for me."[65]

---

63 Sprengel, *Scheunenviertel-Theater*, 39.
64 Alfred Döblin, *Kleine Schriften I*, ed., Anthony W. Riley (Olten-Freiburg i.Br.: 1985), 385; qtd. in Sprengel, *Scheunenviertel-Theater*, 30 and Sprengel, *Scheunenviertel-Theater*, 74.
65 Alexander Granach, *Da geht ein Mensch. Autobiographischer Roman* (Munich: Weismann, 1992), 219. Born in 1890 as Isaiah Szaiko Gronach in Werbiwici, Galicia (Austro-Hungary), Granach arrived in Berlin at the age of 16, after having appeared in the Yiddish traveling theater. In 1909, he was accepted to Max Reinhardt's *Schauspielschule*, the premier drama academy of its time.

This potential for social contestation may explain the five-year silence of *Ost und West* concerning Yiddish theatre. In a December 1902 article—the only one to appear on the subject until 1907—"A Jewish Stage in Galicia" is exalted. This Lemberg-based theatre which influenced Granach to become an actor in the first place is praised for its directness and lack of (Western) sophistication. Its actors are further lauded as "simple children of nature," their style of theatre comparing favourably with the popular farces (*Schwänke und Possen*) which constituted the broad mass of performances by the brothers Herrnfeld.[66]

Perhaps Schach's 1901 call for Jewish theatres to be granted concessions in neighbourhoods heavily populated by Jews served only to further alert the Berlin police.[67] Winz's papers amply attest to the difficulties of being an Eastern Jewish entrepreneur in Germany in the first years of the century. And it was no accident that the earliest financial backers of *Ost und West* were (established) Western Jews such as Heinrich Meyer-Cohn, Otto Warburg, and Eduard Lachmann, for Prussian policy virtually required Russian (and other foreign) Jews to render themselves invisible.[68] Winz's magazine, then, was taking a risk in openly displaying Eastern Jewish leanings. In 1906, however, *Ost und West* became a self-sustaining enterprise, completely and unquestionably under Winz's control. The Yiddish stage had by that time acquired a degree of respectability.[69] The Berlin police had also become more accustomed to it, and performances were becoming more frequent.

In 1907, after Asch's *God of Vengeance* had been performed in

---

[66] See M. S. [Binjamin Segel], "Ein jüdisches Überbrettl in Galizien," *Ost und West* (December 1902), 847–852. This article is purportedly a description of the Gimpel Theater in Lemberg. For Granach's description of the performances, see Granach, *Da geht ein Mensch*, 219–227. Cf. Sprengel's discussion of the "Orientalische Operetten-Gesellschaft," also in Lemberg, to which Segel (himself a Lemberger) is likely referring; Sprengel, *Scheunenviertel-Theater*, 34–43.

[67] Schach, "Das jüdische Theater," column 356.

[68] See the Leo Winz Papers, Central Zionist Archives, Jerusalem, file A136/41.

[69] While David Pinski's drama, *Ayzik Sheftl*, is something of an anomaly in the history of Yiddish theater in Wilhelmine Germany, it was likely staged both in Yiddish and in German translation as early as 1905; Sprengel, *Scheunenviertel-Theater*, 131–32, fn. 190. See also David Pinski, *Eisik Scheftel. Ein jüdisches Arbeiterdrama in drei Akten*, trans. Martin Buber (Berlin, 1905). This volume was for many years the only translation of a Yiddish drama to be found on the list of its publisher, the Jüdischer Verlag.

German translation, *Ost und West* cautiously revived discussion of Yiddish drama, albeit in terms recalling Schach's Western-inflected discourse. Critic A. Coralnik, in a July 1907 review in the magazine, thus pans Asch and his Naturalist dramas, arguing that Asch is

> by no means the most talented of Jewish writers. His literary productions have soul, but not a deep and strong one; moods, but no toned-down, nuanced, fine ones; rhythm, but a monotonous one like the buzzing of a bee on a humid summer day; truths, but everyday, banal ones. There are realms of art that are inaccessible to him, corners of the soul that are invisible to him.[70]

Asch simply failed when compared with the recently canonised "classical" writers of Yiddish, Mendele Moykher-Sforim (1835–1917) and Isaac Leib Peretz, or with nineteenth-century German writers such as Christian Friedrich Hebbel (1813–1863).

Samuel Meisels, the cultural editor of the liberal-Jewish *Israelitisches Familienblatt*, also attacked Asch for his Naturalist aesthetic. In a contribution to *Ost und West*, he directed his fire first at Asch and then at Yiddish literature as a whole. For the Western Jew Meisels, Yiddish literary history was "backward," paralysed through "rhymed sermons," in desperate need of the Impressionist-Symbolist virtues of "emotional ambience [and] natural sentiment."[71] Yet, despite finding such fault, Meisels was himself actively engaged in translating and transmitting the culture of the *Ostjuden*, acknowledging the function of Yiddish theatre as an educational institution for the Jewish masses. And it is worth recalling that his Jewish contemporaries in Eastern Europe shared similar biases concerning "high" and "low" culture.[72] To Sholem Asch, despite all the negative reviews of his work, it was worth raving that his dramas had been performed in Germany at all. According to the

---

[70] A. Coralnik, "Schalom Asch als Dramatiker," *Ost und West* (July 1907), col. 459–60.

[71] German "Gefühlsstimmung, Seelenerguß, [and] Naturempfinden"; S. Meisels, "Zur Geschichte des jüdischen Theaters," *Ost und West* (August/September 1908), col. 509.

[72] See also Luba Kadison's recently published memoir of the Vilna Troupe and her life with Joseph Buloff; L. Kadison and J. Buloff (with I. Genn), *On Stage, Off Stage: Memories of a Lifetime in the Yiddish Theatre* (Cambridge, MA: Harvard University Press, 1992).

critic Samuel Niger, to succeed in Germany in those days was a form of *yikhes* (distinction).[73]

As German-Jewish writers such as Kafka, Kurt Pinthus (1886–1975), and Theodor Lessing (1872–1933) were gingerly beginning to attend and write about the theatre of Eastern Jews, the most popular venue for Yiddish performance in late Imperial Germany was actually the so-called Young Jewish Evening (*Jungjüdischer Abend*) or Evening of Songs (*Liederabend*). Kafka himself organised one such evening, introducing the performances with a famous speech on the Yiddish language. From 1908 on, a considerable number of these pageantlike performances of music and poetry were produced by Winz and his *Ost und West* publishing firm.[74] The 1912 Berlin *Liederabend* was by all accounts a success, prompting Winz to take his ensemble on two highly acclaimed tours of Germany, with concerts in Leipzig, Breslau, Munich, Nuremberg, Hamburg, Hannover, and elsewhere.[75]

A typical *Ost und West*-sponsored evening of "living literature and music" proved that recitation and folksong had more cachet than the pre-*Dybbuk* Yiddish theatre. Standards of the *Ost und West* song evenings were performances of folksongs (from Winz's unrivaled personal collection) and readings from the translations of Yiddish prose published in *Ost und West*. These renderings into German, most of them by writer Theodor Zlocisti (1874–1943), were published in a two-volume edition by Winz in 1909. That book, *Aus einer stillen Welt* (From a Serene World) included works by Mendele, Peretz, Sholem Aleichem, Asch, Pinski, Reuben Braudes, Mordecai Spector, Abraham Reyzen, and

---

73   See Samuel Niger, *Shalom Ash zayn lebn zayne verk: biyografye, opshatsungen, polemik, briv, bibliyografye* (New York: S. Niger bukh-komitet baym Alveltlekhn Yidishn Kultur-kongres, 1960).

74   *Ost und West* reported on what was perhaps the first *jungjüdischer Abend* organized by Buber in February 1902; for Buber's account, see his letter to Herzl of May 3, 1902, in Martin Buber, *Briefwechsel aus sieben Jahrzehnten*, ed., Grete Schaeder (Heidelberg: Gütersloher, 1972), 1:173.

75   For a "public relations" portfolio on the folksong evenings, see "Urteile der Presse über die Jüdischen Volksliederabende," *Ost und West* (December 1912), col. 1169–1200. For an negative, "purist" review, see Fritz M. Kaufmann, *Vier Essais über ostjüdische Dichtung und Kultur* (Berlin: Welt-Verlag, 1919), 61; see also the positive review by Kaufmann's mentor, Nathan Birnbaum (under the name "Matthias Acher"), "Auf dem Volksliederabend von 'Ost und West,'" *Ost und West* (January 1912), col. 17–24.

Hersh David Nomberg.

The only other work that Winz published should come as no surprise: it was Ansky's *Dybbuk* in a 1920 translation prepared jointly by Winz and Arno Nadel (1878–1943). This first rendering of Ansky's drama into German had been commissioned by the author himself just prior to his death. It would exceed the scope of this chapter to chart Winz's further activities on behalf of the *Dybbuk*, which included an opera version for the German stage and an attempt at filming the drama with the Hebrew-language troupe, Habima.[76] Suffice it to say that he was very involved—legally as well as artistically.[77]

The same was true in 1919 when Winz went to considerable expense to bring to Berlin the Alexander Azro/Sonja Alomis "spin-off" troupe of the Vilna Art Theatre. This was one of many guest engagements of Eastern Jews that Winz sponsored over the years, prompting writer and jurist Sammy Gronemann (1875–1952) to dub him "perhaps the most active friend and supporter of Jewish art in all areas."[78] For his initial involvement with Azro and Alomis, however, Winz lost more than 5,000 (pre-inflation) marks, even though he would later succeed in bringing the entire Vilna Troupe to Berlin for a two-year engagement.[79] Clearly, there was a great deal of money at stake in promoting the Yiddish theatre in Weimar Germany. The competition was arguably fierce. Between 1919 and 1924, there were numerous agents and producers doing business in Berlin and at least 20 Yiddish publishing houses.[80]

That "sophisticated" Yiddish theatre by 1920 had become at least as

---

[76] Winz's contract selling the opera rights to Ansky's *Dybbuk* is available in the Leo Winz Papers, Central Zionist Archives, Jerusalem, file 136/52.

[77] For litigation concerning rights to the Ansky's *Dybbuk*, see Winz's letter of justification to Rechtsanwalt Dr. Wenzel Goldbaum dated 31 October 1921: Leo Winz Papers, Central Zionist Archives, Jerusalem, file 136/94. Alfred Nossig's wife, Rosa, had made a counterclaim for the rights to the German translation.

[78] Winz's letter to Rechtsanwalt Dr. Wenzel Goldbaum, 31 October 1921, in the Leo Winz Papers, Central Zionist Archives, Jerusalem, file A136/52.

[79] See the Leo Winz Papers, Central Zionist Archives, Jerusalem, file A136/52.

[80] On Yiddish publishing in Berlin, see Glenn Levine, "Yiddish Publishing Activities in Berlin and the Crisis in Eastern European Jewish Culture," *Year Book of the Leo Baeck Institute* 42 (1997), 85–108.

respectable as it was profitable in Germany and much of Central Europe may to a large extent be on account of Winz's efforts to make Yiddish attractive. *Ost und West* and Winz's other enterprises contributed significantly to the cultural (and commercial) capital of Yiddish. Winz was, to be sure, a sufficiently clever cultural observer to wait for a critical mass before taking a risk himself. The timing was certainly right after 1906, at the latest after 1911 when the Berlin police began to stop cracking down on Yiddish performances in the *Scheunenviertel*. After that, Winz was also safe to promote his *Liederabende* on a broad scale.

Because he lived in and "between" two cultures, Winz understood how to balance *Ost und West*'s advocacy of East European Jewish culture with the demands of its Western Jewish audiences. Although *Ost und West* was the first significant publication to bring together Western and Eastern Jewish intellectuals and artists, its accomplishments lie more in the realm of cultural transmission than artistic innovation. The same can be said of its depiction of Yiddish theatre. Yiddish-language drama, music, and song appeared frequently in the magazine from its inception, but the treatment of these texts valorised the middlebrow more than anything avant-garde. As seen, the earliest arrival of Yiddish theatre in Germany was not as dignified as it might have appeared in the "authoritative" versions promulgated about it in *Ost und West*.

What few people have acknowledged, however, is that prior to Buber's translations—or better "rewritings"—of Hasidic tales, *Ost und West* was the largest transmitter of Eastern Jewish literature, art, and folklore to the Western Jewish public.[81] Besides acting as an editor and publisher, Winz was also a collector of Eastern Jewish art and music and a patron to those who produced it.[82] Besides earning money for Winz and Eastern Jewish artists, *Ost und West*'s practical functions included spotlighting relief efforts for Russian, Rumanian, and other Jews in need; the magazine was a leading publicity organ

---

[81] Cf. Victor Klemperer, who argued that Winz and his associates treated Eastern Jews "more kindly"; Victor Klemperer, *Curriculum Vitae: Jugend um 1900* (Berlin: Aufbau, 1989), 2:489.

[82] According to Sammy Gronemann, Winz was a benefactor to many, from young painters and Russian dancers to boxers and diplomats' wives; see Sammy Gronemann, "Erinnerungen," 1948, unpublished memoir at Leo Baeck Institute in New York, 139.

for Jewish philanthropy in Eastern Europe and elsewhere. Winz and his associates saw no contradiction in championing Eastern Jewish grassroots initiatives while at the same time endorsing Western-based relief efforts.

Ost und West, though, did on occasion misrepresent features of Eastern Jewish culture. Some of the translations into German reveal a selective reinvention of "native" traditions. Yet even when they made mistakes, contributors to the magazine inspired imitators, such as Fritz Mordechai Kaufmann (1888–1921), the founder of *Die Freistatt* (The Sanctuary; Eschweiler, 1912–1914). *Die Freistatt* was indebted to *Ost und West* for its early attempts to publicise Eastern Jewish culture, along with *Neue jüdische Monatshefte* (New Jewish Monthly; Berlin, 1916–1924) and Buber's *Der Jude* (The Jew; Berlin, 1916–1924).[83] Just how envious Buber was of Winz's success as a publicist can be seen in his 1903 sketch for *Der Jude*. This ambitious project, which he conceived along with Chaim Weizmann (1874–1952), and Lilien and Alfred Nossig (1864–1943)—whose wife later sued Winz for the rights to Ansky's *Dybbuk*—was intended to become a literary and cultural monthly similar to Winz's. Because of lack of funds and *Ost und West*'s greater appeal, *Der Jude* was shelved until 1916 when interest in East European Jewry was sufficient to warrant another major pan-Jewish journal. On balance, then, Winz and his magazine should be remembered for pioneering the advocacy of East European Jewry in the West long before the emergence during World War I of what Gershom Sholem dubbed the "cult of the *Ostjuden*."[84]

V

---

[83] On Buber and *Der Jude*, see Jehuda Reinharz, *Chaim Weizmann: The Making of a Zionist Leader* (New York: Oxford University Press, 1985), 183–85; and M. S. Friedman, *Martin Buber's Life and Work: The Early Years, 1878–1892* (New York: Dutton, 1981), 60. The most obvious imitator of *Ost und West* was the Hungarian-Jewish art and cultural journal *Mült és jövő* (Budapest: 1912–1944).

[84] G. Scholem, *Mi-berlin li-yerushalayim* [From Berlin to Jerusalem], expanded Hebrew edition (Tel Aviv: Am Oved, 1982), 47.

When he proposed that his (then) fiancée Felice Bauer catch a performance of his friend Jitzchak Löwy's troupe in the *Scheunenviertel*, Franz Kafka proved himself more ethnographically minded than critics of the culture industry.[85] His warning to Felice that the theatre in question would most likely seem "shabby" should not be misread. Before he had spent much time in Berlin, Kafka already grasped the cultural sociology of the Yiddish theatre, as his lecture on Yiddish and his empathetic encounter with Löwy's troupe in Prague made clear.[86] While Felice may not have acted upon Kafka's suggestion, she appears to have been a regular reader of *Ost und West*, bringing his attention to important reviews published there.[87] Indeed, Kafka may have had this magazine and Eastern Jewish culture in mind when formulating his thoughts on Christmas Day, 1911, in his famous fragment on the culture of "minor" nations:

> [T]he stimulating of minds, the integrated cohesion of national consciousness, often unrealized in public life and always verging on disintegration, the pride and support that a nation derives from a literature of its own in the face of hostile surroundings, this keeping of a diary by a nation which is something quite different from historiography and leads to more rapid (and yet always closely scrutinized) development, the elaborate spiritualization of a wide-ranging civic life, the immediately useful uniting of dissatisfied elements when carelessness can only do harm, the comprehensive organization of a people that is created by the hustle and bustle of *magazines* [...]—all these effects can be produced by a literature whose development is not unusually broad in scope but only seems so because it lacks notable talents.[88]

Since Kafka's reflections here, the field of Yiddish studies has itself

---

[85] See Kafka's letter to Felice Bauer, 3 November 1912, in Franz Kafka, *Briefe an Felice und andere Korrespondenz aus der Verlobungszeit*, ed., E. Heller and J. Born (Frankfurt a.M.: Fischer, 1976), 75.

[86] Kafka noted as well how the Yiddish actors were compelled to perform in a tawdry Prague nightclub, despised and insulted by the doorman (a notorious pimp and brothel owner) and others for their amateurishness on stage.

[87] See Kafka's letter to Felice Bauer of 27 October 1912 in Kafka, *Briefe an Felice*, 59.

[88] Franz Kafka, *Tagebücher 1910–1923*, ed., Max Brod (Frankfurt: S. Fischer, 1983), entry of 25 December 1911, 151; emphasis added.

achieved *academic* respectability, however tenuous. Yet what may be needed today is a movement to unsettle matters, to render Yiddish, its theatre, and its spectators a little *less* respectable.

While the circumstances of Yiddish theatre in pre-Nazi Germany were infinitely more complex than can be reconstructed, its earliest Eastern Jewish participants, both on and off the stage, were quite sophisticated. Their agency and aptitude are verified in two very similar assessments by two very different Jewish theatre mavens in Germany. Theodor Lessing, the liberal *yekke* publicist, concluded that "they're laughing at themselves in bitter seriousness."[89] Alexander Granach, the prototypical *Ostjude* in Germany, concurred: "We griped mercilessly about the bad plays and the bad acting—but kept going back all the same."[90] What unites both interpreters, one Western and the other Eastern born, constitutes a lesson for us today about the complexities that attend the reception of both high and low culture.

---

[89] Theodor Lessing , "Jiddisches Theater in London," *Die Schaubühne* 6, nos. 17 and 18, 28 April 1910 and 5 May 1910, 485; qtd. in Sprengel, *Scheunenviertel-Theater*, p. 286. See also Theodor Lessing, *Der jüdische Selbsthaß* (Berlin: Matthes und Seitz, 1984).

[90] Alexander Granach, *Da geht ein Mensch. Roman eines Lebens* (Munich: Weismann, 1992), 208.

CHAPTER V

"THE RATHENAU CHARISMA": MODERN DESIGN AND ART IN THE SERVICE OF THE RATHENAUS

Elana Shapira

Emil Rathenau (1838–1915), engineer and owner of one of the largest electrical companies in Germany (AEG, Allgemeine Elektrizität Gesellschaft), and his eldest son Walther Rathenau (1867–1922), an industrialist, banker, intellectual, and liberal politician, used modern design and art in order to express their charisma, meaning here their charismatic authority.[1] Emil pursued this goal as a powerful German Jewish industrialist and Walther as an influential and attractive German Jewish public personality. The modernist German architect and designer Peter Behrens expressed Emil Rathenau's authority through his all-product design for the AEG, while the Expressionist Norwegian artist Edvard Munch depicted the self-image and public appearance of Walther Rathenau in two portraits. The Rathenaus' display of their charisma is a response to the crisis of Jewish assimilation and is examined in relation to popular antisemitic beliefs concerning the impossibility of improving the "Jewish character" at the end of the nineteenth century.[2]

---

[1]   I refer here to the German sociologist Max Weber's discussion of charismatic authority as one of three forms of authority (the other two are traditional authority and legal authority). Weber defined *charisma* as follows: "a certain quality of an individual personality, by virtue of which one is 'set apart' from ordinary people and treated as endowed with supernatural, superhuman, or at least specifically exceptional powers or qualities. These as such are not accessible to the ordinary person but are regarded as divine in origin or as exemplary, and on the basis of them the individual concerned is treated as a leader" (Max Weber, *Wirtschaft und Gesellschaft, Grundriss der verstehenden Soziologie* [1922]; English translation: Max Weber, *The Theory of Social and Economic Organization* [New York: Simon & Schuster, 1964, 358]) I thank architectural historian Christopher Long from the University of Texas at Austin for his critical remarks on the meaning of *charisma* and culture historian Lisa Silverman from the University of Wisconsin–Milwaukee for her critical reading of this essay.

[2]   Well-known events and publications document the crisis of Jewish assimilation and

The father and son used modern design and art in different ways. In mid-1907, Emil hired Behrens to create distinguished and unified looks for his electrical company as a representation of the ethics of his engineer profession. Early in 1907, Walther asked the controversial artist Munch to paint a life-size portrait of himself.[3] His portrait was part of Munch's series of German portraits of members of the avant-garde, including two of Walther's friends, the author and art collector Harry Graf Kessler, and the art critic and patron Gustav Schiefler.[4] Munch wanted to capture the psychological depth of his sitter, and described Walther's charisma as a double portrait of a "master" (Rathenau) and a "subordinated woman" (spectre of a naked woman).[5] Both Behrens and Munch expressed the Rathenaus' charisma without appearing to construct progressive German-Jewish identities. They also refrained from referring to the Rathenaus' wish to persuade Jews and Gentiles of the proper way of Jewish acculturation, but simply depicted

---

rework the antisemitic logic of the impossibility of improving the "Jewish character" by Jewish authors. The Dreyfus Affair in France (1894–1906) and the election of the antisemite Karl Lueger as mayor of Vienna (1897–1909) proved the failure of liberal politics in Europe. Max Nordau's play *Dr. Kohn, ein Lebenskampf* (Dr. Kohn: Life Struggle, 1899) supported the idea that there is no future for young Jewish men in Europe. Nordau's protagonist, Dr. Kohn, identifies the "Jewish problem" as the rejection of the wish of Jews to be part of the German nation. Finally, Otto Weininger's book *Geschlecht und Charakter* (Sex and Character, 1903), hailing the unworthiness of the "Jewish character," became a bestseller in Germany and Austria.

3   On January 15, 1907, Rathenau wrote to Munch: "Dear Herr Munch, if you are free we can make a start the day after tomorrow, on Thursday, at one o'clock, in Victoriastrasse. I am free for only half an hour on Thursday, but for the subsequent sessions I shall have an hour. Doubtless you will be needing a large canvas; I think I am over six feet tall" (quoted and translated to English in Ulrich Bischoff, *Edvard Munch: 1863–1944* [Cologn: Taschen, 2000, 80]. Munch's portrait of Walther Rathenau is in the Stiftung Stadtmuseum Berlin.

4   Werner Timm, "Zum Bildnis Walther Rathenaus von Edvard Munch," *Forschungen und Berichte, Kunsthistorische Beiträge* 7 (1965), 59.

5   See my analysis of the iconography of this portrait below. Describing the relationship between Germans and Jews, Rathenau narrated it as a relationship between a master of a house (land) and his disliked, dependent, and inferior dweller: "Dem Stammesdeutschen ist die Frage [about the future position of Jews in the German society] so zuwider wie der Gegenstand. Er ist zufrieden, wenn das schwärzliche Volk ihm vom Leibe bleibt" (Walther Rathenau, "Höre Israel" [1897] reprinted in Christoph Schulte, *Deutschtum und Judentum, Ein Disput unter Juden aus Deutschland* (Stuttgart: Philipp Reclam, 1993, 30.)

their clients' ideal self-image.

A brief reference in an early biography of Emil Rathenau mentions that he suffered from an antisemitic campaign against his business success. His critics compared him to the owner of a department store.[6] This insult undermined Rathenau's idea of a direct relation between the producer and the consumer. Learning some progressive selling tactics from the successful German department store Wertheim, he succeeded in improving the whole operation of production, marketing, and sales. Following an earlier example set by the Wertheim department store of selling modernist interiors in order to familiarize customers with contemporary design and to elevate their customers' aesthetic taste, Rathenau hired Behrens as the in-house designer of AEG. In 1908, the economist Alfred Lansburgh in an article titled *System Rathenau* argued that this system turned the basic principles of economy upside down: "The AEG plans its production not according to the existing demand, but enforces the rise of demand in order to meet its production."[7] Yet that same year Behrens's modernist design of a new corporate identity for AEG secured a supportive review of the company and its trademark by the influential cultural critic Karl Scheffler:

> We have a new sign [Zeichen] that the bourgeois enterprising spirit [Unternehmungsgeist], which till now has only been concerned with the accumulation of material gain, is beginning to idealize; that it—finally! is beginning to feel the need to make ... [its work] moral by considering its duty to beauty; and that it is, in this way, becoming truly aware of its modernity.[8]

---

6   Alois Riedler, *Emil Rathenau und das Werden der Großwirtschaft* (Berlin: Julius Springer 1916), 182.

7   "Die AEG schneidet ihre Produktion nicht auf das Bedürfnis zu, sondern sie peitscht das Bedürfnis auf, bis es die Höhe ihrer Produktion erreicht" (Alfred Lansburgh, "System Rathenau," *Die Bank. Monatschrift für Finanz-Bankwesen* (1908), 768; quoted in Hans Wilderotter, "'Die Mechanisierung der Welt' Emil Rathenau, Walther Rathenau und die AEG," in *Die Extreme berühren sich, Walther Rathenau 1867–1922*, ed. Hans Wilderotter (Berlin: Argon Verlag, 1994, 258.)

8   Karl Scheffler, "Kunst und Industrie," *Kunst und Künstler* 6:10 (July 1908), 434; translated in Frederic J. Schwartz, "Commodity Signs: Peter Behrens, the AEG, and the Trademark," *Journal of Design History*, 9, no. 3 (1996), 153.

Walther Rathenau challenged the relation between art and industry and questioned his father's belief that his financial success guaranteed his integration into German society.[9] In his article "Höre, Israel" in Maximilian Harden's journal *Die Zukunft* (The Future, 1897), signed with his pseudonym, he describes a battle between a dark, Asian, and Jewish race and a northern and Germanic race that reflects his dual self-identification as a Jew and a German. Walther Rathenau thus revealed the identity crisis among individuals in the German Jewish community. Challenging even the mere physical "looks" of his fellow Jews—"Look at yourself in the Mirror! This is the first step of self-critique...."[10] and continuing, "Can you see yourself through strangers' eyes?"[11]—Walther Rathenau demanded that his fellow Jews assimilate unconditionally into the German culture. Yet, according to one "stranger's eyes," those of his close friend Harry Graf Kessler, Walther himself expressed his charisma as an "Outsider" rather than "Insider" in German society:

> He reminded one of Stendhal's Julien Sorel with his dark frock-coat and his piercing eyes, or even more perhaps of another young Jew, who had forced his way into society seventy years before in another country, with an equally brilliant intellect, but adorned with ear-rings and an embroidered Turkish waist-coat—Benjamin Disraeli. With Rathenau it was only the intellect that glittered, the intellect and the rush of images crowding each other in his conversation. His bearing and gestures, and his neat and unobtrusive, but always fashionable dress, revealed a well-considered intention to oppose the simple military style of Prussian Court Society, another still more simple, of his own. Never for a moment did he forget, or allow others to forget that he was a Jew; he seemed to want people to feel that he was proud of his race, that it made of him a

---

[9] In his above-mentioned essay "Höre Israel," he argued, following his note that Germans feel disgusted with Jews, that the Germans respected the rich Jews even less than the poor Jews. See Rathenau, "Höre Israel," 30. His biographer Wolfgang Brenner mentions a rumor that when the article was included in a book of collected articles by Walther Rathenau called *Impressionen* (1902), Emil Rathenau asked in anger that the AEG regional director purchase all copies of the book available in German bookstores and destroy them. See Wolfgang Brenner, *Walther Rathenau, Deutscher und Jude* (München: Piper Verlag, 2005), 110f.

[10] "Seht Euch im Spiegel! Das ist der erste schritt zur Selbstkritik." See Walther Rathenau, "Höre Israel," 34.

[11] Ibid., 35.

distinguished foreigner who had the right to special courtesies and to pass through doors closed to others.[12]

Did their charisma influence the formation of a new model of Jewish acculturation in Germany, or did the Rathenau men prefer to promote their reputation as "standing by themselves" apart from the rest of the German Jewish community?

EXCURSION: THE TOMB OF THE RATHENAU HEROES

In order to answer the question of how the Rathenaus wanted to be remembered, we should begin with the Rathenaus' family burial site in the city cemetery Waldfriedhof Oberschöneweide in the district Treptow-Köpenick in Berlin. In 1902, Emil Rathenau and Max Stuttermann initiated the creation of a new cemetery in Oberschöneweiden, a growing industrial area which included several AEG factories, such as the Kabelwerk (copper and metalworks, rubber fabrication, and insulator fabrication), directed by Emil's second son Erich Rathenau (1871–1903). The oldest burial ground in the cemetery is the grave site of the Rathenau family, which was designed by the prominent Jewish architect Alfred Messel and decorated with sculptures and reliefs made by the Munich artist Hermann Hahn between 1903 and 1904. Rathenau ordered the grave site following the early death of his son Erich. The authority granted to him as the director of the AEG and not as a rich Jewish businessman was grafted onto the burial site. The architectural historian Robert Habel noted that Messel chose a Historicist model of the classical architectural type, the Heroum, for the grave arrangement.[13] The gravestone of the family displayed the names of the deceased with Roman letters, stating their birth and death dates. The whole rectangular court is about 130 square meters. The outer walls are 4.2. meters high. Since one needs to step up the stairs

---

12   Count Harry Kessler, *Walther Rathenau: His Life and Work* (New York: Harcort Brace, 1930), 44.

13   Robert Habel, *Alfred Messels Wertheimbauten in Berlin, Der Beginn der Modernen Architektur in Deutschland*, Mit einem Verzeichnis zu Messels Werken (Berlin: Gebr. Mann Verlag, 2009), 702.

in order to enter the site on a raised ground, the inner walls are lower, at 3.6 meters. The relation of the outside to the inside of the court was established through the processing of shell-lime natural stone from the German town Kirchheim. The outside, with rough walls of freestone, evokes a heroic impression, the inside's smooth walls—created through careful processing of the stones—evokes a more cultivated and calm sense.[14] The portal with its overarching gable is 5 meters high, and decorated by Hahn with larger-than-life-size reclining naked allegories of "Morning" and "Night" on either side. Different architectural elements and sculptures, such as Doric columns, winged figures, two medallion forms of puttee reliefs, and garlands, served as decoration. With this design, the architect Messel and the sculptor Hahn created a monumental setting, securing the feeling of awe at the presence of the dead Rathenaus.[15]

The Heroum (or Heroon) was a shrine or sacred enclosure dedicated to an ancient Greek or Roman hero, used for the commemoration or cult worship of the hero and usually erected over a grave.[16] The cult typically centred around the heroum/heroon and, in a sense, "the hero was considered still to be alive; he was offered meals and was imagined to be sharing feasts. His allegiance was seen as vitally important to the continued well-being of the city."[17] Emil Rathenau preferred to be buried in a city cemetery and not in a Jewish cemetery. He orchestrated his remembrance as a public personality in direct relation to his commitment and contribution to German society. Referring to Emil Rathenau's projected anxiety about his family at the beginning of his career as an engineer and owner of a machine factory concerning the possibility that the machines would fail to operate, Harry Graf Kessler quoted Walther from his text "Apology," stating: "I grew up in an atmosphere, not of want, but of anxiety."[18] The experience of anxiety was transformed into the experience of triumph: the fast expansion

[14]   Ibid., 703.
[15]   Ibid., 704.
[16]   Cyril M. Harris, *Illustrated Dictionary of Historic Architecture* (New York: Dover Publications, 1983), 283.
[17]   http://en.wikipedia.org/wiki/Heroon (accessed September 1, 2010).
[18]   Quoted in Kessler, *Walther Rathenau*, 10.

of AEG factories and operations granted him enough self-confidence and power to order a burial site fitting to his charismatic authority. I suggest that the evocation of the ancient cult hero was not accidental but rather intentional, to mask the biographical details such as the Jewish identification of the Rathenaus with a mythological aura. The Rathenaus' ambitious cooperation with the renowned architect Messel took place five years before Emil hired Behrens and Walther was portrayed by Munch.

Emil Rathenau was highly aware of the value of public opinion, and from the beginning of the AEG firm he maintained a "literary office" to be responsible for public relations. This office carefully followed the reports in the media about the electrical industry and helped shape media reports on its own company through its own AEG-Zeitung (AEG Newspaper).[19]

THE COLLECTIVE SELF-PORTRAITS OF EMIL RATHENAU—THE GLORY OF AEG MODERN DESIGN

Emil Rathenau's aim was to establish a superior professional position and to familiarize the public with his electrical products by promoting himself as a German Jew, and his electric enterprise and the new machines as part of the Western high culture tradition. Behrens's all-product-modern design for AEG supported Rathenau's success and expressed his charismatic authority.

The art historian Tilmann Buddensieg argues that Peter Behrens was asked to design different plans and projects for AEG following the third German Applied Arts exhibition in Dresden in 1906. Behrens had a special role in this exhibition, since he developed a new type of highly stylized exhibition pavilion for the industrial products of the linoleum factory Anker.[20] Moreover, he offered new and unified

---

[19] Michael Kunczik, "PR-Theorie und PR-Praxis—Historische Aspekte," in *Theorien der Public Relations, Grundlagen und Perspektiven der PR-Forschung*, ed. Ulrike Röttger (Wiesbaden: VS: Verlag für Sozialwissenschaftne, 2004), 203f.

[20] Tilmann Buddensieg, "Behrens und Jordan, Das Programm von 1907 und die Folgen," in *Industriekultur, Peter Behrens und die AEG 1907–1914*, ed. Tilmann Buddensieg (Berlin: Gebr. Mann Verlag, 1979), 14.

visual references for the Anker factory by using the same architectural image of the pavilion as a graphic illustration for the ad of the Anker factory in the exhibition brochure. Behrens was expected to supply the AEG electrical company with an aesthetic, memorable, and unified appearance.[21] Buddensieg refers to the manager Paul Jordan's conviction of Behrens's authority as an industrial designer. I suggest that Behren's visual reference to sacred architecture, matching two columns at the entrance with cupola on top in his Anker Pavilion, appealed as well to Emil Rathenau. The first ambitious exhibition pavilion Behrens designed for AEG after he was hired as the in-house designer in the German shipbuilding exhibition in 1908 followed sacral architectural prototypes such as the baptistery of Florence and the imperial Chapel at Aachen. The goal was to show that the product was not only useful but also impressive. The architectural historian Stanford Anderson argues that the choice of architecture reflected the company's recognition of the political and cultural implications of its corporative power as well as "the necessity of representing industry as a forceful agent within society."[22] This was Rathenau's clear aim from his first hiring of the Historicist architect Franz Schwechten, who also designed for AEG the monumental Beamtentor (Clercks Gate) for AEG factories in Wedding in 1896. The monumental gate, designed in bricks following Gothic style, with short, heavy towers, was decorated with mosaics with mystical religious associations in order to communicate the importance of AEG as a new "religious force" in society and to foster belief in the machine age. Above the side entrances in the towers, in frames imitating the shape of the arched Gothic windows, mosaics were placed showing the logo of AEG in the *Jugendstil* artist Otto Eckmann's printing style, symbolically highlighted by a surrounding chain of lightbulbs; thus, lightbulbs replacing the traditional divine aura granted the logo AEG religious authority. The big E at the centre of the AEG logo could be seen as a reference both to electricity and consciously or unconsciously also to the name of the founder of the

---

[21]   Ibid., 15.
[22]   Stanford Anderson, *Peter Behrens and a New Architecture for the Twentieth Century* (Cambridge, MA: The MIT Press, 2000), 98.

firm, Emil.

Rather than raising the question of who invited Peter Behrens to work for AEG for different, rather small, projects in 1906, it is important to ask how Behrens managed to convince Rathenau to hire him as the in-house designer in mid-1907.[23] The early success of Behrens as Rathenau's AEG "court artist" was a smart match between familiar sacral imagery and modernist at first Jugendstil decorations,[24] and immediately afterward geometric abstract aesthetic concepts. Behrens's development of a functionalist and geometric aesthetic concept eventually allowed Rathenau to be truer to his professional identification and to his workaholic lifestyle in the marketing of his products. The fertile cooperation between Rathenau and Behrens resulted in the seminal AEG-Turbine factory in the Moabit district of Berlin in 1909. The AEG-Turbine factory championed Rathenau's engineer aesthetics and the ethics of his professionalism: the design represented simplicity, calmness, usability, cleanliness, and overall control of the operation.[25] The AEG-Turbine factory was also compared to Romanesque architecture:

> In the turbine factory, which required a great deal of light, the large window surfaces are set between slender supporting pillars. The massive corners conceal the steel frame that actually bears the load; they create a solemn monumentality which, coming just as the new building materials were first making possible lightness of construction, is reminiscent of Romanesque architecture. Out of the original intention—to develop

---

[23] See the discussion in Elana Shapira, "Jewish Identity, Mass Consumption, and Modern Design," in *Longing, Belonging, and the Making of Jewish Consumer Culture*, ed. Gideon Reuveni and Nils Roemer (Leiden, Boston: Brill, 2010), 82.

[24] An enlightening example is Behrens's graphic design of the document by the Association of German Engineers honoring Rathenau for his great contribution to electricity production in Germany, on June 17, 1907, reproduced and analyzed in Gabriele Heidecker, "Das Werbe-Kunst-Stück," ed., Buddensieg, *Industriekultur,* 182f (reproduced also in colour, Ibid., D215). See also Henning Roge, "Ein Motor muß aussehen wie ein Geburtstagsgeschenk," ed., Buddensieg, *Industriekultur,* 108. Heidecker refers to Behrens's graphic letters as reminiscent of the royal manuscripts of the court school of Charles the Great; this reference could explain how Behrens's subtle use of Jugendstil ornament produced the impression of a grand historical document.

[25] Buddensieg, *Berliner Labyrinth, neu besichtigt* (Berlin: Wagenbach, 1999), 53.

buildings especially suitable for factories—a quasi-religious kind of building is developed. The factory's function is expressively enhanced by the dramatic emphasis on the corners. The building becomes an "architectural monument."[26]

Behrens succeeded in expressing both Emil Rathenau's professionalism and his political power by granting the packaging of the AEG factories and products sacral garb, including designing the logo of AEG as a modern icon and parallel representation of the AEG enterprise's superior position through geometric uniformed imagery, thus evoking the impression of a *Gesamtkunstwerk* (total artwork).

Rathenau attached great importance to the design of his products. He knew that in the growing competition with other electrical companies he would gain economic advantage from producing his products more cheaply; giving his product a unique artistic form would also place them in a superior position.[27] Moreover, he had to prove the advantage of his products over the cheaply produced items sold in department stores. Rathenau was not a man who promoted a luxurious lifestyle but a man who identified with the practical quality of his products.

Rathenau may have known Georg Wertheim, owner of "A. Wertheim" in Leipzigerstrasse, since it was the street where Rathenau opened the first offices of DEG (Deutsche Edison-Gesellschaft, the original electrical firm founded by Rathenau in 1883). To be sure, he followed the model set by the department store Wertheim of giving mass consumption a cultured appearance through fitting architectural "packaging" as well as through the promotion of modern design. In 1905, Rathenau once again hired the architect Messel, this time to design the office building of AEG on Friedrich-Carl-Ufer, asking Messel to consider the self-image of the client, meaning the firm, in his design. Messel was hired at the same time as he was working on the final extension of the Wertheim department store in Leipzigerstrasse, transforming the department store into a ground-breaking architectural monument. Messel chose the neo-Gothic style for the Wertheim department store in order to relate the

---

26   Albert Schug, *Art of the Twentieth Century* (New York: Harry N. Abrams, Inc. 1969), 38.
27   Tilmann Buddensieg, *Berliner Labyrinth, neu besichtigt*, 56.

phenomenon of mass consumption to European history and German national pride.[28] In comparison with the Wertheim department store, however, Messel's design for the AEG office building was sober and rigid. Messel almost completely renounced decorative forms, and the monumental architectural impression relied on the choice of material and its natural effect.[29] Rathenau demanded that the artistic form should demonstrate the ethics of his profession as an engineer and not disguise the professional character of his enterprise.

Two years later, Rathenau's choice of Behrens as his house designer may have followed another example set in the Wertheim department store in Leipzigerstrasse. In the autumn of 1902, the artistic advisor of the Wertheim department store, Curt Stoeving, opened an exhibition which included the interiors of two apartments, each room designed by an individual contemporary architect or designer, including himself. In 1903, in a short text entitled "Kunst dem Volke" (Art for the People), published in the journal *Deutsche Kunst und Dekoration*, Stoeving argued that his interest was to satisfy the public's longings for "reshaping [their apartments, their nation, and possibly also themselves] and for the newest [design]."[30] The Jewish art critic Max Osborn's review of the modern interior design exhibition in the department store followed Stoeving's text. Osborn pointed out that the main principle of modern applied arts is similar to the principle of the department store, which is democratic.[31] Osborn further noted the contribution of the Wertheim department store to modern applied arts.[32] In contrast to the interest of the Wertheim department store in "democratizing" modern design, Rathenau helped produce modern design in order to maintain authority over producing distinct "intelligent objects." His aim was to use art to convince his clients

---

28 Helmut Frei, *Tempel Der Kauflust. Eine Geschichte der Warenhauskultur* (Leipzig: Edition Leipzig, 1997), 92.

29 Brigitte Jacob, "Alfred Messel," in *Baumeister. Architekten. Stadtplaner, Biographien zur baulichen Entwicklung Berlins*, ed. Wolfgang Ribe and Wolfgang Schäche (Berlin: Historische Kommission zu Berlin; Stapp Verlag, 1987), 315.

30 Curt Stoeving, "Kunst dem Volke," *Deutsche Kunst und Dekoration* 6:1 (1903), 258. The additions in brackets are mine.

31 Max Osborn, "Die modernen Wohn-Räume im Waren-Haus von A. Wertheim zu Berlin," *Deutsche Kunst und Dekoration* 6:1 (1903), 259.

32 Ibid., 259.

that machines carried the potential to improve standards of living.

Osborn noted how important it was for Wertheim to match fine arts with applied arts. Furthermore, he declared that the mere fact of the existence of artistically furnished rooms in such a place is of great value for the distribution of good taste and for the education of the public. Behrens designed a dining room for the Wertheim exhibition, and Osborn paid special attention to this modernist design as one of the most interesting interiors in the exhibition. He described Behrens's projection of *Gesamtkunstwerk*: "It is a unified design, rigidly executed, in which each detail submits itself to an organized determination."[33] The formal design theme was a rectangle, and Osborn criticized Behrens's pedantic execution of his total scheme. Osborn's critique may have appealed to Rathenau in his search for an artistic advisor for his company. Through the publication of his interior design for the Wertheim department store, offering a rigid scheme that emphasizes the straight line—in contrast to the emphasis on the wavy line in Art Nouveau—Behrens proved his qualifications as the future artistic advisor for the AEG electrical company. Behrens was hired to design a uniform appearance for the AEG that would include factories, product design, and advertisement.[34]

The architectural historian Frederic J. Schwartz noted that members of the *Deutscher Werkbund* (German Work Federation) "repeatedly and mysteriously invoked the brand name commodity and its logo as some sort of answer to the problem of the relation of culture and economy in modernity: the trademark was an object of obsessive concern."[35] The trademark granted a face to the firm and its products within a mass consumption setting. Behrens may have designed the AEG logo in a symmetrical hexagon with the letters A, E, and G contained in three large hexagonal facets, the A above and the E and G below next to each other, as a formal allusion to the "Holy Trinity," replacing the Father, the Son, and the Holy Ghost with the three letters. His inspiration may have been the mosaics in the Beamtentor showing the AEG signet

33   Ibid., 263.
34   Buddensieg, *Berliner Labyrinth, neu besichtigt*, 51.
35   Frederic J. Schwartz, "Peter Behrens, the AEG, and the Trademark," 154.

highlighted with a modern aura of a chain of light bulbs.[36] Behrens thus expressed Rathenau's and the AEG's authority as a powerful and political agent in society.[37]

In June 1910, Rathenau invited the members of the Deutscher Werkbund for a tour with Behrens in the new buildings of AEG in Humboldthain. Rathenau welcomed the group on the roof garden and invited them to enjoy a small snack on Behrens's chairs and benches near Behrens's tables. The frame of the cultural happening produced the impression of a "Gesamtkunstwerk."[38] Rathenau did not leave anything to chance, or any space for a personal exchange between him and his guests. His commanding authority was demonstrated through the total design. At this event, Rathenau delivered a speech on the roof of AEG Humboldthain, speaking about the mass production of electrical parts and the importance of producing high quality parts cheaply in order to make them profitable.[39] The grand image of the AEG logo designed as part of the roof garden depicted the charisma of Emil Rathenau. Yet the logo may have appeared bigger than Rathenau himself—the "garden logo" magnified and at the same time depersonalized Emil's ideal self-image.

Rathenau did not necessarily associate his choice of modern design with the need to evoke aesthetic pleasure. He aimed for a new physiognomy that would identify his products with what he considered a superior German stance in technology. Similarly, Behrens did not create a sense of artistic enjoyment from the decorative and individual form of a specific machine, but expressed its professional authority through the organizational design of a product series and its formal unity with the buildings, the stores, and the advertisements.[40]

Behrens succeeded in meeting Rathenau's expectation of an intelligent corporate image presented in depersonalized, clear, and

---

[36] One of Behrens's first signets for AEG (1908) was a simplified adaptation of Schwechten signet (1896). See Buddensieg, ed., *Industriekultur*, D233.

[37] See also Schwartz's explanation of the magical aura of the AEG logo, Schwartz, "Peter Behrens, the AEG, and the Trademark," 168ff.

[38] Buddensieg, *Berliner Labyrinth, neu besichtigt*, 48.

[39] Ibid., 53.

[40] Ibid., 54. Here it should be noted that only after World War I did household electrical appliances become more accessible to the wider public. Until then, the advertisements of AEG addressed only a small and exclusive circle of clients.

abstract forms. The appreciation of the firm and its products did not depend any more on a personal like or dislike of an object (or of the like or dislike of the Jewish owner of the firm), but on an objective consideration of the collective persona of the firm. Rathenau's charisma was transformed into and expressed through "collective self-portraits"—which included the consumers, the workers, and the stockholders—as a collective organism.[41] The majority of art critics praised the role of Emil Rathenau and his contribution to the synchronization of industry and art as an important contribution to German culture.

MODERN JEWISH CHARISMA?—WALTHER RATHENAU AS A CULTURAL ICON

Early in his career Walther Rathenau acknowledged the privilege of appearing on the German public stage. He loved to pose in front of the camera, for example, in the renowned photo studio Dührkoop and Perscheid and in front of artists.[42] As his biographer Wolfgang Brenner noted, he always made a statement in order to be unforgettable.[43] He may have tried to cover his anxiety of failing to leave an impression by always adorning his sentences with colourful, beautiful imagery, even if the sentence was understood by itself. Some of his statements were meant to question the legitimacy of his own public persona as a tall and rich Jewish man; he criticized the materialism of Jews and their alleged

---

[41] I rephrase here an interesting observation made by Sigrid Meyer zu Knolle in her dissertation *Die Gebändigte Vertikale. Materialien zum frühen Hochhausbau in Frankfurt* (1998) about Walther Rathenau's wish to depersonalize the economic and political relations. I relate her interpretation that Walther Rathenau aimed at removing the divisions in society through replacing the subjective personal appreciation with an objective depersonalized evaluation to the wish of his father Emil Rathenau to depersonalize the relations in consumption and design in order to combat the prejudice that was addressed against him as a Jewish entrepreneur. Sigrid Meyer zu Knolle, "Die Gebändigte Vertikale: Materialien zum frühen Hochhausbau in Frankfurt" (Ph.D. diss., Philipps-Universität Marburg, 1998), 86ff.

[42] Stefan Pucks, "'Eine Weichliche, Leidende, dem Beruf nicht Genügende Natur'?" in *Die Extreme berühren sich, Walther Rathenau 1867–1922*, ed. Hans Wilderotter (Berlin: Argon Verlag, 1994), 90.

[43] Brenner, *Walther Rathenau, Deutscher und Jude*, 119.

physical degeneration.[44] Yet, Rathenau's wish to be photographed and portrayed could also be understood as a desire to materialize himself over and over again as an aesthetic product (competing with the electrical products of AEG). The art historian Janis Bergman-Carton observed in regard to another brilliant public performer, the French Sarah Bernhardt, that she could not find an "essential Sarah Bernhardt" in the actress because "both on the stage and in the metatheater of French public life, she continuously slipped between the categories of assimilated Jewess and anti-semitic cliché. She vexed the very terms of assimilation."[45] Walther Rathenau also slipped between the categories of acculturated Jew and antisemitic cliché of a Jewish snob. The philosopher and cultural critic Hannah Arendt's conclusion about the attractiveness of Rathenau's possible role model, the Jewish politician Benjamin Disraeli, whose Jewishness was only accepted among the discriminating few, could also apply to Rathenau himself:

> Significantly, it was Disraeli who said "What is a crime among the multitude is only a vice among the few"—perhaps the most profound insight into the very principle by which the slow and insidious decline of nineteenth century society into the depth of mob and underworld morality took place. Since he knew this rule, he knew also that Jews would have no better chances anywhere than in circles which pretended to be exclusive and to discriminate against them; for inasmuch as these circles of the few, together with the multitude, thought of Jewishness as a crime, this "crime" could be transformed into an attractive "vice."[46]

Munch's portrait of Walther Rathenau (Stiftung Stadtmuseum Berlin) was painted at the same time Rathenau was preparing his entry into German politics. In July 1906, the editor Maximilian

---

[44] Ibid., 110ff. See reference to Rathenau's "physical defect" in Ernst Schulin, "Walther Rathenaus Diotima, Lili Deutsch, ihre Familie und der Kreis um Gerhart Hauptmann," in *Die Extreme berühren sich, Walther Rathenau 1867–1922*, ed. Hans Wilderotter (Berlin: Argon Verlag, 1994), 55.

[45] Janis Bergman-Carton, "Negotiating the Categories: Sarah Bernhardt and the Possibilities of Jewishness," *Art Journal* 55, no. 2 (Summer 1996), 60.

[46] Hannah Arendt, "The Jews and Society," II: The Potent Wizard (on Benjamin Disraeli), in *The Origins of Totalitarianism* (Cleveland and New York: Harcourt, Brace and Company, [1951] 1968), 69. The quote from Disraeli is from his novel *Tancred* (1847).

Harden recommended in his journal *Die Zukunft*, "If I were Chancellor, I would consider this man very carefully. He could become useful in London, New York and also in a large colony."[47] Rathenau welcomed the challenge and was working on his political manifesto during the same period Munch was painting his portrait. His moderate liberal manifesto presented in the article "Die Neue Ära" (The New Era) was published in the *Hannoverscher Courier* shortly after the Reichstag elections in February 1907. Rathenau argued about how Germany could improve its international politics and recommended a "middle-class evolution" which could bring industry to the centre of political power.[48]

Rathenau's choice to be portrayed by Munch at this point in his career was not accidental. He identified his purchasing of Munch's paintings as part of his personal achievements. In 1893, Rathenau bought from his first business profit a Munch painting called *Regenwetter in Kristiania* (Rainy Day in Christiania). In 1902, after three years of serving on the board of AEG, Walther left the company following a conflict with his father and began to work for the bank of his father's friend Carl Fürstenberg, Berliner Handelsgesellschaft. At that time he bought a double portrait by Munch of the painter Paul Hermann and the doctor of medicine Paul Contard. Shortly afterwards, he bought etchings by Munch.[49] In June 1906, Walther resigned from the board of the bank and set his departure date as July 1907. His request from Munch was therefore an expression of his literally new positioning in the house of his father (since the portrait was made in his apartment in his parents' house) and consequently in German society.

Munch's works provoked scandal in Berlin, and they were rejected because of their modernist psychological content and their style. Munch depicted Rathenau in a life-size portrait (200 x 110 cm) as a ruler and master. The Expressionist artist transformed the banker and industrialist Rathenau into a modern icon. Art historian Stefan Pucks

---

47 Harmut Pogge von Strandmann, ed., *Walther Rathenau, Industrialist, Banker, Intellectual, and Politician, Notes and Diaries 1907–1922* (New York: Oxford University Press, 2001), 29 footnote 6. (Originally published in German by Droste Verlag in Dusseldorf in 1967.)

48 Ibid, 28f.

49 Brenner, *Walther Rathenau, Deutscher und Jude*, 109.

noted that almost no other banker, businessman, or industrialist in the German Reich at the time was portrayed so often and displayed with such high artistic quality as Walther Rathenau. Yet Pucks argues that it was not Rathenau's high sense of self-awareness that drove him to be portrayed but that rather this was a compensation for a deep feeling of inferiority.[50] Munch's depiction of Rathenau as a "master" relates to Rathenau's conclusion of his work as a director at the Berliner Handelsgesellschaft and to his planned journey to the colonies in order to advise the German government on how to improve their colonial politics.

His planned visit to the colonies may have granted Walther Rathenau's narration in "Höre, Israel" of German "masters" and Jewish unrespected and disrespectful "servants" a certain urgency.[51] Yet, he used the emotional intensity and erotic appeal of this narrative in the context of the cultural conflict between Germans and Jews in order to express his personal charisma. Examining his art collection, Pucks suggests that Rathenau, with his theoretical idealism and his pragmatic art promotion, revealed himself as a conservative revolutionary but, above all, a patriot, "indeed, almost chauvinist."[52] His "chauvinistic" claim, however, was "freely" constructed following chosen intellectual ideas borrowed from, for example, the nationalist and antisemitic author and cultural critic August Julius Langbehn concerning the un-German character of several modern artistic movements, and the humanist scholar and statesman Wilhelm von Humboldt, who promoted the ideal of educating the whole nation to become free citizens in the early nineteenth century.[53] Yet, Rathenau's German chauvinism made him an

---

[50] Pucks, "'Eine Weichliche, Leidende, dem Beruf nicht Genügende Natur'?" 90.
[51] In a letter to Maximilian Harden from September 27, 1906, months before accepting the assignment and traveling to East Africa with the German delegation headed by his friend and Secretary of Colonies Bernhard Dernburg, Rathenau wrote: "No, dear Friend, no Bülow [future Chancellor] can take a crust of bread from me, if it is a case of sending me dishonorably to the Colonies Office, to the negro women and other tasks, which I cannot carry out." (BA Koblenz, Nachlass Harden, 85; quoted and translated in Pogge von Strandmann, *Rathenau, Industrialist, Banker, Intellectual, and Politician*, 29 footnote 7.)
[52] Pucks, "'Eine Weichliche, Leidende, dem Beruf nicht Genügende Natur'?" 88.
[53] Lothar Gall, *Walther Rathenau, Portrait eine Epoche* (Munich: C. H. Beck, 2009), 108.

"Einzelgänger" as the narrow entrance door to his future private villa showed.[54] In 1909, two years after Munch's portrayal of him, Rathenau bought and renovated a small castle originally designed for the widow of King Friedrich Wilhelm II. Rathenau together with the architect Johannes Kraasz designed his house in accordance with German country houses in the Biedermeier period with interiors showing a stylistic mix, borrowing from styles ranging from eighteenth-century to early-twentieth-century.[55] The question arises, can one witness the essential Walther Rathenau as a self-crowned "German master" in the Munch portrait? His heroic portrayal was further celebrated in a bronze bust by Hermann Hahn.

The portrait of Munch did not accompany Walther Rathenau in his move to his private villa but remained in his parents' house: more than a decade later, Walther wrote to Munch and mentioned it.[56] Rathenau's friend, the author and army officer Gustav Steinbömer, was present at one of the sitting sessions and described Rathenau's conscious self-posing: "Rathenau stands drawn up to his full height, legs apart, his head arrogantly back, his gaze aloofly authoritative, his big feet in narrow, shiny patent leather shoes that stab sharp into the eye."[57] Rathenau who possibly observed the expression on his friend's face while watching him posing or while checking the portrait, confirmed the aggressive impression he wanted to convey by stating: "An awful character, isn't he? That's what you get for having your portrait done by a great artist—you look more like yourself than you really are."[58] Does the description of himself as an awful character testify to Pucks' suggestion that Rathenau suffered from inferiority? What supposed "inferiority" and what projected "mastership" is grafted onto Rathenau's portrait? Could this portrait be a visualization of the battle between

---

54 Pucks, "'Eine Weichliche, Leidende, dem Beruf nicht Genügende Natur'?" 84.
55 Ibid., 84. Rathenau's private house did not receive positive feedback, and until today scholars address the question of his choice of a Biedermeier and Historicist eclectic setting. See Fredric Bedoire, *The Jewish Contribution to Modern Architecture 1830–1930* (Jersey City, NJ: Ktav Publishing House, 2004), 274ff.
56 Timm, "Zum Bildnis Walther Rathenaus von Edvard Munch" (1965), 59 and 61.
57 Quoted and translated in Bischoff, *Edvard Munch*, 80. My emphasis.
58 Ibid., 59. Quoted in Gustav Hillard (pseudonym of Gustav Steinbömer), *Herren und Narren der Welt*, 1954, 240.

a dark, Asian, and Jewish race and a northern and Germanic race as a reflection of his dual self-identification as a Jew and a German as described in his essay "Höre Israel"?

Rathenau's patronizing look from above with his confident pose dressed in a dark suit and the cigarette in his hand, is a depiction of a self-confident master. He is standing between an abstract, sensually coloured orange canvas possibly referring to "warm" gold and symbolizing Rathenau's richness or his rich family and a "cold" pink shadow of an anonymous naked woman with no face, whose arms have no hands, or whose hands appear to be held behind her back, and cut lower legs. The presence of the female spectre suggests that Munch may have intended to paint a double portrait. The double portrait followed a tradition of portraying artists and their models.[59] Similarly to the power relations and the erotic tension between artist and model, we witness Rathenau's cigarette pointing at the naked woman's genitalia. Is the naked woman representing his "servant"?

At the time the portrait was painted, Rathenau had a romantic relationship with Lili Deutsch née Kahn, the wife of his rival in AEG, Felix Deutsch.[60] The romantic relationship celebrated in passionate letters supposedly did not cross a certain line of physical intimacy. Yet, a few months after Munch's portrait was completed, Lili Deutsch complained about Walther in a letter to her brother that "he wants to have and dominate everything ..."[61] If Walther is standing erect as a German master, is Lili supposedly the Jewish inferior servant? The German playwright and author Gerhart Hauptmann, who was a house guest at the salon of Lili and Felix Deutsch and a friend of Walther Rathenau, also spoke with Rathenau about the latter's race theories. On November 30, 1905, presumably at the beginning of the relationship between Rathenau and Lili Deutsch, Hauptmann noted in his diary: "Rathenau. His racial ideal. The aspirations of Mrs. D[eutsch]: to become blonde. What a crazy notion! There is nothing more beautiful than to be

---

[59]   See, for example, Ernst Ludwig Kirchner, *Erich Heckel and Model in Studio*, 1905, Brücke-Museum Berlin.

[60]   Schulin, "Walther Rathenaus Diotima, Lili Deutsch, ihre Familie und der Kreis um Gerhart Hauptmann," 56.

[61]   Ibid., 62. My translation.

driven to madness by a young man or a woman?"[62] Did Rathenau treat Deutsch as "not good enough" for him because she did not fit his racial (blonde) ideal?

Walther Rathenau never married. It is possible that he used his racial theories in order to keep a certain distance from women as well as from men; in other words, celebrating his experience of duality as a German and a Jewish man helped him maintain a certain alienation and a sense of shock of physical intimacy with the people around him in a manner that expressed his charisma as an unattainable man.[63] Munch expressed this loaded situation through Rathenau's patronizing facial expression and with the hand holding the cigarette near the curve of the rounded hips of the naked woman. The white, blue, and pink colours of the woman express the fact that she is a white woman. Her hair appears dark. In the place where her breasts should be seen, there is also a white curvy line. This line is identified through the image of a golden handle in the second portrait of Walther Rathenau, which was presumably painted simultaneously.[64]

---

[62]   Gerhart Hauptmann, *Tagebücher 1895–1905*, ed., Martin Machatzke (Frankfurt a.M: Propyläen, 1987), 456; quoted in Schulin, "Walther Rathenaus Diotima, Lili Deutsch, ihre Familie und der Kreis um Gerhart Hauptmann," 59. My translation.

[63]   Another example is the mixed reaction of admiration and distancing of the Austrian poet and playwright to Rathenau and his talks on race and Jewish matters, noted in Oswalt von Nostitz, "Hofmannsthal und das Berliner Ambiente, Persönliche Begegnungen," in *Hugo von Hofmannsthal. Freundschaften und Begegnungen mit deutsche Zeitgenossen*, ed. Ursula Renner und G. Bärbel Schmid (Würzburg: Königshausen und Neumann, 1991), 67f.

[64]   It is not clear if Munch's second portrait was painted simultaneously or if it was painted after the first portrait. Werner Timm noted that the portrait in the Bergen Art Museum was in accordance with Munch's habit to paint a second portrait and that it was painted after the first: "So wurden eine Reihe von Details geändert, die das Bergener Bild 'Korrekter' erscheinen lassen, die Gesamtkonzeption blieb jedoch unverändert." (Timm, "Zum Bildnis Walther Rathenaus von Edvard Munch," 59.) Arne Eggum, the former curator and director of the Munch Museum, suggests in his book on Edvard Munch's portraits that the two portraits of Rathenau were made simultaneously. Rathenau had to sit for the portrait several times, and he probably came in different suits. Rathenau is depicted in different suits in the two paintings. He also holds a cigarette in his right hand in one painting (Stiftung Stadtmuseum Berlin), while he holds a cigar in the other painting (Bergen Art Museum). Eggum argues that painting both portraits simultaneously helped Munch to try the outcome in one painting which he could use in a way or another in the other one (Arne Eggum,

Munch's second life-size portrait of Walther Rathenau (Rasmus Meyer Collection, Bergen Art Museum, Norway) positioned Rathenau next to a door. The door is almost unrecognizable since it is coloured with white like the wall, only with a golden door handle next to his hand, which here holds a cigar, revealing the fact that it is a door. There is also a blue outline of a woman near the left part of the painting, which refers back to the spectre of the woman in the first portrait. Munch used a brief reference to the "woman" in order to evoke the experience of the uncanny. Did Munch suggest that the woman's presence is a threat to her "master"? Did Munch, who was known for his psychological reflections on his sitters, refer in the second portrait to Rathenau's wish to escape? Or his need to control his entrees and exits from his parent's house and the German public stage by having the security of the door next to him. It is certain that Walther Rathenau is capturing the eyes of his viewer outside the painting to confront him with a "master" gaze.

A year after Munch's portrait, 1908, Walther Rathenau asked Hermann Hahn—for no obvious reason that could explain the special order[65]—to create a bronze bust portrait of himself (Stiftung Stadtmuseum, Berlin). Walther appears in a frontal view with empty eye holes and with a frozen, almost stoic, expression, and viewers at the time recognized in the bust his claim to be seen as a Roman leader like Caesar.[66] The Hahn bust of Rathenau is also related to Rathenau's trip to the German colonies in East Africa as a preparation for the possibility of him becoming the future minister of the colonies.[67] Yet

---

"Edvard Munch, *Portretter* (Oslo: Labyrinth Press, 1994), 133. I am grateful to Petra Pettersen, Curator of Paintings at the Munch Museum, Oslo, for this reference and information (e-mail correspondence from September 29, 2010). Still, it is possible that Munch painted the second portrait later with the wish to make a clearer statement about Rathenau's authority and hoping to achieve this by reducing Rathenau's "psychological conflicts" (turning the "gold" canvas to Rathenau's left into a decorative wallpaper pattern and the naked woman to his right into a blue outline of a shadow figure).

65 Pucks, "Eine Weichliche, Leidende, ..." 91.

66 Ibid., 91. Original quote from Georg Jacob Wolf, "Herman Hahn," *Kunst für Alle* 20 (1914), 298.

67 Exh. Cat. Dorothee Hansen ed., *Munch und Deutschland* (Hamburg: Verlag Gerd Hatje, 1994), 72.

Rathenau remained second in charge to the minister of the colonies office, Bernhard Dernburg.[68] What is interesting to note in relation to the shape of the sculpted head is his friend Harry Graf Kessler's remark in his biography of Walther Rathenau: "And one who met him then will remember a slim and very tall young man, who startled one by the abnormal shape of his head, which looked more negroid than European!"[69] Did Kessler's comparison between the shape of Rathenau's head and the shape of a head of a "negro" suggest that Rathenau identified himself with the inferior "subordinate citizen"? Yet at the same time, Hahn carefully shaped the bronze bust of Rathenau as a Roman leader.[70] This duality of a leader and a servant is also exposed in Munch's portrait: his positioning next to the subordinated "second sex" increased Rathenau's charismatic authority. Rathenau avoids gazing at the naked woman, proving that he is above any earthy temptations; thus Walther Rathenau remained untouched (unattainable) due to his duality as a German master and a Jewish (negro? woman?) subordinate.

After World War I, Rathenau was one of the founders of the German Democratic Party. In 1921 he became the minister of reconstruction and, in 1922, as noted above, the minister of foreign affairs. In June 1922, the liberal politician Rathenau was assassinated in a plot led by two right-wing German army officers. A historical narrative refers to his insisting on fulfilling the conditions of the Treaty of Versailles and his signing of the Treaty of Rapallo with the Russians as an expression of German defeatism as a possible direct motive for his murder. Yet, it is more likely that his authority as an important minister was undermined due to circulating antisemitic conspiracy theories against Jews that led to his "public execution."

---

[68]   See further Dieter Heimböckel, *Walther Rathenau und die Literatur seiner Zeit: Studien zu Werk und Wirkung* (Würzburg: Königshausen und Neumann, 1996), 152f.

[69]   Kessler, *Walther Rathenau*, 43.

[70]   It is possible to compare this bust portrait with an earlier sculpted portrait of Rathenau in marble in the form of a Herme (1905, missing). The philosopher's concentrated look of the early portrait is contrasted by the more directed and unwavering look of the portrait made three years later. The gaze is the ultimate identification of the power of control and his ability of arresting "the Other"—namely us, the viewers (the two bust sculptures are reproduced in Buddensieg, ed., Industriekultur, D.325).

CONCLUSION

The Rathenau charisma was not granted as a gift of god but evolved as part of a trend of Jewish "self-stylization," integral to the development of modern culture in Germany. Emil and his son Walther expressed the ideals of two different generations. The father Emil welcomed the stylization of his electrical products to promote the sales and as an expression of his professional and good reputation as an engineer and the director of one of the largest electrical company in Germany. The son Walter stylized his experience of duality as a German and a Jew into a cultural icon, choosing an Expressionist artist to depict his political ambition and to secure a lasting impression in public—the German public—by keeping his viewer in an "eye contact" with his ideal self- image.[71] The two men were aware of their responsibility toward the Jewish community. Yet, their charismatic authority as demonstrated in their burial site showed that they were "set apart" both from the Jewish community and the German society. This expression of the Rathenau charisma may have led to the fact that neither the National

---

[71]   The portrait of Rathenau (Stiftung Stadtmuseum Berlin) was first exhibited in the Kunstsalon Fritz Gurlitt in 1914. In 1921, a year before he was murdered, it was exhibited first in Cassirer Gallery in Berlin and later in Arnold Gallery in Dresden. In both cases, it was identified as a *Herrenbildnis* (Portrait of a Man). After Rathenau's murder, the portrait was exhibited in the Akademie der Künste in Berlin (1923) and in the Kunsthalle Mannheim (1926) where it was identified as the portrait of Walther Rathenau. It was further exhibited in the National Galerie, Berlin (1927), in the National Gallery, Oslo (1927), in the Museum Folkwang, Essen (1928), in the Kunsthütte Chemnitz (1929), in the Leipziger Kunstverein (1929) and in the Hamburger Kunstverein (1930). I thank Dominik Bartmann, Curater of Paintings at the Stiftung Stadtmuseum Berlin, and Petra Pettersen for this information (e-mail correspondence from Bartmann, October 1, 2010, and from Pettersen, September 28, 2010). It appears as if Rathenau or his mother hesitated to exhibit the portrait, and either they waited for Walther to gain public recognition or used the portrait to promote his public reputation by lending it to exhibitions. The second portrait of Rathenau remained with Munch until he sold it to Rasmus Meyer (Bergen Art Museum), and it was exhibited in two exhibitions in Germany, in the Franz Hancke Gallery in Breslau and in the 15th Berlin Secession exhibition in Berlin, in 1908, and in two exhibitions in Norway, Blomqvist auction house in Kristiania and Bergens Kunstforening in Bergen, in 1909 (Gerd Woll, *Edvard Munch, Catalogue Raisonné*, Vl. 2, [Oslo: 2008], 737. I thank Knut Ormhaug, Chief Curator of the Bergen Art Museum for this information [e-mail correspondence September 28, 2010]).

Socialist dictatorship nor the Communist regime ordered to destroy their burial site in the city cemetery in East Berlin.[72] Moreover, these modern expressions of the Rathenau charismatic authority were used as a defense measure against antisemitism and as an assertive claim to their own grand contribution to German culture.

---

[72] Habel, *Alfred Messels Wertheimbauten in Berlin*, 702. It should be noted that there was an antisemitc vandalism attack against the site in 1992.

---------- CHAPTER VI ----------

THE JEWS AND THE GERMAN WAR EXPERIENCE, 1914–1918

George L. Mosse

Dedicated to Robert Weltsch

The role of the German Jew in the First World War has been analyzed often, with the hope that the "spirit of 1914" would lead to a more complete union of Germans and Jews and an end to the discrimination and suspicion which dogged Jews even in wartime. There were those German Jews who recalled Gabriel Riesser's remark that only blood spilled in the struggle for fatherland and liberty would lead to emancipation,[1] and there were other German Jews whose faith in such baptism by fire decreased over the course of the war. It is time to go beyond such attitudes in attempting to illuminate certain fundamental problems in the German-Jewish dialogue which the war laid bare and which cannot be subsumed under the familiar dichotomy of assimilation and antisemitism.

The war provides us with a glimpse of the position of the Jew in Germany under extreme conditions. The lives of soldiers in the trenches must be our concern, as they inhabit a unique world isolated not only from the normalcy of home and family life but also at war with its military surroundings, such as the base camp or the regimental headquarters. Typically enough, at the end of the war a guide for returned veterans was published (1918) "because for the most part veterans are completely alienated from bourgeois existence." Through their overwhelming war experiences, they have lost any sense of the so-called necessities of life.[2] Soldiers at war had indeed left the ordered society they knew and had to make a new life for themselves in the

---

[1]   I. Karl Hilmar, *Die deutschen Juden im Weltkriege* (Berlin: n.d.), 48.

[2]   J. Jehle, ed., *An was hat der heimkehrende Kriegsteilnehmer zu denken? Praktische Wegeweise* (Munich: Bayr. Kommunalschriften, 1918), 3.

trenches, largely underground and exposed to constant discomfort, danger, and death.

From the winter of 1914 to the spring of 1918, the trench system was fixed, belligerents' positions moving only a few yards or miles over terrain covered with the bodies of dead and wounded combatants. This new "world of myth," as Paul Fussell has called it, had its own rules, superstitions, miracles, legends, and rumours.[3] The personal issues at stake were indeed momentous: the expectation of death, injury, and disease, and yet there was also a certain exaltation in battle and in that camaraderie which was vital for any survival at all.

The war experience created patterns of thought which were to last into the postwar world. Myths and symbols, cults such as that of the fallen soldier, became central to the self-understanding of the nation. The necessity of transcending the horror of trench warfare created a new world of myth which affected German-Jewish relations in a multitude of ways. Jews had to take part in this world, although it demanded a still more thorough assimilation. A new ideal of manhood grew out of the war, providing a stereotype which was not new but which became more firmly rooted as a German ideal. The Jew was to become the foil not only of this ideal of manhood but also of the myth of the front-line soldier.

War, one combatant wrote, "compresses the greatest opposites into the smallest space and shortest time."[4] Rainer Maria Rilke was not unique in viewing the outbreak of the war as a new release of primeval energy, an intrusion of supposed reality into the realm of illusion.[5] Rilke wrote under the spell of the "spirit of 1914," but while he himself grew disillusioned with war, others fled from reality to myth. With heightened sensibility, a new appreciation of nature rose from the mud of the trenches, together with all sorts of superstitions, prophecies, signs, and portents. All of these reactions to the unparalleled

---

3   Paul Fussel, *The Great War and Modern Memory* (London: Oxford University Press, 1975), 114 and 115. I am greatly indebted to this epoch-making book. Hanus Bächtold, *Deutscher Soldatenbrauch und Soldatenglaube* (Strassourg: K. J. Trübner, 1917) repeats in a German context the superstitions listed for England by Paul Fussell.

4   J. Glenn Gray, *The Warriors: Reflection on Men in Battle* (New York: Harper and Row, 1973), xiv.

5   Sir Maurice Bowra, *Poetry and the First World War* (Oxford: Clarendon Press, 1961), 11.

confrontation with the horrors of war were integrated into myths and symbols which would explain the present and give hope for the future.

At this point, Christian patterns of belief gained new vitality not only as safeguards against danger but also in making the close proximity of death to life bearable. Christian belief under such circumstances tended to be neither Protestant nor Catholic, but rested upon shared myths and symbols. The difference between Protestant and Catholic troops in the reception of the war experience remains to be examined, as military units from Protestant and Catholic German states fought separately from each other. The sources for this essay are Protestant rather than Catholic. However this may be, the war became infused with Christian meaning and vocabulary.

The initiation into the world of the trenches was so momentous that it became natural to speak of the "baptism of war."[6] Death was so close, with bodies all around, that it made men think about Christ's passion and resurrection, an analogy basic to the cult of the fallen soldier. The one celebration in the year which seemed most meaningful was Christmas, a symbol of peace, family, and home, for one moment breaking the isolation of the trenches. These basic patterns of myth and symbol will occupy us, for they are relevant to the place of the Jew in the war and to the peace that was to follow. As we shall see, many Jews accepted the structures of Christian mythology without their specific religious content.

Christian analogies were everywhere. The most popular writer of wartime Germany, Walter Flex, stated in 1914 that "the sacrifice of the best of our people is only a repetition willed by God of the deepest miracle of life ... the death of Christ."[7] Ludwig Ganghofer, another best-selling author, likened Germans to the Three Kings who are led by the star to Bethlehem.[8]

We must focus upon such Christian themes which informed the new "world of myth" of the trenches, for without realizing their impact

---

6   Paul Fussell, op. cit., 115.
7   Walter Flex, *Vom grossen Abendmahl: Verse und Gedanken aus dem Feld* (Munich: C. H. Beck, 1915) 43. The citation is from "Machtgedanken," written in 1914.
8   Ludwig Ganghofer, *Reise zur deutschen Front 1915* (Berlin: Ullstein, 1915), 74.

the Jewish position cannot be understood. Moreover, in order to make our point we will deal with details, even with trifles, the perception of which dominated the daily life of the trenches. The trench experience was taken as representative of human experience.[9] Of course, it needs stating that we are dealing here with only one major theme of the war experience, but one which throws an important light upon the position of Jews in Germany. After we have analyzed these themes and their consequences for Jewish integration, we will have to evaluate whether the attitudes of some important Jews towards the war did not in fact differ from those of non-Jewish Germans, even if Jews by and large accepted the new world of myth trench warfare created. Finally, the adversary habit of mind and the stereotypes the war advocated helped to transform apparent differences between Germans and Jews into a racial reality by the end of the Weimar Republic.

I

Mass death was central to the First World War, a new experience for most Germans and therefore a reality difficult to confront. The only possible confrontation was to transcend it, and this was done by the analogy of death for the fatherland to the passion and sacrifice of Christ. This was not new but strengthened a tradition going back to the wars of liberation against Napoleon. German poets had likened these wars to a German Easter, and later Christ's holy blood was harnessed to German legend in several of Richard Wagner's operas. The Holy Grail was said to be in the custody of the German Volk. When Walter Flex coined the First World War the "Last Supper," he was refurbishing this tradition. Now it was projected upon the fallen comrades and on one's own imminent death: "Christ's wine consists of German blood."[10]

One memorial book may stand as exemplary for a great many others: the fallen have found no rest; they return to earth in order to rejuvenate the Volk. "To fight, to die, to be resurrected, that is the essence of being. From out of your death (in the war) the nation will

9   Paul Fussel, op. cit., 145.
10   Walter Flex, op. cit., 5.

be restored."[11] Such sentiments are not merely typical of the Right but can be duplicated from the official guide to war monuments issued by the Weimar Republic.[12] Clearly, a Christian theme became symbolic of sacrifice for the nation. Moreover, Germany was not unique in proclaiming such a synthesis: across the channel in England, the fourth day of August, 1914, which marked England's entry into the war, was often depicted as the nation's crucifixion and resurrection.[13] Life and death became united, linked by the *imitatio Christi*, pictured after the war through the "cross of sacrifice" in military cemeteries or even in frescoes showing the fallen soldier resting in the lap of Christ. Decades of secularization had not markedly affected the symbolism and the iconography surrounding heroic death. It was still the saviour who drew deaths' sting.

That sometimes Jews were buried under crosses on the battlefield becomes meaningful in this context, and so does the fact that one Jewish officer immediately connects his presumed death with the plain wooden cross under which he will rest, and this in a poem published in a Jewish wartime pamphlet.[14] Moreover, even where Jewish graves were marked with the Star of David, they were apt to rest in the shadow of a giant cross of sacrifice in a chapel which stood as a symbol of the resurrection of Christ. Soldiers' burials were roughly the same in all warring nations. For example, the American Battle Monuments Commission also at first automatically placed crosses on the graves of Jewish soldiers. When eventually the Star of David was substituted, one American Jewish leader protested against this "mischievous act." Matters of faith were irrelevant as "Jews and Christians fought shoulder to shoulder, actuated

---

11 *Ehrendenkmal der Deutschen Armee und Marine* (Berlin & Munich: Deutscher National Verlag, 1926), 654.

12 That is, *Deutschen Ehrenhein für die Helden 1914–1918* (Leipzig: 1931).

13 Albert Marrin, *The Last Crusade: The Church of England in the First World War* (North Carolina: Duke University Press, 1974), 135.

14 Immanuel Saul, "An meine Kinder," *Im Deutschen Reich, Feldbücherei der CFJG* (Berlin: n. d.) 55. Other examples of Jews buried under crosses: M. Spanier, *Leutnant Sender* (Hamburg: M. Gloga, 1915), 77; *Unsere Gefallenen Kameraden: Gedenkbuch für die im Weltkrieg gefallenen Münchner Juden* (Munich: B. Heller, 1929), 212. Julius Marx writes about a Jew buried under a cross, and that such a cross and the praying soldier in front of it became symbolic for the war. *Kriegs-Tagebuch eines Juden* (Zürich: Die Liga, 1939), 33.

by the same patriotic impulse."[15] The cross became a national symbol for a war which was regarded as holy by all combatants. War graves became part of this myth: for Ludwig Ganghofer travelling along the front, individual graves with their crucifixes were not places of death but "verdant temples of resurrection."[16]

We are apt to take Jewish acceptance of certain Christian symbolism for granted: the Iron Cross of Valour, if not the cross over the grave. But this was not always the case. During the Wars of Liberation, the Prussian government, hesitant to offend Jewish sensibilities, sometimes withheld from Jews the Iron Cross or the Luisen Cross, the medal of valour for women on the home front. Thus, a Jewish banker's wife merely received a medal instead of the decoration, whereupon she protested that she was proud to wear a cross. For, in any case, eventually she would be buried next to her son, who had fallen in battle and whose grave was marked by a cross.[17] As late as 1853, Carl Meyer Rothschild received the Prussian Red Eagle in a form especially designed for Jews, which substituted a round base for that in the form of a cross.[18] But such times were past. The common war experience meant accepting a shared symbolism.

To make such a statement does not deny that for the most part Jews tried to make use of their own religious symbolism in order to confront the war. In fact, during the Wars of Liberation, Prussian rabbis had already justified enlistment through the use of biblical analogies. Following this tradition, in the Great War, Russia became Goliath, while the president of one German-Jewish community proclaimed that "German courage and the heroism of the Maccabees are one and the same."[19] We shall discuss Jewish reservations about the war, which

---

[15]   Charles Reznikoff, ed., *Louis Marshall, Champion of Liberty: Selected Papers and Addresses* (Philadelphia: The Jewish Publication Society of America, 1957), 247. 248. I owe this reference to Professor L. Gartner of the University of Tel Aviv.

[16]   Ludwig Ganghofer, op. cit., 150.

[17]   Unidentified newspaper clipping of 8 February 1816, Stern collection, item 212, p. 17. Archives of the Jewish People, Jerusalem.

[18]   Cited in Fritz Stern, *Gold and Iron; Bismarck, Bleichröder, and the Building of the German Empire* (New York: Knopf, 1977), 16.

[19]   M. Güdemann, "Der jetzige Weltkrieg und die Bibel," *Monatsschrift fur Geschichte und Wissenschaft des Judetums* 23 (1915), 5; *Zum Gedächtuis an Dr. Moritz Levin, 13. Dezember 1914*, 6.

sprang from a still vigorous ethical tradition, later in this essay. But here, it is important to point out that the shared camaraderie of the trenches did mean a further assimilation.

After all, the Jewish soldier was a part of this comradeship, even though Julius Marx believed that this was only true during times of danger.[20] We have no concrete knowledge of what such comradeship actually meant to the front-line soldier. To be sure, officers wrote about it, writers like Walter Flex and propagandists behind the front. But there is no survey in Germany such as that taken in France in 1917; and even in that case, only some 50 soldiers replied and attempted to formulate the meaning of wartime friendship. Often this was assumed to be instinctive, based upon common affinities, and these in turn were thought to be both products of a shared hatred of the enemy and also of shared traditions reaching back into the past. Religion and regional ties usually defined such traditions.[21] This survey comes to us from the Right, from admirers of Maurice Barrés, and must be viewed with suspicion: but in Germany, glorification of shared hatreds and common religious and volkish ties was carried into the postwar world. For the National Socialists, but not for them only, this *Bund* of males was the cell from which all states have their origins.[22] The postwar tendency to endow the war with dramatic unity was especially effective in making the myth of the camaraderie in the trenches symbolic for the fate of the entire nation.

The immediate symbol of the wartime camaraderie was the military cemetery: linking the living comradeship of the trenches with the fallen comrades. Already in 1915, the distinction was made between bourgeois' and soldiers' cemeteries. Bourgeois' cemeteries are materialistic in the boastfulness of their monuments; in soldiers' cemeteries, "gravestones through their simplicity and uniformity lead in to a serious and reverential mood."[23] The camaraderie in life is continued in death. The historical background of this kind of cemetery cannot concern us,

---

20   Julius Marx, op. cit., 129.
21   That is, J. H. Rosny Aîné, *Confidences sur l'amitié des des tranchées* (Paris: E. Flammarion, 1919), passim.
22   George L. Mosse, *The Crisis of German Ideology* (New York: Grosset & Dunlap, 1974), 216.
23   Emil Högg, *Kriegergrab und Kriegerdenkmal* (Wittenberg: Ziemsen, 1915), 29.

except to mention that it owes something to the classical revival of the eighteenth century, and that the simple row graves date from the quest for equality in the Enlightenment and during the French Revolution. But now a myth grew up around the simple, uniform graves with their serried crosses: they symbolized Germany. As we read in the previously cited war memorial published by the Republic, it is from these graves that the fallen are said to rise and visit the living in their dreams in order to command them to continue the battle. War cemeteries are the symbols of war turned to stone.

Uniformity was crucial here, and so were the walls that enclosed the war cemeteries. They were meant to form a sacred space, analogous to a church, centred upon a cross or a chapel. Jewish cemeteries did not, of course, entirely follow this plan, although the separately enclosed space was kept, and so were the row graves. Instead of crosses, these resting places sometimes adapted another German tradition which had become an alternative to crosses of sacrifice, if not in military cemeteries then in war memorials: huge boulders, symbols, so it was said, of primeval power (*Urkraft*), exemplifying reverence, exaltation, and iron force. These, we are told, had been used by ancient Germans to represent an *Ehrenmal*. Jewish cemeteries were at times centred upon such a boulder; in the Jewish cemetery of Nuremberg, it took the form of an altar.[24]

The iconography of death in war was similar among Jews and Gentiles, although of course there were no crosses or chapels of resurrection among the Jews. Yet, more often than not, Jews and Gentiles were buried in a common cemetery in Flanders or in the east. Sammy Gronemann tells of the difficulty of persuading a Jewish parent that his son should be torn from his comrades and buried separately in Jewish soil.[25]

The war produced one new form of military cemetery: the *Heldenhain* or Heroes' Wood, first proposed in 1915. War heightened the sense of nature: from out of the trenches, soldiers stared at a ravaged no man's

---

[24] That is, *Kriegsgenkbuch der israelitschen Kultusgemende Nürnberg*, ed., Marx Freudenthal (Nuremberg: J. L. Schrag, 1920), passim. For the symbolisms referred to, see George L. Mosse, *Nationalization of the Masses: Political Symbolism and Mass Movements in Germany from the Napoleonic Wars Through the Third Reich* (New York: H. Fertig, 1975).

[25] Sammy Gronemaun, *Hawdoloh und Zapfenstreich* (Berlin: Jüdischer Verlag, 1924), 102.

land and looked for an enemy they could never see. But what they did see were the woods of Flaudel, which seemed to suffer much like themselves. "The Murdered Wood" is the title of a story in *Die Feldgrauen* (The Field-Grey), a journal written by soldiers at the front. "This wood, battered and beaten like myself, nevertheless lives on."[26] Walter Flex's *The Wanderer between Two Worlds,* that most famed of war books, is filled with descriptions of nature. For Flex, nature is a means of transcending the war experience; for example, fields full of flowers directly behind the trenches are reminders of beauty and hope. Here, typically enough, nature is Christianized, as it were, and Flex's hero reads the New Testament even as he admires the "breath of religious spring."[27]

The image of the crucifixion was very much a part of the Belgian and Flemish landscape: the numerous calvaries visible at the crossroads. Paul Fussell has pointed out the role that these calvaries played in the imagination of British soldiers who, coming from a Protestant country, were much impressed. The sacrificial theme in which each soldier becomes analogous to the crucified Christ was not confined to English war poetry.[28] Walter Flex spoke to his friend Wurche for the last time in the shadow of just such a cavalry: a few days later, Wurche was killed while on patrol.[29] The heightened feeling for nature was infused with such Christian symbols, which seemed an integral part of the countryside.

The Heroes' Wood, however, while linked to the heightened sensibility towards nature in wartime, was based upon the tradition of the Germanic landscape with its sacred trees and forests. "Emperor's oaks" (*Kaisereichen*) had already been planted as a thanksgiving for the victory of 1871. The renewal of a Germanic nature was now seen as symbolic of the resurrection of the dead. The German wood itself should form the sacred burial space. Field Marshall von Hindenburg in praising this new concept of burial wrote about the "German tree, gnarled and with solid roots, symbolic of individual and communal

---

26 *Die Feldgraue. Illustrierte Kriegszeilschrift der 50. I.-D.* (June 1916), 12.
27 Walter Flex, *Der Wanderer zwischen beiden Welten* (Munich: Beck, n.d.), 46.
28 Paul Fussell, op. cit., 118,·119.
29 Walter Flex, *Der Wanderer zwischen beiden Welten*, 73.

strength."[30] "Oaks of honour" were common in Jewish as well as Christian military cemeteries. Heldenhaine were ecumenical, fusing Germanic and Christian symbolism for all of those who had made the ultimate sacrifice.[31]

A common mood united Jews and Gentiles, but it was a mood subsumed under Germanic and Christian symbolism. Sermons preached on days of mourning by Christian ministers and rabbis might well be compared. Such a comparison made on a very limited scale emphasized once more a joint approach to the fallen heroes. The day of mourning was conceived of as a festival: a worthwhile death has climaxed a worthwhile life in the service of the fatherland. Such themes are hardly surprising, but some sermons of Jewish chaplains show a confusion of Christian symbolism and Jewish identity, especially as services at the front were sometimes held in churches. Thus was Bruno Italiener carried away when he praised the combination of organ music, bright light falling through the church windows, and the power of ancient Germanic song. In such a moment, he said, there exist no Jews, Catholics, or Protestants, but only Germans.[32] Ecumenical cooperation between all faiths was the rule during the war, *communio sanctorum* as a Protestant court preacher called it,[33] but here such a community is found but within a specific Germanic and Christian context.

Christmas in the trenches became the festival which best symbolized the longing for an end of isolation, for home and family, for camaraderie, and for the return of the fallen. It is curious that this festival has never been analyzed, although the "war Christmas" became a cliché in both world wars; it was accompanied by an outpouring of poetry and prose claiming to be symbolic of the true national spirit. Christmas was a festival of peace, a "secret armistice" as it was called, which in the first year of the war did in fact become real, as enemies met in the no man's land between the trenches. But when such fraternization was

---

30   Stephan Ankenbrand, ed., *Heldenhaine, Heldenbäume* (Munich: Dettelbach a. Main and K. Triltsch, 1918), 28.

31   That is, *Kriegsgedenkbuch der israelitischen Kultusgemeinde Nürnberg*, 25, 43.

32   Bruno Italiener, *Heimat und Glauben: Kriegsbetrachtungen* (Darmstadt: H.L. Schlapp, 1917), 9.

33   Johannes Kessler, *Ich schwöre mir ewige Jugend* (Leipzig: P. List, 1935), 285.

stopped (in 1915, anyone repeating such fraternization was ordered shot), Christmas in the trenches still mimicked that in times of peace: the decorations, the Christmas tree, the presents from home, and the festive board. "Everyone's face lit up at the thought of home." Yet a short sermon by an officer was supposed to exhort the men, to strengthen their will to fight in the realization that peace can only be attained through war. Moreover, once more thoughts of home were mixed with memorials to the fallen.[34]

Walter Flex, that great myth maker, in his "Christmas fable" has a war widow drown herself and her son. They are restored to life through an encounter with the ghosts of dead soldiers. "Christmas night the dead talk in human voices."[35] Flex likens the fallen to the angels who brought the news of Christ's birth to the shepherds—a repetition of the motif which Ganghofer made symbolic for the role of Germany in the war. Small wonder that a rabbi justified his leading such a Christmas celebration: it also symbolized to him a camaraderie which knew no barriers of faith; it was a festival symbolic of German unity and the bonds of friends and family back home. His rejection of the belief that the Saviour was really born on this day was of little importance, he tells us, compared to the wartime meaning of Christmas.[36]

We might see in the war Christmas, as in the other symbols and myths discussed, a secularization of Christianity, an ecumenicism which was so broad as to lose its specific Christian relevance. It is indeed possible that the references to Christ and Christianity were rhetoric, a shorthand for dilemmas and longings shared by everyone at the front. Certainly they could become form without content, as, for example, in the constant Nazi use of Christian vocabulary which transferred terms like *apostles* and *evangelical* to their own substitute religion. But there was no such substitute religion in the trenches; worship of the nation was expressed through the passion and the resurrection, and the national landscape was replete with Christian symbolism. As

---

[34] D. E. Dryander, *Weihnachtsgedanken in der Kriegszeit* (Leipzig: Hirzel, 1935), 21; *Die Feldgrauen, Kriegszeitschrift aus dem Schützengraben* (mimeographed, February, 1916), 30, 31.

[35] Walter Flex. *Vom grossen Abendmahl*, 15.

[36] *Gefallene Deutsche Juden: Frontbriefe 1914–1918* (Berlin: Vortrupp Verlag, 1935), 92.

the Christian metaphors of war were transferred into the postwar world, nationalism increasingly took the lead in a badly defeated and disorganized nation.

Yet if it had not been for the crisis that followed the war, Jews might not have been affected by the mood and piety we have analyzed. As it turned out, the details and even the trifles which have concerned us opened a deep gulf between Germans and Jews because they operated on the level of myth and symbol, within an extreme human situation. The folk community, the camaraderie, were wrapped in a Christian analogy which had to be accepted.

Not all Jews went so far in their acceptance of this as did Walther Rathenau. During the war, he wrote that he was taking his stand on the Acts of the Apostles, but this did not prevent him from going his own way and remaining a Jew, just as his pious Christian friends believed in religion without dogma. "I want a Christian state" but without state power or a state church.[37] In fact, many important Jews attempted to disentangle themselves from the German mood, or at least to mitigate its effects.

Amidst all the enthusiasm, there were reservations. One need only read Leo Baeck's sermons or his official reports as field chaplain to the Jewish community to feel his love of peace and hatred of all war.[38] For Leo Baeck, the war was a necessary evil, and there can be no greater contrast than that between his thoughts and those of the Protestant chaplain. Chauvinism of any kind is rejected by Baeck but accepted by nearly all of his official Christian colleagues. The ethical ideals of Reform Judaism held fast in this case.

On the home front, where on the one hand enthusiasm ran high but on the other hand voices of dissent did exist, some though by no means all Jewish publications were remarkable in their outspokenness. Not only did Leo Baeck's reports and articles in the *Gemeindeblatt* bear witness to this fact, but so too did certain Zionist papers. For example, after first sharing the "spirit of 1914," the *Jüdische Rundschau*

---

[37]   Walther Rathenau, *Eine Streitschrift* (Weilheim/Obb.: O. W. Barth, 1917), 20–28.
[38]   Leo Baeck's report appeared regularly in the *Gemeinedeblatt der Jüdischen Gemeinde Berlin* from 1914 onwards.

emphasized that the war proved the importance of nationalism, but immediately qualified this statement by referring to the brotherhood of man.[39] Robert Weltsch clung to his ideal that the nation was but a step towards the unity of mankind. In the midst of the myth of the fallen soldier, the *Herzl-Bund* of young Zionist merchants stressed the awfulness of death and war, and the burdens which they impose upon life. In the halcyon days of the "spirit of 1914," even as it defended the Jews against the charge of cowardice, *Ost und West* exclaimed that the moral grandeur of a people is not only revealed in war but, above all, in the solid accomplishments of peace. This is certainly a unique dissent in the chorus of German voices.[40]

To be sure, all Jewish papers exhorted young Jews to do their best and called upon them to volunteer for the colours. Yet there is enough meaningful difference that we can talk, even if not consistently, of an ethical imperative which remained intact. If Jews were prone to accept Christian metaphors because ideas and rituals taken from the non-Jewish environment had penetrated to the heart of Judaism during the process of assimilation, so the ideals of the Enlightenment lasted longest among the Jews. The *Israelitische Wochenblatt* as early as September 1914 warned against "unhealthy chauvinism" and appealed to reason instead.[41]

We call cite as additional evidence for the attitude of large parts of the German Jewish and Zionist establishment their rejection of Ernst Lissauer's hymn of hate against England. This poem became the most popular war poem in Germany. It received praise from the emperor and the Crown Prince of Bavaria, but not from many of his fellow Jews. When Binjamin Segel surveyed 60 important Jewish personalities, they unanimously rejected the *Hassgesang* as un-Jewish.[42] *Ost und West*, once more in the forefront, wrote a whole article against Lissauer called

---

[39]   That is, *Jüdische Rundschau* (August 7, 1914), 343, ibid. (October 16, 1914), 387, but also Kurt Blumenfeld "am deutschen Wesen soll die Welt genesen," ibid. (19 February 1915), 65.

[40]   *Protokoll des II. Ordentlichen Bundestages des Herzl-Bundes Berlin,* 17–20, April 1918, 7; *Ost und West* (January-May, 1915), 14ff.

[41]   Quoted in *Jüdische Rundschau* (September 4, 1914), 361.

[42]   Binjamin Segel, *Der Weltkrieg und das Schicksal der Juden* (Berlin: G. Stilke, 1915), 143.

"Education in Hate." Jews generally, it asserted, have rejected Lissauer, towards whose poems one can feel only revulsion and horror.[43]

Here, then, there was no easy acceptance of the new world of myth of the trenches, and this in spite of the acceptance of the common mood. This persistence of ethical attitudes, of a refusal to join in the symphony of hate and the deification of the nation, separated some important Jews from most Germans. Once more, we face a phenomenon which will continue into the postwar world, when Jews in their liberalism and cosmopolitanism will face ever greater isolation in Germany, where the war experience led to a heightened chauvinism. This alienation worked hand in hand with the covert rather than overt exclusion of Jews from the *communio sanctorum* of the embattled fatherland.

At the same time, the war led to several other attitudes which were to prove dynamic in destroying the precarious German-Jewish relationship. The hatred Leo Baeck rejected dominated the war. The adversary relationship led to a state of mind which craved an enemy, and which was ready for the politics of confrontation in postwar Germany. The crises of the Weimar Republic took the form of an undeclared civil war which the Nazis eventually exploited and won. The Jews became the real victims of the continuation of war in peace time. Just so, the war deepened an already present German stereotype of manliness. This "totally new race," as Ernst Jünger called it,[44] which emerged from the war was to take the Jew as its foil.

Eventually all the ideals we have discussed, the glorification of sacrifice and the reward of resurrection, the exaltation of simplicity and equality as the essence of comradeship, and the love of home and of nature, were turned against the Jews. What started as Jews coming to terms with national Christian myth and symbols ended with the expulsion of the Jew from participation in the national myth. He became the enemy who had to be destroyed.

---

[43] *Ost und West,* 14.
[44] Ernst Jünger, *Der Kampf als inneres Erlebnis* (Berlin: E.S. Mittler, 1933), 33.

II

The hatred of the enemy in wartime needs no documentation. To be sure, there was at times respect for the adversary as well as fraternization during the first war Christmas. Whatever the soldiers may actually have felt, the barrage of propaganda and the loss of their comrades can hardly have left them without moments of hate. As the entire war experience was constantly lifted into a world of myth and symbol, so the adversary relationship was transformed into a general principle of life by influential writers and poets. Ernst Jünger was the most famous of these, and his war diary, *The Storm of Steel* (1919), which sold 244,000 copies in 26 editions and which was translated into seven languages,[45] put it bluntly: "For I cannot too often repeat, a battle was no longer an episode that spent itself in blood and fire; it was a condition of things that dug itself in remorselessly week after week and even month after month."[46] This was a total confrontation for, so we are told, "war means the destruction of the enemy without scruple and by any means. War is the harshest of all trades, and the masters of it can only entertain humane feelings so long as they do no harm."[47] Such passages seem to anticipate the Nazi future, and indeed Hitler greatly valued *The Storm of Steel*. But then the book was received with universal praise by the *Tagebuch* on the moderate left as well as from the right, where the welcome was warmest.[48]

Jünger revised his book from edition to edition during the Weimar Republic. It is not without significance that he now omitted the beginning of his diary and took the acceptance of war as a necessary and higher reality for granted. Within the diary itself, personal experience is changed into the shared experience of comradeship in the trenches and in battle.[49] Such an emphasis on camaraderie brought Jünger's work into line with many other books about the war, but also

---

45 Karl Prümm, *Die Literatur des Soldatischen Nationalismus der 20er Jahre*, 2 vol. (Kronberg, Taunus: Kronberg, 1974), vol. 1, 101.
46 Ernst Jünger. *The Storm of Steel* (New York: H. Fertig, 1975), 109.
47 Ibid, 126–127.
48 Karl Prümm, op. cit., 101.
49 Ibid, 1031f.

reflected the search for a new nation which would restore German power and glory.

Jünger, despite his rejection of the Nazis, must have approved of the words which Joseph Goebbels addressed, in the midst of the victories of the Second World War, to the dead of the First: "Germany is beginning to glitter in the dawn of your sacrifice." Already in 1928 he wrote that the young Nazi movement was led by the fallen soldiers.[50] Not only the Nazis annexed the myths of the war and its aggressive attitude of mind. The political Right under the Republic fed and grew fat on it, while much of the Left proved unable to cope with the war experience, although it also dominated the lives of its followers.

Jünger did not stand alone. War novels and war poetry echoed the constant refrain that Germany must remain hard as steel, that sentimentality, even during Christmas, must not sap the fighting spirit. It is no accident that these hackneyed sentiments dating from the First World War were repeated by Himmler in the midst of the Second World War. Telling his SS execution squads in 1943 that they must know what it means to see a hundred Jewish corpses lie side by side, or five hundred, or a thousand, he continues: "To have stuck this out ... to have kept our integrity, that is what has made us hard."[51] This comparison does not telescope history but tells us about one consequence of the First World War: the adversary relationship, the acceptance of mass death, led to an ever greater brutalization of the human mind.

This brutalizing effect was noticed in the first year of the war by a psychologist who otherwise fully shared the "spirit of 1914": "The marvelous enthusiasm, heroic courage and willingness to sacrifice ... which sprang from a shared devotion to the fatherland," wrote Otto Binswanger, "have been sadly perverted into degrading ... feelings of cruel hate, of lust for revenge and desire to ruthlessly exterminate the enemy."[52] The confrontation politics of the Weimar Republic continued

---

[50] Joseph Goebbels, *Der Angriff: Aufsätze aus der Kampfzeit* (Munich: F. Eher, 1942), 251, 274.

[51] Quoted in Lucy S. Dawidowicz, *A Holocaust Reader* (New York: Behrman House, 1976), 133.

[52] Otto Binswanger, *Die seelischen Wirkungen des Krieges* (Stuttgart and Berlin: Dt. Verlags-Anstalt, 1914), 27.

this trend. Yet such brutalization was not merely the product of the enthusiasms Binswanger cited but also of the efforts to transcend the horrors of war through the myth of the fallen soldier and the other myths and symbols which we have discussed. They made it easier to confront mass death, made it easier for soldiers to not only face their own deaths but also the task of killing the enemy.

The contrast between "we" and "them" was used as the spearhead for the post–world war attack against liberalism. Liberalism, so Jünger tells us, relativises everything on behalf of its business interests, and the political philosopher Carl Schmitt praised decisiveness without giving quarter, which alone was said to be worthy of the sovereign state.[53] Such attitudes gave solid support for the onslaught on the Weimar Republic's ideals of freedom and pluralism. That not only the Republic but its Jews as well were victims of such anti-liberalism needs no demonstration. Jewish existence had always depended upon the pluralism and the liberalism of society. That such an onslaught was made in the name of the war experience gave it a frightening dimension. That the Republic was watering down the myths of the war was one of the most fundamental accusations made against the freedom and tolerance it championed.[54]

The veterans organization, *Der Stahlhelm*, for example, opposed the Republic in order to transmit the "spirit of the front line soldier" to future generations.[55] According to the *Stahlhelm*, the new nation was to be built upon the "camaraderie of the trenches." Yet the Jewish soldier was now excluded from such comradeship. As Jews formed their own veterans' organization, the cooperation between all faiths which had taken place on the front collapsed—Christianity had become too Germanized, an integral part of the *Vollksgmeineschaft* embattled against the enemy.

It is all the more significant that the *Stahlhelm* leader, Franz Seldte,

---

53   Karl Prümm, op. cit., 45ff; Carl Schmitt, *Politische Theologie* (Munich and Leipzig: Duncker & Humblot, 1934), preface.

54   Kurt Sontheimer, *Antidemokratisches Denken in der Weimarer Republik* (Munich: Nymphenburge, 1962), 132.

55   Volker R. Berghahn, *Der Stahlhelm: Bund der Frontsoldaten in der Weimarer Republik* (Düsseldorf: Droste, 1962), 91.

was no passionate antisemite. His novel, *Vor und hinter den Kulissen* (In Front and Behind the Scenes, 1931), praised one Jewish officer as an exemplary German patriot, modest and of pleasing appearance. At the same time, Seldte demanded a clear-cut division between German and Jew.[56] While he regarded the Jews as a separate people, many of his followers came to regard them as a separate race as well. In 1932, when it was revealed that the *Stahlhelm*'s deputy leader had some Jews in his family tree, a veritable storm broke over Theodor Duesterberg's head in spite of his own unquestionable volkish allegiance. In vain Duesterberg gave his word of honor that he was not related to any Jews himself or through his children, and that he never borrowed money from Jews, nor had Jewish clients.[57] Nothing can demonstrate more clearly how exclusive the *Frontgeist* had become: a clean separation between Germans and Jews was now part of the "spirit of the trenches," in spite of Seldte's noble Jewish officer or the Stahlhelm delegations which appeared at memorials to the Jewish fallen.

Such a separation might have been inherent in the mythology of the war, but it became explicit only after the war. To what degree the Jewish war veterans' association attempted to reestablish the lost comradeship, and to what extent they attempted to revitalize a shared myth once more—now volkish rather than Christian—must be left to further research. But it is possible to trace the German-Jewish dialogue based on shared Germanic and Christian myths,[58] just as it is possible to trace the ethical imperatives which separated important Jewish leaders like Leo Baeck from the commonly accepted war experience.

Hatred of the enemy, the adversary relationship, became a total commitment for important and powerful segments of the population. Hans Oberlindober, the leader of the disabled veterans' organization, wrote that though the First World War was finished, the war against the German people continues, and that 1914–1918 was merely its bloody beginning.[59] The politics of struggle, of clear and unambiguous

---

56   Fran Seldte, *Vor und Hinter den Kulissen* (Leipzig: Koehler, 1931), 56ff.
57   Volker R. Berghahn, op. cit., 241.
58   That is, George Mosse, *German and Jews: The Right, the Left, and the Search for a "Third Force" in Pre-Nazi Germany* (New York: Grosset & Dunlap, 1970), 105ff.
59   Hans Oberlindober, *Ein Vaterland, das allen gehört!* (Munich: Eher, 1925), 10 and 11.

decision making, was thought to be the consequence of facing an enemy, foreign or domestic. Great revolutions are decided by blood and iron, wrote Oswald Spengler, without the kind of hesitation about violence which characterized many left-wing revolutionaries as well as many Republicans. The German revolution, he continued, must go forward until the nation becomes once more a community like that of the trenches. Typically enough, Spengler believed that such politics were the politics of power, the only politics that count. Power belongs to the whole nation; the individual is merely its servant.[60]

Those who wrote about the trenches often stressed the primitivism of such a life, glorifying it as the breakthrough of elemental forces which had slumbered within all artificial civilization. The rage of which Jünger and others spoke as they went over the top was exalted as an ecstasy which revealed the true nature of man. The myth of the storm troopers existed during the war and was not merely a creation of the postwar world. Such men were endowed with certain characteristics, so it was thought, which went beyond mere courage and the will to fight. Contemporaries believed that this stereotype was new, of the iron-hard man of decision, slim and lithe, with fair skin and clear eyes. In reality, this was a stereotype present in European aesthetic consciousness ever since the eighteenth century, sinking still deeper into the German mind through its reaffirmation during the war.[61]

Such stereotypes were not confined to Germany. In England, Siegfried Sassoon described George Sherston's friend, the young officer Dick Tiltwood, in terms almost identical to those with which Walter Flex characterized his hero Ernst Wurche: "He had the obvious good looks which go with fair hair and firm features, but it was the radiant integrity of his expression which astonished me."[62] *The Wanderer between Two Worlds* began with a description of Wurche, student of Christian theology, whose outward appearance mirrors his inward beauty. Wurche's integrity is symbolized by his light and clear eyes,

---

[60] Oswald Spengler, *Preussentum und Sozialismus* (Munich: O. Beck, 1925), 15.

[61] For this see, George L. Mosse, *Toward the Final Solution: The European Experience of Race* (New York: Howard Fertig, 1978), chapter xi.

[62] Paul Fussel, op. cit., 57.

his good looks, and his slender and well-proportioned body.[63] When Sassoon followed up his description of Tiltwood by writing that, "His was the bright countenance of truth ... incapable of concealment but strong in reticence and modesty,"[64] he unwittingly duplicated the ideal of manliness which Walter Flex popularized in Germany.

Wurche, however, loved nothing better than his naked sword and rejoiced in battle. If the English ideal type included vulnerability and innocence, as Paul Fussell tells us,[65] the German model was hard, wise, and invulnerable. There exist vital differences in national traditions which surface in times of deep stress and anxiety. Dick Tiltwood is not particularly religious, and his patriotism is tempered by his gentleness. Wurche, who reads Goethe and the New Testament even while rejoicing in his sword, is reconciled to a heroic death as part of his joyful duty to the fatherland and to his men. And so is Otto Braun, the *Frühvollendete* (one who dies young), who unlike Flex cannot be counted on the political right. The body, so he tells his war diaries, must become hard, steely, grave, and austere, pregnant with future deeds and manly beauty. For Otto Braun, this ideal warrior corresponded to the stereotype of Greek beauty which had formed the Germanic ideal ever since the eighteenth century.[66]

Ernst Jünger once more summed up this stereotype in all its mixture of brutality and beauty, so common in Germany. "This was a totally new race, all energy ... slim, lithe and muscular bodies, finely chiseled faces ... These were men who overcame, natures of steel, ready for any struggle however ghastly," and Jünger thought that such a struggle was a permanent condition of life. The foils of this hero were the Philistines, the bourgeois, and the Liberals, the "retail merchant and the glove makers," as Jünger characterized them.[67] It was the Jewish stereotype which became the foil of this manly ideal. For like the new race of which Jünger spoke, the Jewish stereotype had over a century of history behind it and was quite ready for use. Werner Sombart's

[63] Walter Flex, *Der Wanderer zwischen beiden Welten*, 5, 6.
[64] Siegfried Sasson, *Memoirs of a Fox-Hunting Man* (New York: Faber and Faber, 1929), 321.
[65] Paul Fussel, op. cit., 272.
[66] Otto Braun, *Aus Nachgelassenen Schriften eines Frühvollendeten*, ed., Julie Vogelstein (Berlin-Grünewald, 1921), 120.
[67] Ernst Jünger, *Der Kamp als inneres Erlebnis*, 33, 56.

contrast between merchants and heroes (*Händler und Heiden*, 1915) projected the opprobrium of the antiheroic upon the English enemy, but it was easily transferred back to the Jews. It is not necessary to cite further proof that the Jew was excluded from this heroic ideal.

The specific monuments to the fallen which we find in the Heroes' Woods often present the dying young Siegfried,[68] a figure thought especially effective when juxtaposed with the darkness of the trees. We have already mentioned earlier the role played by massive boulders as war monuments, but in this case the symbolism was not so limited that Jews could not follow, in spite of the frequent references to ancient Germanic traditions. Young Siegfried was another matter. The emphasis in such monuments was on simplicity and youth. Simplicity, as we have already seen, was thought essential for military cemeteries because it was said to reflect the manliness of the comradeship of the trenches. Greek ideas were operative here, reinforced by the stress of youth. The young hero was modelled on Greek sculpture whose concept of beauty had determined the German stereotype ever since J. J. Winckelmann wrote in the eighteenth century. In 1931, looking back over the war memorials of the last decade, Karl von Seeger was moved to wonder about the persistence of the ideal of Greek art. The "naked, lithe, muscular youth, filled with spirit and will, still represents an ideal of humanity."[69] The eros which was always part of the camaraderie of the trenches was worshipped as youth. Poetry and prose were filled with admiration for "youthful steps" and "youthful exuberance." Much of the best English war poetry was also erotic, with its delight in blond and tender youth, but in Germany this kind of eroticism became politicized. Such heroes' memorials, so we are told in 1915, are symbolic of the eternal youth of the people. Siegfried was a young Apollo, and so was Germany.[70] The struggle between young Germany and the old nations of the West was popularized by Moeller van den Bruck, but it subtly drew much of its strength from the image of heroic youth during the war.

---

68   That is, *Das Deutsche Grabdenkmal* (Februar-März, 1926); Albert Maennchen, *Das Reichsehrenmal der Eisenbolz am Rhein* (Koblenz: Breuer, 1927), n.p.

69   Karl von Seeger, *Das Denkmal des Weltkrieges* (Stuttgart: H. Matthaes, 1930), 22.

70   Willy Lange, *Deutsche Heldenhaine* (Leipzig: J. J. Weber, 1915), 27; *Das Deutsche Grabdenkmal* (April 1926), 11.

The Jews were considered an old people, and the Jewish stereotype was consistently one of age, not of youth. In German literature, even young Jews usually have old faces.[71] This Jewish stereotype is once again a part of a long tradition which cannot be analyzed here. The epithet "old," people attached to the image of the Jew, but now this confronted a nation which adopted the symbol of heroic youth.

Not only the Germanic stereotype received renewed impetus through the war experience, but so did the ideals of simplicity and modesty, which were a part of the myth of camaraderie as symbolized in the resting places of the fallen. Once more, the Jewish stereotype ran squarely counter to this ideal. The Jew as arrogant and showy was a myth over a century old by the time of the war, but now it was heightened by the supposed qualities of the front-line soldiers, which were so contrary to what the Jew was meant to represent. Finally, the concept of beauty and eros, which symbolized the ideal German, confronted a Jewish stereotype which was its opposite: small and puny, ill-proportioned, and with shambling gait. The dash of stereotypes is well enough known, but the war gave it a dimension unknown before this time. To be sure, without a long tradition behind them neither stereotype would have acquired the force given to it by the war and the defeat which followed. The commonplaces of antisemitism received a new importance when transposed upon the myths and stereotypes of the war.

Germany saw itself defending European civilization. The myths and symbols we have discussed were thought to be specifically German. Germany in turn was the guardian of Europe, and more than that, God's instrument to pass judgment upon the world. As Klaus Vondung has shown, ideas of the Jewish and Christian apocalypse became one means of interpreting the war: Germany is lifted from an instrument through which God judges to the executor of the Last Judgment. Jewish war sermons at times echoed such thoughts.[72] Through this self-appointed task, some racism penetrated the war experience, directed not against Jews but against blacks.

---

[71] That is, George L. Mosse, "Die NS-Kampfbühne," in *Geschichte im Gegenwartsdrama*, ed., Reinhold Grimm and Jost Hermand (Stuttgart: Kohlhammer, 1976), 35.
[72] Klaus Vondung, "Geschichte als Weltgericht," *Zeitschrift für Literaturwissenschaft und Linguistik*, Beiheft 2 (1977), 147–168; Dr. Jelski, *Aus grosser Zeit* (Berlin: L. Lamm, 1915), 91.

The Entente was accused of importing inferior races to Europe in order that they might fight God's chosen people. Such racism strengthened German feelings of exclusiveness and mission, which later flowed into Weimar racism and antisemitism. Indeed, when the Entente used black troops to occupy Germany after the armistice (1919–1920), the cry that culture was being raped coincided with the first and as yet merely social restrictions against the Jews because of their race.[73] Walter Bloem, writing in 1916, had already likened the black and coloured troops used by the English to Hagenbeck's famous circus.[74] War literature and war memoirs show a special hostility to blacks, and no fine distinctions were made between the Moroccans, Indian Sepoys, or Africans from Senegal. Stefan George, from his ivory tower, pontificated against the "Blutschmach," that is, the destruction of the white by black and yellow races.[75] The war not only furthered the stereotype of the German hero but also encouraged racial myths. France and England were not yet seen in racial terms, but the war helped Germans see the world as a struggle between races. By 1939, the Jews also became the victims of this inheritance of the war.

German Jews like Leo Baeck shared a common German tradition but bent it to different purposes. They continued to combine German idealism with the heritage of the Enlightenment. Leo Baeck, with some justice, blamed the Lutheran tradition for the worst in German thought and thus connected it with the destructiveness of the war. The Lutherans had created a paternal police state, a tradition Baeck contrasted to that of the Prussian Enlightenment. This Enlightenment put the state in the service of morality and attempted to improve all that was human. Significantly, looking at the destruction of the war, he added in 1919: "Prussian idealism with its optimistic belief in the future of all mankind has retained a home within the Jewish communities."[76] Historically that was a true observation, and one which helps to explain Baeck's own

[73] George L. Mosse, *Towards the Final Solution*, chapter xi.
[74] Walter Bloem, *Vormarsch* (Leipzig: Eisentraut, 1916), 306. Some Englishmen seemed to have agreed with the Germans in viewing the use of imperial black or colored troops in the war as an atrocity. Robert Graves, *Goodbye to All That* (New York: Longmann, 1957), 185.
[75] Eckart Koester, *Literatur und Weltkriegsideologie* (Kronberg, Ts: Scriptor-Verlag, 1977), 246.
[76] Leo Baeck, *Wege im Judentum* (Berlin: Schocken, 1933), 390.

attitude towards the war, the more so as he saw such enlightenment as part of the essence of Judaism. But this mixture between German idealism and the Enlightenment also influenced Zionists like Robert Weltsch, who wanted to give nationalism a human face.

To be sure, most German Jews succumbed to the almost irresistible temptation to share to the full the German war experience. But after the war, many had a rude reawakening and recaptured the liberal and Enlightenment tradition. At that time, establishment figures like Baeck had more in common with the left-wing Jewish intellectuals than they might have cared to admit. Both believed that man must be the end and never the means, and that war perverted the inherent virtues of man. It must be left to another time and place to show the similarity of thought between Baeck and the young Lion Feuchtwanger, between Robert Weltsch and Kurt Eisner. All that needs to be stated is the existence of a certain German-Jewish tradition, widely shared among Jews of different political persuasions, retaining ideals the war experience had helped to defeat. It is hardly surprising that so many Jews were willing to pay a high price in order to complete the process of assimilation, even if it meant accepting foreign and inherently hostile myths and structures of thought. But that a quite different German-Jewish tradition existed, which though it thought of itself as loyally German, opted to stand aside—this should fill us with pride and wonder.

CHAPTER VII

GEMEINSCHAFT AND GEMEINDE: THE IDEOLOGICAL AND INSTITUTIONAL TRANSFORMATION OF THE JEWISH COMMUNITY

Michael Brenner

Das Idol dieses Zeitalters ist die Gemeinschaft. Wie zum Ausgleich für die Harte und Schalheit unseres Lebens hat die Idee alles Süße bis zur Süßlichkeit, alle Zartheit bis zur Kraftlosigkeit, alle Nachgiebigkeit bis zur Würdelosigkeit in sich verdichtet.
—Helmuth Plessner, *Grenzen der Gemeinschaft* (1924)

The trauma of World War I dashed the hopes German Jews had, to be finally included in a German *Volksgemeinschaft*. Still, they shared with their non-Jewish neighbours the need to establish new forms of community. Some satisfied this need by emphasising their Germanness; others became socialists or communists; and many found refuge in the rediscovery of a Jewish Gemeinschaft. Only a few weeks after the outbreak of World War I, Martin Buber anticipated this strengthening of Gemeinschaft in a speech later reprinted as the opening essay in *Der Jude*:

> In the tempest of events the Jew has had the powerful experience of what Gemeinschaft means.... The most essential weakness of the Western Jew was not that he was "assimilated" but that he was atomized; that he was without connection [to the Jewish community]; that his heart no longer beat as one with a living Gemeinschaft ... ; that he was excluded from the life of the people and their holy Gemeinschaft. Judaism was no longer rooted, and the uprooted roots [*Luftwurzeln*] of his assimilation were without nourishing force. Now, however, in the catastrophic events that he experienced with his neighbors, the Jew discovered with shock and joy the great life of Gemeinschaft. And [this discovery] captured him.[1]

Buber and his fellow Zionists believed that the nineteenth-century confessionalisation of Judaism had led to an atomisation among German Jews, whose Judaism was now defined not as a framework

---

[1]   Martin Buber, "Die Losung," *Der Jude* 1 (1916), 1–2.

for communal life but as a private religious faith of individual German citizens. Indeed, by the end of the nineteenth century religion had become a divisive force among a populace split into Orthodox, liberals, and nonbelievers. Unlike in Eastern Europe, the Jewish population of Germany was not distinguished from its non-Jewish surroundings by such visible factors as languages or neighbourhoods. What then was the source of this image of communion that was in the minds of the members of this fragmented community?[2]

Buber's reference to a "community of blood" was familiar to many Zionists, who employed ethnic terms to define their ties to other Jews.[3] Liberal Jews, though rejecting the concept of a Jewish nation, also employed such ethnic terms as *Abstammungsgemeinschaft* (community of common descent) to express their belonging to a Jewish Gemeinschaft.[4] This definition of Gemeinschaft included all children of Jewish parents, regardless of what they believed or how they acted. When such acculturated German Jews as Walther Rathenau spoke of a Jewish *Stamm* (and compared it to the Bavarians or the Saxons) to emphasise their Germanness, they clearly departed from the nineteenth-century conception of Jewish identity as purely religious.[5] This Gemeinschaft of common descent remained, however, an invisible community, whose members could not be identified by dress, language, or religious practice.

Weimar Germany's organised Jewry aimed to change this rather vague sense of Gemeinschaft into a concrete culture, thus transforming

2   For a stimulating interpretation of community, see Anderson, *Imagined Communities: Reflections on the Origin and Spread of Nationalism* (London: Verso, 1991), 6.
3   For a discussion of German Zionists' view of a Jewish race see Efron, *Defenders of Race: Jewish Doctors and Race Science in Fin-De-Siècle Europe* (New Haven: Yale University Press, 1994), 123–174.
4   Jehuda Reinharz, *Fatherland and Promised Land: The Dilemma of the German Jew, 1893/1914* (Ann Arbor: University of Michigan Press, 1975), 227. On the concept of ethnicity, see Anthony D. Smith, *Ethnic Origin of Nations* (New York: Oxford University Press, 1986).
5   In a letter to the German nationalist Wilhelm Schwaner, Walter Rathenau wrote on 18 August 1916, "Mein Volk sind die Deutschen, niemand sonst. Die Juden sind für mich ein deutscher Stamm, wie Sachsen, Bayern oder Wenden." Walther Rathenau, *Briefe*, vol. 1 (Dresden: Carl Reissner, 1926), 220.

an invisible community into a visible one.[6] The sections of this chapter explore three aspects of the changing conception of community among German Jews: the influence of the debate about Gemeinschaft on the self-conception of liberal German Jews; the transformation of the Gemeinde, the local Jewish community, from an essentially religious congregation into a mainly secular institution; and the central role of cultural institutions within such a transformed Gemeinde.

THE IMPACT OF INTELLECTUAL TRENDS ON LIBERAL JUDAISM

German Jews probably had stronger ties to nineteenth-century German liberalism than most other segments of the German population, because their legal equality and acceptance in German society depended to a large extent on the success of liberal politics. The liberals promised to emancipate German Jews not because of love for Judaism but because of their firm principle that the inhabitants of a country should not be divided into first- and second-class citizens.

German Jews adopted many of liberalism's principles. Most Jews voted for the liberal parties and supported constitutional government;[7] they adhered to the principle of free trade, which suited their economic interests; and most German Jews replaced their traditional synagogue service with modern liturgy and introduced such aesthetic innovations as choir and organ. They firmly defended such liberal principles as personal freedom, individualism, rationalisation of religion, and the belief in progress. They welcomed their transformation from the ethnically distinct German Jewish society of the ghetto into a denomination of German citizens of Mosaic (or Israelite) faith.

Jews adhered to liberal doctrines as long as they were convinced that liberalism would pave the way for them to be accepted into German society. When the influence of liberal parties in German politics decreased, however, the social integration of Jews was blocked, and new antisemitism

---

6   On the concept of an "invisible subculture" among nineteenth-century German Jews, see David Sorkin, *Transformation of German Jewry, 1780–1840* (New York: Oxford University Press, 1987), 6–7.
7   Toury, *Politischen Orientierungen*, 110–169.

became more visible in the Bismarck era. When even the liberal parties hesitated to attack antisemitism openly and refused to admit Jewish candidates in the leading positions in national elections at the end of the *Kaiserreich*, many German Jews lost their faith in liberalism.

An increasing number of Jews thus shifted their vote to the Social Democratic Party (SPD). Although the economic interests of most German Jews conflicted with those of the Social Democrats, 12 out of 14 (unbaptised) Jewish members of the Reichstag of 1912 belonged to the SPD. In Weimar Germany, when the SPD gained respectability and the liberals lost further political ground, Jewish votes went equally to the SPD and the liberal parties and, to a smaller extent, to the conservatives and the Catholic Centre Party.[8]

In comparison to German society as a whole, in which the ideals of nineteenth-century liberalism were rapidly waning and liberal parties gradually disappeared from the political scene, Weimar Jewry appeared to be one of the last strongholds of liberal traditions. Contrary to the consensus among historians, however, the "symbiosis between Liberalism and the Jews" did not persist from emancipation until the years after 1933.[9] Most Jews in Weimar Germany would not have objected to being characterised as liberals, and the major Jewish organisations still referred to themselves as liberal, but their understanding of liberalism had undergone a profound transformation. During the two decades preceding the Nazi rise to power, liberal Jews abandoned such traditions as a purely religious definition of Judaism, dominance of rationalist thought, and cultural optimism.

Three facets of the quest for community characterised the transformation of liberal Judaism in Weimar Germany: the construction

---

[8] Ernest Hamburger and Peter Pulzer, "Jews as Voters in the Weimar Republic," *Leo Baeck Institute YearBook* 30 (1985), 3–66.

[9] George L. Mosse, "German Jews and Liberalism in Retrospect," *Leo Baeck Institute YearBook* 32 (1987), xiii-xxv, here xxiv. The main source for Mosse's analysis of liberal German Jews in the radical Reformgemeinde of Berlin. See also George L. Mosse, *German Jews Beyond Judaism* (Bloomington: Indiana University Press, 1985), 72–73. Similarly, Donald L. Niewyk maintains that German Jews "attached themselves to the liberal movement, and they retained that association until well into the Weimar Republic years." See Donald L. Niewyk, *Jews in Weimar Germany* (Baton Rouge: Louisiana State University Press, 1980), 3.

of a community based on common ethnicity rather than individual faith, as expressed by Germany's most important Jewish organisation, the CV; the emphasis on nonrational elements within the Jewish religion by a new generation of liberal rabbis; and the Romanticist antimodernism of the Jewish youth movement. All three elements signified a gradual departure from the nineteenth-century ideology aimed toward the acquisition of political equality. This departure signalled a shift in the traditional affinity between liberals and Jews and the construction of a new collective Jewish identity.

When the CV was founded in 1893, it defined itself as an *Abwehrverein*, an association whose purpose was to defend the legal equality of German Jews and fight antisemitism. By the First World War, however, significant changes in the CV's ideology had taken place. The CV had assumed the role of a *Gesinnungsverein*, which regarded the strengthening of the Jewish identity of its members as one of its most important tasks. Ironically, increasing antisemitism led to the political organisation of German Jews and ultimately to a rediscovery of positive values in Judaism.[10]

This change was first expressed clearly in a speech that Eugen Fuchs, the CV's chief thinker who would later become its president, made in 1913. Fuchs admitted that the original purpose of the CV was no longer sufficient: "We started as an Abwehrverein, and the more we practiced Abwehr the more we realized that Abwehr could not be done without knowledge, and without pride.... We became more contemplative, more positive, and more Jewish."[11] Fuchs introduced a new element into the self-definition of liberal German Jews when he emphasised that they were bound not only by a common religion but also by the

---

[10] This development is recognised in Ismar Schorsch, *Jewish Reactions to German Anti-Semitism, 1870–1914* (New York: Columbia University Press, 1972). A history of the CV in Weimar Germany, however, remains a desideratum. Sydney M. Bolkosky's *Distorted Image: German-Jewish Perceptions of German and Germany, 1918–1935* (New York: Elsevier, 1973), 16, presents a rather distorted image of the CV, identifying it with assimilation and not taking into account its internal development. Similarly, Donald L. Niewyk subtitled his chapter on liberal German Jews "The Search for an Assimilationist Identity." See Niewyk, *Jews in Weimar Germany*, 96.

[11] Eugen Fuchs, *Um Deutschtum und Judentum*, ed., Leo Hirschfeld (Frankfurt: Kauffmann, 1919), 236–237.

consciousness of common descent (*Stammesbewußtsein*).[12] Fuchs concluded that the term *Centralverein deutscher Staatsbürger jüdischen Glaubens* was outdated: "If I could create a new formula today, I would say, 'We are a Centralverein of Jewish Germans.'"[13]

The new emphasis on Jewish Stammesbewußtsein and on positive values of Judaism brought a renewed sense of Gemeinschaft to German Jews. One ought not to forget that Fuchs's speech was directed mainly against Zionism and its notion of a Jewish nation. Because liberal Jews vehemently rejected the existence of a Jewish nation (at least in Germany), they had to find an alternative to the Zionist sense of Gemeinschaft. In a relatively secularised society, religion was no longer a sufficient basis for community, and defence against antisemitism could hardly be regarded as an ideal common ground. Therefore, such terms as *Stammesgemeinschaft* and *Schicksalsgemeinschaft* (community of common fate) were gradually integrated into the ideology of the CV during World War I and in the Weimar period. Both terms indicated the search for a new sense of *Gemeinschaft*, a word much used and often misused in Germany, especially with reference to Ferdinand Tönnies's sociological study *Gemeinschaft und Gesellschaft* (Community and Society).

Originally published in 1887, *Gemeinschaft und Gesellschaft* attracted little attention beyond the academic realm. When a second edition appeared in 1912, however, the book was widely discussed, and during the Weimar years it was republished in several editions and popularised in many different versions.[14] The sudden interest in Tönnies's study was part of a passion for the term *Gemeinschaft* in Weimar Germany. Nationalist ideologues and politicians propagated a *Volksgemeinschaft*, Protestant theologians and Catholic social reformers spoke of a new religious community, philosophers discussed a *Philosophie der*

---

[12]   The German word *Stamm* literally means "tribe" or "race" and was often used as self-identification by German Jews who disliked the term nation and religion. It is related to *Abstammung* (descent) and *Stammesgemeinschaft* (community of descent). The popularity of its use can be partly explained by its vagueness. Assimilationists interpreted it in the sense of a German Stamm analogous to Bavarian or Saxons, but for Zionists, it became a synonym for a Jewish Volk.

[13]   Fuchs, *Um Deutschtum und Judentum*, 242.

[14]   See Alois Baumgartner, *Sehnsucht nach Gemeinschaft: Ideen und Strömungen im Sozialkatholizismus* (Munich: Ferdinan Schönigh, 1977), 40.

Gemeinschaft and an artificial Gesellschaft, and the youth movement aimed for the ideal of a genuine Gemeinschaft.[15] Opponents of an idealised sense of Gemeinschaft, such as the philosopher Helmuth Plessner, seemed like lonely prophets who had to admit that the quest for community had become the "idol of our time."[16]

Tönnies did not explicitly evaluate the terms *Gemeinschaft* and *Gesellschaft*. For him, Gemeinschaft represented "organic" relations, such as families, neighbourly relations, and village communities, whereas he saw Gesellschaft reflected in "mechanical" relations like business associations and urban administration. Tönnies envisioned the integration of certain forms of Gemeinschaft within a modern Gesellschaft, but the popularisers of his theories condemned modern Gesellschaft for representing a society of uprooted individuals and longed for a renewal of a genuine Gemeinschaft.[17]

Eugen Fuchs's comments must be seen in the context of the public discussion of Tönnies's book. Fuchs made it clear that Jews formed an organic Gemeinschaft rather than a mechanical Gesellschaft. What Fuchs only cautiously mentioned in 1913 was openly adopted by a younger generation of CV leaders in the 1920s. In February 1928, the CV's syndic, Ludwig Holländer, rejected the definition of German Jewry in terms of religious denomination. He was not reluctant to express bluntly that German Jewry was partly an *Unglaubensgemeinschaft* (community of lack of faith) rather than a *Glaubensgemeinschaft* (community of faith) and left no doubt that common descent united German Jews.[18]

---

[15] I shall mention only a few of the numerous lectures, essays, and studies discussing the renewal of Gemeinschaft. See, for example, Pau Natorop, *Individum und Gemeinschaft* (Jena, Germany: E. Diederichs, 1921); Erich Stern, *Über den Begriff der Gemeinschaft* (Langensaza: Beyer and Söhne, 1921); Hans Pichler, *Zur Logik der Gemeinschaft* (Tübingen: J. C. B. Mohr, 1924); and Franz Wilhelm Jerusalem, *Gemeinschaft und Staat* (Tübingen: J. C. B. Mohr, 1930). The motto of the 1928 conference of the German Philosophical Society was Philosophie der Gemeinschaft.

[16] Helmuth Plesner, *Grenzen der Gemeinschaft: Eine Kritik des sozialen Radikalismus* (Bonn: Bouvier Verlag Herbert Grundmann, 1972), 26.

[17] For a discussion of Tönnies and his reception by the German academic community, see Fritz K. Ringer, *The Decline of the German Mandarins: The German Academic Community, 1890–1933* (Cambridge, MA: Harvard University Press, 1969), 164–172.

[18] Ludwig Holländer, *Deutsch-jüdische Probleme der Gegenwart: Eine Auseinandersetzung*

In a much discussed article in the *Europäische Revue* of October 1930, Erich von Kahler, a Jewish historian and philosopher, tried to integrate the theory of Jewish descent into a systematic philosophical framework based on the difference between the character (*Wesensart*) of Jews and that of other Germans. Kahler was well known in German intellectual life primarily because of his critique of Max Weber's "Wissenschaft als Beruf" (Wissenschaft as vocation), which he published under the title "Der Beruf der Wissenschaft" (The profession of Wissenschaft),[19] Influenced by the neo-Romantic ideas of the George circle, Kahler rejected Weber's liberal rationalism as well as that of the principal philosopher of liberal Judaism, Hermann Cohen, and the founders of the CV. Kahler believed that Jews should admit that they were a distinct Stamm, different from the German *Stämme*. Unlike the antisemites, however, Kahler denied that this difference should lead to the exclusion of Jews from German society. Quite the contrary: *because* of their difference, Kahler argued, German Jews could contribute much to German society. This was exactly the reverse of the original ideology of the CV. Instead of claiming that individual Jews should be integrated into society on the basis of their equality with non-Jewish Germans, Kahler maintained that the German Jewish Stamm should be tolerated in German society because of its differences.[20]

Kahler did not represent the CV, but one of the younger CV leaders explicitly endorsed Kahler's view. The CV's Bavarian syndic, Werner Cahnmann, assured Kahler that "there are no basic differences whatsoever between our views and yours." In a second letter, Cahnmann went further:

> I am of the opinion that our friends in the camp of liberalism and Enlightenment ... are dangerous friends for us. Because rationalism dissolves all kind of distinctive existence [Sonderart] ... , it also dissolves distinctive Jewish existence.... The maintenance [of a distinctive Jewish existence] is only possible in alliance with the Romantic forces in German Bildung.[21]

über die Grundfrage des Central-Vereins deutscher Staatsbürger jüdischen Glaubens E. V. (Berlin: Philo-Verlag, 1929), 14.

[19] For a discussion of this essay, see Ringer, *German Mandarins*, 358–359.

[20] Erich von Kahler, "Juden und Deutsche," *Europäische Revue* 6 (1930), 744–756.

[21] Werner Cahnmann to Erich von Kahler, 27 November 1930, 31 December 1930, Erich von Kahler Collection, LBI-AR, 3890.

Cahnmann explicitly referred to Kahler when he published an article in *Der Morgen* in which he demanded the integration of German Jews, as a group with distinctive characteristics, into German society. As Cahnmann recalled, a "small-scale internal revolution" took place in the CV during the late 1920s; and his ideas, reversing nineteenth-century emancipation ideology, were shared by an increasing number of leading CV members.[22]

The changing position of the CV represented only one facet of Jewish liberalism in Weimar Germany. Its emphasis on the Stammesgemeinschaft should not be confused with the abandonment of religion. In his memoirs, Caesar Seligmann, a Frankfurt rabbi and long-time president of the Union of Liberal Rabbis in Germany, juxtaposed the passivity of liberal Judaism at the end of the nineteenth century with its fresh spirit in the first decades of the twentieth century.[23] Seligmann may have exaggerated the extent of revitalisation of liberal Judaism, in which he played a leading part, but a variety of documents and personal recollections leave no doubt that a changing spirit was perceived among liberal German Jews around the turn of the century. In many respects, this change was a reaction to contemporary Jewish and non-Jewish movements: the rise of Zionism, the popularity of East European Jewish spirituality as Buber presented it, and a parallel renewal of religiosity in Protestant and Catholic circles.[24] More deeply, it had the same causes as

---

[22] Werner Cahnmann, "Judentum und Volksgemeinschaft," *Der Morgen* 2 (1926), 291–298; Werner Cahnmann, "The Nazi-Threat and the Central-Verein: A Recollection," manuscript, Werner Cahnmann Collection, LBI-AR, 556, p. 6. Two of the younger CV leaders who argued against a purely religious definition of Judaism were Ludwig Tietz and Friedrich Brodnitz. The participation of such liberal Germans Jews as Leo Baeck and Julius Blau in the enlarged Jewish Agency created by the World Zionist Organization in 1928 was a further indication of the CV's shift in attitude.

[23] Caesar Seligmann, *Erinnerungen*, ed., Erwin Seligmann (Frankfurt: Waldemar Kramer, 1975), 119–120. See also the contemporary statement of another liberal German rabbi, Felix Goldmann of Leipzig, who characterised the last remnants of nineteenth-century radical reform congregations in Germany as "able neither to live nor to die." Felix Goldmann, "Das liberale Judentum," in *Das Deutsches Judentum: Seine Parteien und Organisationen. Eine Sammelschrift* (Berlin: Verlag der Neuen Jüdischen Monatshefte, 1919), 19–20.

[24] Some of the most popular products of the "new thinking" in Jewish theology were reactions to the contemporary debates in Bible scholarship that attacked the most important sources of Judaism. Franz Delitzsch's *Babel und Bibel* (Leizig: J. C. Hinrichs, 1902) questioned the originality of many central concepts of the Hebrew Bible, and

those movements: the search for spiritual support in an age increasingly dominated by materialism, and the longing for religious and ethnic roots in a rapidly urbanising, anonymous society.

One of the main features of the transformation of liberal Judaism in Weimar Germany was its gradual detachment from the optimistic belief in human reason and progress. This development must be seen in relation to the general intellectual framework and especially in relation to contemporary Protestantism. Belief in human reason, scientific progress, and the settlement of theological questions by historical analysis had characterised Protestant liberalism from Friedrich Schleiermacher to Adolf von Harnack, but these beliefs were shattered in the early twentieth century. In 1906, Albert Schweitzer pointed to the self-deception of historical analysis in *The Quest for the Historical Jesus*; a decade later, Rudolf Otto rediscovered the "numinous element" in the Old Testament and stressed the nonrational elements in Luther in *The Idea of the Holy* (1917), the most widely read theological work in Weimar Germany. Between 1922 and 1933, "postliberal" thinking was published in the journal *Zwischen den Zeiten* (Between the times), a forum in which a younger generation of theologians rejected their teachers' rational belief in progress.

A similar development occurred in the field of philosophy. The official summary of the tenth convention of the German Philosophical Society in Leipzig in 1928 emphasised that, "The discussions in Leipzig and their after-effects revolved in large part around the problem of the irrational."[25] It was certainly no coincidence that the rising star among German philosophers in the last days of Weimar was Martin Heidegger, whose Philosophy of Being repudiated both rationalism and scientific progress.

In Jewish thought this trend was best characterised in Franz Rosenzweig's *Star of Redemption*, the three parts of which reflected different aspects of the "new thinking" as expressed by a liberal German

---

Adolf Harnack's *Wesen des Christentums* (Leipzig: J. C. Hinrichs, 1900) called for Christians to remove themselves from the Old Testament.

[25] Felix Krueger, *Philosophie der Gemeinschaft: 7 Vorträge, gehalten auf der Tagung der Deutschen Philosophischen Gesellschaft vom 1.-4. Oktober 1928 in Leipzig* (Berlin: Junker und Dünnhaupt, 1929), 155.

Jew. The first section stresses the subjectivity of truth; in the second section, Rosenzweig analyses the continuous relationship between humans and God on the basis of revelation; the final portion argues for the existence of Jewish history outside the course of general history.[26]

The Star of Redemption was a reaction to the elimination of the concept of revelation in Judaism by many nineteenth-century German Jewish thinkers. This development was related to the more general cleansing of nonrational elements from Judaism, which found a last expression in *The Religion of Reason out of the Sources of Judaism* (1919), the posthumously published work of Rosenzweig's own teacher, Hermann Cohen. Cohen, the neo-Kantian philosopher of Marburg who in his last years taught at the liberal rabbinical seminary in Berlin, represented a nineteenth-century view shared by the bulk of contemporary liberal rabbis and the first generations of scholars of Wissenschaft des Judentums. In their view, the emphasis on revelation and other concepts originating beyond human reason constituted an aberration from the rational course of Jewish history and the rational essence of Judaism. They had a special disdain for Jewish mysticism, as illustrated by the words of the Posen rabbi Philipp Bloch, told in anecdotal form by Gershom Scholem. Impressed by Bloch's immense collection of Kabbalistic works, a young scholar inquired of him why he read so much mystical literature. The old rabbi looked at his library and replied, "What, am I supposed to *read* this rubbish, too?"[27]

The premier figure of liberal Judaism in Weimar Germany, Rabbi Leo Baeck, signalled the changing spirit of liberal German Judaism in his second edition (1922) of *The Essence of Judaism,* originally published in 1905 as a reply to Adolf Harnack's *Essence of Christianity*. In the first edition, Baeck basically had adopted the rational framework of Hermann Cohen, but the second edition included significant modifications.

---

[26] On the Star of Redemption see Stéphane Moses, *System und Offenbarung Die Philosophie Franz Rosenzweigs* (Munich: W. Fink, 1985), and Paul Mendes-Flohr, *The Philosophy of Franz Rosenzweig* (Hanover: University Press of New England, 1988).

[27] Gershom Scholem, *From Berlin to Jerusalem: Memories of My Youth* (New York: Schocken, 1980), 150. Bloch, one of the most learned and respected liberal rabbis in Germany and long-time president of the liberal rabbinical association, was in fact the author of several essays on Kabbalah.

Baeck never refuted his rationalist outlook, but as historian Michael Meyer summarises, in the revised version of *Essence of Judaism*, the "moral and rational elements in Judaism, as well as its universal goals, are increasingly balanced by their polar counterparts, which achieve equivalent importance. However strong the moral bond between God and humans, Baeck came to believe that religion encompassed more. It was forced to acknowledge the unfathomability of the Divine, to appreciate what reason could not fully grasp."[28]

As Albert Friedlander noted, Baeck's prototype in Jewish philosophy was not the rational Maimonides, who was celebrated by Baeck's predecessors, but the nonrational Yehudah Halevi.[29] Unlike Philipp Bloch and many of his older colleagues, Leo Baeck considered Kabbalistic literature a source of inspiration for modern liberal Judaism. Baeck's publications after World War I concentrated increasingly on topics of Jewish mysticism.[30] In his obituary for Nehemias Anton Nobel, an Orthodox rabbi of Frankfurt, Baeck appreciated first and foremost Nobel's reintegration of mystical elements into Judaism.[31]

Leo Baeck succeeded Nobel as president of the General Rabbinical Association of Germany in 1922 and became the leading representative of the German rabbinate throughout the remainder of the Weimar period. His colleagues also integrated nonrational elements into liberal Judaism. When asked to define liberal Judaism in a short essay, Leipzig liberal rabbi Felix Goldmann stressed the relations between Hasidism and liberal Judaism. Goldmann saw Hasidism no longer as a

---

[28] Michael A. Meyer, *Response to Modernity: A History of the Reform Movement in Judaism* (New Zork: Oxford University Press, 1988), 207–208. Baeck's biographer, Albert Friedlander, expresses a similar view when he calls the change from Baeck's earlier writings to his later ones the "move from essence to existence." Albert H. Friedlander, *Leo Baeck: Teacher of Theresienstadt* (New York: Holt, Rinehart and Winston, 1968), 103.
[29] Friedlander, *Leo Baeck*, 101.
[30] Baeck's new interest in nonrational aspects of Judaism was best expressed in his essay "Geheimniss und Gebot" in *Wege im Judentum: Aufsätze und Reden* (Berlin: Schocken, 1933), 33–48. On this subject see also Alexander Altmann's important essay, "Leo Baeck and the Jewish Mystical Tradition," *Leo Baeck Memorial Lecture* 17 (1973).
[31] Leo Baeck, "Nehemias Anton Nobel zum Gedenken," in *Korrespondenzblatt für die Gründung und Erhaltung einer Akademie der Wissenschaft des Judentums* 3 (1922), 1–3.

"daughter of darkness which is born in the dark and continues to walk on dark paths" (Graetz) but as "born in the spirit of liberalism." On the other hand, the Enlightenment philosopher Moses Mendelssohn, the undisputed hero of nineteenth-century liberal Jews, was now seen as "having contributed little to the religious development" of Judaism; his friends and successors—much celebrated a generation before—were called by Goldmann in 1919 the representatives of "Protestantism in Jewish garb" [ein jüdisch frisierter Protestantismus].[32]

The changing mood among liberal German rabbis was clearly reflected in their annual conventions. During the first postwar meeting, in 1921, Rabbi Max Dienemann of Offenbach delivered a speech called "On the Importance of the Irrational for Liberal Judaism." In this lecture, which amounted to a systematic criticism of nineteenth-century religious Jewish liberalism, Dienemann voiced his deep shame over "our superficiality and our lack of depth." Dienemann confessed that the rationalisation of Judaism by liberal Jews had torn the roots from the tree of Judaism and gradually dried it out. He complained that the partial replacement of Hebrew by German as the language of prayer and the abolition of several Jewish rituals and laws had negative repercussions. "One thought purely rationally; one imagined that the better one understands his prayers, the more one would pray. But one did not think of the nonrational element of the emotion, which is tied to the Hebrew language." The time of rationalism had passed: "It is a characteristic of our time that the irrational is dominant, that one cannot answer questions—as has been done in the previous era—out of contemplation, cool examination, rational thought, explanation, and scientific orientation, not at all out of clarity, but out of the dark, the instinctive, the inexplicable, the mystical forces."[33]

Dienemann, who later became the editor of the most prestigious liberal German Jewish journal, *Der Morgen*, and the last president of

---

[32] For Goldmann see *Deutsches Judentum*, p. 19–20; for Heinrich Graetz, see *Geschichte des Judentums von den ältesten Zeiten bis auf die Gegenwart*, vol. 11 (Leizig: Oskar Leiner, 1900), 94.

[33] Max Dienmann, "Über die Bedeutung des Irrationalen für das Liberale Judentum," *Liberales Judentum* 13, nos. 4–6 (1921), 29.

the Union of Liberal Rabbis in Germany, welcomed this development. He believed that it brought new life to Judaism and that therefore the task of liberal Judaism was to integrate nonrational elements into its ideology: "Today, thank God, one again knows that reason is not the ultimate force. One feels mysteries and is willing to immerse oneself in them. One hungers for positive emotions, for steadfastness and support, one is tired of the individual way of life and recognizes community and feelings of togetherness.... It is our task to create a synthesis of the rational and the irrational forces."[34]

An even stronger push away from rationalism was visible among the younger generation of liberal German rabbis, as represented by Max Wiener. Wiener, born in 1882, grew up in the Silesian town of Oppeln while Leo Baeck, then a young rabbi, was serving there. Wiener's and Baeck's paths were to cross several times. On completion of his rabbinical studies, Wiener became an assistant rabbi to Baeck in Düsseldorf, and after Wiener went to Stettin for a short stay, they became colleagues as *Gemeinderabbiner* of Berlin. While Baeck was still wavering between rationalism and nonrational elements, Wiener's break with nineteenth-century liberal traditions was complete. In his programmatic speech at the convention of liberal German rabbis in Berlin in January 1922, Wiener held Judaism's nineteenth-century rational *weltanschauung* responsible for the poor condition of modern Jewish religiosity.[35] He demanded a religious renewal based on the integration of nonrational elements—the feeling of belonging to the Jewish people and the self-consciousness of the particularity of the Jews as a chosen people—into modern Judaism. As Wiener's biographer, Robert S. Schine, has observed, Wiener's "historical-metaphysical irrationalism" constituted an assimilation of Romantic nationalism into liberal Judaism.[36]

For Wiener, religious acts based on revealed law, not rational doctrines, were the basis of Judaism. His critical position toward the

---

[34] Ibid., 32.

[35] "Verhandlungen und Beschlüsse der Versammlungen der Liberalen Rabbiner Deutschlands," *Liberales Judentum* 14, nos. 1–3 (1922), 5–9.

[36] Robert S. Schine, *Jewish Thought Adrift: Max Wiener (1882–1950)* (Atlanta: Scholars Press, 1992), 109–120.

development of German Judaism in the nineteenth century was also reflected in his book *Jüdische Religion im Zeitalter der Emanzipation* (Judaism in the time of emancipation). This work was one of the most important studies written by a liberal rabbi in the Weimar period and served as an epitaph for liberal Judaism in Germany. When it was published in 1933, both Liberalism and Judaism had become invectives.

Leo Baeck, Max Dienemann, and Max Wiener represented the new leadership of the liberal German rabbinate.[37] While such scholars as Gershom Scholem started to grasp the importance of the mythical element in the Jewish religion, such rabbis as Baeck, Wiener, and Dienemann tried to reintegrate nonrational elements into theological interpretations of contemporary Judaism. This process constituted a reversal of the rational Enlightenment traditions that had emphasised the common elements of all monotheistic religions and culminated in the propagation of one deistic faith. The renewal of nonrational traditions paved the way for marking once again the borderlines that separated religions. After a century of increasing acculturation, liberal German rabbis felt the need to stress the distinct character of Judaism and thus strengthen the collective identity among German Jews.

In an increasingly nonliberal environment, many German Jews were hesitant to continue liberal traditions. Franz Rosenzweig most eloquently summarised the crisis of liberal Judaism in his poignant words, "The Liberal German-Jewish standpoint on which almost all of German Judaism had enough room for nearly a century has become so tiny that apparently only one person—I myself—can live there. Poor Hermann Cohen."[38]

The transformation of liberal Judaism was most dramatically

---

[37] Their critical view toward the rational tradition of liberal Judaism was shared by numerous other liberal rabbis. Cologne rabbi Isidor Caro rejected the elevation of reason to the ultimate ideal of Judaism (*Gemeindeblatt der Deutsch-Israelitischen Gemeinde Hamburg*, 10 January 1927, 1), and Rabbi Max Elk of Stettin held rationalism responsible for the long passivity of liberal Jews (Bayerische Israelitische Gemeindezeitung, 13 December 1927), 373.

[38] Franz Rosenzweig, *Briefe und Tagebücher*, ed., Rachel Rosenzweig and Edith Rosenzweig-Scheinemann. *Vol. 1 of Franz Rosenzweig. Der Mensch und sein Werk* (The Hague: M. Nijhoff, 1979), 980.

expressed by the younger generation. In his pioneering study on the German youth movement, Walter Laqueur distinguishes the prewar *Wandervogel* era from the Weimar period, dominated by the *Bunde*. Emerging out of the hiking traditions of the Wandervogel, the Bunde clung to a blend of Romanticism, teetotalism, nationalist thought, and a strong belief in the principle of leadership. When antisemitism in the youth movement became palpable shortly before World War I, Jews founded their own movements. The first was Blau-Weiss (established in 1907 in Breslau and in 1912 nationwide), a Zionist organisation that transformed elements of German nationalism into Jewish nationalism. The influence of the German Wandervogel youth movement on the Blau-Weiss was obvious. Its hiking tours and songs expressed a Romantic love for nature and the collective experience. Zionist ideals were prominent in the Blau-Weiss program, but often, as the seventeen-year-old Gerhard (Gershom) Scholem criticised, these ideals remained theoretical.[39]

Liberal Jewish youth also adopted the essential elements of the German youth movement, giving first priority to ties with nature and organising countless hiking tours. The bulletins of the liberal youth movement were full of letters in which idealistic Jewish youngsters explained to their worried bourgeois parents or to "effeminate" brothers why they went for one-week hikes, slept in tents, and ate from tin plates. The Jewish youth movement shared with its non-Jewish counterpart a general rejection of the bourgeois home, with the added incentive that the Jewish homes may have been even more bourgeois than those of many of their non-Jewish comrades.

The Jewish and non-Jewish youth movements shared an immense admiration for spiritual leaders. What Gustav Wyneken and Hans Bluher had been for the Wandervogel and the Bunde, Martin Buber

---

[39] In three pamphlets entitled "Die blau-weiße Brille," Scholem demanded that the Zionist youth take emigration to Palestine more seriously and promote the knowledge of Hebrew and Judaism. The essence of Scholem's criticism appeared in his essay "Jüdische Jugendbewegung," *Der Jude* 1 (1917), 822–825 (translated in Gershom Scholem, *On Jews and Judaism in Crisis: Selected Essays*, ed., Werner J. Dannhauser [New York: Schocken, 1976], 44–53. See also Moshe Rinott, "Major Trends in Jewish Youth Movement in Germany," *Leo Baeck Institute YearBook* 19 (1974), 87–90.

was for many young Jews.[40] Without taking Buber's philosophy too seriously, the youth movement adopted his Romanticism and his call for originality and saw in the East European Hasidim an equivalent to the German peasant ideal. The terminology of the Jewish youth movement imitated that of the German youth movement. There were Jewish *Knubbels* and *Pimpfe*, *Führer* and *Schwarze Haufen*. In letters of 1925 among members of the Kameraden youth group, the greeting *Heil* was still commonly used. It was partially replaced by the Hebrew *Shalom* in later years.[41]

In the 1920s, about one-third of young German Jews belonged to one of the Jewish youth organisations. The mainstream Verband der jüdischen Jugendvereine had 41,000 members. Although most of them were children of CV adherents, this organisation differed from its parent organisation in its idealisation of healthy rural life and small-town Jewish communities. Like Zionist youth groups, it "rejected liberalism, rationalism, materialism, and solutions that revolved around the individual."[42] For all the youth groups, Jewish issues were important. Most German Jewish families practiced shallow forms of Judaism, and Jewish children rejected this shallowness as part of the bourgeois spirit of their parents. The *Kameraden* began to study Hebrew and organise reading sessions of the new Buber-Rosenzweig edition of the Bible. As one of them recalled, they "somehow sought a Jewish way of life. All this search was based more on Romanticism than on a deep religious urge .... One section of the Kameraden came to the conclusion that they were Germans by language, way of life, and homeland, but Jews by 'blood.'"[43]

Another section of the Kameraden stressed its ties to the German homeland. But both groups expressed their affiliations in similar terms; while the German Jews gathered around their campfires and recited

---

[40] See Chaim Schatzker, "Martin Buber's Influence on the Jewish Youth Movement in Germany," *LBIYB* 23 (1978), 151–171.

[41] Bundesarchiv, Potsdam, Wanderbund Kameraden 75 C Wa 1, folder 16.

[42] Glenn Richard Sharfman, "Jewish Youth Movement: in Weimar Germanz, 1900-1936; A Study in Ideology and Organisation." Ph.D dissertation, University of North Carolina, 1989, 436.

[43] Eliyahu Maoz, "Werkleute," *Leo Baeck Institute YearBook* 4 (1959), 167.

Martin Buber's *Hasidic Tales*, the Jewish Germans met at medieval castles to read Stefan George. Although they rejected the Zionist idea of a Jewish nation, the liberal Jewish youth organisations adopted much of the Zionist agenda of a revival of Jewish solidarity. If they read Buber or George (and most read both), they did it as Jews who were in search of a new sense of Gemeinschaft, one that was no longer phrased in the language of rationalism.

Hiking tours, though important to all German youth groups, were more significant for young Jews. No other group had undergone as rapid an urbanisation as German Jews. At the beginning of the nineteenth century they lived almost exclusively in villages and small towns; a hundred years later, they were highly concentrated in big cities. In 1933, one-third of Germany's half million Jews lived in Berlin. Jews were often stereotyped as urban dwellers, and both youths and adults were eager to prove that Jews actually had strong ties to nature.

In his article "Community in the Big City," Leo Baeck summarised the dangers of urban life, its anonymity, and its numerous temptations, which had not existed in the traditional rural Jewish community, but Baeck also mentioned the social and cultural advantages of the urban Jewish community.[44] Criticism of modern urban life and idealisation of rural Jewish life and East European Jewry were sometimes voiced in the language of neo-Romanticism and cultural pessimism. As members of Zionist youth organisations recalled, Hermann Hesse's *Demian* and Oswald Spengler's *Decline of the West* were just as popular as Theodor Herzl's *Old-New Land* and Martin Buber's *Hasidic Tales*.[45]

Spengler's cultural pessimism was not restricted to the youth movement or Zionist circles. When the B'nai B'rith lodge of Germany published a special journal for its 1921 meeting, it stressed the difference between culture and civilisation. Lodge member Fritz Kahn, author of *Die Juden als Rasse und Kulturvolk* (The Jews as a race and a people of culture, 1920), expressed in specifically Jewish terms the

---

[44]   Leo Baeck, "Gemeinde in der Großstadt," *Der Morgen* 5 (1929), 583–390.
[45]   See Ernst Noam, "Erinnerungen und Dialog," LBI-AR ME, 70, and Herbert Nussbaum, "Weg und Schicksal eines deutschen Juden," LBI-AR, ME, 8. On the radical rejection of urban Jewish life and its materialism, see Alfred Lemm [Lehmann], "Großstadtkultur und Juden," *Der Jude* 1 (1916–1917), 316–317.

ideas of Spengler, Thomas Mann, and others who juxtaposed German culture and Western civilisation. Civilisation, Kahn maintained, was modern urban life adopted by Jews only after they had been absorbed into European society in the nineteenth century, whereas culture was truly representative of Judaism: "*Zivilisation* surrounds us when we ride on the electric streetcar through the bustle of the streets, when we hear the evening telegrams on illuminated squares ... , and when a Mercedes whizzes by with sixty horsepower.... But when we have entered our house, and see from inside the splendor of the Sabbath candles ... , when we enter the room from which the millennia-old *Schir hamalaus* sounds ... in this hour we are surrounded outwardly and inwardly by culture."[46]

By the end of the 1920s, when the youth movement had become a substantial part of the cultural life of German Jews, its activities were increasingly integrated into the institutional framework of the Jewish community. The demand of Brunswick rabbi Paul Rieger that Jewish communities grant generous financial subsidies for youth activities and establish permanent homes for Jewish youth (*Jugendheime*) was realised in most large communities.[47] The Jewish community of Breslau, for example, established a Jugendheim that became the centre of a rich cultural program, with a library and a number of special events in music, literature, and sports. The Jewish community of Hamburg opened a *Jugendamt* (youth welfare office) in 1921, which was followed by a *Landjugendheim* (countryside youth centre) ten years later. Some communities employed special youth rabbis, who would concentrate all

---

[46]　Fritz Kahn, "Neue Wege jüdischer Kultur," *Festnummer zum Ordenstag: Großloge für Deutschland VIII. U.O.B.B.* (October 1921), 93–95. Kahn's distinction between civilization and culture reflected one aspect of a transformation of the German B'nai B'rith lodges in the Weimar period. By the end of the 1920s, the lodge was for many members no longer a place for sociability and charity but an Erlebnisbund (association of common experience). See, for example, Fritz Wielunder, "Der Weg der Loge von der Gesinnungsgemeinschaft zum Erlebnisbunde," *Der Orden Bne Briss* (June- July 1928), 77–80.

[47]　Siegfried Bernfeld Collection, YIVO, RG 6, folder 41: "Die jüdischen Jugendvereine und die Gemeinden: Leitsäte von Landesrabbiner Dr. Rieger" (n. d.). See also Max Grunwald, "Jüdische Jugend und jüdische Gemeinde," *Jüdische Wolfahrtsplege und Sozialfürsorge* 2 (1931), 65–72.

local youth activities under the auspices of a distinct *Jugendgemeinde* (youth community).[48]

The Jewish youth movement arose on the eve of World War I in opposition to the established Jewish organisations and institutions.[49] During the 15 years of the Weimar period, it contributed significantly to the transformation of the Jewish establishment and its most important pillar, the local Jewish community. In the youth movement, the new sense of Gemeinschaft among German Jews first found its institutional expression.

THE TRANSFORMATION OF THE LOCAL JEWISH COMMUNITY

English makes no distinction between *Gemeinschaft* and *Gemeinde*, and both words are usually rendered as community. In German, the two terms have different meanings: *Gemeinschaft* refers to a general communal solidarity, and *Gemeinde* usually stands for an institution representing a certain form of Gemeinschaft, such as a municipal administration or a religious congregation. The traditional Jewish Gemeinde, the *Kehillah*, was a semi-autonomous institution representing the local Jewish population. When Jews began to gain political equality, the Kehillah lost its legal and cultural autonomy in Central European and Western European countries. In contrast to the Jewish congregations of most other countries, which were voluntary unions fulfilling mainly religious purposes, the Jewish Gemeinde in Germany retained some of the characteristics of the premodern Kehillah.[50]

The German Jewish Gemeinde remained a publicly constituted corporation based on the principle of compulsory membership and

---

[48]   See, for example, Max Grünwald, "Zur Errichtung der Jugendgemeinde," Die Jugendbewegung: Beilage zum Israelitschen Gemeindeblatt Mannheim, 25 Mannheim 1926, 1. On Hamburg: Lorenz, *Juden in Hamburg*, 869–893. On Breslau: Jüdisches Gemeindeblatt Breslau, vol. 8, no. 2 (February 1931), appendix.

[49]   The rise of the Jewish Youth Movement in Germany was parallel to the development of interwar French Jewry. See Paula Hyman, *From Dreyfus to Vichy: The Remaking of French Jewry, 1906–1939* (New York: Columbia University Press, 1979), 179–198.

[50]   See Kurt Wilhelm, "Jewish Community in the Post-Emancipation Period," *Leo Baeck Institute YearBook* 2 (1957), 47–75.

empowered by the state to levy taxes on its members. It included all the Jews in anyone place of residence, and anybody who left it left Judaism at the same time. In 1876, this rule changed slightly when the Prussian *Austrittsgesetz* enabled Jews to be members of separatist communities without leaving Judaism. Neither this nor later legal reforms, however, significantly altered the character of Jewish communities. Most German Jews remained within the structure of the Gemeinden, to which they paid their taxes.

The modern German Jewish Gemeinde had lost much of the traditional Kehillah's autonomy, but it was more comprehensive than a religious congregation. The representatives of the Gemeinden could emphasise different aspects of the communities' activities at different times. In the early nineteenth century, most communities adopted as their official designation the term *Israelitische Religionsgemeinde* or *Kultusgemeinde*, thus underlining their religious character. In the nineteenth century, the Religionsgemeinde contained such secular institutions as schools, hospitals, and old-age homes, but the synagogues were its undisputed centre. Consequently, internal debates between liberal and Orthodox representatives focused mostly on issues of synagogue decorum, such as the introduction of organ music and the status of the rabbi.

With the emergence of Zionism at the turn of the twentieth century, this situation began to change. Following Theodor Herzl's appeal for the "conquest of the *Gemeindestube*," the Zionists soon emerged as a third party in the elections for the assemblies of representatives of the Gemeinden.[51] By reopening the debate on the self-definition of Judaism, they also questioned the self-definition of the Jewish Gemeinde. According to the Zionists, Jews were united not by religion but by nationality, so they intended to transform the Gemeinde from a Religionsgemeinde or Kultusgemeinde into a broad local framework representing a national minority (*Volksgemeinde*).

Before World War I, major changes could not be made in the Gemeinden because of the undemocratic voting system and the

---

[51] See Shmu'el Ma'ayan, *Ha-behirot be-kehilat Berlin, 1901–1920* (Givat Haviva: Zvi Lurie Institute for the Study of Zionism, 1977), and Ma'ayan, *Ha-behirot be-kehilot Köln, 1900–1921* (Givat Haviva: Zvi Lurie Institute for the Study of Zionism, 1979).

small size of the Zionist electorate. After 1918, however, the Jewish communities underwent a process of democratisation that ultimately led to their profound transformation. The most visible change occurred on the supralocal level. The liberal establishment successfully resisted Zionist attempts to establish a democratically elected Jewish Congress in Germany, but such elections took place in the supracommunal organisations that had been established shortly after World War I in the two largest German states. Jewish parliaments were elected for the first time in Bavaria in 1921 and in Prussia in 1925.[52]

Members of the old establishment in the local Jewish communities initially resisted such a development, without being able to prevent it. Most Jewish communities, reflecting other political developments in Germany, introduced universal suffrage on the basis of proportional representation in the Weimar period. With a few exceptions, they granted voting rights to women, immigrant citizens, and non-taxpayers.[53]

The democratisation of the Jewish community was intimately connected with its politicisation. The *Jüdisches Jahrbuch für Gross-Berlin* described this change: "The question of 'liberal or conservative' was not enough to describe all the problems. The profound question, what Judaism and Jewishness meant, broadened the hitherto existing questions and led, by its divergent answers, necessarily to the creation of new parties."[54] The new parties emerging within the Jewish community were built around political platforms, not religious concepts. In Berlin, parties ranged from the socialist Poalei Zion, led by Oskar Cohn, former Social Democratic member of the Reichstag, to the Deutsche Liste of Max Naumann's extremely conservative Verband nationaldeutscher Juden. A manifesto of the Poalei Zion from

[52] On Prussia, see Max P. Birnbaum, *Staat und Synagoge*, 1918–1938: Eine Geschichte des Preußischen Landesverbands Jüdischer Gemeinden (Tübingen: J. C. B. Mohr, 1981).
[53] The fight for universal suffrage took many years and encountered considerable resistance in most communities. In Leipzig, Chemnitz and a few other places with a high percentage of Ostjuden, German immigrants who were not citizens never attained equal voting rights, and neither did women in Cologne. See Marioin Kaplan, *Jewish Feminist Movement: The Campaign of the Jüdischer Frauenbund, 1904–1938* (Westport: Greenwood Press, 1979), 271.
[54] *Jüdisches Jahrbuch für Gross-Berlin auf das Jahr 1926* (Berlin: Scherbel, 1926), 115–116.

1920 illustrates the degree to which the Jewish community's election campaigns had become politicised and secularised: "The legend that the Jewish people is only a religious community must be brought to an end. All concerns of worship [*Kultusangelegenheiten*] must be eliminated from the tasks of the community and shall be given to a voluntary organisation. The community must contain all affairs of culture and learning, education and instruction, immigration and migration, legal and political protection, economic need and housing problems, gymnastics, sports, and statistics." The Nationaldeutsche Juden also advocated the secularisation of the Jewish community, although its members had different motives. In the same election campaign, they distributed leaflets saying, "The election campaign must not be a struggle of religious conceptions, it must be a decisive struggle about our Germanness [*Deutschtum*]!"[55]

The most important party to emerge after World War I was the Jüdische Volkspartei (JVP), an alliance of Zionist, Ostjude, Orthodox, and lower-middle-class Jews. The principal goal of the JVP was to transform the Jewish community into a Volksgemeinde. Although it sought to care for the religious needs of its members, the JVP considered social welfare and cultural activities most important. In a pamphlet of 1919, a leading JVP activist envisioned the Volksgemeinde as the "representation of the Jews as a national minority that autonomously determines its cultural activities based on its particular *Volkseigenart*."[56]

The main rivals of the JVP were the long-established Liberals, who fought officially for the continuation of the Kultusgemeinden, in which religious institutions would remain central. By the end of the 1920s many elections had been reduced to a duel between the Liberals and the JVP. Those two parties received 87 percent of the vote in the 1930 Berlin Gemeinde elections, although ten parties had nominated candidates. The third major faction, the Orthodox, received less than 5 percent of the vote.[57]

The biggest success for the JVP was the overthrow of the Liberals in Berlin, where they had been the majority party for more than half a

---

[55] Both quotes are from Central Zionist Archive, Jerusalem, Alfred Klee Collection, A 142/87/2.
[56] Emil Simonsohn, *Die Jüdische Volksgemeinde* (Berlin: Jüdischer Verlag, 1919), 29.
[57] *Jüdische Rundschau*, 2 December 1930, 639.

century. In the elections of 1926, the Liberals lost their absolute majority, and a coalition of JVP and Orthodox determined the community's fate during the next four years. For the first time a Zionist, Georg Kareski, became the head of Germany's largest Jewish community.[58]

In most other communities, the Liberals suffered perceptible losses but held sway. In Hamburg and Cologne, they lost their absolute majorities and were dependent on coalitions with their long-time opponents, the Orthodox.[59] In Dresden, Leipzig, and Chemnitz, the Liberals maintained their majorities only because of an undemocratic voting system, according to which the minority of German Jews was reserved a majority of seats in the assemblies. In Breslau, the shifting of power was arranged by peaceful agreement: the assembly of representatives was enlarged in 1930 from 21 to 23 members, and the number of liberal members was reduced from 13 to 11.[60] In some smaller communities with large numbers of East European Jews, the JVP succeeded in gaining the absolute majority; for example, in Duisburg in 1928, the JVP won more than 60 percent of the vote.[61]

Even where the Liberals retained the majority, the concept of a Religionsgemeinde was sacrificed for the concrete needs of German Jewry. No matter which party dominated, by the late 1920s, the large Gemeinden had in fact become "cities within cities," administering hospitals, old-age homes, orphanages, banks, unemployment assistance, schools, adult education institutions, art collections, libraries, statistics offices, and more. The annual budget of the Berlin Jewish community, with 170,000 members and 1,500 paid officials, was more than 10 million marks. The segment of the communities' annual expenses distributed in the religious sector decreased steadily. By the late 1920s, synagogue attendance on the High Holidays slipped below 50 percent in Berlin, Frankfurt am Main, and other large cities. At the same time,

[58] For more details, see Michael Brenner, "Jüdische Volkspartei—National-Jewish Communal Politics during the Weimar Republic," *Leo Baeck Institute YearBook* 35 (1990), 219–243.
[59] For Hamburg see Central Archives for the History of the Jewish People, Jerusalem, AHW 348; for Cologne see *Ma'ayan, Ha-behirot ha-kehilat Köln*, 117–118.
[60] *Jüdische Zeitung für Ostdeutschland*, 7 November 1930, n. p.
[61] *Jüdisch-Liberale Zeitung*, 8 June 1928, n. p.

participation in the secular community elections increased. Even in Berlin, 60 percent of the community (more than 77,000 people) went to the polls in 1930; in many smaller places, election turnout was about 90 percent.[62]

Although the Weimar period clearly witnessed a progressive secularisation—in the Catholic and Protestant communities as well as in the Jewish one—there were also tendencies of religious revival. Not only did such figures as Leo Baeck, Martin Buber, and Franz Rosenzweig engage in creative religious thought, but everyday religious practice also made a comeback. Among the liberals, a growing number of young rabbis hoped to attract younger people to Judaism with educational programs, and the opening in 1929 of the first Berlin community synagogue with mixed seating appealed to women, who demanded a more equal role in prayer. The Orthodox segment of the community changed, too. A new type of rabbi, like Nehemias Anton Nobel of Frankfurt and Joseph Carlebach of Hamburg, reached out to non-Orthodox Jewish students and intellectuals. By their new approaches toward Jewish mysticism or by their modern pedagogical techniques, these leaders of Weimar's Orthodox Jewry were indeed able to awaken new interest in Judaism—though not necessarily in Orthodoxy—on the fringes of Jewish society.

FROM *KULTUSGEMEINDE* TO *KULTURGEMEINDE*

The development of three cultural institutions—local Jewish newspapers, modern Jewish libraries, and Jewish schools in urban areas reflected the transformation of the Jewish community. The Gemeinde attempted to halt the spread of private Jewish cultural institutions and associations and instead advocated that they be included under its auspices. Before World War I, less than a handful of Jewish communities

---

[62] On the community budget and synagogue attendance, see Niewyk, *Jews in Weimar Germany*, 102–105. A similar decline in involvement in religious life could be observed in rural areas. See Jacob Borut, "Hayei ha-dat be-kerev yehudei ha-kefarim veha-ayarot be-ma'arava shel Germaniah bi-tekufot Weimar," *Yehudei Weimar: Hevrah haßmashber ha-moderni'ut, 1918–1933*, ed. Oded Heilbronner (Jerusalem: Magnes Press, 1994), 90–107. On election turnout, see Brenner, "Jüdische Volkspartei," 223.

issued their own news bulletins, but in 1932, there were more than 40 local Jewish newspapers, which had a combined circulation of about 310,000.[63] The Gemeinden integrated formerly private Jewish libraries into their framework, took over or subsidised Jewish schools, and replaced such private associations as the Associations for Jewish History and Literature and the B'nai B'rith lodges as the centres of Jewish adult education.

In the premodern Kehillah, the transmission of essential information about the principles and activities of the Gemeinde, from the administration to its members, was arranged on the daily basis of informal contact. The members of a Jewish community lived close to each other, met for regular prayer, and were subject to the authority of the local Jewish community. With the loss of communal ties in the age of political equality and the rapid population increase of urban Jewish communities, many Jews were no longer informed about the activities of their community. The Frankfurt community, for example, had grown from 3,000 to almost 30,000 during the nineteenth century, and the Berlin Gemeinde, with more than 170,000 members, had become an entirely anonymous apparatus for most of them.

The increasing atomisation of a rapidly urbanising Jewish population forced the Gemeinden to create institutional frameworks that would renew the contact between the communities' administration and their membership. The Gemeinden thus established their own publication organs, usually called *Gemeindeblatt* or *Gemeindezeitung*. In the late nineteenth century, such local newspapers existed only in a few communal or supracommunal organisations, such as those in Baden (founded in 1884) and Cologne (founded in 1888). Berlin launched its Gemeindeblatt in 1909, when the community already had more than a hundred thousand members.

During the Weimar years, every large community and many small ones created a Gemeindeblatt. By 1933, 42 such communal newspapers had appeared, constituting almost half the Jewish journals circulating

---

63   Adolf Kober, "Jewish Communities in Germany from the Age of Enlightenment to Their Destruction by the Nazis," *Jewish Social Studies* 9 (1947), 220.

in Germany.[64] They reported news from the Jewish world, announced regular activities of the community and its institutions, and published lists of those who joined and defected from the communities. The officials of the Jewish communities realised that the Gemeindeblatt provided a unique opportunity to promote Jewish knowledge among a highly assimilated urban Jewish population. In contrast to such older Jewish journals as the liberal *Allgemeine Zeitung des Judentums* (founded in 1837) and the Orthodox *Der Israelit* (founded in 1860) or the later-established mouthpieces of the CV (*Im deutschen Reich*, 1895) and the Zionist movement (*Jüdische Rundschau*, 1896), the local Gemeindeblatt was distributed freely to every household registered in the Jewish community and was the only means the community had of reaching all its members.

The publications had two tasks, as formulated in the programmatic statement of the first issue of the Berlin Jewish Gemeindeblatt. First, they filled the gap between the community administration and its members and encouraged everyone to participate in Jewish life: "The knowledge of the individual member about the community events has dwindled, and as a consequence interest in community activities has declined as well. In this respect, the Gemeindeblatt wants to create a change." Second, the Gemeindeblatt had a more general aim: "It should publish articles about the essence of Judaism, its tasks, and its particular character, its teachings and its writings."[65]

Many communal newspapers went far beyond the role of local news bulletins and developed into attractive journals concerning all matters of interest to Jews. During the late 1920s, the communal newspapers increased their efforts to attract the attention of members whose contact with the Jewish community was tenuous. In 1928, the Berlin Jewish community hired the former editor of *Ost und West*, Leo Winz, to professionalise the management of the local Gemeindeblatt. He significantly changed the appearance of the paper and its advertising

---

64 See Herbert Strauss, "Jewish Press in Germany, 1918–1943 (1943)," in *The Jewish Press That Was: Accounts, Evaluations and Memories of Jewish Papers in the Pre-Holocaust Europe*, ed., Arie Bat (Tel Aviv: Jerusalem Post, 1980), 350–351.

65 *Gemeindeblatt der Jüdischen Gemeinde zu Berlin* 1, no. 1 (1 July 1909).

strategies.[66] The Gothic script was modernised into Latin letters, and the title page became an aesthetically refined frontispiece. Winz transformed the Gemeindeblatt into a voluminous journal of 48, sometimes even 68, pages with numerous illustrations. Some issues included competitions for prizes, and some were special editions on topics chosen to attract readers. Winz's advertising strategies were so successful that the Berlin Gemeindeblatt no longer depended on community subsidies. Its circulation rose from an average of 58,000 in 1928 to 77,000 in 1931, with individual issues reaching 87,000. Winz left no doubt about the purpose of those measures: "The Gemeindeblatt has to become a publicity tool of the first rank, in order to promote the Jewish interests of the members of the Jewish community. As a result of such an aroused interest there will naturally be an increasing participation in community activities."[67]

The Gemeindeblatt of the Berlin Jewish community was the Jewish newspaper with the highest circulation in Germany. All other communal newspapers had a circulation of less than 10,000. Nevertheless, many of them were of high literary quality and were significant in their promotion of Jewish culture in Weimar Germany.[68] Among the smaller community newspapers, the *Bayerische Israelitische Gemeindezeitung* (*BIGZ*), published by the Bavarian Union of Jewish Communities, must be singled out. Edited (from 1930) by Ludwig Feuchtwanger, a brother of the writer Lion Feuchtwanger, the *BIGZ* followed the first cautious steps in the Christian-Jewish dialogue, analysed the contemporary development of Zionism, reviewed the most recent Jewish literature, discussed modern Jewish philosophy, and reported on matters of communal life. Like most community newspapers, the *BIGZ* recorded

---

[66] Winz had recognised the importance of local Jewish newspapers long before his employment in Berlin. When still editing *Ost und West*, he proposed the creation of an illustrated Jewish weekly that would contain a main section and different local section for each Jewish community, to be published with an average circulation of 2,000 in the 16 largest Jewish communities. Leo Winz Collection, CZA, A 136/39.

[67] Leo Winz Collection CZA, A 136/42. On circulation numbers and advertisement strategies see Leo Winz Collection CZA, A 136/46.

[68] In 1928, the largest Gemeindeblätter other than the one in Berlin were in Breslau (with a circulation of 8,700), Hamburg (8,000), and Frankfurt (6,000). Leo Winz Collection CZA, A 136/49.

the views of the factions within the community without taking sides in internal struggles. (The neutrality of the communal bulletins was generally respected.) The *BIGZ* succeeded in recruiting many young, first-rate Jewish intellectuals as contributors, among them Gershom Scholem, Hannah Arendt, and Leo Lowenthal.[69]

Newspapers and journals were a relatively new way to express Jewish culture, but the classical medium of the book was also used to promote a modern Jewish cultural identity. Traditionally, every Jewish community had its beth midrash (house of study), with a library consisting of the classic religious texts and their interpretations. During the nineteenth century, those texts became irrelevant for most German Jews, and the libraries were used almost exclusively by rabbis, scholars, and the small minority of Orthodox Jews. When at the end of the nineteenth century Jewish libraries became popular again, their shelves were filled with a different kind of literature: novels, dramas, poems, and critical essays written in German about Jewish history and contemporary issues. Most of the users of these libraries were unable to read Hebrew or follow the traditional Talmudic interpretations. The first director of the World Zionist Archives, Georg Herlitz, wrote in 1928: "It is a long way from those [traditional] synagogue libraries to the community libraries of our time.... Those synagogue libraries contained Jewish books for experts of Jewish knowledge, whereas the community libraries of today contain mainly instructional books about Judaism for general readers.... Today, the main purpose is not the deepening of already existent knowledge about Judaism but the initial spread of such a knowledge."[70] The first Jewish reading halls to hold modern and mostly secular Jewish literature were opened in Germany's larger cities at the end of the nineteenth century by private associations. In Berlin, the first such organisation to establish a Jewish library was the Verein Jüdische Lesehalle und Bibliothek in 1895, and similar foundations in other cities followed suit. Within ten years the Berlin Jewish library

---

[69] On the Bayerische Israelitische Gemeindezeitung, see Max Grünewald, "Critic of German Jewry: Ludwig Feuchtwanger and his Gemeindezeitung," *Leo Baeck Institute YearBook* 17 (1972), 75–92.

[70] Georg Herlitz, "Jüdische Gemeindebibliotheken," *Orden Bne Briss: Festschrift zum Ordenstage* (October 1928), 171–172.

was significantly enlarged. With an annual average of 24,000 readers, the library moved several times to larger locations, increased its stock of books, and established additional reading hours.[71]

In 1920, the Lesehalle, shattered by the postwar economic crisis, was integrated into the Jewish community as a branch of its library, which had been founded in 1902.[72] This measure initiated a broad extension of the Berlin Jewish community's library network. By 1932, the Gemeinde had set up nine branches, with about 70,000 volumes, in various sections of the city.[73] The main reading room of the library had become a meeting point for the local Jewish population. There Gershom Scholem met the Hebrew writer Shmu'el Yosef Agnon, "where he tirelessly leafed through the Hebrew card catalogue." Asked by Scholem what he looked for, Agnon supposedly replied, "Books that I have not read yet."[74] Although the Gemeinde library had acquired some remarkably rare books and Hebrew manuscripts, they were not its most important holdings. In contrast to other large Jewish libraries in Berlin, such as the rabbinical seminary libraries or the Staatsbibliothek and the Universitatsbibliothek, the main objective of the Jewish community library was not to become a place of scholarly research but to provide popular books and a large selection of newspapers for a highly acculturated Jewish audience.

Franz Rosenzweig compared the potential readers of Jewish libraries with the four types of children discussed in the Passover Haggadah. Whereas professional libraries were for the "clever child," the natural audience of the Gemeinde library was the "child who does not know how to ask"—those assimilated Jews who had to be taught how to approach their lost cultural heritage. The main task of the Gemeinde library was, according to Rosenzweig, to make such an audience curious to learn more about Judaism. The Berlin library was Rosenzweig's model for such an approach.

---

[71] Josef Linn, "Die Berliner Jüdische Lesehalle in ihrem neuen Heim," *Ost und West* (November 1908), 683–690; Johannes Giskala, "Zum zehnten Stiftungstage des Vereins Jüdische Lesehalle und Bibliothek," *Ost und West* (February 1905), 137–142.
[72] JJB,1926, 151–152.
[73] *Verwaltungsbericht des Vorstandes der Jüdischen Gemeinde zu Berlin*, 26–27.
[74] Scholem, *From Berlin to Jerusalem*, 91.

Next to the main lending library there is a reading room, whose open stacks hold not only the volumes that serve the expert as indispensable tools but also modern works that provide the non-expert with the ability to take the first steps into the world [of Judaica]: books of history, philosophical representations of Judaism, modern Bible commentaries, finally—and especially important—the classics in modern translation. This is a collection of books for the curious. And this curiosity is today the natural situation of three-quarters of the members of an urban Jewish community.[75]

On Rosenzweig's initiative, the Frankfurt Jewish community enlarged its library in the 1920s and established a reading room according to the Berlin prototype. Similarly, in 1920, the Jewish community of Munich revived its "completely neglected" Jewish library.[76] Other communities followed, and by 1932 libraries existed in more than 30 Jewish communities. Among these towns were such small places as Neuwied and Speyer, where every community member was asked to donate one book.[77]

As in Berlin, the local Jewish reading hall in Hamburg had been founded as a private initiative around the turn of the century. It was closed during the economic crisis of 1921, when the Jewish girls' school claimed its rooms. The private association that had established the library urged the Jewish community to finance its reopening, arguing that "several Jewish students had to leave Hamburg in order to write their dissertations on Jewish topics in other cities."[78] After protracted negotiations the Gemeinde agreed in 1923 to finance and extend the library, "with regard to the middle and lower classes of the Jewish population who are no longer able to keep Jewish newspapers and buy Jewish books."[79]

---

[75] Franz Rosenzweig, *Zweistromland: Kleinere Schriften zu Glauben und Denken*, ed., Reinhold Mayer and Annemarie Mayer, vol. 3 of *Franz Rosenzweig. Der Mensch und sein Werk* (The Hague: M. Nijhoff, 1984), 511–512.

[76] *Das Jüdische Echo*, 24 December 1920. An incomplete list of community libraries can be found in the Führer durch die jüdische Gemeindeverwaltung 1932/33, 527–528.

[77] Synagogenausschuß of the Israelitsche Kultusgemeinde to community members 28 Februarz 1919, CAHJP, PF XIII, 21. On Neuwied see CAHJP, Rh/Nw 75. The library of the Jewish community of Cologne had 3,000 volumes in 1932. See *GBJK* no 2 (22 January 1932), 17.

[78] Jüdische Lesehalle und Bibliothek to Gemeindevorstand, 7 December 1922, CAHJP, AHW 887.

[79] Gemeindevorstand to JOINT, 19 March 1923, CAHJP, AHW 887.

The Gemeinde took over the formerly private library, united it with smaller local Jewish libraries, and reopened it in 1928 as the *Gemeindebibliothek*, the official community library. Professor Isaak Markon, a leading Hebraist who had taught at the universities of Petersburg and Moscow and at the Orthodox rabbinical seminary in Berlin, was hired to be its director. He intellectually enriched the library and the entire Jewish community of Hamburg.

During the remaining years of the Weimar era, the number of readers at the reopened Hamburg library grew steadily from an average of 500 per month in 1929 to 600 per month a year later to a thousand readers per month in 1931.[80] The most popular books were novels by German Jewish authors, such as Jakob Wassermann, Max Brod, Stefan Zweig, Arnold Zweig, and Jacob Loewenberg, a local author. Translations from Yiddish literature and Hasidic tales were also well liked. Only three years after its reopening, the library was called the "intellectual center of the Jewish community."[81]

Other institutions also claimed to be the community's intellectual centre. First among them was the Jewish school. When acculturation progressed and the number of Jewish pupils at non-Jewish schools increased in the second half of the nineteenth century, the Jewish school lost its predominance in the education of Jewish children. At first glance, the further decline in the number of Jewish schools until the rise of Nazi Germany appears a continuation of this trend. Although 492 Jewish elementary schools existed in 1898, only 247 remained in 1913, and 141 were left in 1932.[82] This dramatic development was caused by the rapid urbanisation of German Jewry, which forced the closure of many Jewish schools in rural areas, and by the belief of most liberal Jews that the abolition of separate Jewish schools would constitute an important step toward their complete integration into German society.

---

[80] *Gemeindeblatt der Deutsch-Israelitischen Gemeinde Hamburg*, 10 July 1930, 5, and *Gemeindeblatt der Deutsch-Israelitischen Gemeinde Hamburg*, 25 January 1932, 1–2.

[81] *Gemeindeblatt der Deutsch-Israelitischen Gemeinde Hamburg*, 25 January 1932, 1–2.

[82] See Schatzker, *Jüdische Jugend*, 37, and *Führer durch die jüdische Gemeindeverwaltung und Wohlfahrtspflege 1932/33* (Berlin: Zentralwohlfahrtsstelle der deutschen Juden 1932), 522.

As a more detailed analysis reveals, however, the closure of Jewish schools in rural areas was one of two major currents in the development of Jewish educational institutions during the Weimar period. In big cities, new Jewish schools were reestablished and already existing schools were enlarged and increasingly supported by the Jewish communities. The rural schools threatened by closure usually had fewer than ten pupils, but most of the new schools in large cities soon counted a few hundred students. In some Jewish communities with established Jewish school systems—Hamburg, Frankfurt, and Cologne—about every second Jewish child attended a Jewish school in 1932. Berlin never reached such a ratio, but the opening of five Jewish elementary schools in the German capital between 1919 and 1927 marked a clear revival of separate Jewish education. In other cities, such as Munich, Nuremberg, and Duisburg, no Jewish schools had existed for decades, but such institutions were reestablished during the 1920s, either by the Jewish community or by Orthodox associations.

Children of Orthodox Jews, Zionists, and East European Jews constituted most pupils in Weimar Germany's Jewish schools. Despite the vehement opposition of liberal leaders to education that separated students along religious lines, a minority of liberal Jews also began to send their children to Jewish schools. They were motivated partly by the realisation that most interfaith schools (*Simultanschulen*) remained dominated by the guiding principles of the Christian religion, celebrated Christian holidays, and required attendance on the Sabbath. Of the few schools that distanced themselves from Christian doctrine, most were situated in workers' neighbourhoods and were unattractive to middle-class Jewish parents.[83] An additional reason for the increased attendance at Jewish schools in big cities was the spiralling rate of antisemitic incidents in non-Jewish schools. Two years before the Nazi rise to power, a former student of both Jewish and non-Jewish schools recommended that Jewish children attend the Jewish school in Breslau, and his main argument was the absence of antisemitism in a Jewish

---

[83] In Breslau, for example, there were only five Simultanschulen, compared to more than 100 conspicuously Christian schools. See *Jüdische Zeitung für Ostdeutschland*, 27 March 1931, n. p.

milieu: "How happy is the child who spends his time free of the hatred of Gentile companions."[84]

Most of the new Jewish schools of the Weimar years were established by the Orthodox separatist communities. Those schools, however, often recruited pupils who were not Orthodox. When the Orthodox congregation Ohel Jakob in Munich opened a Jewish elementary school in 1924, its 64 pupils hailed mainly from the Orthodox and East European Jewish communities. By 1932, its student body had doubled, with 42 percent of the pupils coming from liberal Jewish homes. During the same period, the attendance of Jewish pupils at non-Jewish public elementary schools dropped from 586 to 278.[85]

In Bavaria's second largest community, Nuremberg, the situation was similar. Jewish schools were nonexistent until the Orthodox association Adas Israel established an elementary school in 1921, which five years later became an institution of the local Gemeinde. This school grew from 80 pupils in 1921 to 180 pupils in 1928. Thus, before 1933, 30 to 40 percent of Jewish children in Bavaria's two largest cities attended a Jewish elementary school. Those numbers are especially significant given that for decades, there had been no Jewish school in those communities.[86] Outside Bavaria, new Jewish elementary schools were established in Breslau (in 1920 and 1921), Duisburg (in 1925), and several other cities.[87]

The development of Jewish education in Weimar Germany was best reflected in its centre, Berlin. Before World War I Germany's largest Jewish community had two lower-grade secondary schools but no elementary school. During the Weimar years, five Jewish elementary schools were founded. One of them belonged to the Orthodox separatists,

[84] *Jüdische Zeitung für Ostdeutschland*, 27 March 1931, n. p. See also Schatzker, *Jüdische Jugend*, 83–89.

[85] *Statistisches Handbuch der Stadt München 1928*, 261.

[86] Claudia Prestel, *Jüdisches Schul-und Erziehungswesen in Bayern* (Göttingen, Vandenhoeck and Ruprecht, 1989), 135–139. In Nuremberg's neighboring city Fürth, a young Henry Kissinger was among the pupils of the local Jewish high school, the only one left in Bavaria. Ibid., 262.

[87] On Breslau, see *Jüdische Zeitung für Ostdeutschland*, 27 March 1931, n. p. The Duisburg school had about 200 pupils in 1930; see *Gemeinde-Zeitung Duisburg*, 17 February 1930, n. p. On Berlin see *Jüdisches Jahrbuch Berlin 1932*, 142.

and another one remained a private school, but three schools were integrated into the framework of the Jewish community. The Rykestraße school was founded in 1924 as a private school but was taken over by the Jewish community in 1929. The two other schools were opened as *Gemeindeschulen* during the rule of the alliance between the JVP and the Orthodox. When the Liberals regained power in 1930, they cut the schools' subsidies but let them remain institutions of the community. The number of students attending Jewish schools in Berlin rose from 1,170 in 1913 to 2,713 in 1930 and reached a peak of almost 3,000 in 1932. The proportion of Jewish pupils in Berlin who attended Jewish schools thus had increased to about 20 percent by 1932.[88] In many smaller cities of Prussia, almost every second Jewish child attended a Jewish school. In 1930, when the Orthodox high school of the separatist Adass Jisroel congregation in Berlin held its first *Abitur* exams (which qualified students to attend a university), the Berlin Jewish community made public its plan to establish its own high school and a yeshivah, but neither of those institutions was created before 1933.[89]

In other cities, however, the Jewish high school system started to expand before 1933. Four of Germany's ten Jewish high schools existing in the 1920s had been established during the previous decade, and many of the others were significantly enlarged during this period. All the new schools—Leipzig (1913), Cologne (1919), Berlin (1919), and Breslau (1921)—were founded by the Orthodox community but included students who were children of non-Orthodox parents. In Breslau, the initial resistance of liberal and some Orthodox Jews to the school had diminished by the time of its tenth anniversary in

---

[88] For 1913, see *Handbuch der jüdischen Gemienverwaltung und Wohlfahrtspflege 1913*; for 1930, see *Gemeindezeitung für die israelitische Gemeinden Württembergs* 20, no. 10 (October 1930), p. 459; for 1932, see *Führer durch die jüdische Gemeindeverwaltung 1932–1933*, 512–515. See also Selma Schiratzki, "The Rykestraße School in Berlin," *Leo Baeck Institute YearBook* 5 (1960) and Kochavi, "Beyn Tsionim le-Liberalim be-Berlin 1929–1932: ma'avakim tsiburi;im be-kehilat Berln uva-yahadut Germaniah ba-shanim she kadmu le 'reich ha-shilishi,'" Manuscript, CZA, 69.

[89] *GJGB*, October 1930, 462. See also Max Sinasohn, *Adass Jisroel Berlin: Entstehung, Entfaltung, Entwurzelung, 2869–1939* (Jerusalem: Private printing, 1966), 58. On Prussia, see the numbers provided in Levinson, *Ha-tenu'ah ha'ivrit ha-golah* (Warsaw: B'rith Ivrith Olamith, 1935), 70.

1931.[90] At other places too, Jewish schools were initially rejected by the liberal establishment as an attempt at renewed ghettoisation but were gradually accepted as necessary institutions in times of virulent antisemitism.

Because of the economic crisis, most Jewish schools—founded as private institutions—could no longer exist with exclusively private funding and therefore turned to the Gemeinde for financial support. At the same time, Jewish high schools received official state recognition and enabled their students for the first time in the history of Jewish education in Germany to graduate with the *Abitur*. Both developments occurred in the three cities with the best developed Jewish educational systems in Weimar Germany: Hamburg, Cologne, and Frankfurt.

Although the mostly liberal establishment of the communities did not favour the creation of religious schools, they avoided the closure of already existing Jewish schools and granted increasing financial support. The Cologne Jewish community, for example, concluded a contract in 1928 with Jawne, its Orthodox high school, that guaranteed annual subsidies for a period of five years in exchange for community control over the school.[91] In Hamburg, the girls' high school of the Jewish community grew from 350 to 600 pupils in the Weimar years because it absorbed the students of a private Jewish girls' school that had to be closed.[92]

For the first time in its 124-year history, the Frankfurt Philanthropin (the only non-Orthodox Jewish high school in Weimar Germany) enabled its students to graduate with an *Abitur* degree after the school was recognised as a *Realreformgymnasium* in 1928. Jawne followed a year later, and the Hamburg Talmud Tora high school for boys was accredited the equivalent status as an *Oberrealschule* in 1932, after the school underwent pedagogical reforms under the direction of Joseph Carlebach in the early 1920s.[93]

---

[90] *Jüdische Zeitung für Ostdeutschland*, 27 March 1931, n. p.

[91] Adolf Fürst, "Höheren jüdischen Schulen," *MGWJ* 75 (1931), 57–58.

[92] Inga Lorenz, *Juden in Hamburg zur Zeit der Weimarer Republik: Eine Dokumentation*, 2 vols. (Hamburg: Hans Christians, 1987), vol. 2, 413–414.

[93] On Cologne, see Alexander Carlebach, *Adass Zeshurun of Cologne: The Life and Death of a Kehila* (Belfast: W. Mullon and Sons, 1964), 100–102.

The development of the Frankfurt Philanthropin reflects the increase in numbers of students attending Jewish schools and their new self-perception. During the 1920s, the Philanthropin established an elementary school and a kindergarten. This expansion enabled Frankfurt Jewish children to attend a Jewish school from kindergarten until high school graduation. As a result, in 1930 the number of students at the various Philanthropin schools reached an unprecedented high of 900. About the same time, the Orthodox schools of Frankfurt had 1,160 pupils.[94] As in Hamburg and Cologne, every second Jewish pupil in Frankfurt attended a Jewish school during the Weimar years.

Founded in 1804, the Frankfurt Philanthropin, offering courses in secular subjects and the German language to as yet unemancipated German Jews, furthered equality and acculturation throughout the nineteenth century. In the Weimar years, however, the Philanthropin began to promote Jewish knowledge and Jewish consciousness. Religious education was expanded from three to five hours per week. Boys were required to cover their heads during Hebrew lessons in obedience to religious ritual, and for the first time, strictly Orthodox teachers were employed. Books with Jewish content became more widely read, and in the late 1920s, a permanent study group was established to discuss "problems of Judaism."[95]

Most Jewish schools similarly strengthened their Jewish education. The study of modern Hebrew, as introduced by Joseph Carlebach in Hamburg, soon became obligatory in other Jewish high schools.[96] Non-Jewish subjects were taught regularly, but curricula allowed Jewish matters to be emphasised even in courses on nonreligious subjects. The director of the Breslau Jewish high school encouraged teachers to assign essays on "Jewish experiences" in German lessons, discuss Jewish heritage in history lessons, sing Jewish melodies in music

---

[94] *Führer durch die jüdische Gemeindeverwaltung 1932–1933*, 516–517. See also the statistics in Paul Arnsberg, *Geschichte der Frankfurter Juden seit der französischen Revolution* (Frankfurt: Eduard Rother, 1983) vol. 2, 502–505. On the Philantropin see Inge Schlotzhauer, *Philantropin, 1804–1942 Die Schulen der Israelitschen Gemeinde in Frankfurt am Main* (Frankfurt a. M.: Waldemar Kramer, 1990), 90.

[95] Fürst, "Höheren jüdischen Schulen," 54–56.

[96] On Carlebach's pedagogical principle, see Miriam Gillis-Carlebach, *Hinukh ve-emunah* (Tel Aviv: Moreshet, 1979).

classes, and introduce female students to the customs of a Jewish home in home economics classes.[97]

In spite of those efforts, Jewish subjects remained restricted to three to five hours per week. The study of Hebrew was mostly rudimentary, and basic religious education was still the major objective of those lessons.

More important was the creation—partly voluntary and partly forced—of a Jewish milieu, caused by the return of the Jewish denominational school. Together with the extension of the Jewish community's social welfare network and the establishment of the Jewish youth movement, the exclusively Jewish social environment in these schools nourished the ideals of a Jewish Gemeinschaft within Weimar Germany.

Although the Jewish high schools promoted the study of a modern curriculum within a Jewish milieu, a small but visible movement advocated a return to a premodern framework of Jewish education. About the middle of the nineteenth century, the last *yeshivot*—academies for the study of Talmud—in Germany had disappeared, although they were still flourishing in Eastern Europe.[98] With the influx of East European Jews in the late nineteenth century, the *yeshivah* returned to Germany. In 1890, Salomon Breuer, the Hungarian-born rabbi of the local separatist community, opened a *yeshivah* in Frankfurt am Main. Although it drew a few students from local Orthodox families, most of its pupils came from Eastern Europe, especially from Hungary. With the establishment of the Breuer Yeshivah, Germany won a place on the map of religious Jewish education in Europe. For the first time in more than a century, Jewish parents sent their sons from distant places to Germany in order to study Talmud.[99] After World War I, Joseph Breuer succeeded his father as director of the *yeshivah*, and he significantly expanded and reorganised it. To cope with the increasing number of students of both German and East European background, four additional teachers had

---

[97] *Jüdische Zeitung für Ostdeutschland*, 27 March 1931, n. p.

[98] Mordechai Eliav, *Ha-hinukh ha-yehudi bi-yamei ha-haskalah veha-Imancipasiah* (Jerusalem: Jewish Agency, 1960), 238.

[99] Among the sons were Nahum Glatzer and Jacob Katz, who later became important scholars. See Katz's recollection in Rivka Horwitz, ed., *Yitshak Breuer, Iyunim be-mishmato* (Ramat Gan: Bar Ilan University, 1988), 39–49.

to be employed in the early 1920s.[100] Immigration from the East helped
to establish *yeshivot* in other German cities as well, such as Berlin,
Cologne, Leipzig, and Nuremberg.[101] What to East European Jews was
a continuation of traditional learning appeared to German Jews to be
innovation. When Rabbi Joseph Carlebach established a *yeshivah* in
Hamburg in 1921, a contemporary observer stressed the extraordinary
importance of this development for German Jewry: "We felt that what
was taught to this youth was something *totally new,* something never
heard of in Hamburg during the last hundred years."[102]

Germany's three rabbinical seminaries, founded in the last third of
the nineteenth century, flourished in the Weimar period. The Orthodox
Hildesheimer Rabbinerseminar in Berlin's Artilleriestraße increased
its student body to accommodate the influx of East European Jews.
The number of students soon exceeded the number of vacancies in
the rabbinate. The Rabbinerseminar began to offer Bible and Talmud
courses for a broader Orthodox audience, ranging from schoolchildren
to businessmen. According to its annual report of 1924, the institution
had "come much closer to what was undoubtedly the intention of the
founder of this Seminary, that is, to make it a centre for all those who
wish to train in the spirit of Orthodox Judaism."[103]

The liberal Hochschule für die Wissenschaft des Judentums—located
on the same street—also recruited a new type of student, but one of a
different kind:

---

[100] *Der Israelit*, 25 March 1922, 3.
[101] On Berlin, see *Führer durch die jüdische Gemeindeverwaltung 1932–1933*, 51–52; on Hamburg, see *Gemeindeblatt der Deutsch-Israelitischen Gemeinde Hamburg*, no 7 (10 July 1926), 1–2, and Lorenz, *Juden in Hamburg*, 776, 792–808; on Cologen *yeshiva* on St. Apern Street see Alexander Carlebach, "Orthodoxie in der Kölner jüdischen Gemeinde der Neuzeit," in *Köln und das rheinische Judentum: Festschrift Germania Judaica, 1959–1984*, ed. Jutta Bohnke-Kollwity (Cologne: J. P. Bachem, 1984), 353; on Nuremberg see Prestel, *Jüdisches Schul-und Erziehungswesen*, 135. On Leipzig see *Der Israelit*, 16 February 1922, 12, and S. J. Kreutner, *Mein Leipzig: Gedenken an die Juden meiner Stadt* (Jerusalem: Rubin Mass, 1992), 49–59. In Lübeck a *yeshivah* had been established in 1920. See Carlebach, *Adass Yeshurun*, 21.
[102] *Gemeindeblatt der Deutsch-Israelitischen Gemeinde Hamburg*, 11 July 1926, 7.
[103] Quoted in Eisner, "Reminiscences of the Berlin Rabbincal Seminary," Schiratzki, "The Rykestraße School in Berlin," Leo Baeck Institute *YearBook* 12 (1967), 41.

The "new student" had neither shared the traditionalist climate of the small Jewish community, nor did he possess any sizable fund of Jewish learning. In all probability, one of the Jewish youth movements which had sprung up in recent years had made him aware of the Jewish problem. He had read, though not necessarily understood, Buber and later Rosenzweig, and he was bursting with questions and eager to acquire a Jewish philosophy. He was deeply emotive, penitently aware of his insufficiency of Jewish learning, and sincerely anxious to acquire it together with a firmly founded Jewish *Weltanschauung*. The difference between learning and *Weltanschauung* was not settled in his mind either. He looked forward to a university education, but felt strongly that getting only a university education, as perhaps his family expected, was wrong from the Jewish point of view. Some of those post-war students were considering professional careers in the Jewish field, possibly the rabbinate, but all that would depend on the clarification of their Jewish problems and the answer of the *Lebensfragen* which they expected to get in the classrooms of the *Hochschule*.[104]

One of the regular guests at the Hochschule in the winter of 1923 was a rather unusual figure, who had just come to Berlin from Prague. Franz Kafka found a second home in the Artilleriestraße, as he wrote to a friend. The Hochschule was for him a "refuge of peace in wild and woolly Berlin and in the wild and woolly regions of my mind.... A whole building of handsome lecture rooms, large library, peace, well heated, few students, and everything free of charge."[105]

The Jewish Theological Seminary in Breslau, the centre of positive-historical Judaism (the German counterpart to Conservative Judaism), enrolled its largest student body in 1930, just a year after its 75th anniversary. Like the Berlin Rabbinerseminar and the Hochschule, the Breslau Seminary extended its reach by offering evening courses for adults and members of Jewish youth groups.[106]

104 Fritz Bamberger, "Julius Guttmann: Philosopher of Judaism," *Leo Baeck Institue Year Book*5 (1960), 11.
105 Frany Kafka, *Letters to Friends, Family, and Editors*, trans. Ernst Kaiser and Eithene Wilkins (New York: Schocken, 1977), 402–403.
106 Lothar Rotschild, "Geschichte des Seminars von 1904 bis 1938," in *Das Breslauer Seminar: Jüdisch-Theologisches Seminar (Fraenckelscher Stiftung) in Breslau 1854–1938*, ed. Guido Kisch (Tübingen: J. C. B. Mohr, 1963), 145–156.

The range of educational possibilities illustrates the ambiguity that characterised Weimar Germany's Jews: one segment of Jewish students received very little Jewish education (or none at all) in school—mostly reduced to a weekly lesson in religion—while another growing segment attended Jewish elementary schools and high schools or even *yeshivot* and rabbinical seminaries, grew up in a Jewish milieu, and obtained at least a basic knowledge of Judaism.[107]

Although the end of separate Jewish schools in Germany seemed close at hand at the beginning of the twentieth century, most observers agreed that a revival of Jewish education was well underway during the Weimar years:

> The Jewish elementary school is no longer the problem child of responsibility-conscious Jewish circles. It has forcefully proved itself.... . All levels of the Jewish population in its social, religious, and political varieties today send their children to the Jewish elementary school.... The present growth of Jewish elementary schools in big cities clearly reflects the living spirit of certain streams within German Jewry.[108]

Indeed, the increasing attendance at urban Jewish schools reflected a more general trend among adults. Many German Jews who had not attended Jewish schools and had grown up in assimilated Jewish families began to participate in the newly established Jewish adult education system, which will be discussed in the next chapter.

---

[107] At the same time, systematic attempts were made underway to improve Jewish education in the afternoon schools and Sunday schools. In Stuttgart, for example, 60 pupils attended a Talmud-Tora-Schule with supplementary Hebrew lessons. *Das jüdische Echo*, 9 May 1919, 214–215.

[108] *Jüdisches Gemeindeblatt: Mitteilungsblatt der Israelitsachen Gemeinde Bremen*, 1 April 1930, n. p.

CHAPTER VIII

GERMAN JEWS BEYOND BILDUNG AND LIBERALISM: THE RADICAL JEWISH REVIVAL IN THE WEIMAR REPUBLIC

Steven Aschheim

The liberal German-Jewish position, which has been a meeting ground to almost the whole of German Jewry for nearly a century, has obviously dwindled to the size of a pinpoint.
—Franz Rosenzweig (1924)[1]

Today, as at the very beginning, my work lives in this paradox, in the hope of a true communication from the mountain, of that most invisible, smallest fluctuation of history which causes truth to break forth from the illusions of development.
—Gershom Scholem (1937)[2]

Only the Messiah himself consummates all history, in the sense that he alone redeems, completes, creates its relation to the Messianic. For this reason nothing historical can relate itself on its own account to anything Messianic.
—Walter Benjamin (1940)[3]

Finally the pride of being Jewish has awoken. It stirs within us restlessly.
—Ernst Bloch (1918)[4]

---

[1]   Not only can this be taken as a *leitmotif* of the Weimar Jewish revival, but Rosenzweig's gnomic remark immediately following was typical of its overall paradoxical style as well. After "pinpoint," he wrote: "so that just one man—I, that is—can occupy it." See the letter to Gertrud Oppenheim, July 1924, in *Gesammelte Werke* 1, ed., Rachel Rosenzweig and Edith Rosenzweig-Scheinmann (The Haag: M. Nijhoff, 1979), 980.

[2]   Letter of 29 October 1937 to Zalman Schocken on his 60th birthday entitled "A Candid Word about the True Motives of My Kabbalistic Studies," reproduced in David Biale, *Gershom Scholem: Kabbalah and Counter-History* (Cambridge: Harvard University Press, 1979), 74–6 in English and 215–16 in German.

[3]   "Theologico-Political Fragment," in Walter Benjamin, *Reflections*, ed., Peter Demetz (New York: Schocken, 1978), 312–13.

[4]   *Geist der Utopie* (Munich and Leipzig: Duncker & Humblot, 1918), 319.

Over the past few years, there has emerged a rather persuasive paradigm delineating the distinctive qualities of the modern German Jewish experience. As expounded by David Sorkin[5] and especially George Mosse in his *German Jews Beyond Judaism*,[6] it holds that in the course of the special protracted circumstances underlying their emancipation and acculturation, German Jewry forged what has to be understood as an essentially new (and indeed unique) form of Jewish identity and culture. The timing of German Jewish emancipation, they argue, determined the definition and the content of this new "Jewishness." For its beginnings—the first decade of the nineteenth century—coincided with the autumn of the German Enlightenment. From that time on, Jewish self-definitions and hopes were shaped in its image. Its accompanying postulates—liberalism, the notions of progress and gradual perfectibility, and the optimistic belief in a humanity making its way from darkness to light—became deeply ingrained within German Jewry.

But beyond that, according to this paradigm, it was the peculiar nature and ideals of German culture in the age of emancipation that provided the substance of this German Jewish identity.[7] For Enlightenment in Germany was accompanied by that unique construct known as *Bildung* (a notion so bound to its native context that no precise English or Hebrew equivalent exists).[8] *Bildung*—or self-cultivation—combined what we conventionally understand as formal education with that of character formation and moral and aesthetic refinement. To be sure the idea of *Bildung* underwent various transformations in the course of modern German cultural history, but Jews internalised and (even after

---

5   David Sorkin, *The Transformation of German Jewry 1780–1840* (New York: Oxford University Press, 1987).

6   George Mosse, *German Jews Beyond Judaism* (Bloomington: Indiana University Press, 1985).

7   Mosse, *German Jews Beyond Judaism*, ix.

8   I discovered the best—and most recent—account of *Bildung* well after this paper was first written. See the illuminating study by Aleida Assmann, *Arbeit am national Gedächtnis: Eine kurze Geschichte der deutschen Bildungsidee* (Frankfurt a.M.: Campus, 1993). See too W. H. Bruford, *The German Tradition of Self-Cultivation: "Bildung" from Humboldt to Thomas Mann* (Cambridge: Cambridge University Press, 1975).

1933) tenaciously clung on to its original classic meaning as formulated by giants such as Goethe and Wilhelm von Humboldt.[9]

What was the inner content of this ideal? *Bildung* referred to a continuous process of self-formation, the gradual unfolding of the harmonious, autonomous personality through the cultivation of reason, aesthetic taste and the moral imperative. Jews found this ideal so congenial and adopted it so quickly because it held that potentially *everyone* could attain it. *Bildung*, as Mosse puts it, "transcended all differences of nationality and religion through the unfolding of the individual personality."[10] It was thus an ideal perfectly suited to the requirements of Jewish integration and acculturation (especially into the middle class), rendering it the animating ideal of modern German Jewry, "basic to [the] Jewish engagement with liberalism and socialism, fundamental to the search for a new Jewish identity after emancipation." Over the years, so this argument goes, Jewishness and the classical notion of *Bildung* became more and more synonymous. "Above all," Ludwig Strauss once said, "in a study of Goethe one finds one's Jewish substance"; Kurt Blumenfeld defined himself as "a Zionist by the grace of Goethe."[11]

The connection between *Bildung* and Jewishness was never stronger, Mosse claims, than during the Weimar Republic, when "most Germans themselves had distorted the original concept beyond recognition." During this polarised period when more and more segments of German society (especially its originators, the bourgeoisie) were jettisoning the ideal, the Jews, so goes the argument, most stubbornly clung on to its liberal-humanist precepts: the belief in the progressive powers of reason, the (perhaps politically naive) insistence upon the primacy of culture, self-cultivation, and the critical mind.[12] Jewish intellectuals,

---

9   See Sidney M. Bolkosky, *The Distorted Image: German Jewish Perceptions of Germans and Germany, 1918–1935* (New York: Elsevier, 1975). The interpretive frame in which Bolkosky sets these examples is open to question.
10 Mosse, *German Jews Beyond Judaism*, 3–4.
11 Ludwig Strauss, quoted in Mosse, *German Jews Beyond Judaism*, 14; on Blumenfeld, see Hannah Arendt's letter of September 7, 1952, in *Hannah Arendts-Karl Jaspers Correspondence 1926–1969*, ed., Lotte Kohler and Hans Saner (New York: Mariner Books, 1992), 198.
12 Jewishness here is envisaged not as a particular community or set of contents but,

Mosse holds, had always been the primary advocates of these values within German society. But it epitomised their role in Weimar culture even more acutely. In a society engulfed by waves of extreme nationalism and confrontation politics, Jewish intellectuals more than ever sought to perpetuate and transmit this classical ideal of *Bildung* and "to exorcise the irrational by examining it rationally and dissecting it in the rational mind."[13]

Mosse is here seeking to distil a fundamental impulse, to capture that which was most characteristic of the German Jewish psyche and to discern its enduring legacy. He does not claim that all Jews necessarily partook of the *Bildungs* sensibility in equal measure—there were clearly illiberal, narrow-minded, even "reactionary" Jews; city dwellers internalised it more than those who lived in small towns, and it was most clearly expressed by an articulate, educated minority. Nevertheless, he insists, "most were touched by its ideal of self-cultivation and liberal outlook on society and politic," an ideal that became "a part of German-Jewish identity, infiltrating to some extent most aspects of Jewish life in Germany"[14] (including Orthodoxy and the Zionist fringe).

To be sure, critics have directly challenged the validity of this paradigm as *the* key to German Jewish identity. Shulamit Volkov has argued for a more heterogeneous notion of *Bildung*. Volkov reminds us that the "autumn of the Enlightenment" was also the beginning of romanticism and points to the attraction that less "rational," morally elevated aspects of German culture possessed for Jews throughout the post-Enlightenment period.[15] "Jewishness," Paul Mendes-Flohr has argued from another point of view, "is more than a mere sensibility or even an identity in the existential and psychological sense"; a sociologically meaningful identity requires a shared community,

---

as Walter Benjamin once put it, as "noble bearer and representative of the intellect." Quoted in Anson Rabinbach, "Between Enlightenment and Apocalypse: Benjamin, Bloch and Modem German Jewish Messianism," *New German Critique* 34 (Winter 1985), 97.

13 Mosse, *German Jews Beyond Judaism*, 19.
14 Mosse, *German Jews Beyond Judaism*, 1–2.
15 This appears in the as yet unpublished paper "The Ambivalence of Bildung: Jews and Other Germans."

culture, and sense of solidarity with other Jews.[16] It may also be that more of the tradition may have lingered on in German Jewish lives than Mosse is prepared to allow. Nevertheless, I believe that it does at least capture something essential about the impulses and assumptions that German Jewish intellectuals[17] and the educated bourgeoisie (liberal, socialist, even religious and Zionist) lastingly brought to bear: the belief in the primacy of culture, the humanising emphasis on "the autonomy of personal relationships," and so on.[18]

Many of these insights I thus take to be essentially valid. Nevertheless, to argue as Mosse does that it was the *Bildungs* German Jewish tradition that largely determined what today we take to be the essence of "Weimar culture" (p. I) in some critical respects obscures more than it illuminates. Indeed, it is my contention that Weimar culture's most vital impulses were informed by an explicit suspicion, even outright negation, of many of the essential postulates that made up the *Bildungs* tradition and that it was not only the increasingly brutalised nationalist camp that jettisoned the notion, as Mosse would have it. In some important ways, it also characterised the projects of a remarkable generation[19] of intellectuals like Walter Benjamin, Ernst Bloch, Franz Rosenzweig, and Gershom Scholem, who formulated novel—and at times astonishing—fusions of radical and Jewish thematics. Each of their endeavours was distinctive and merits separate, detailed study. But they were linked by a thick network of personal (not always harmonious) relationships and a common set of concerns and dispositions.[20] Each, in their own distinctive way, has taken on

---

16 See Paul Mendes-Flohr's review of *German Jews Beyond Judaism* in *Studies in Contemporary Jewry 5* (1989), 377–9. The quote appears on p. 398.

17 The German edition of the book is, perhaps, more accurately entitled *Jüdische Intellektuelle in Deutschland* (Frankfurt a.M.: Campus Verlag, 1992).

18 Mosse, *German Jews Beyond Judaism*, 11.

19 There were, of course, differences in age as well as opinions. Bloch was born in 1885, Rosenzweig 1886, Benjamin 1892 and Scholem 1897. Nevertheless, they did constitute an intellectual generation. Rosenzweig and Benjamin died relatively young while Bloch and Scholem enjoyed longer lives.

20 Leo Lowenthal has vividly described the way in which this worked: "About a year after my first meeting with [Siegfried] Kracauer [around the end of World War I], he introduced me to Adorno, who was then eighteen years old. I introduced him to my friend Ernst Simon, who like myself, was studying history, *Germanistik*, and

almost paradigmatic status as embodiments of an emergent Jewish and Weimarian sensibility that has become part of the overall cultural and intellectual legacy of the twentieth century.[21]

We shall presently examine these projects in greater detail. But it is necessary first to recognise that—for all its many distinguishing qualities—this manifold Jewish renaissance was of a piece with some of the fundamental animating themes characteristic of the Weimar Republic and an age that had just experienced a war of unprecedented upheaval and dislocation. The figures to which we refer all defined themselves as in opposition to mainstream liberal, "bourgeois" Jewry. Certainly none of them were representative of official communal positions. In that sense, they may have been "marginal." But, quite contrary to what Mosse believes, their thought was quintessentially stamped by the times in which they lived. Far from being isolated remnants of a classical tradition rendered irrelevant by contemporary events they were very much in touch with contemporary currents, their projects resonant with the characteristic concerns, categories, and assumptions of a restless and radical age. For the purposes of this

---

philosophy, and who won me over to a very messianic version of Zionism. Through Ernst Simon, Kracauer met Rabbi Nobel, then a revered figure in our Jewish circle, to whose *Festschrift,* on the occasion of his 50th birthday, Kracauer contributed. Through Nobel, Kracauer first met Martin Buber and later Franz Rosenzweig. In the spring of 1922, I introduced him to Ernst Bloch, and he in turn introduced me to Horkheimer, who was already a good friend of Adorno's." See his "As I Remember Friedel," *New German Critique* 54 (Fall 1991), 6. Those very close friends Scholem and Benjamin were, of course, either in contact or familiar with most of these figures.

21 I am not arguing that this is the only possible legacy of Weimar (nor is this the legacy with which I would necessarily identify). The left and Marxist traditions of Kurt Tucholsky, Georg Lukacs, and Karl Korsch can be considered another, as can the writings of more liberal-minded thinkers and writers discussed by Mosse. But if present cultural fashions are any indication, the growing emphasis on the thinkers (and kind of thinking) discussed here increasingly seems to be regarded (together with its right-wing opposition and mirror) as somehow its most pertinent contemporary legacy. The dynamics of its reception process still need to be studied. Clearly it operates differently within different cultures; the American is not the same as, say, the Israeli or German case. The manifold psychological as well as intellectual functions these Jewish thinkers presently play within German cultural life certainly merits study. Jürgen Habermas seems to have been one of the major early pioneers successfully promoting this interest. See his essays on these topics (beginning in 1961) in *Philosophical-Political Profiles,* trans. Frederick G. Lawrence (Cambridge: Cambridge University Press, 1985).

paper, it is important to stress that their thought was animated by explicitly antibourgeois and postliberal impulses. Here was a revival dependent upon and made possible by the construction of what can only be described as *post-Bildung* conceptual frameworks. The guiding themes of this renaissance—and its respective emphases on cataclysm, apocalypse, and redemption, and on radical anti-evolutionary Utopian modes and the rediscovery of (Jewish) mystic and messianic materials[22]—must be understood as particular expressions of concerns that today are, by and large, regarded as most novel and characteristic of the Weimar intellectual enterprise.

It is of course no easy task defining the distinctive signature of a culture.[23] "Pure" distillations are seldom to be found. In the Weimar Republic, as elsewhere, older patterns of thought and behaviour persisted and existed side by side with newer creations. Moreover, much that then came to fruition originated in the prewar *Kaiserreich*. Nevertheless, despite an admittedly highly complex, plural constellation, I do think it useful to try and identify those core creative—spiritual, intellectual, and artistic—features that most decisively seemed to capture what was most epochally peculiar. I am clearly rejecting as too partial (and obvious) the argument that attitudes and perceptions in the Republic were so deeply fragmented and contradictory, the right-left cleavages so great that no common parameters whatsoever may be found:[24] "German culture at the time of the Weimar Republic," writes Eberhard Kolb, "was a deeply divided culture—we may even say that there were two cultures which had scarcely anything to say to each other and were mutually alien and hostile, each denying (though with different degrees of justification)

---

[22] While lumping these aspects together here, it should be clear that these all have separate histories and structures. Radical utopianism is obviously not the same as messianism. Nevertheless, salvation appears at the end of history or as an event within history but never produced by it. As such, it can be discussed together with messianic strains.

[23] For an attempt to define these distinctive characteristics, see Detlev J. K. Peukert, *The Weimar Republic: The Crisis of Classical Modernity*, trans. Richard Deveson (London: Hill and Wang, 1991). See especially parts I and VI.

[24] See, in this connection, Kurt Sontheimer, "Weimar Culture," in *The Burden of German History*, ed., Michael Laffan (London: Methuen Publishing, 1989), especially 1.

that the other was a culture at all."[25]

At one level, this is of course indisputable. But beyond the obvious differences, the notion of a hopelessly driven culture diverts attention from the common inheritance and predicament that constituted the transformed post–World War I German reality. In this common informing context, articulate elites of very different intellectual stripes shared more in sensibility and ways of thinking than they would have cared to admit.[26] What we take to be quintessentially Weimarian intellectual projects are, I submit, those essentially postliberal ruminations, posited on the ruins of a destroyed political and cultural order, that sought novel—and usually radical—answers to the problems of a fundamentally transformed European civilisation. Intellectuals of both the left and the right (especially those who, for whatever reason, find the most echo in our own late twentieth century) shared the desire for a kind of "root" re-thinking. The coherence lay less in the various preferred solutions than in the modes of conceptualisation—the drive to think everything anew—and above all, in a certain messianic or even apocalyptic temper.[27]

It is common knowledge that the right, given its postwar dislocation and disempowerment, became increasingly radical, revolutionary, and even apocalyptic. Precisely because it too felt dislocated and disempowered, it now adopted such radical stances.[28] What Karl Loewith

---

[25] Eberhard Kolb, *The Weimar Republic*, trans. P. S. Falla (London: Routledge, 1988), 84.

[26] It is a little known but telling fact that none other than Carl Schmitt arranged for the publication of Ernst Bloch's *Geist der Utopie* by Duncker & Humblot in 1918. Personal communication from Raphael Gross.

[27] This holds even in the face of the apparent (and always illusory) stabilization that is supposed to have characterised the years 1924–1929. Indeed, even the *Neue Sachlichkeit*, the "new sobriety," the cultural expression of that politico-economic period, presented itself within these terms of reference as an overt alternative to what was recognised as the prevalent revolutionary, redemptive, apocalyptic discourse of the time. As the expressionist playwright Paul Kornfeld put it in his 1924 comedy *Palme oder der Gekraenkte:* "Let us hear no more of war and revolution and the salvation of the world! Let us be more modest and turn to other, smaller things." Quoted in Kolb, *The Weimar Republic*, 85.

[28] On the radicalisation of the right, see my *The Nietzsche Legacy in Germany 1890–1990* (Berkeley: University of California Press, 1992), especially chapters 5 and 6; Jeffrey Herf, *Reactionary Modernism: Technology, Culture, and Politics in the Third Reich* (Cambridge: Cambridge University Press, 1984), and Martin Greiffenhagen, *Das*

has written about its conceptual armoury—the perception of decline and impending European catastrophe and the concomitant radical "will to rupture, revolution, and awakening"[29]—was, however, by no means limited to the right. Many of the same strains animated much of what was new on the intellectual left and, often in interdependent ways, the Jewish radical revival. As George Steiner has remarked,[30] the representative "master" texts of Weimar culture—Martin Heidegger's *Being and Time* (1927), Ernst Bloch's *Spirit of Utopia* (1918), and Oswald Spengler's *Decline of the West* (1918 and 1922)—were all characterised by an acute sense of rupture and nihilistic breakdown, and all explored novel and radical ways in which to both comprehend and address this new predicament. He could as easily have added to this list, perhaps as the master text of the Weimar Jewish renaissance, Franz Rosenzweig's similarly motivated *The Star of Redemption*.

These kinds of texts have a bearing on our central theme, for they were expressions of an overall sensibility that either explicitly challenged, opposed, or jettisoned many of the most cherished presuppositions inherent in classical *Bildung* (and in so doing, formulated significantly revised conceptions of both Jewishness and general culture). For what underlay the notion of *Bildung* and gave it plausibility was the essentially liberal-Enlightenment belief in notions of totality and the gradual evolution of humankind,[31] in "progress." *Bildung* envisaged a gradual, unfolding process of self-formation that applied not only to the life of individuals but eventually to its realisation for all of humanity. As one historian of *Bildung*, Rudolf Vierhaus, has shown, the notion was predicated upon the concepts of individuality and "development." *Bildung*, defined as "inner self-contained development leading outwards" [*selbstaendige Entwicklung von innen heraus*], presupposed rational Enlightenment ideas of gradual

Dilemma des Konservatismus in Deutschland (Frankfurt a.M.: Duncker & Humblot, 1986), especially 241–56.

29   Karl Loewith, "The Political Implications of Martin Heidegger's Existentialism," trans. Richard Wolin and Melissa J. Cox, *New German Critique* 45 (Fall 1988).

30   George Steiner, "Heidegger, Again," *Salmagundi* 82–83 (Spring-Summer 1989), 31–55.

31   See Assmann, *Arbeit am Nationalen Gedächtnis*, 9, 29–30, 74–5.

historical progress, development, and *process*.[32] Moreover, as Mosse himself stresses, the substance and style of "*Bildung* was not chaotic or experimental but disciplined and self-controlled."[33] It also, I should add, took for granted what modernists would later seriously doubt: the assumption of the unity and the continuity of the self.

The Weimar Jewish revival was based on rejecting virtually every one of these presuppositions (although it is worth noting that the intellectuals who articulated it were also the inheritors of this tradition and their sophisticated ruminations were in part made possible by it). The rejection can be clarified by contrasting it to what Martin Buber later wrote. A Jewish revival that was solely future oriented, he argued, should not be satisfactory; just as important as the quest for arrival was consciousness of the point of departures.[34] But this is not what I have in mind. As Mosse argues, the varieties of modern German Judaism from Orthodoxy to Zionism (including the *Voelkish* nationalism of Buber[35]) definitionally integrated Jewish origins into some kind of a forward-looking, humanising *Bildungs* outlook. Indeed, Buber cannot be considered a part of this kind of Weimar radicalism because his vision of Jewish renewal was predicated upon a typically *Bildungs* basis—the radical self-reformation of the individual Jew and his *inner* world.[36] The Weimar Jewish revivalists recognised this and, in part, modelled their renaissance on explicitly anti-Buberian premises, rejecting Buber's pre-1914 call for a return to a personal Judaism of

---

[32]   Rudolf Vierhaus, "Bildung," in *Geschichtliche Grundbegriffe: Historisches Lexikon zu politisch-sozialen Sprache in Deutschland*, ed., Otto Brunner, Werner Conze, Reinhart Koselleck (Stuttgart: Klett, 1972), vol. 1, 508–551. The quote appears on 508. See too especially 516.

[33]   Aschheim, *German Jews Beyond Judaism*, 7.

[34]   Martin Buber, "*Bildung* und Weltanschauung" (Frankfurter Lehrhausrede), *Mittelstelle für Jüdische Erwachsenen Bildung, Reichsvertretung der Juden in Deutschland* (Frankfurt, April 1937), 1. Quoted in Mosse, *German Jews Beyond Judaism*, 36 and note 53, 88.

[35]   See "The Influence of the Volkish Idea on German Jewry," George L. Mosse, *Germans and Jews: The Right, the Left, and the Search for a "Third Force" in Pre-Nazi Germany* (London: Howard Fertig, Inc, 1971) especially 89; Mosse, *German Jews Beyond Judaism*, 36.

[36]   See Paul Mendes-Flohr, "Nationalism as a Spiritual Sensibility: The Philosophical Suppositions of Buber's Hebrew Humanism," in *Divided Passions: Jewish Intellectuals and the Experience of Modernity*, ed., Paul Mendes-Flohr (Detroit: Wayne State University Press, 1991), especially 190.

renewal and pure *Erlebnis*.[37]

This revival, it is true, shared some of the convictions that young radicals were already voicing in the years immediately prior to 1914. The revolt against bourgeois elders, the rejection of the assimilation, and doubts about the *Deutschtum-Judentum* synthesis[38] all preceded the war. But now under the vastly changed conditions of war and a polarised republic, they adopted new critical perspectives and novel ways not only of casting the problems but also of answering them. Theirs was an eclectic radicalism that characteristically fused Messianic, utopian, and modernist modes of thought. The period abounds with numerous examples of its experimental (often esoteric) character. It was expressed atmospherically in such diverse institutions as the famous *Juedisches Lehrhaus* in Frankfurt, the *Juedische Volksheim* and the utopian socialist Safed society in Berlin, the Heidelberg sanitarium (1924–1928) that combined Judaism with psychoanalysis (the "Thorapeutikum," as it was known!), and the "metaphysical magicians" in Oskar Goldberg's circle.[39] Although this paper concentrates on four of the most significant embodiments of this new radicalism, historians have included other such diverse figures as Georg Lukacs, Gustav Landauer, Kurt Hiller, Salomo Friedlaender,[40] Erich Fromm, and Leo Loewenthal within its contours. (Characteristically, the young Loewenthal's Zionism had little to do with Palestine. It was rather, as he wrote to Ernst Simon in 1920, a mode of consciousness, the most appropriate way in which Jews could realise Bloch's *Spirit of Utopia*.[41])

Bloch, Scholem, Rosenzweig, and Benjamin knew each other—or

---

[37] See the fascinating article by Anson Rabinbach, "Between Enlightenment and Apocalypse," *New German Critique* 34 (Winter 1985), especially 88ff.

[38] For a history of these developments, see my *Brothers and Strangers: The East European Jew in German and German-Jewish Consciousness 1800–1923* (Madison: University of Wisconsin Press, 1982), chapters 5, 6.

[39] See respectively *Brothers and Strangers*, 193–8; Reinhard Blomert, "Das vergessene Sanitorium," in *Jüdisches Leben in Heidelberg: Studien zu einer unterbrochenen Geschichte*, ed., Norbert Giovannini, Johannes Bauer, Hans-Martin Mumm (Heidelberg: Das Wunderhorn, 1992), 249–62; Gershom Scholem, *From Berlin to Jerusalem: Memories of My Youth* (New York: Schocken, 1980), 131, 146–8.

[40] See Rabinbach, "Between Enlightenment and Apocalypse," 82–3.

[41] Unpublished Loewenthal letter to Simon of April 9, 1920, kindly provided to me by Guy Meron.

at the very least, about each other—and the critical, highly complex perspectives they developed about each other's work and person[42] are testimony to the separate nature of their undertakings, their divergent conceptions of Judaism, and their varying degrees of commitment to it. Yet all—Scholem and Rosenzweig in their respective reconceptualisations of Judaism and Benjamin and Bloch as they appropriated Judaic ingredients into their eclectic recasting of Marxism—nevertheless rejected crucial ingredients of the *Bildungs* inheritance. They did so because the quasi-messianic, utopian, and apocalyptic temper, those critical and prophetic tools which so widely pervaded the Weimar Republic (and which, at least in part, prompted these thinkers to turn to the Jewish messianic and mystic traditions for inspiration[43]), subverted many of the foundations of the *Bildungs* world. They all questioned the very idea of gradual historical progress and emphasised in its place the importance of historical cataclysm, caesurae, and rupture. Small wonder that in 1919 a shocked (and politically very conservative[44]) Franz Rosenzweig—faced with the

---

[42] The complexity of the relationships can be gleaned from a brief look at Gershom Scholem, *Walter Benjamin: The Story of a Friendship*, trans. Harry Zohn (Philadelphia: Jewish Publications Society of America, 1981); Gershom Scholem, ed., *The Correspondence of Walter Benjamin and Gershom Scholem 1932–1940* (Cambridge; Harvard University Press, 1991); Franz Rosenzweig, *Briefe*, ed., Edith Rosenzweig (Berlin: Schocken, 1935), and many other sources mentioned in this chapter.

[43] There is, of course, another side to this—the problematic relation (yet continued attraction) to tradition that characterised these modernists. As Hannah Arendt wrote, Benjamin's choice to study baroque (in a double sense) had "an exact counterpart in Scholem's strange decision to approach Judaism via the Cabala which is untransmitted and untransmittable in terms of Jewish tradition, in which it has always had the odor of something downright disreputable. Nothing showed more clearly—so one is inclined to say today—that there was no such thing as a "return" either to the German or European or the Jewish tradition than the choice of these fields of study. It was an implicit admission that the past spoke directly only through things that had not been handed down, whose seeming closeness to the present was thus due precisely to their exotic character, which ruled out all claims to a binding authority." See the 1968 essay "Walter Benjamin" reproduced in her *Men in Dark Times* (New York: Schocken, 1968), 195. Of all four men, Benjamin was of course the most resistant to salvationary solutions (see 189–90).

[44] Rosenzweig had extreme monarchist views, was "outraged at the prospects of a President [*sic*] Scheidemann or an Emperor Max," and in November 1919 exclaimed that it is "most natural, normal and inevitable ... to be in the reactionary camp." See

magnitude of the European catastrophe—said of Oswald Spengler, author of that right-wing, apocalyptic work *The Decline of the West*, that he was objectively probably the greatest philosopher of history that has appeared since Hegel.[45] (Bloch, incidentally, originally envisaged the title *Music and Apocalypse* for what became known as *Spirit of Utopia*.[46])

For all these men it was no longer the rational process of "self-formation" and "development" that would ultimately bring salvation but rather epiphanic events, flashing moments that by disrupting the flow of history would provide intimations of redemption or, as in the case of Rosenzweig, conceive of redemption entirely outside of history.[47] (For Rosenzweig, precisely because the Jews constituted a metahistorical community—a nation beyond history—they were the realisation of the future redemption within pre-Messianic time and could act as custodians of human eschatological hope.[48])

While the notion of *Bildung* may have had pietistic roots, its centrality to German culture from the second half of the eighteenth century epitomised its secular, entirely self-referential nature, denoting "a process of integral self-development ... that was an inherent part of the individual."[49] What could have been further away from this world than the quasi-theological (almost heteronomous) categories of the Weimar

---

Stefan Meineke, "A Life of Contradiction: The Philosopher Franz Rosenzweig and his Relationship to History and Politics," *Leo Baeck Institute YearBook* 36 (1991), 477.

[45] See the letter to Rudolf Ehrenburg of May 5 1919 in Franz Rosenzweig, *Briefe*, 359.

[46] Ludwig Feuchtwanger, the editor of the Duncker and Humblot publishing house, rejected Bloch's title, Scholem writes, "because it might scare readers away. Benjamin described to me Bloch's impressive appearance and told me that Bloch was now working on his magnum opus, *System des theoretischen Messianismus* [System of theoretical messianism]; he grew wide-eyed when he mentioned this." See *Walter Benjamin: The Story of a Friendship*, 79.

[47] Given the manifold, complex nature of the *Bildungs* idea, it has been pointed out (in conversation with Joel Golb), that in some of its versions it contains an epiphanic, flashing quality. It is possible that the thinkers we have considered here even drew from that particular tradition. But, even if this is so, this strain remains distinct from what Mosse regards as *Bildungs* classical core, the one to which German Jewish intellectuals remained most steadfastly loyal.

[48] On this (and related themes) see the interesting reflections by Paul Mendes-Flohr, "The Stronger and the Better Jews: Jewish Theological Responses to Political Messianism in the Weimar Republic," *Studies in Contemporary Jewry* 7 (1991), 159–85, especially 165–9.

[49] See Sorkin, *The Transformation of German Jewry*, 15.

Jewish revival? In Rosenzweig's case, this requires no illustration. But it was similarly the Marxist Benjamin who wrote: "My thinking relates to theology the way a blotter does to ink. It is soaked through with it."[50] Benjamin's thought is so idiosyncratic precisely because it is permeated by this sensibility, creating a historical materialism that, as he put it, "establishes a conception of the present which is shot through with the chips of Messianic time."[51] In ways similarly alien to mainstream Marxism, Bloch was fascinated with subterranean religious phenomena, his explosive utopian project nurtured by the religious imagination. His *Spirit of Utopia* ends with the words "truth as prayer" (*Wahrheit als Gebet*).[52] He was certainly perceived in the theological mode. Emil Lask asked, "Who are the four evangelicals? Matthew, Mark, Lukacs and Bloch."[53] And careful philological scholar and critical historian though he may have been, Scholem's language and writings were throughout laden with the theological dimension, the "hope," as he put it, "of a true communication from the mountain."[54]

---

[50] See his "Re The Theory of Knowledge, Theory of Progress," in *Benjamin: Philosophy, Aesthetics, History*, ed., Gary Smith (Chicago: University of Chicago Press, 1989), 61. Characteristically gnomic, Benjamin went on to say: "If one were to go by the blotter, though, nothing of what has been written would remain." As for Scholem, see the remarkable letters that he wrote to Benjamin (July 9 and 17, 1934). There his insistence on the theological mode is completely apparent. See *The Correspondence of Walter Benjamin and Gershom Scholem*, 122–7.

[51] Walter Benjamin, "Theses on the Philosophy of History," in *Illuminations*, ed., Hannah Arendt and trans. Harry Zohn (New York: Schocken, 1969), 263.

[52] Bloch, *Geist der Utopie*, 445.

[53] Quoted in Hans Saner, *Karl Jaspers* (Hamburg: Rowohlt, 1970) 33. On the Heidelberg experience of these "Jewish Apocalyptics," see Eva Karadi, "Ernst Bloch and Georg Lukacs in Max Weber's Heidelberg," *Max Weber and His Contemporaries*, ed., W.J. Mommsen and J. Osterhammel (London: HarperCollins, 1987), 499–514.

[54] This remained a constant from 1916 on. For a late statement, see his remarkable 1974 essay, "Reflections on Jewish Theology," where he addresses the limits of Zionist "normalization" and of secularization in general: "The position of the man of the secularistic age *vis-à-vis* his society is more helpless than ever in his confrontation with nihilism (293)... I admit that this unshakable belief in a specific moral centre, which bestows meaning in world history on the Jewish people, transcends the sphere of pure secularization. I would not even deny that in it a remnant of theocratic hope also reaccompanies that reentry into world history of the Jewish people that at the same time signifies the truly Utopian return to its own history (294–5)....
I consider a complete secularization of Israel to be out of the question so long as the faith in God is still a fundamental phenomenon of anything human and cannot be

This theological sensibility was animated by an acute consciousness of messianic themes. Benjamin's Marxism is unthinkable without it. Which other historical materialist could have written that "the Messiah comes not only as the redeemer, he comes as the subduer of the Antichrist"?[55] Bloch's entire *oeuvre* can be regarded as a sustained meditation on the vibrant and radiant possibilities of an "atheistic messianism"[56] and eschatological hope as an *a priori* of human existence, culture, and politics.[57] As we have seen, Rosenzweig was also acutely aware of the messianic dimension, rendering the Jews its realisation within premessianic historical time.[58] Scholem's brilliant sensitivity to its internal dynamics is well known. He did, after all, later become the primary incisive analyst of the paradoxical dialectics inherent in the messianic—and related apocalyptic—idea.[59] But it was not merely as analyst that Scholem approached the matter. To be sure, he was as aware of the dangers of messianism as he was fascinated by to it. Yet throughout, it provided him with a (critical-redemptive) perspective that rendered it more than a simple historical category.[60] Its normative

---

liquidated 'ideologically'" (297). This is reproduced in Gershom Scholem, *On Jews and Judaism in Crisis: Selected Essays*, ed., Werner J. Dannhauser (New York: Schocken, 1976), 261–97.

55 Benjamin, "Theses on the Philosophy of History," 255.

56 See Paul Mendes-Flohr, "'To Brush History against the Grain': The Eschatology of the Frankfurt School and Ernst Bloch," *Divided Passions*. Bloch's "atheistic messianism" opposes religious messianism in that the latter limits man's capacity to create his own future. In effect, Bloch defers to the infinite, unrealizable future. Still, he too rejects progressive, linear development.

57 For an excellent overview of Bloch's work, see chapter 5 of Martin Jay, *Marxism and Totality* (Berkeley: University of California Press, 1984); see too George Steiner, "Sojourns in the Wondrous," *Times Literary Supplement* (October 4, 1985).

58 Paul Mendes-Flohr has pointed out that although Rosenzweig failed to integrate the historical-apocalyptic ingredients of messianism into his theology, he had a profound phenomenological appreciation of its role. See "The Stronger and the Better Jews,"165–9.

59 See his *The Messianic Idea in Judaism And Other Essays on Jewish Spirituality* (New York: Schocken, 1971).

60 "The utopian, messianic element," Henry Pachter writes, "in the problematic of neo-Marxism constituted the major point of contact with Scholem, who drew attention to the Jewish source of utopian thinking in the Frankfurt School, for it *is* evident that messianism is the basic pattern on which both he and they built their particular methods of criticizing the present system." (Interestingly, both Bloch and

role in his thought was most clearly expressed in his 1931 critique of what he perceived to be Rosenzweig's neutralisation of the apocalyptic strain in Jewish messianism. This neutralization undermined what Scholem regarded to be the profound truth of apocalyptic messianism: the "recognition of the catastrophic potential of all historical order in an unredeemed world ... the truth that redemption possesses not only a liberating but also a destructive force."[61]

This messianic mode of thinking and its variegated thematic—the dismissal of gradual change, the emphasis on origins and restoration to a golden age, a radical utopianism (in which salvation appears either at the end of history or as an event within history but never produced by it), and the apocalyptic-catastrophic dimension in which a qualitative rent utterly divides the Messianic age from the past,[62] operates with a notion of "redemption" that is diametrically opposed to the optimistic notions of progress and process inherent in the liberal-Enlightenment notion of *Bildung*.

One look, for instance, at the structure of restorative messianism and its notion of origin as goal[63]—traces of which can be found in the thought of all these thinkers—demonstrates an overturning of the insistence upon growth and development that lay at the heart of *Bildung*. Paradoxically, the idea of return to an original, paradisical state lies in both the past *and* the future. As Bloch put it: "The world is not true, but it will successfully

---

Max Horkheimer at the end of their lives recognized religion as an expression of their aspirations; Scholem was vindicated.) "Masters of Cultural History: Gershom Scholem—The Myth of the Mythmaker," *Salmagundi* 40 (Winter 1978), 9–39. The quote appears on p. 22.

61 "On the 1930 Edition of Rosenzweig's Star of Redemption." This appeared originally in the *Frankfurter Israelitisches Gemeindeblatt* 10 (1931) and is reproduced in Gershom Scholem, *The Messianic Idea in Judaism* (New York: Schocken, 1971). The quote appears on p. 323. As a Zionist, moreover, Scholem seems to have been disturbed by the historical quietism implied by Rosenzweig's conception of messianism.

62 This outline of the restorative, utopian, and apocalyptic elements of messianic thought rests upon the brilliant schema and analysis of Rabinbach, "Between Enlightenment and Apocalypse," especially 84–8. Rabinbach also argues that this thinking is characterised by a profound ethical ambivalence, a mood caught between doom and hope, and the poles of contemplation and action.

63 On this theme, especially in Benjamin, see Richard Wollin, *Walter Benjamin: An Aesthetic of Redemption* (New York: Telos Press, 1982), 36–44.

return home through human beings and through truth."[64]

More importantly, restorative messianism entailed a curious view of language as the most powerful, almost magical, key to and medium of redemption. We must be careful to identify what was new here. German-speaking Jewish intellectuals had always been sensitive to the shaping powers of language.[65] But prior to 1914—in keeping with the activities of rational *Bildung* intellectuals—they were prone to stress its duplicities and dangers. Men like Karl Kraus and Felix Mauthner were the most penetrating critics of language, unmasking its limits and untruths (a tradition later radicalised by Ludwig Wittgenstein).[66] At that time (in an astonishing 1911 diary entry), no one pointed more tellingly to its deficiencies and limits than did Franz Kafka:

> Yesterday it occurred to me that I did not always love my mother as she deserved and as I could, only because the German language prevented it. The Jewish mother is no "Mutter," to call her "Mutter" makes her a little comic ... "Mutter" is peculiarly German for the Jew, it unconsciously contains together with the Christian splendor Christian coldness also.[67]

With their messianic and modernist predispositions, the Weimar Jewish revivalist intellectuals now *went beyond critique and sought the ultimate redemptive possibilities of language*. Emphasis on origins focused thought

---

[64]   Ernst Bloch, *Geist der Utopie* (Frankfurt a. M. Suhrkamp, 1964), 347. Quoted in Rabinbach, "Between Enlightenment and Apocalypse," 85. The first edition appeared in 1918, the second in 1923.

[65]   For German Jewish modernizers, Yiddish (or the *Jargon*) was synonymous with *Unbildung*. Indeed, as Moses Mendelssohn wrote in 1782, it had "contributed not a little to the immorality of the common man; and I expect a very good effect on my brothers from the increasing use of the pure German idiom." It was typical of this *Bildungs* faith in culture that it held that immorality could somehow be countered by the proper use of language. See the quote in Michael A. Meyer, *The Origins of the Modern Jew* (Detroit; Wayne State University Press, 1967), 44. See also *Brothers and Strangers,* chapter 1.

[66]   For an analysis of these developments see Allan Janik and Stephen Toulmin, *Wittgenstein's Vienna* (New York: Simon and Schuster, 1973). See also Sander Gilman, *Jewish Self-Hatred: Anti-Semitism and the Hidden Language of the Jews* (Baltimore and London: Johns Hopkins University Press, 1986).

[67]   See the entry for October 24, 1911, in *The Diaries of Franz Kafka 1910–1913*, ed., Max Brod (New York: Schocken, 1965), 111.

on the recovery of lost meanings and on truth as hidden, part of a primal, esoteric structure waiting to be revealed. The many differences in the conceptions of these Weimar intellectuals notwithstanding, there were important underlying commonalities (although these were not always perceived as such).[68] Thus, strikingly, Rosenzweig believed in a human *Ursprache*, a kind of pre-Babel speech in which he posited a primordial unity between name and thing. (One need only mention the similarity to Heidegger in this context.[69]) Rosenzweig's view of the redemptive powers of language[70]—the belief that, given God's eternal presence, the lost *Ursprache* could be reconstituted—rendered translation a peculiarly potent medium:[71] "Every translation is a messianic act, which brings redemption nearer."[72] Similarly, Walter Benjamin, that materialist metaphysician, proclaimed the existence of a paradisical linguistic condition in which, as he put it, "language and revelation are one without any tension."[73] Despite the differences, Benjamin

---

[68] For a comparative examination see Stephane Moses, "Walter Benjamin and Franz Rosenzweig," in *Benjamin,* ed., Gary Smith, 228–46, and Martin Jay, "The Politics of Translation: Siegfried Kracauer and Walter Benjamin on the Buber-Rosenzweig Bible," *Leo Baeck Institute Year Book* 21 (1976), especially 18ff.

[69] Not only in this, but in many other respects as well, the similarities between Rosenzweig and Heidegger have been variously noted. See Karl Loewith, "M. Heidegger and F. Rosenzweig or Temporality and Eternity," *Philosophy and Phenomenological Research* 3 (1942–1943), 53–77; Steven S. Schwarzschild, "Franz Rosenzweig and Martin Heidegger: The German and the Jewish Turn to Ethnicism," and Alan Udoff, "Rosenzweig's Heidegger Reception and the reorigination of Jewish Thinking" in *Der Philosoph Franz Rosenzweig* (1886–1929), Internationaler Kongress—Kassel 1986. Band II—*Das Neue Denken und seine Dimensionen,* ed., Wolf Dietrich Schmied-Kowarzik (Freiburg/Munich: Karl Alber, 1988), 887–9 and 923–950; Stephane Moses, *System and Revelation: The Philosophy of Franz Rosenzweig,* trans. Catherine Tihanyi (Detroit: Wayne State University Press, 1992), 290–3.

[70] See Franz Rosenzweig, *The Star of Redemption,* trans. William W. Hallo (Boston: Notre Dame, 1971), especially 109–11, 125–32, 141–2, 150–1.

[71] See Rosenzweig's "The Function of Translation," *Franz Rosenzweig: His Life and Thought,* Nahum N. Glatzer (New York: Schocken, 1961), 252–261. Originally Part Two from the essay "Die Schrift und Luther," Rosenzweig's *Kleinere Schriften,* 141–66 (Berlin: Schocken, 1937).

[72] Quoted in George Steiner, *After Babel: Aspects of Language and Translation* (London: Oxford University Press, 1975), 244.

[73] See "The Task of the Translator" in Benjamin, *Illuminations.* The quote appears on p. 82. See too "On Language as Such and on the Language of Man," in *Reflections.* To be sure, unlike Rosenzweig, Benjamin believed that after the fall, language degenerated into the profane medium of communication. The act of translation had an almost

posited an archaic-mythical "language of revelation," while Rosenzweig regarded it as eternally present, "language as revelation"[74]—their conceptions of the role of origins and revelation clearly undercut the secular, unfolding, and self-forming idea of *Bildung*.

Scholem too imbibed this view of the potency of original language, especially the holy tongue. This is most remarkably illustrated in his letter to Rosenzweig (on the occasion of the latter's fortieth birthday in 1926). In this "Confession on Our Language" [Bekenntnis ueber unsere Sprache],[75] Hebrew, as Robert Alter puts it, "is imagined as a system of deep taps into the abyss ... which, once having been activated, will open up an irresistible resurgence of the depths."[76] As Scholem wrote:

> This land is a volcano: It inhabits the language.... People here actually do not realize what they are doing. They think they have turned Hebrew into a secular language, that they have pulled out its apocalyptic sting. But that is untrue. The secularization of a language is a mere phrase, no more than a slogan.... A language is composed of names. The power of the language is bound up in the name, and its abyss is sealed within the name. Having conjured up the ancient names day after day, we can no longer suppress their potencies. We roused them, and they will manifest themselves, for we have conjured them up with very great power.[77]

I concede that Scholem's relationship to my general argument here is a complex one. Still I would take issue with Mosse's paper on Scholem—an extension and application of his overall thesis—which renders Scholem's project (though centred upon the quest for Jewish nationhood rather than integration into Germany) comprehensible only in terms of its

---

magical reconstitutional function, revealing original truth and meaning from the obscurities of mere communication.

[74] Moses, "Walter Benjamin and Franz Rosenzweig," op. cit., especially 238–9.

[75] On the complex nature of the relationship, see Michael Brocke, "Franz Rosenzweig und Gerhard Gershom Scholem," in *Juden in der Weimarer Republik*, ed., Walter Grab and Julius H. Schoeps (Stuttgart and Bonn: Wissenschaftliche Buchgesellschaft, 1986), 127–52.

[76] See Robert Alter's excellent *Necessary Angels: Tradition and Modernity in Kafka, Benjamin, and Scholem* (Cambridge: Harvard University Press, 1991), esp. 36–7.

[77] Gershom Scholem, *Od Davar* (Tel Aviv: Am Oved, 1989), 58–9. The original, "Bekenntnis ueber unsere Sprache," is reproduced in Brocke, op. cit., 148–50.

Bildung's base: the moral, humanist posture, never at ease with normative nationalism; the insistence on the primacy of culture; the perception of the historical process as an open, not a finished, product.[78]

These elements are certainly there. But the interpretation is strained because it is unable to comfortably incorporate the many essentially postliberal, even anarchistic, ingredients of Scholem's thought that Mosse himself emphasises: the profound anti-bourgeois convictions, the irrepressible attraction to the unconventional and even the bizarre, the notion of Zionism as a highly experimental wager, and so on.[79] Classical *Bildung*, Mosse stresses elsewhere, "was not chaotic or experimental but disciplined and self-controlled." That may have characterised Scholem's method of work, but it did not fit his anarchistic predilections nor the way he believed history operated. Indeed, as early as 1916, in a fashion quite antithetical to the philosophy of *Bildung*, he dismissed outright "the illusions" of "development" as an obstacle to truth (see the opening motto).

I would like to suggest that the discourse of this Jewish renaissance, like that of the Weimar radical right (Ernst Jünger, Martin Heidegger, Oswald Spengler, and so on),[80] was couched in clearly post-Nietzschean terms. It is not surprising that in the postwar Weimar context, far removed from the refined, cultivated world of *Bildung*, they all took as their starting point a heightened awareness of the nihilistic predicament and its simultaneously destructive and liberating possibilities. Unlike Bloch, Rosenzweig, and Benjamin, who albeit in complex ways admired Nietzsche,[81] Scholem consistently denied any such affinity. Yet the tonal resonance and thematic resemblance is obvious: the notions of abyss, immoralism, catastrophe and apocalypse, nihilism, and antinomianism inform his conceptual universe and everywhere permeate his writings.

---

[78] George L. Mosse, "Gerschom Scholem as a German Jew," *Modern Judaism* 10 (1990), 117–33. See especially 124–5.

[79] Ibid., p. 129.

[80] See *The Nietzsche Legacy in Germany,* especially chapters 5 and 6.

[81] On Rosenzweig's and Bloch's relation to Nietzsche, see my *The Nietzsche Legacy,* 101–2, 182–4, 217–8, 288–9. On Benjamin, see R. Reschke, "Barbaren, Kult und Katasrophen. Nietzsche bei Benjamin," *Aber ein Sturm weht vom Paradiese her. Texte zur Walter Benjamin* (Leipzig: Reclam, 1992), 303–41.

Moreover, I would argue, it was precisely these contemporaneously familiar and radical categories (whether they were also mined from the Jewish tradition is here not relevant) which rendered his presentation of the most esoteric byways of Jewish history immediately accessible and exciting to the modern reader.

The years 1916–1918, Scholem has testified, were decisive in the making of this kind of thinking and lay behind his startling and original application of these categories to the world of Kabbalah, where, as he stated, he found "intuitive affirmation of mystical theses which walked the fine line between religion and nihilism ... [and] courage to venture out into an abyss, which one day could end up in us ourselves."[82]

Contemporaries were aware of this very un-*Bildung*-like fascination: in 1922, Rosenzweig labelled Scholem simply as a "nihilist."[83] He wrote the following in 1960, but its animating spirit and categories derived from his formative World War I and Weimar years: "Every acute and radical Messianism that is taken seriously tears open an abyss in which by inner necessity antinomian tendencies and libertine moral conceptions gain strength."[84] His preoccupation with and fascination for nihilism and the radical transgression of limits, the connections between nihilistic powers of destruction and vital powers of national renewal" most classically expressed in his 1937 Hebrew essay "Mitzsva haba'ah ba'averah" (Redemption Through Sin), exploring how "messianism was transformed into nihilism,"[85] could not have been further away from the ways in which *Bildungs* intellectuals regarded the world and its potential.[86] To be sure, as David Biale has persuasively demonstrated,

---

[82] Letter to Zalman Schocken in Biale, *Gershom Scholem*, 75–6. The modernist connection here should be clear: immediately afterward Scholem commented that it was in Kafka that he found "the most perfect and unsurpassed expression of this fine line."

[83] See his letter to Rudolf Hallo of March 3, 1922, where he refers to "der boese Scholem. Warum disputierst du? ... Am wenigsten mit einem Nihilisten wie Scholem. Der Nihilist behaelt immer recht ... In Scholem steckt das Resentiment des Asketen." See Franz Rosenzweig, *Briefe*, 431.

[84] Gershom Scholem, "The Crypto-Jewish Sect of the Doenmeh (Sabbatians) in Turkey," in his *The Messianic Idea in Judaism*, 164. The article was originally written in German.

[85] *Keneset* II (1937), 347–92. The English version, "Redemption through Sin" is in *The Messianic Idea in Judaism*, 78–141. The quote appears on p. 109.

[86] In 1935, Scholem wrote to Benjamin that this essay—on "the ideology of religious nihilism in Judaism"—could "only be written in Hebrew ... if the author is to remain

Scholem was "at once the child of the vitalistic counterculture of turn of the century Europe but also its critic, a kind of anti-Nietzschean Nietzschean" whose attraction to the irrational and the demonic was tempered by an awareness of its catastrophic potentialities.[87]

Scholem's acute, lifelong awareness of what he called the "abyss" provides an even deeper insight into the ways in which he and this generation left the *Bildungs* inheritance far behind.[88] It reflected a basic assumption concerning the ultimate nature of reality. The stability of the world is illusory and potentially filled with terror: "reassuring orderliness and coherence [were] not intrinsic to it."[89] Scholem's historical world is characterised by a deep grasp of its interrelated destructive and radiant possibilities. To be sure, classical *Bildung* stressed a certain open-endedness; but this was always predicated upon the belief in progressive development, in a civilising and humanising process far removed from Benjamin's (now-famous) dictum that there "is no document of civilization which is not at the same time a document of barbarism."[90]

Our Jewish Weimarians could no longer automatically accept these progressive, civilising propositions which had been deeply punctured by the traumatising experience of World War I. In his diary of 1916, the young Scholem already registered the death and burial of Europe.[91] In November 1918, Rosenzweig wrote: "The 'culture' that was ours will be destroyed even in our lifetime ... Something

---

free from apologetic inhibitions." See Gershom Scholem, ed., *The Correspondence of Walter Benjamin and Gershom Scholem 1932–1940*, 174. See letter 79 (December 18, 1935), 172–4. While that may be so I would also argue that, at least in part, the *Fragestellung*, categories, and mode of thinking were very much related to the post-1916 German cultural milieu.

87 See the interesting unpublished paper by David Biale, "Scholem and Modem Nationalism."

88 Mosse, "Gerschom Scholem...," 121, which notes that Scholem's notion of history had absolutely no conception of progress or organic, steady development without perceiving the concomitant undermining of the *Bildungs* ideal.

89 See the unpublished paper by Robert Alter, "Scholem and Modernism," esp. 5.

90 Benjamin, "Theses on the Philosophy of History," op. cit., 256.

91 See the unpublished paper by Stephane Moses, "Benjamin, Rosenzweig, Scholem: The Critique of Historical Reason," given at the International Conference on *Walter Benjamin's Jewish Constellation* (July 14, 1992), 147.

new will take its place, of course. But it will not be ours."[92] He now regarded history as a purely destructive force, and it was to Jewish eternality that he turned for redemption. At any rate, a progressive philosophy of history—an assumption that had provided *Bildung* with its ontological and epistemological underpinnings—was no longer viable for any of these thinkers. Ernst Bloch, with all of his visions of future hope, nowhere posits a system of historical development; he explicitly opposes the notion of "progress." There is no continuum. True humanity, rather, can emerge at any time, at flashing, chosen moments, and ultimate realisation is pushed into the never realizable future.[93] While humanization remains the goal, it is far removed from the liberal-Enlightenment model: "History," he wrote, "is no entity advancing along a single line ... It is a polyrhythmic and multi-spatial entity with enough unmastered and as yet by no means revealed and resolved corners."[94]

These thinkers shared a kind of neo-eschatological bias characterised by the conviction that there was a radical disjunction between history and redemption.[95] Rosenzweig, the anti-Hegelian, dismissed history as an endless cycle of wars and revolution in principle unable to redeem itself. As Stéphane Moses has demonstrated, historical reason and the notion of historical telos were rejected and a new conception of time developed.[96] *Bildung's* twins—growth and self-formative progress—were dismissed.[97] Rifts, ruptures, and revolutions took precedence over the continuum of homogeneous time. But this was not, as we have seen, a merely negative critique, for a redemptive

---

[92] Unpublished letter to Magrit Rosenstock, 11 November 1918 quoted in Stefan Meineke, "A Life of Contradiction...," 481.

[93] See the comments by Hans Meyer, "Ernst Bloch in der Geschichte," *Reden ueber Ernst Bloch* (Frankfurt a.M.: Suhrkamp, 1989), 60.

[94] Ernst Bloch, *Erbschaft dieser Zeit* (Zuerich, 1935), 58; see the translation by Neville and Stephen Plaice, *Heritage of Our Times* (Berkeley: University of California Press, 1991), 62.

[95] This point is nicely developed in Paul Mendes-Flohr, "'To Brush History against the Grain': The Eschatology of the Frankfurt School and Ernst Bloch," *Divided Passions*.

[96] Moses, "Benjamin, Rosenzweig, Scholem: The Critique of Historical Reason," op. cit.

[97] As Benjamin put it: "The concept of the historical progress of mankind cannot be sundered from the concept of its progression through a homogenous, empty time. A critique of the concept of such a progression must be the basis of any criticism of the concept of progress itself." "Theses on the Philosophy of History," in *Illuminations*, 261.

alternative—surprisingly similar in structure despite the obvious differences separating these thinkers—was offered.[98]

This consisted of the notion of actualisation, redemption as a constant immanent possibility, now or at any given time (*Jetztzeit*). In place of an uninterrupted progressive totality, time is now conceived in terms of qualitative moments. Thus, Rosenzweig replaced the conventional Enlightenment notion of time with the eternal Jewish cycle and linked it to *Jetztzeit*, where redemption was possible at all times. The Marxist Benjamin (and similarly Bloch) no longer regarded revolution as the culmination of a progressive process but as the sudden eruption of a deeper truth that exploded the continuity of history. Here the rents and fractures are what counts, for continuity, according to Benjamin, was a category of the victors while discontinuity represented the realm of the oppressed and their uprisings.[99] History was thus a nonlinear process fuelled by the possibilities of new beginnings. If Scholem did not subscribe to Benjamin's view, he certainly understood its inner structure, describing it as "the secularization of Jewish apocalyptic doctrine," where "the noble and positive power of destruction ... now becomes an aspect of redemption, related to the immanence of the world, acted out in the history of human labor."[100]

It must be noted that this post-*Bildung* sensibility typically went together with what I can only call a "modernist" cast of thought. This was manifested in numerous ways.[101] It characterised the stylistic tendencies attendant upon "the breakdown of a causal, linear sense of

---

98 For a comparative examination, see Ulrich Hortian, "Zeit und Geschichte bei Franz Rosenzweig und Walter Benjamin," *Der Philosoph Franz Rosenzweig*, 815–27; Stephane Moses, "Walter Benjamin and Franz Rosenzweig," 228–46. While Bloch certainly dismisses "progress," his eruptive, flashing moments, important as they are, do not bring ultimate redemption. This is infinitely deferred into the future.

99 For an exposition of Benjamin's view of history, see Stéphane Moses, "Eingedenken und Jetzzeit: Geschichtliches Bewusstsein im Spaetwerk Walter Benjamins," in *Memoria Vergessen und Erinnern: Poetik und Hermeneutik* XV, ed, Anselm Haverkamp and Renate Lachmann (Munich: Fink Verlag, 1993).

100 "Walter Benjamin," in Gershom Scholem, *On Jews and Judaism in Crisis*, 194–5.

101 It is surely no accident that Rosenzweig's *Star of Redemption*, that anti-Hegelian treatise, begins in rhapsodic praise of that important founder of modernism, Nietzsche. See too Robert Alter, "Scholem and Modernism."

time and development."[102] It had much to do with the self-conscious montage form in which Bloch constructed much of his work (most famously in *Heritage of Our Times*). As he wrote there: "The combinations of manifold montage hold no expired totalities, no fraudulently idolised 'eternal values,' but rather interrupted ruins, in new figurations which possessed redemptive potential."[103] It also accounts for much of Benjamin's mode of writing, epitomised in his "One-Way Street," that densely personal record combining observations, dreams, aphorisms, and prose epigrams.[104] Modernism in general challenged those narrative modes, tellingly known as the *Bildungsroman*, that endorsed a life of continuity or growth within a single biography or even across generations.[105] Bloch made it clear that the times had rendered this an impossibility. "When the bourgeois world was still revolutionary ... the path was still from the *Sturm und Drang* period to [Goethe's] *Wilhelm Meister* as the bourgeois *Bildungsroman* through the 'world'; the imagined balance culminated ... as Hegel's 'reconciliation of the subject with necessity' ... today ... in the perfect non-world, anti-world or even ruin-world of the upper middle-Class hollow space, 'reconciliation' is neither a danger nor possible for concrete writers."[106]

But there is a deeper point here that is integrally related to the theme of our paper. This (once again post-Nietzschean) modernist consciousness challenged perhaps the most fundamental presupposition underlying *Bildung*—the notion of a unified, continuous self. As Bloch admiringly wrote of Benjamin's work: "Its 'I' is very near, but variable, indeed there are very many 'I's ... Constantly new 'I's ... extinguish one another."[107] Benjamin's brilliant study of surrealism not only explicitly

---

[102] This applies too to Bloch's central notion in *Erbschaft dieser Zeit* of "Ungleichzeitigkeit" in which social and cultural structures of the past are active in the present alongside aspects pregnant with the future.

[103] Neville and Stephen Plaice, *Heritage of Our Times,* 197. But see generally 195–208.

[104] "One-Way Street" is reproduced in Benjamin, *Reflections,* 61–94. See the comments in Demetz's "Introduction," xviii-xix.

[105] On this, see Ricardo J. Quinones, *Mapping Literary Modernism: Time and Development* (Princeton: Princeton University Press, 1985).

[106] Neville and Stephen Plaice, *Heritage of Our Times,* 228.

[107] See "Revue Form in Philosophy (1928)," in *Heritage of Our Times,* op. cit., esp. 334–5. Bloch refers to Benjamin's style as "photomontage."

addresses this problem but demonstrates how, in Charles Taylor's words, the modernist quest for "the liberation of experience can seem to require that we step outside the circle of the single, unitary identity and that we open ourselves to the flux which moves beyond the scope ... of control or integration ... the epiphanic centre of gravity begins to be displaced from the self to the flow of experience, to new forms of unity, to language conceived in a variety of ways."[108] Whereas in *Bildung*, it is the formative powers of the self that are redemptive, they are now to be found without. "Language takes precedence," wrote Benjamin. "Not only before meaning. Also before the self. In the world's structure dream loosens individuality like a bad tooth."[109]

The Weimar Jewish revival, we must conclude, provides a paradoxical challenge to the *Bildungsparadigm* and its conception of the intellectual substance and legacy of German Jewry.[110] Its makers defined their Jewishness not, as Mosse would have it, in terms of an ongoing *Bildungs* view of the world but rather by exploding many of its most cherished assumptions (and perhaps hanging on to selected others such as the ongoing belief in the humanising capacities of culture and the personalising of relationships). This was a renaissance whose

---

[108] Charles Taylor, *Sources of the Self: The Making of the Modern Identity* (Cambridge: Cambridge University Press, 1989), 462 and 465. The whole chapter "Epiphanies of Modernism" is relevant. Nevertheless, as Taylor shows, this decentering process was a paradoxical way of reestablishing unity at a deeper level, reinforcing the radically reflexive (and thus inward) posture of (an always manifold) modernism.

[109] "Surrealism: The Last Snapshot of the European Intelligentsia" is reproduced in Benjamin, *Reflections*, 177–192. The quote appears on p. 179. The piece was originally written in 1929. The vitality of the *Bildungs* idea, as Aleida Assmann has observed, was a function of an unproblematised notion of a "centre," whether of the person or the nation (something which in our own time is no longer conceivable). My argument is that such problematisation was already present in the writings we have considered here. See Assmann, *Arbeit am National Gedächtnis*, 111.

[110] When this paper was first presented at a conference in Madison, Wisconsin, in October 1993, it was objected that these intellectuals indeed remained constant to the original *Bildungs* idea but that its emphases shifted according to the dictates of changing circumstances. The critique of reason, it was argued, was built into *Bildung* itself: when the reason of critique failed, it became the critique of reason. But this provides the notion of *Bildung* with a remarkably potent protean quality—one which, at least in Mosse's book, does not appear in the original and enduring conception which informed its Jewish appropriation.

predispositions, sensibility, and categories were not isolated from but linked to many of the most definitive currents of the time, currents which also helped to determine which (usually neglected and esoteric) Jewish sources and materials would be integrated into the respective visions. Indelibly stamped by contemporary circumstances, their novel reconceptualisations of Judaism and affirmations of Jewishness were rendered possible, assumed their peculiar vitality, and found their resonance precisely by proceeding well beyond the calmer worlds of classical liberalism and *Bildung*.

CHAPTER IX

BETWEEN *DEUTSCHTUM* AND *JUDENTUM*: IDEOLOGICAL CONTROVERSIES WITHIN THE *CENTRALVEREIN*

Avraham Barkai

In purely legal terms, the period of the Weimar Republic is considered the heyday of Jewish emancipation in Germany, but the political antisocial reality was quite different. During the first, turbulent years of the Republic, antisemitism reached a new peak in political and public life. It was disseminated in an unprecedented flood of popular pamphlets, novels, and pseudoscientific racist publications, and it erupted in violent outbreaks on the streets. Then, after a few more peaceful years between 1924 and 1929, economic and political upheaval caused the rise of the Nazi Party and its neoconservative right-wing satellites, and the so-called Jewish Question became a major political topic.

Historians have long been aware that despite increasing pressure from the outside, which should have enhanced unity and the closing of ranks, internal Jewish conflicts did not diminish. The editor of the *Jüdische Rundschau*, Robert Weltsch (1891–1982), has argued that "at this time, despite—or probably because of—the danger from outside, the party differences among the Jews were not laid aside and were indeed not irrelevant. Each of the two leading groups believed its policy was right and that of the others injurious."[1] Nowadays, one may doubt if this is a sufficient explanation.

Probably the most violent polemical clashes occurred during the election campaigns of 1926 and 1930 for the leadership of the Jewish community of Berlin, where one-third of all German Jews lived at that

---

[1]   Robert Weltsch, "Schlussbetrachtung," *Entscheidungsjahr* 1932. *Zur Judenfrage in der Endphase der Weimarer Republik,* ed., Werner Mosse and Arnold Paucker, 2nd ed. (Tübingen: J. C. Mohr, 1966), 555.

time, and for that of the Prussian Association of Jewish Communities (*Preussischer Landesverband jüdischer Gemeindcn*, PLV). The temporary loss of the "Liberal" majority to a coalition of Zionists, Orthodox Jews, and organisations of East European Jews in 1926 was a severe shock to the members and followers of the *Centralverein deutscher Staatsbürger jüdischen Glaubens* (CV).[2] Despite these conflicts, the leadership of the principal nationwide Jewish political organisations, the *Zionistische Vereinigung für Deutschland* (ZVfD), and the Centralverein succeeded in creating a united election committee for the Reichstag elections of September 1930 in order to support the democratic parties and to counter antisemitic propaganda. On the other hand, although the Liberals regained their position in the Berlin community in the elections of November 1930, the alliance between the two organisations was not renewed before the far more crucial general elections of 1932.[3] Although the power struggles in Berlin and other communities did play some role in aggravating internal Jewish conflict, the real reasons for the radicalisation of the two sides' ideological and political positions are the internal disputes within the main political camps, the Zionists and the Centralverein.

Neither the CV nor the ZVfD campaigned in community elections. The main, though not the only, Zionist list was the *Jüdische Volkspartei* (JVP), while most followers of the CV voted for the Vereinigung für das Liberale Judentum (VLJ). In the case of the Zionists, recent research has disclosed that this was not just a functional "division of labor" produced by tactical considerations. The leaderships of the JVP and that of the ZVfD were not identical. Their prominent spokesmen differed in their sociological, occupational, and, in part, educational backgrounds,

---

[2]   See Gabriel E. Alexander, "Berlin Jewry and Its Community during the Weimar Republic (1919–1933)," Ph.D. diss., Hebrew University of Jerusalem, 1995 (in Hebrew), esp. 214ff; Michael Brenner, "The Jüdische Volkspartei National Jewish Communal Policies during the Weimar Republic," *LBIYB* 3 (1990), 219–43. I am grateful to Gabriel Alexander for letting me use his unpublished thesis.

[3]   See Arnold Paucker, *Der jüdische Abwehrkampf gegen Antisemitismus und Nationalsozialismus in den letzten Jahren der Weimarer Republik*, 2nd ed. (Hamburg: Leibniz, 1969); idem, "Der jüdische Abwehrkampf," in *Entscheidungsjahr 1932: Zur Judenfrage in der Endphase der Weimarer Republik. Ein Sammelband*, ed. Werner E. Mosse and Arnold Paucker (Tübingen: Mohr Siebeck, 1965), 423–24.

as well as in their political orientations.[4] So far, no adequate study exists of the VLJ leadership and its relations with CV. I would suggest, however, that although all the activists and most of the voters of the VLJ were members or supporters of the CV, substantial differences in political outlook and ideological tenets are discernible between these two organisations.[5]

The founding of the Centralverein deutscher Staatsbürger jüdischen Glaubens on March 28, 1893 was a reaction to a renewed wave of antisemitism in Imperial Germany.[6] Two years earlier, the hoary blood

---

[4]   I wish to thank Michael Brenner for letting me use his unpublished M.A. thesis, "Die jüdische Volkspartei-Nationaljüdische Gemeindepolitik in der Weimarer Republik", Hochschule für Jüdische Studien, Heidelberg, 1988. His article "The Jüdische Volkspartei" (see note 2 above) summarizes his findings.

[5]   Alexander's chapter on the VJL in "Berlin Jewry," 97–119, is a commendable pioneering study on the history of this organization.

[6]   A comprehensive history of the CV is still outstanding. For the pre–World War I period, see Paul Rieger, *Ein Vierteljahrhundert im Kampf um das Recht und die Zukunft der deutschen Juden* (Berlin: Centralverein, 1918). Informative for the same period is Ismar Schorsch, *Jewish Reactions to German Anti-Semitism, 1870–1914* (New York: Columbia University Press, 1972). See also Jehuda Reinharz, *Fatherland or Promised Land: The Dilemma of the German Jew, 1893–1914* (Ann Arbor: University of Michigan Press, 1975), which deals mainly with the ideological controversies between CV and the Zionists. Arnold Paucker, "Zur Problematik einer jüdischen Abwehrstrategie in der deutschen Gesellschaft," in *Juden im Wilhelminischen Deutschland*, ed., Wener Mosse and Arnold Paucker (Tübingen: Mohr Siebeck, 1976), 479–548, contains an account of the political activities.

Two outstanding leaders of the CV who survived the war, Eva and Hans Reichmann, produced some important but fragmentary contributions on internal discussions and developments within the CV; see Eva Reichmann, "Der Bewusstseinswandel der deutschen Juden," in *Deutsches Judentum in Krieg und Revolution*, 1916–1923 ed., Werner Mosse and Arnold Paucker (Tübingen: Mohr Siebeck, 1971), 511–612; Hans Reichmann, "Der Centralverein deutscher Staatsbürger," in *Festschrift zum 80. Geburtstag von Rabbiner Dr. Leo Baeck* (London: Council for the Protection of the Rights and Interests of Jews from Germany, 1957), 63–75.

Elsewhere, Hans Reichmann has lamented the lack of archival sources that makes the writing of an objective, scientifically adequate history of the CV extremely difficult. He explained that in March 1933 none other than Hermann Göring advised the leaders of the CV to destroy the material that they had collected in their campaigns against the Nazi Party. This had partly already been done before at the CV's own initiative. On the other hand, the files of Jewish organizations were confiscated by the Gestapo and other National Socialist agencies because the Nazis wanted to efface the traces of their terrorist regime. (See Reichmann's essay "Der drohende Sturm" in the volume *In zwei Welten. Siegfried Moses zum 75. Geburtstag*, ed., Hans Tramer [Tel Aviv: Bitaon,

libel had reappeared at Xanten. In 1892, overtly antisemitic tenets were incorporated into the Tivoli program of the Conservative Party. In the parliamentary elections of 1893, the antisemitic parties won 16 seats in the Reichstag. That same year, Raphael Loewenfeld (1854–1910), a well-known writer and the founder and director of the popular Schiller Theatre in Berlin, published a pamphlet called *Schutzjuden oder Staatsbürger?* that was to become the most important "founding paper" of the CV. Loewenfeld's brochure argued against the intentions of the executive board of the Jewish community in Berlin to appeal to the Kaiser for protection against rising antisemitic propaganda.

The CV's intention to fight antisemitism via an open and public confrontation ("im Lichte der Oeffentlichkeit") had to overcome the opposition of community leadership, both Liberal and Orthodox, mainly in Berlin and other large cities.[7] Taking up Loewenfeld's rhetoric, the new organisation declared its aim of refraining from the traditional political practices of preemancipation Schutzjuden: no more behind-the-scenes petitioning and buying of the protection of sympathetic or self-interested Gentiles. Instead, the Jews themselves should fight openly, as German citizens, for their full and equal rights and against antisemitic slander and discrimination. The CV claimed these rights not only on the basis of the constitutional emancipation of 1869 but also on the basis of the centuries-old history of the German Jews and their allegiance to the sacred and time-honoured values and predominant

---

1962], 557–58) Reichmann was wrong: some years ago, a stock of more than 4,300 files containing what is believed to be the main body of the archives of the CV main office in Berlin was discovered in the Moscow Sonderarchiv and may now enable the writing of the history of the largest and most important political organization of German Jewry.

7   Arnold Paucker, "Zur Problematik einer jüdischen Abwehrstrategie," 486ff, quotes the *Leitsätze* of the new organization as "closely relying upon Löwenfeld's theses, yet divested of any religious polemic." The proviso refers to the attacks against Orthodoxy and the Talmud in Löwenfeld's brochure; according to Paucker, this proves that "he was not exactly a spiritual giant" (488); Jacob Borut, "A New Spirit among Our Brethren in Ashkenaz: German Jewry in the Face of Economic, Social, and Political Change in the Reich at the End of the 19th Century," Ph.D. diss. (in Hebrew), Hebrew University of Jerusalem, 1991, esp chapter 6, 198–236, and, within that discussion, 2161f. See also idem, "The Rise of Jewish Defense Agitation in Germany, 1890–1895: A Pre-History of C.V.?" *Leo Baeck Institute YearBook* 36 (1991), 59–96.

nationalist ideals of *Deutschtum*; this allegiance had been proclaimed and proven under the fire of war by their forefathers and by themselves.

Very soon, however, the ideological tenets of the movement went beyond those of a mere defensive organisation. The CV's most prominent ideologue, Eugen Fuchs (1856–1923), led the way in the definition of the CV as not only an association of defence (*Abwehrverein*) but also as one of conviction (*Gesinnungsverein*). Outlining this theory of unifying conviction in 1917, in a famous polemic against Kurt Blumenfeld, Fuchs stressed his German identity: "I speak German and feel German. I am more fulfilled by German culture and German spirit than by Hebrew poetry and Jewish culture. When abroad, I yearn for Germany, for German nature, and German *Volksgenossen*."[8] But in the same article, he also declared: "If it were so that the Centralverein enhances apostasy and the disintegration of Judaism, and that Zionism furthers antisemitism, I would not hesitate for one moment to move with flying banners into the Zionist camp ... because, compared with apostasy, I regard antisemitism to be the lesser evil."[9]

There is no doubt that Eugen Fuchs's Jewish consciousness, so aptly expressed in these declarations, voiced the sentiments of a significant number of his contemporaries in the CV's leadership.[10] But I doubt that this consciousness deeply penetrated the ranks of the CV members and followers. Around 1900, the Deutschtum element in the ideological formula was indeed played down in the guidelines in favour of more Judentum, but this was less prominent in the widely circulated publications of the CV.[11] During and after the war, under the dual pressure of antisemitism and Zionism, the CV's public rhetoric increasingly featured extremely nationalistic pronouncements of German patriotism.

During the interwar years, the task of an ideological redefinition of the synthesis between Deutschtum and Judentum was taken over by Ludwig Holländer (1877–1936), who from 1908 on was the *Syndikus*

---

8   Eugen Fuchs, *Um Deutschtum und Judentum. Gesammelte Reden und Aufsätze* (1894–1919) (Frankfurt a.M.: M. J. Kauffmann, 1919), 25f.
9   Ibid., 258.
10   Schorsch, *Jewish Reactions*, 112ff.
11   Ibid., 137.

(legal counsel) and later the director of the CV and its most outstanding spokesman. Holländer presented his interpretation of the synthesis in a set of nine theses and a lengthy lecture at the convention of the CV in February 1928. An extended version was published the following year by the organisation's publishing house (Philo-Verlag), founded by Holländer in 1919.[12] Aware of the politically charged connotations of Deutschtum under the prevailing conditions, Holländer went out of his way to justify the CV's continuous adherence, since 1893, to the main ideological commitment in the first paragraph of the statutes of the CV, the "cultivation of German sentiment" (die Plege deutscher Gesinnung):

> I remember ... that in this question there were always differences of opinion.... But as friends who are seeking the truth I have to tell you that the term "cultivation of German sentiment" is justly an extraordinarily multifaceted one to this very day. The development of our present public circumstances has created so many possible interpretations in this direction that clarity cannot easily be found, ... because these emotionally inflated, rational definitions are open to thousands of possible mental modifications.[13]

Holländer found himself in perhaps even deeper waters when he redefined the contents of Judentum. If the CV wanted to be an association of conviction and "not only call itself so, it has to face the questions of *our connection with Jewry and Judaism.*" Holländer's first leading principle with regard to this connection was a negative "denial of the unity of these two entities." "We regard the absolute unity of Jewry in the whole world to be not even a beautiful aim, not to mention an existing reality ... Even the Middle Ages could not unify the Jews in the diverse ghettos of the world."[14] The ideal of Jewish unity was to be sought only in the spiritual sphere of Judaism, that is, in "the unity of religious conceptions and moral perception lead us to conceive the unifying idea of God and unifying morals as essential to Judaism and thereby for us."[15]

---

[12] Ludwig Holländer, *Deutsch-Jüdische Probleme der Gegenwart* (Berlin: Philo-Verlag, 1929).
[13] Ibid., 10–11.
[14] Ibid., 21.
[15] Ibid., 23.

Holländer had to admit that even this broad definition of Judaism was subject to different interpretations. He could not ignore the fact that a sizeable portion of the German Jews of that time, whom the CV claimed to represent, had little interest in religion. A good number even regarded themselves as atheists who nonetheless belonged to the German-Jewish entity and wanted to remain part of it. "Today we can no longer cling to the principle that their religion alone distinguishes the Jews of a country from their fellow citizens…. We recognize that the viewpoint of a community of fate and common descent also creates important cohesion …. We know today that the question, 'Why are we and why do we remain German Jews?' has to be asked and explored again and again."[16]

The concept of a "community of fate" (*Schicksalsgemeinschaft*) was Holländer's contribution to an ongoing process of ideological clarification in the search for a new definition of modern Jewish identity. The "community of common descent" (*Stammesgemeinschaft*) had already been introduced before the war by Eugen Fuchs in an important speech at the CV's convention in March 1913: "Judaism is for me a community of religion and of common descent, not a nation …. It would be insincere to deny that as a Jew I possess a special peculiarity, that my Jewish origin and Jewish home bestowed on me not only religious but also a special spiritual, maybe also physical, stamp … but in the national sense this kind of tribal stamp does not separate me any more from the German Christian … than the tribal stamp separates the Frisian peasant from the Rhenish industrial worker or from the proletarian of Berlin."[17]

Fuchs's conception of the Jews as a *Stamm* (literally, "tribe") was aimed at integrating the German Jews, at placing them beside and making them equal to the other German tribes in the entity of not only the German state but the German folk as well. In a lecture of December 1932, Ludwig Holländer went further when he spoke of a common Jewish Stamm, united across national borders by millennia of a "heritage of memory" (*Erinnerungserbe*). Jews had been a folk in

---

16   Ibid., 9.
17   Fuchs, *Um Deutschtum und Judentum*, 252–53.

the past, but being today a part of the German folk they, "like every other German Stamm, have to be proud of our tribal history."[18] Hans Bach (1902–1977), one of the editors of *Der Morgen*, went even further, reconnecting the German Jewish Stamm to its ancient historical origins: "Since the Babylonian exile they have not been a *Volk*. They are less and more: A *Stamm*. Only as a *Stamm* can ... the unity of blood and spirit, of character and religion, of physical and metaphysical cohesion that is peculiar to Judaism be created and preserved."[19]

Eugen Fuchs's definition and almost all the following soul-searching efforts to reduce the tension between Deutschtum and Judentum appeared in the context of anti-Zionist polemics. Considering the relatively small membership of the ZVfD in 1913, and even in early 1930s, one wonders why it was that Zionism occupied the minds of CV spokesmen. After all, they could rightly claim to represent the vast majority of German Jews. Even most CV followers who were members or supporters of the ZVfD did not regard this as a contradiction of their German patriotism. The undeniably defensive note of the arguments in some articles by Eugen Fuchs and Ludwig Holländer suggests that the dispute with the Zionists reflected differences of opinion within their own ranks. The more the CV conceived of itself as a Gesinnungsverein, rather than as a mere Abwehrverein, the more important internal ideological conflicts became.

In the lecture by Fuchs quoted above, he reacted to the radicalisation of the ZVfD, led by Kurt Blumenfeld, at its convention in Posen June 1912. The CV convention then countered the Zionist challenge with a decision to "separate ourselves ... from those Zionists who deny a German national sentiment, regard themselves as guests, of a [foreign host people], and feel themselves to be only Jewish nationals."[20] The resolution reiterated the CV's commitment to the maintenance of *deutsche Gesinnung*, but the selective differentiation among Zionists

---

[18]   *JR*, December 16, 1932.

[19]   *Der Morgen* 8/1 (April 1932), 14. For the passages referred to here and in note 18 and for an insightful analysis of them, see Kurt Loewenstein, "Die innerjüdische Reaktion auf die Krise der deutschen Demokralie," in *Entscheidungsjahr* 1932, ed., Mosse and Paucker, 354–55.

[20]   Fuchs, *Deutschtum und Judentum*, 249.

allowed for quite a flexible interpretation of that concept. In fact, although the ZVfD reacted with a declaration that from then on simultaneous membership in the ZVfD and in the CV was no longer tenable,[21] many Zionists ignored this directive, and there is no evidence of massive ejections from the CV on its own initiative.

The growing antagonism between the CV and the Zionists in the interwar years reflected increasing differences of opinion within the "sown ranks." The Balfour Declaration and the League of Nations mandate for the British administration of Palestine bestowed a new aura of feasibility on the Zionist "utopia." At the same time, the rise of antisemitism dashed hopes for a full integration into German society in the near future. Although the Zionist movement still had not attained a large mass membership, its influence and self-assurance were increasing, especially among the younger generation. In this situation, it was unavoidable that the tension between Deutschtum and Judentum, and the attitude toward the construction of the developing Jewish national home in Palestine, became major sources of internal dispute within the CV.

Immediately after the war the differences of opinion between the CV and the ZVfD appeared to have diminished. Reactions to both an American Jewish initiative for the establishment of a Jewish congress, and even to the idea of seeking internationally granted and supervised minority rights for the Jews of certain countries, were quite similar. Some CV leaders, led by Eugen Fuchs, did not entirely exclude the possibility of a German Jewish congress to support the minority rights of Jews in Eastern Europe, and even serve as a common platform for the representation of German Jewry. On the other hand, most Zionists showed little sympathy for the idea of assuring the status of national minority for the Jews in Germany. For a while, a rapprochement between the positions of the two main opposing parties within German Jewry seemed possible.[22]

---

[21] See Jehuda Reinharz, ed., *Dokumente zur Geschichte des deutschen Zionismus* 1882–1933 (Tübingen: J. C. Mohr, 1981), 111–12.

[22] See Jacob Toury, "Organizational Problems of German Jewry: Steps Towards the Establishment of a Central Jewish Organization (1893–1920)," *Leo Baeck Institute YearBook* (1968), 57–90, esp. 84ff; *Dokumente*, ed., Reinharz, 235ff. The positive

But very soon the antagonism gained new and stronger momentum. In my view, the greater share of responsibility for this must be attributed to the Palestinocentric orientation of the ZVfD leaders at Berlin's Meinekestrasse. Some of them believed that the rattled ideological self-confidence of the CV opened the way to recruiting support for Zionism among the CV's membership, especially among the younger followers of the organisation, by means of intensified polemical attacks.[23] To some extent, these tactics could claim success, although it may well be that a more objective and conciliatory method might have resulted in even greater influence than was actually exerted.

But what concerns us here is the discussion of principles inside CV that, in my opinion, would have occurred in any case. As a result of the changing situation, the "radicalization of Jewish aims and perceptions" inside the CV that had already begun between 1907 and 1913[24] now continued even more vigorously among the young members of the CV, as it did among the Zionists. And as before, this process did not bridge ideological and political differences. On the contrary, it increased the tensions between the two camps and inside each of them.

Reassessment of the priority of Deutschtum or Judentum was a major subject of dispute not only within the youth movements that still identified with the CV, such as the Deutsch-Jüdische Jugendgemeinschaft (DJJG) and the Kameraden. Some of the younger members of the CV also challenged what they regarded as the exaggerated "German-oriented" or "assimilationist" tendencies of an older generation that still comprised the vast majority of members. In early 1927, Ludwig Foerder (1885–1954) replied to an anti-Zionist

---

approach of Eugen Fuchs appeared in his article "Was Tun?" in the *Neue jüdische Monatshefte* (1919), 137ff, reprinted in Fuchs, *Deutschtum und Judentum*, esp. 269–270.The negative reaction of the majority of the CV to the Jewish Congress initiative appeared in an anonymous brochure under the title *Zeitfragen. Die Kongresspolitik der Zionisten* (Berlin: 1919).

[23]   See Reinharz, ed., *Dokumente*, 390–91: Anlage I—Streng vertraulich! 30 Oktober 1927: *Unsere Stellung zu den jüdischen Organisatione in Deutschland.*

[24]   Evyatar Friesel, "A Response," *Leo Baeck Institute YearBook* 33 (1988), 110. This article concludes a discussion of the same author's thesis presented in "The Political and Ideological Development of the Centralverein before 1914," *Leo Baeck Institute YearBook* 31 (1986), 121–46.

pamphlet by the chairman of the CV in Chemnitz, Georg Mecklenburg (1869–1932); it had been distributed by the CV main office. Foerder claimed that it endangered "the unity and concord of German Jewry, which are an important condition for our fight."[25] Quoting the first article of the CV bylaws, Foerder stressed the unchanged and unequivocal agreement on the first part, the "safeguarding of German Jews' civic equality"; but he criticised current interpretations of the second part on the "cultivation of German sentiment."

Foerder objected in particular to the demand that all present or new members declare their allegiance to Deutschtum because the CV was first of all an "association for the cultivation of German sentiment." Instead, he argued, the positive attitude of each member to his German nationality should be taken for granted, but in a purely legal sense, while his German sentiment should remain no more a matter for concern than his Jewish beliefs. "The special demand for *deutsche Gesinnung* would violate the parity of *Deutschtum* and *Judentum* that has rightly always been underlined. We do not demand any Jewish *Gesinnung* … but are satisfied with the formal Jewish confession … Do we have any right to act differently with regard to *Deutschtum*?"[26]

One year later, much more outspoken voices emanated from a circle of active members of the younger generation. In a programmatic brochure for the forthcoming convention, Friedrich Brodnitz (1899–1997), Kurt Cohn (1899–1987), and Ludwig Tietz (1897–1933) set out to sketch the guidelines for the "Centralverein of the future":

> We, together with the generation of young men, have first of all the true desire not to be compelled any longer to speak of our *Deutschtum* … [in situations or environments] where we are among ourselves we have no need to speak of it. This seems to be obvious, but closer observation shows that there are many among us who can never sufficiently overemphasize their conscious *Deutschtum*.… We believe that one can assume *deutsche Gesinnung* as an unconscious function of life, especially among the young generation.… For us this is the basis of our work in the CV, but not the

---

25 Ludwig Foerder, *Die Stellung des Centralvereins zu den innerjüdischen Fragen in den Jahren* 1919–1926 (Breslau: Volkswacht, 1927), 1.
26 Ibid., 8.

principle of work.... On this basis we now demand the unperturbed cultivation of our *Judentum* .... A *Judentum* that Jewish youth deeply yearns to see become a really insoluble part of its life.[27]

What did the protagonists of more Judentum really have in mind? Was it a mere demand for sentimental *yiddishkeit* in the movement's educational programs or for a return to religious beliefs and practices in the spirit of Liberal Judaism? A close examination will show that, essentially, it was neither of the two but rather a search for identity and a sense of belonging. As we have seen, the spiritual leaders of the CV had grappled with this problem from its very beginnings. Starting with definitions of German Jewry as a mere confessional *Religions* or *Glaubensgemeinschaft*, they had advanced to concepts of a historical and ongoing *Schicksals* or *Stammesgemeinschaft* without marking the boundaries of this community of fate or common descent. This is probably the reason their propositions now appeared to be unsatisfactory in the eyes of some, mostly younger members.

We should keep in mind, however, that this group constituted a very small minority within the CV. Just how small it was became apparent in the Berlin community elections of 1930, in which Tietz and Brodnitz appeared as a separate "Postiv-liberale Liste" and gained 723 votes, less than 1 percent of the total.[28] Nevertheless, they were not lacking influence. Tietz was elected deputy chairman of the CV and, together with Brodnitz, held leading posts in nationwide Jewish youth and welfare organisations. After 1933, Brodnitz became the official spokesman of the Reichsvertretung der deutschen Juden (National Representation of German Jews).

The real target of the young opposition was not the CV's top leadership, which actually tried to find a conciliatory middle way. Rather, the target was the host of second-rank functionaries in the CV's regional *Landesverbände* and its local chapters in the provinces, among whom the most ardent defenders of an explicitly national and conservative concept of Deutschtum were to be found. The practical

---

[27] Friedrich Brodnitz, Kurt Cohen, Ludwig Tietz, *Der Central-Verein der Zukunft. Eine Denkschrift zur Hauptversammlung 1928* (Breslau: M. Lichtwitz, 1927), 1.

[28] Alexander, "Berlin Jewry," 220.

political issues, discussed at the national conventions of 1926 and 1928, were the motions to join the German section of the *Keren Hayesod* and later the non-Zionist German representation in the enlarged Jewish Agency. Both motions were, time and again, defeated by the majority of delegates from the provinces. They did not have enough power to explicitly prohibit the personal membership of outstanding personalities such as Leo Baeck (1873–1956), who served on the executive boards of both the CV and the Keren Hayesod. Baeck, Tietz, Otto Hirsch (1885–1941) and other prominent members of the CV's board of directors also became members of the Jewish Agency after its establishment in 1929. But the bulk of the provincial delegates manifested their misgivings and suspicions by passing riders that expressed "expectations" that these "individual delegates" would always represent the CV's true "patriotic sentiments" (*vaterländische Gesinnung*) in all places and on all occasions.

The most ardent anti-Zionists found it hard to live with this compromise. The local chapter of the CV in Chemnitz circulated a brochure in which the anonymous author criticised a decision of the CV executive, according to which "it trusts all its members to defy any Jewish-national propaganda ... in the Jewish Agency."[29] He explained, not without reason, that this contradicted the legal basis of that organisation, namely, the Palestine Mandate based on the Balfour Declaration. The Jewish Agency, he argued, was nothing other than the political executive of the Zionist movement, and the Keren Hayesod was its financial tool. Therefore, the Chemnitz chapter demanded the immediate resignation of all CV members from the Jewish Agency.

This did not happen, of course, but the argumentation in this brochure reveals an interesting reaction, shared by many members of the CV, to the rising tide of antisemitism:

---

[29]   *Aufklärungschrift der Ortsgruppe Chemnitz des Centralvereins deutscher Staatsbürger jüdischen Glaubens* (n.p., n.d.), 2–3. The decision of the board of directors at its session of February 16, 1930, read, "Der Hauptvorstand ... hat das Vertrauen, dass alle seine Mitglieder jede national-jüdische Propaganda auch im Rahmen deer Jewish Agency abweisen."

> The duty of the CV is to fight anti-semitism. Zionism nurtures anti-semitism .... The CV demands equal rights for the Jews because they belong to the *German people*, ... and [it] fights the libelous allegation that the Jews are a foreign people in Germany. The Zionists declare themselves to be a part of this foreign people.... Our defense is constantly weakened by compromises, based on some cloudy sentiments, between these two absolutely contradictory ideologies.[30]

This was an almost verbatim repetition of the Mecklenburg Resolution, which passed by a small margin against the opposition of most of the CV's prominent leaders, at the CV's general convention of 1928.[31] Georg Mecklenburg may well have been the author of the unsigned paper. It was certainly no coincidence that this appeal emanated from a community in which native German Jews were the minority and which to the very end led a vigorous and successful fight against granting equal voting rights to the majority of Ostjuden.[32] It was also no coincidence that the paper referred approvingly to a strongly worded decision of the Vereinigung für das Liberale Judentum (VLJ), dated February 29, against participation in the Jewish Agency.

The history of the VLJ is still to be written, and one can only surmise that this organisation contained the staunchest, most inveterate defenders of an extremely nationalistic Deutschtum among the German Jews, outdistanced only by the vociferous but quantitatively insignificant *Verband nationaldeutscher Juden* led by Max Naumann (1875–1939), or the even less significant *Deutscher Vortrupp* of Hans-Joachim Schoeps (1909–1980), whose affiliation or membership with the VLJ is not clear.

The VLJ was founded in 1908, following an appeal signed by liberal rabbis and laymen. On the face of it, the proclaimed aims were purely religious: the adjustment of the Jewish faith and its practice to modern life, as a barrier against religious indifference and apostasy. These were without doubt the objectives of the liberal rabbis, organised since 1898

---

30   Ibid., 15–16.
31   CV calendar, 1929, 62.
32   See Trude Maurer, *Ostjuden in Deutschland* 1918–1933 (Hamburg: H. Christians, 1986), 621ff.

in their own Vereinigung der liberalen Rabbiner.[33] Very soon, however, they detected that their lay cofounders, who from the beginning secured the majority in all forums, were less seriously concerned with religious problems and used the Vereinigung as a political instrument to assure their hold on the administration of the Jewish communities. These differences had already appeared in 1912 at the convention of the VLJ in Posen, where rabbis Caesar Seligmann and Leo Baeck presented a set of guidelines for Liberal ritual and observance after it had been ratified by a convention of Liberal rabbis. The lay majority rejected the institution of "a liberal *Shulkhan Arukh*" (the ritual code of Orthodox Jews) and arranged for what Seligmann later described as "a first-class burial" of the guidelines.[34]

In 1912, the militant anti-Zionist attitude of the VLJ came to the fore when its chairman, Bernhard Breslauer, initiated the establishment of a Reichsverband zur Bekaempfung des Zionismus, afterwards renamed Antizionistisches Komitee, at the VLJ's offices in Berlin. The two most prominent leaders of the CV, Eugen Fuchs and Maximilian Horwitz, who were discreetly approached, declined to be connected with this initiative, but Ludwig Holländer seems to have supported it.[35] At the CV convention of May 1913, Holländer demanded a clear break and the expulsion of Zionists, but he had to give way to his more moderate elders, who advocated the already mentioned "selective" anti-Zionist decision.

After the war, the movement's monthly, *Liberales Judentum*, edited in Frankfurt am Main by Seligmann, was transferred to Berlin and became

---

[33] The organization of the Liberal rabbis continued to exist after 1908 and had 94 members in 1933. See Walter Breslauer, "Die 'Vereinigung für das liberale Judentum in Deutschland' und die 'Richtlinien zu einem Programm für das liberale Judentum: Erinnerungen aus den Jahren 1908–1914," *Bulletin of the Leo Baeck Institute 9* (1966), 302ff. The following discussion is based on this article and on Michael A. Meyer, "Caesar Seligmann and the Development of Liberal Judaism in German at the Beginning of the Twentieth Century," *Hebrew Union College Annual* 40/41 (1969–1970), 529–54; on Caesar Seligmann, *Erinnerungen*, ed., Erwin Seligmann (Frankfurt a.M.: W. Kramer, 1975); and on Alexander, "Berlin Jewry," esp. 97–119.

[34] Quoted in Meyer, "Caesar Seligmann," 545n; see also Seligmann, *Erinnerungen*, 146ff.

[35] Schorsch, *Jewish Reactions*, 198–99; Marjorie Lamberti, "From Coexistence to Conflict-Zionism and the Jewish Community in Germany 1897–1914," *Leo Baeck Institute YearBook* 27 (1982), 78ff.

the weekly *Jüdisch-Liberale Zeitung*, edited by Bruno Woyda, a member of the Berlin Reformgemeinde and an ardent German nationalist. The new weekly was transformed into a mouthpiece of the Liberal factions in the communities. Caesar Seligmann had fought this transfer and, like many Liberal rabbis, distanced himself from the activities of the VLJ and its weekly, as both "descended to become mere instruments of community politics in a purely anti-Zionist vein." In March 1927, a conciliatory resolution of the Association of Liberal Rabbis, leaving the attitude towards Zionism to the personal decision of each Liberal rabbi or layman, provoked the wrath of the lay leadership of the VLJ. The weekly's editors declared that the rabbis had ceased to be the leaders of Liberal Judaism, and from then on, most rabbis refrained from participating in the VLJ's activities and publications.[36]

The VLJ was, from early on, an essentially political organisation, not a religious one. Its "lay leadership was composed mainly of community politicians whose interest was often limited to gaining and holding onto positions of power in their communities."[37] Although most of its leaders and followers were at that time members of the CV, the political orientation of the two organisations differed in some important respects. Actually, this was more evident in the prewar period. As we have seen, the CV established its policy and tactics of Abwehr against antisemitism in opposition to the liberal "notables" who governed the communities. During the Weimar years, both organisations underwent substantial changes. The CV shed the character of a mere, absolutely neutral Abwehrverein, while the VLJ withdrew almost entirely from religious matters and became primarily an instrument for political power struggles in the Jewish communities. It remains to be determined why, in this process, many leaders of the VLJ appear from the very beginning to have been the most radical German nationalists and extreme anti-Zionists in the ranks of the CV. In any case, perusing the pages of the Jüdisch-Liberale Zeitung, one understands whom Leo Baeck had in mind when he deplored, in a letter to Seligmann thought to have been written in 1926, "the

---

[36] Seligmann, *Erinnerungen,* 159–60; Meyer, "Caesar Seligmann," 552–53.
[37] Meyer, "Caesar Seligmann," 547.

spiritual dreariness of some CV members who try to create from their Deutschtum a kind of substitute religion."[38]

The confrontation with the JVP in the election campaigns of the 1920s are at best only a partial explanation. There may also be sociological reasons, as in the case of the *Gemeindezionisten*, but even more distinctly the "Gemeinde Liberals," who belonged to the CV and were the second tier of the movement's leadership. The first-tier leaders of the CV and the ZVfD were professionals with a broader intellectual and ideological outlook, while among those of the JVP and certainly of the VLJ there were many middle- or upper-class businessmen. But despite these perhaps superficial and schematic similarities, some differences in attitude are perplexing: among the Zionists, the most radical opponents to closer cooperation with the CV were Kurt Blumenfeld and Siegfried Moses of the ZVfD, while men such as Alfred Klee or Max Kollenscher of the JVP took a more conciliatory stand. As we have seen, the opposite is true in the case of the CV, where the Gemeinde Liberals outvoted the leaders at the top on issues such as the Keren Hayesod, the Jewish Agency, and financial assistance to Hechaluz.

Also of interest are the different attitudes of the young generation in the two camps. In the CV, as we have seen, Ludwig Tietz, Friedrich Brodnitz, and their followers had consistently fought for internal Jewish rapprochement and, though a minority, achieved growing influence on the board. In contrast, inside the VLJ, the young spokesmen of the Jüdisch-Liberale Jugendvereine (JLJ) outdid their elders in German nationalism and radical anti-Zionism.[39] During the election campaign of October 1930, their column in the *JLZ* accused the JVP of hiding its Zionist commitment behind false pretenses; the JVP was compared to the Nazis: "Through fanaticism, phrases, and unrealistic yet idealistic-sounding programs, the National Socialists have brought people over to them who, according to their mentality, belong somewhere quite different. The same phenomenon manifests itself with Jewish-Nationals. Here too there were fanaticism and idealistic programs, which must affect every "feeling." Moreover, the populist ring of the Jüdische

---

[38]   See the facsimile copy of the letter in *Leo Baeck Institute YearBook* 2 (1957), 44ff.
[39]   Breslauer, "Die 'Vereinigung,'" 312–13.

Volkspartei was akin to that of the NSDAP, which called itself a *workers'* party.[40] These Liberal youth groups seem to have attracted only a small membership in some larger communities and had almost no influence on the young Jewish generation of the Weimar period. Still, these differences in attitude deserve further study in future research.

The community elections of 1926 and 1930 in Berlin coincided in time with the rising political crisis and the upsurge of antisemitic propaganda. It is difficult to determine the role of these developments in the aggravation of inter-Jewish conflicts, including the tensions between the VLJ and the CV. In any case, toward January 1933, and even more so during the first month of the Nazi regime, the *Jüdisch-Liberale Zeitung* and the official declarations of the Liberals adopted an ever more pronounced right-wing nationalist and anti-Zionist vocabulary. This was without doubt influenced by the vociferous public campaign launched in the press and on the street kiosks by the Verband nationaldeutscher Juden. [41] Naumann and his followers believed their time had come, and Liberals such as Bruno Woyda or his successor as editor of the *Jüdisch-Liberale Zeitung*, George Goetz (1892–1968), were dangerously close to them. In April 1933, Naumann convinced even the leaders of the veterans' organisation, the Reichsbund jüdischer Frontsoldaten (RjF), to join his Verband along with the right-wing Jewish youth movement Schwarzes Faehnlein and other marginal groups in an effort to unite all German Jewish nationalists in an Aktions-Ausschuss der jüdischen Deutschen, but the coalition fell apart after only a few weeks.[42]

This was not the end of Liberal initiatives to accommodate the new regime, nor of their attacks on the CV's leaders, who at that time took part in the establishment of the Reichsvertretung der deutsche Juden. George Goetz openly accused them of "letting the German Jews down" and of handing over the provisional chairmanship of the CV to a man (evidently Ludwig Tietz) "whose position on the question *Deutschtum*

---

40   "Aus der ILI—Bewegung," *JLZ*, October 8, 1930.
41   See Carl J. Rheins, "The Verband nationaldeutscher Juden," *Leo Baeck Institute YearBook* (1980), 243–68, esp. 265ff.
42   See Klaus J. Herrmann, *Das Dritte Reich und die deutsch-jüdischen Organisationen* 1933–1934 (Cologne: Heymann, 1969), 12–13.

and *Judentum* has never been … in the tradition of the CV and who, to our taste, has always been too much interested" in Palestine.[43]

This was the overture to a concerted campaign against allegedly increasing Zionist influence among the leading ranks of the CV. In October Bruno Woyda published in the *Berliner jüdisches Gemeindeblatt* what he defined as "programmatic guidelines" for the future of the Jews in Germany. His main thesis was that the German Jews expect "to have their rights granted only by … the German *Volk* and its leaders … Therefore the German Jews must not hesitate to integrate themselves into a state organism that is compelled to restrict their rights, because it regards a certain community of blood the foundation for the community of the *Volk* …" Woyda stressed that he was speaking only of those "who have only one fatherland, one homeland: Germany," not of those who want to emigrate, or of Jewish foreigners, who can only expect to be treated like other foreigners.[44] The publication of Woyda's article led to the resignation of the chairman of the ZVfD, Siegfried Moses (1887–1974), from the executive board of the Jewish community of Berlin. The community's liberal chairman, Heinrich Stahl (1868–1942), declared in response that Woyda's conceptions "were by no means obsolete … and are agreed on by the majority of the Jews of Berlin and of Germany."[45]

In November 1933, Bruno Woyda and a few like-minded friends founded a Revival Movement of Jewish Germans (*Erneuerungsbewegung der juedischen Deutschen*). In its first, and to my knowledge only, public appeal, the movement acknowledged the fundamental change in the situation of the German Jews, who evidently "had lost their equal standing and equal rights, but not their consciousness of being and remaining Germans who are connected, for better or worse, with the fate of our German fatherland." In the name of those Jewish Germans, the initiators of the appeal demanded complete separation from the "Zionists of all shades, who should be left to attend to their own affairs,"

43 Georg Goertz, "Gefahren, Versäumnisse, Aufgaben. Eine notwendige Kritik," *JLZ*, May 1, 1933, supplement.
44 Bruno Woyda, "Um die künftige Stelllng der deutschen Juden. Programmatische Richtlinien," *JLZ*, October 31, 1933, supplement.
45 Stahl to Moses, October 18, 1933, in *JLZ*, October 24, 1933, supplement.

while the "Jewish Germans unite and subordinate under the discipline and order of a determined German-Jewish leadership."[46]

This appeal was an open call for war against the newly established Reichsvertretung and a short-lived attempt to cotton to the new rulers who, as in the case of Naumann's approaches, showed little interest.[47] In this case the executive of the Berlin Jüdische Gemeinde, replying to repeated accusations by Siegfried Moses, distanced itself from Woyda's Revival Movement and declared its loyalty to the Reichsvertretung.[48]

In the current historical events, the Jewish Germans and their most radical leaders inside the JLV fought a losing battle. The *Jüdisch-Liberale Zeitung* had to restrict publication to twice a month, and even after it adjusted to the new reality and, under a new editor, changed its name to *Jüdisch-Allgemeine Zeitung*, its readership constantly declined. The CV also had to fight the desertion of growing numbers of its members to the Zionist camp.[49] But for the last years of the Weimar period, it is still difficult to discern which group, the intransigent "Jewish Germans" in the provinces or the more moderate leaders in Berlin, could more rightfully claim to represent the majority of the CV's membership. Nor do we have a clear sense of those German Jews, who had already severed substantive connections with any Jewish establishment or organisation, even if formally they still belonged and paid their taxes to the Jewish communities. Now, following the discovery of the CV's files in Moscow and the addition of other sources, until recently inaccessible, from other archives, we may hope that a younger and more distanced, or less biased, flock of historians will be able to answer these and similar questions that remain.

---

[46] "Erneuerungsbewegung der jüdischen Deutschen," *JJZ*, November 14, 1933.
[47] See Herrmann, *Das Dritte Reich*, 70ff.
[48] "Berliner Gemeinde für Einigkeit," *JLZ*, November 21, 1933.
[49] See Avraham Barkai, "Der CV im Jahre 1933: Neu aufgefundene Dokumente im Moskauer 'Sonderarchiv,'" *TJBDG* 28 (1994), 233–46.

CHAPTER X

INSIDE/OUTSIDE THE UNIVERSITY: PHILOSOPHY AS WAY AND PROBLEM IN COHEN, BUBER, AND ROSENZWEIG

Willi Goetschel

Philosophy as a discipline as well as Jewish philosophers as individuals faced a particular set of challenges between 1871 and 1933. There were internal institutional pressures within the university, which underwent during this period a rapid process of growth, expansion, and disciplinary differentiation that had direct implications with regard to the repositioning of philosophy and its role within the institution. Once a leading discipline, philosophy had become during that time the subject of renegotiation of its academic and social standing. At the same time, the German university had witnessed a significant increase in enrolment of Jewish students, the maturing of that student population, and a steady increase in the production of Jewish candidates in line for teaching and research positions. Ever since Leopold Zunz's failed attempts from 1848 onwards to secure a place for Jewish history *intra muros*, that is, to establish an independent field of Jewish scholarship within the German university, it had become clear that the university's claim to universality was poised to remain fiercely selective.[1] For Jewish philosophers, the signs of the time were clear. But if the university left no doubt where the glass ceiling was set that would limit Jewish students to the academic career prospects of the rank of *Privatdozenten* or private lectures, that is, unsalaried adjuncts, the push into academic education was too strong to be further delayed. Jewish communities would develop alternatives to the university as opportunities in the

---

1   Cf. Willi Goetschel, "A House of One's Own? University, Particularity, and the Jewish House of Learning," chapter 4 in Goetschel, *The Discipline of Philosophy and the Invention of Modern Jewish Thought* (New York: Fordham University Press, 2012).

Jewish education system were created that would provide Jewish academics with employment and some minimal job security as teachers, school directors, journalists, and intellectuals. The options were few, and the careers of Hermann Cohen (1842–1918), Martin Buber (1878–1966), and Franz Rosenzweig (1883–1929) illustrate in exemplary ways three creative responses to this situation.

In 1876, Hermann Cohen was the first Jew at a German university to assume a chair in philosophy without the requirement of baptism. To ascend to the office of a professor in philosophy had not been impossible for Jews before, but they were forced to leave the country to look for opportunities elsewhere. Moritz Lazarus, for instance, had been appointed to the university of Berne in Switzerland in 1860 and became rector there in 1864 but resigned in 1866 to choose to return to the life of a *Privatdozent* in Berlin, where he would continue to work with his brother-in-law, Heymann Steinthal, on their joint project of research in "Cultural Psychology" (Völkerpsychologie), a forerunner of cultural philosophy.[2] But Cohen's predicament was that he served as the token Jewish philosophy professor who by a lucky coincidence would beat the system, mainly due to the generously unwavering sponsorship of Friedrich Albert Lange, his predecessor in Marburg. In Berlin, Georg Simmel's experience in attempting to secure a position at the university highlights the difficulties Jewish academics would confront. Facing some of the same faculty that saw to it that Zunz's initiative, promoted by the government, would be shelved, Simmel was first taught a lesson when he was examined for his credentials as private lecturer. He was sent home with the recommendation to acquire first the finer etiquette of subservient academic conduct that he seemed to lack in the eyes of the members of the examination committee. Back a year later, he was admitted to the lecture hall in 1885 and was awarded the title of an extraordinary (and unsalaried) professor in 1901. But he had to wait until 1914 to be appointed to a chair in philosophy. Far away from the scene of his sphere of popular success in Berlin, the position at the

---

2   See the fine collection of essays of Moritz Lazarus, *Grundzüge der Völkerpsychologie und Kulturwissenschaft*, ed., and intro. Klaus Christian Köhnke (Hamburg: Felix Meiner, 2003).

University of Strasbourg was, however, in a city at the time considered to be located at the fringe of the German Empire and certainly away from the vibrancy of Berlin's metropolitan life.[3]

PROFESSION AND CONFESSION: HERMANN COHEN

Hermann Cohen's appointment to the chair of philosophy in Marburg occurred at a time that was not particularly promising with regard to the hopes and the aspirations for equal opportunities. The pressures of assimilation were strong and required careful negotiating between integration and self-assertion. Just recently consolidated as a modern Prussian state and driven by the economic boom and expectations of the founding years, Germany finally could claim a state of its own. At the same time, the dynamics of consolidation with its nation-building implications exposed the Jews in a new way as precariously positioned if it came to the question of membership of the German state and nation, or so many Germans liked to think. The late 1870s witnessed the breakout of a new controversy on antisemitism, as the newly coined term introduced by publicist Wilhelm Marr gained popular currency. Hermann Cohen entered the debate of the Berlin antisemitism controversy with his self-consciously assertive intervention: "A Confession Concerning the Jewish Question" (Ein Bekennntis in der Judenfrage).[4]

Cohen's intervention opens with the words that the time has yet again come to *bekennen*. But *bekennen* does not just mean "confess" but also "profess," and the emphatic accentuation of Cohen's stance that confession and profession do not need to stand in opposition but can in fact coexist side by side is central to his philosophical position:

> The point thus has again been reached that we are forced to confess. We, the younger generation, may well have hoped that we eventually would

---

3   For the details of Simmel's life, see Klaus Christian Köhnke, *Der junge Simmel*, in *Theoriebeziehungen und sozialen Bewegungen* (Frankfurt a.M.: Suhrkamp, 1996).

4   Hermann Cohen, *Jüdische Schriften* (Berlin: Schwetschke & Sohn, 1924), vol. 2, 73–94. For the significance of the "Confession" as Cohen's inaugural public intervention, see Franz Rosenzweig's introduction to the edition, ibid., vol. 1, XIII-LXIV, XXVI-XXIX.

succeed in being settled in "Kant's nation"; that the existent difference with the principled support of an ethical politics and the historical sense of the individual would continue to balance each other; that with the passing of time it would become possible to give voice in an unprejudiced way to the patriotic love in us and to the consciousness of the pride of participating in the tasks of the nation in equal measure. This confidence has been broken: the old trepidation is being awaked again.

(Es ist also doch wieder dahin gekommen, daß wir bekennen müssen. Wir Jüngeren hatten doch wohl hoffen dürfen, daß es uns allmählich gelingen würde, in die "Nation Kants" uns einzuleben; daß die vorhandenen Differenzen unter der grundsätzlichen Hilfe einer sittlichen Politik und der dem einzelnen so nahe gelegten historischen Besinnung sich auszugleichen fortfahren würden; daß es mit der Zeit möglich werden würde, mit unbefangenem Ausdruck die vaterländische Liebe in uns reden zu lassen, und das Bewußtsein des Stolzes, and Aufgaben der Nation ebenbürtig mitwirken zu dürfen. Dieses Vertrauen ist uns gebrochen; die alte Beklommenheit wird wieder geweckt.)[5]

For Cohen, knowledge and faith stand in profoundly reciprocal relation. Rather than taking philosophical thought as the opposite of religious faith, both originate for Cohen from the same faculty of reason, and it is the universal scope of a universally open faith that grounds reason in the universal vision whose idealist force rests on the faith that makes it universal. Translated into the rhetorics of the time, Cohen argues that what makes Germany modern is its Protestant culture and that its roots, in turn, are to be found in Judaism, from which Protestantism derives. Culturally related to the degree of deep affinity, Judaism and Protestantism not only share the basic principal values that define modernity, but also represent the guarantee for the exemplary universal significance of this modernity. During World War I, Cohen would return to this argument and intensify its rhetorics in "Deutschtum und Judentum."[6] But what makes his approach so important for his philosophical position is that he not only sees Judaism as completely compatible with the exigencies of modern academic philosophy but also

---

5   Hermann Cohen, *Jüdische Schriften* (Berlin: Schwetschke and Sohn, 1924), vol. 2, 73.
6   Hermann Cohen, *Jüdische Schriften*, vol. 2, 237–301.

comprehends Jewish tradition as a pillar on which universal thought grounds.

It is telling that from the start of his university career, Cohen never viewed himself as part of a "minority" religion but rather as a fully entitled citizen with a legitimate stake in German culture and society. Cohen's project of grounding philosophy in rigorous fashion on a universalism that would meet the critical standards of the emancipatory vision of humanity that the philosopher of the Enlightenment Immanuel Kant had advanced is entirely continuous with the very core of his identity. In other words, Cohen makes the central issue of his identity the very point of departure of his philosophical work. In self-consciously positing his vision of Jewish tradition as the correlative anchor of his philosophical project, Cohen addresses the predicament of the Jewish philosopher head on and with all the hopeful directness that had become possible to embrace the promise academe held out for the first generation of German Jews who assumed careers at the university against all odds and the obstacles the majority of the German professorate had thrown in their way.

On the one hand, Cohen's neo-Kantian approach represents a trailblazing, rigorous approach to philosophy. His version of Kantian idealism advanced a constructivist approach that signalled purity and epistemological sophistication. Its claim for universal validity was firmly grounded in Kantian thought but in such a way that Cohen's own original approach to philosophy was centrally inscribed at the heart of this version of neo-Kantianism. The exemplary manner in which Cohen sought to claim the university as a home for a philosophy that would heed the commitment to a rigorously universalist outlook combined his philosophical and Jewish concerns in an inspiring new way. On the other hand, Hermann Cohen was equally firmly grounded in his Jewish tradition, which he viewed as not merely fully compatible with modern philosophy and German culture but more assertively as a crucial element that contributed to the universal promise of modern German culture as well as that of philosophical thought. What to many seemed a tenuous if not entirely contradictory proposition, that is, the profound affinity between German and Jewish modernity, was in Cohen's eyes a culturally decisive fact whose link between Judaism and modernity was no longer to be eclipsed if philosophy was to be truly universal. The core idea of Cohen's notion of constructivism represented a form of universal vision that would not lead to the erasure of Jewish particularity but rather highlighted its critical role as a pivotal moment in grounding a non-exclusionary vision of universalism.

In other words, Cohen renegotiated the relationship of universal and particular as correlative aspects at the heart of Kant's critical philosophy. And he did so in a way that presented itself as not just concomitant with the Kantian intention but as one that would bring its impulse to full fruition. In doing so, Cohen at the same time marked his stance in the context of late nineteenth-century academic philosophy. Returning to Kant, as Otto Liebmann reminded his readers in his *Kant und die Epigonen*,[7] the rallying call for the neo-Kantian movement, meant to move beyond the dead-end situation of post-Hegelianism, neo-Aristotelianism, and neo-Thomism that dominated the German universities during the second half of the nineteenth century. In other words, if the rejection of Jews and Jewish philosophers in particular was motivated by refusing them entrance to the sacred halls of the German spirit, whose universality seemed uncontested—at least in the eyes of the dominant voices of German academic philosophy—Cohen inverted the situation by arguing a position that established the Jewish philosopher as a fully co-equal participant already at the very inside of the philosophical project from which Jews had been excluded.

Bold as this move was, it did not come without problematic implications. If Cohen bravely grasped the dilemma by the horns and set the conditions of his terms in terms of philosophy, this pointedly philosophical move triggered the reiteration of the very fronts of the debate on the "Jewish Question" that Cohen had hoped to leave behind but that returned, now transposed as a controversy of demarcating contesting schools of philosophy. Cohen's hopeful appeal to philosophy's universalism led thus to philosophical border disputes where Cohen's aspirations were met by the factions of the philosophical establishment, nervous about the challenge to their claims to universalism. In an

---

[7]   Otto Liebmann, *Kant und die Epigonen. Eine kritische Abhandlung* (Stuttgart: Carl Schober, 1865)

ironic twist, the factional divisions concerning the task and the nature of philosophy rendered different visions of universality incompatible, pitting them, as it were, against each other. Differences in philosophy curiously repeated the schematism of the "Jewish Question" as they "re-entered" the problem of distinguishing the universal and the particular and mapped it onto the question of philosophical method. If the attitude with regard to the "Jewish Question" correlated with the preference to affiliation with particular schools of philosophy, the nexus was not always in the open but more often loomed under the surface and can certainly not be reduced to it. Rather, it complicates the story of the formation of schools and factions during the period. The stance on the "Jewish Question" thus informs the discourse of German philosophy in its structure and cannot be separated from it. If German culture could always be distinguished along the lines of attitudes towards Judaism and Jews and this had also been true for philosophy, Cohen's move as it were *intra muros* signalled a new challenge of philosophy on its very own terms. The fact that most of the university politics seemed to pay little attention to this sea change makes it no less momentous but complicates the picture in an interesting way. Spinoza had never been an academically accredited philosopher, and he had even made a point of that.[8] So had Mendelssohn in equal measure. But Cohen had not only successfully complied with the protocol of the institutional requirements of the German university but went on to become the undisputed head of the Marburg school of Kantianism, arguably the most prominent school of philosophy during his leadership.

When Cohen retired in 1912, he moved to Berlin to teach at the Institute for the Wissenschaft des Judentums, where he lectured until his death in 1918. In Berlin, Cohen focused his attention on the examination of Jewish tradition and its thought. While some considered Cohen's work on Judaism a separate line of thought that he would cultivate in his retirement, other critics argued for consistency and continuity in Cohen's philosophic work beyond the retirement from

---

[8]   See Spinoza's letter of March 30 1673, to Johann Ludwig Fabritius, where he politely refuses the offer of appointment to the chair of philosophy at the university of Heildelberg.

his "professional" life. Franz Rosenzweig was one of the first to broach this issue in his introduction to the three-volume edition of Cohen's *Jewish Writings*.[9] Arguing critically against the view that there was a neat and clean division between Cohen's philosophical and his Jewish writings, Rosenzweig maintained that the thought of the mature Cohen came to its full fruition during the Berlin period, whereas others wished to discern a clear break between the pre-retirement and post-retirement phase. For Rosenzweig, however, Cohen's trajectory also marked a critical break with what Rosenzweig considered the Kantian straitjacket of philosophy. The discussion about this issue has remained controversial, as it poses the question of what exactly is philosophy in principal terms.

The question of Cohen's place in the history of German nineteenth- and early twentieth-century philosophy has been a question that has remained open as it poses the problem of the terms of such ascription as one inseparable from his double identity as German and Jewish philosopher. But one point has been irrefutably clear: Cohen continues to present a challenge to any attempt at streamlining the history of philosophy along the lines of conventional narratives of philosophy. Cohen's unafraid straddling of both the philosophical and Jewish visions of universalism, which he understood to be intrinsically correlated and mutually constitutive aspects and thus of one piece, represents a paradigmatic stance that changed not just the self-perception of Jewish philosophers but also the discourse of philosophy itself. To be a Jewish philosopher, however, seemed now to mean to be a Kantian and more precisely to embrace Cohen's version of idealism. Cohen's move as it were came with the costs of relying on Kant as his ally, a philosopher from whom many contemporaries felt distanced. Kant had become "Jewish" while German national sentiments had begun to move apart from the critical cosmopolitanism that Kant so rigorously advocated but whose emancipatory promise soon waned with the end of World War I.

When in 1919 Cohen's *Religion of Reason out of the Sources of Judaism* was posthumously published, the book's argument did not

---

9   Hermann Cohen, *Jüdische Schriften*, vol. 1, XIII-LXIV.

come as a complete surprise. At the same time, however, the book posed some questions insofar as it raised the issue of whether or not it was to be seen as part and possibly a concluding cornerstone of the architectonics of the neo-Kantian system Cohen had staked out with his epistemological, ethical, and aesthetic studies. Was the *Religion of Reason* to be seen as a break and departure from Kantian systematics as some argued or, on the contrary, as the completion that Kant himself had failed to deliver but Cohen now eventually offered? Cohen's concept of correlation, however, seemed to precisely pre-empt any response that would mistake Judaism for a case study in Kantian philosophy. Rather, Cohen's posthumous work argues that reason and religion are to be seen as co-equals constituting each other's universal import through correlation. If the point of origin seemed to be constituted in and through reason, reason was at the same time understood as self-constituting, that is, grounded in a self-generating origin that would be reiterated in each and every person anew. Likewise, historical narratives of origin in Jewish tradition were doubled. Genealogies could not be derived from one single historical origin but came always in the plural: in other words, the written and oral traditions, Halakhic and Aggadic. Cohen's critical approach would work both ways: if determining the meaning of the sources of religious traditions required the use of reason, reason itself as self-generating principle represented a unity that could only be argued as consistent insofar as it would be universal, that is, reflecting onto itself its conditions of possibility as well as its rootedness in a universality resistant to any form of exclusionary impulse. For Cohen, Judaism thus did not imply a withdrawal behind a position of ultimate truths or reason's other but represented a case in point that would highlight the reason of reason itself as one that would be grounded in a universalism that envisioned Greek and Jewish tradition as continuous rather than mutually exclusive.

Cohen's approach featured Plato as the quintessential Greek philosopher. This allowed Cohen to position himself in a philosophical trajectory running from Plato to Kant and to the present and could include exponents of Jewish thought such as the medieval Jewish philosopher Maimonides. The reliance on Plato, however, would stress a particular form of idealism. Liberating and emancipatory, it came in Cohen at the same time with a rigorism whose etatist note called for an unquestioned allegiance to the Prussian state. As Cohen carefully distinguished between nation and nationality, he defined the nation state's mission as one that would accommodate a diversity of nationalities within its sphere of jurisdiction. For Cohen, the nation state relies on the diversity of its constituents, the different nationalities, and therefore, he concludes that nationality does not stand in contradiction to the nation of the nation state.[10]

This is the point where Cohen's high-powered idealism has the potential of reverting back into a strikingly coercive impulse of etatist rigorism. His project, promising as it may have been, grounds in a reliance on the very nation state that had become increasingly problematic. Its eventual demise, Cohen was spared to experience.

THE LITERARY MODERNIST
AS ITINERANT MAGGID: MARTIN BUBER

If Hermann Cohen had gracefully entered—and left—academe, his career also highlighted the continuing difficulties for Jews when it came to the choice of philosophy as academic career and discipline. In contrast to Cohen's first generation experience inside the university, Martin Buber's professional career illustrates the situation of the second generation. Less strongly drawn to an academic career, Buber from the beginning pursued an education that would prepare him for a career as a freelance intellectual. His philosophic interests were matched with a lasting interest in the literary aspect of philosophic thought. Indeed, Buber chose *Schriftsteller*, that is, writer or literally "script setter," as the term he felt would best describe his profession.[11]

A student of Georg Simmel, Buber might just like so many of Simmel's other students (from Ernst Bloch to Margarete Susman) have been inspired by Simmel's most significant impact. Simmel's approach would set philosophy and its students free from the constraints and the

---

10   Hermann Cohen, *Religion out of Reason*, 421.
11   See his poem "Bekenntnis eines Schriftstellers" (Confession of a Writer) in Martin Buber, *Nachlese* (Heidelberg: Lambert Schneider, 1966), 11.

limitations of the confines of the academe. In fact, Simmel's hands-on approach to philosophy broke down the academic walls from within as his philosophical sociology opened philosophy's scope to all aspects of human cultural production. Like Cohen, Simmel had been a student of Heymann Steinthal who, together with Moritz Lazarus, developed the project of cultural psychology (*Völkerpsychologie*) that saw the source of creativity as a result of the recognition of diversity and exchange between different national, religious, and ethnic traditions as enabling force. Simmel's position had always been somewhat marginal within German academe. Active for many years as private lecturer and unsalaried associate professor, it was only in 1914 and at the age of 56 that Simmel eventually was appointed a chair of philosophy, however literally at the margins of the German Empire at the university of Strasbourg. But Simmel's success and recognition as one of the internationally acclaimed founding fathers of modern sociology was barely limited by the institutional politics of the domestic academic front. As a lecturer who reached a following well beyond the lecture hall and a writer who made the essay his genre of choice, Simmel showed the way in which philosophy could become a powerful discipline outside the confines of the university.

For Buber, like others of his generation, Simmel had opened the way to a career outside the walls of academe that provided a mission and purpose that no longer lacked the luster the university had seemed to have reserved for itself in the nineteenth century. With the beginning of the twentieth century and its advance of literary modernism, which led to the consolidation of a public intellectual sphere that was no longer defined by scholarship alone but staked out a literary space of its own, Jewish modernity no longer depended on academe as the source for its legitimacy. Along with other movements of literary, intellectual, and cultural renewal, the turn of the century witnessed the emergence of alternative spaces and venues that offered Jewish intellectuals the opportunity to realise visions of modernity that no longer required the stamp of institutional approval. Inspired by currents of *Lebensphilosophie* as the contemporary Nietzsche reception represented it, aspiring young Jewish intellectuals ventured into a new world outside the university that not only offered feasible alternatives to academic employment but promised a new lifestyle, working opportunities, and recognition of creative initiative.

Buber early on recognised the opportunities that this situation presented as no one else did, and went on to become one of the leading figures and a source of inspiration to a whole generation of young Jewish intellectuals. Buber's literary and philosophical approach are inseparably linked as he brought the two concerns together, forging them into a unique trajectory that was as distinctly modernist and literary as it was Jewish and philosophic. The not yet 20-year-old Buber sought to translate Nietzsche's *Thus Spoke Zarathustra* into Polish, while in his 40s he began the collaborative project of translating the Bible into German with Franz Rosenzweig, a project he would eventually complete decades later after Rosenzweig's death in 1929. In addition to these and other translation projects, one of the distinctive features of Buber's literary career was his work as editor of book series, anthologies, and the journal *Der Jude*, a short-lived but crucially seminal venue of cultural production. Buber's dialogical thinking grounds as much in his endeavour to bring different perspectives together and interface them by dialogue as his literary projects ground, on the other hand, in the larger cultural project of bringing out the distinctly different and individual voices. This is a project that thrives by establishing ever new constellations of dialogical contexts through which these voices would gain the individuality and specificity they, taken "in and of themselves," could never assume if understood independently and separately. To be a writer in the emphatic sense that Buber noted in the word *Schriftsteller* meant to recognise the crucial context for a text to speak and be heard. Text and context required each other, and the writer would be the literary custodian who gave the text its context, a context that would change in ever new constellations as some of the mystical, Hasidic, and religious traditions knew that Buber would edit, rephrase, and thus reconstellate in a modernist context.[12]

---

[12] For studies on the early Buber, see especially Hans Kohn, *Martin Buber: Sein Werk und seine Zeit. Ein Beitrag zur Geistesgeschichte Mitteleuropas 1880–1930*, 3rd ed. (Cologne: Melzer, 1961), Maurice Friedman, *Martin Buber's Life and Work, vol 1: The Early Years 1878–1923* (London and Tunbridge Wells: Search Press, 1982) and vol. 2: *The Middle Years 1923–1945* (New York: Dutton, 1983); Paul Mendes-Flohr, *From Mysticism to*

For Buber, the medium of literary expression could not be separated from the philosophical thrust it articulated, and it allowed him to recognise the literary dimension of philosophy as a constituent feature of thought itself. Buber's emphatic concept of reality (*Wirklichkeit*) led him to locate philosophy's task outside the confines of academic exercise, or more precisely, his critically performative accentuation of the notion of *Wirklichkeit* as action and event rather than simply an eidetic entity became as much a theoretical as s a practical necessity to move beyond the confines of the university. The mystic, the *maggid*, the storyteller, and the characters taken from everyday life experience that populate Buber's writings represent all peripheral figures that highlight that reality is less to be grasped as speculative proposition but rather is to be understood as a transformative experience whose concrete specificity challenges the conceptual apparatus of abstract thought. For Buber, the philosopher could thus no longer stay inside the ivory tower but for the very purpose of gaining knowledge had to move beyond the university in order to do his work, that is, to attend to the problem of reality (*Wirklichkeit*) and realization (*Bewährung*), central terms in Buber that accentuate the dynamic meaning of the notion of realization through the proof of self-realization.

Situating his project in the context of the movement of literary modernism, Buber re-imagined modernism in his own way as he inscribed Jewish tradition as a vibrant moment in this movement. Interested in rethinking the phenomenology of religion and cultural renewal as a way to reconceptualise the question of essence and reality, Buber articulated a philosophy that no longer separated conceptual thought from hermeneutics but contextualised the task of philosophy as part of the anthropological necessity to negotiate the world. In Buber's view, there was no theoretically pure space to which philosophical reflections could withdraw to sort out its categories independently from the purpose for which they were constituted. Rather, Buber, for whom the import of

---

Dialogue: Martin Buber's Transformation of German Social Thought (Detroit: Wayne State University Press, 1989); and Martin Treml's detailed introduction to Martin Buber, *Frühe kulturkritische und philosophische Schirften 1891–1924*, Werkausgabe vol. 1 (Gütersloh: Gütersloher Verlagshaus, 2001), 13–91.

Spinoza and Nietzsche remained palpable throughout his life, understood philosophy as just one way to see the world that was no less contingent of its institutional practice as any other. Moving on the periphery and in between conceptual and literary imagination, Buber navigated between Nietzschean, neo-Kantian, and phenomenological currents on the one hand and between impressionism, art deco, and expressionism on the other. As Buber sought realisation of the critical philosophical impetus in life rather than the academe, he set philosophy free from the strictures of its institutional limitations and opened it up to the world. One of Buber's last responses to the request to sum up his teaching was simply his explanation that there was no particular content he wanted to teach but that all he intended to was to carry a dialogue or conversation, *Gespräch*, and lead the listener to the window, open it, and point outside.[13]

If Buber has been taken to task for the artfully literary character of his style, which seems to lack the philosophical rigor and stringency expected of philosophy, such criticism highlights a crucial aspect of Buber's approach. For Buber's choice not to limit himself to the protocol of a particular discipline is an expression of the very impulse that defines his philosophic thought. Positioned as cultural critique of philosophy as academic discipline, Buber's redeployment of philosophic thought in a literary modernist key signals a critical engagement with the problematic proposition of philosophy itself as a discipline that, on Buber's analysis, had left the very needs of thought and knowledge in the lurch. In pointed departure from academic conventions, Buber's style might lack the appearance of rigor and precision, but it is precisely the obsession with the claim to terminological exactness that Buber's writing exposes as a desire if not obsession that drives instrumental rationality yet undermines the very project of critical reason. For in Buber's eyes, philosophy's liberating push does not consist in what could be limited to a purely epistemological task but rather in the recognition that knowledge and its realisation is always already bound up with the ethics of a practice that calls for ever new critical examination.

---

[13] Martin Buber, "Aus einer philosophischen Rechenschaft" in Buber, *Werke 1: Schriften zur Philosophie* (Munich and Heidelberg: Kösel and Lambert Schneider, 1962), 1109–1122, quote 1114.

Buber's work is thus less historically oriented or just a critique of modernity than a bold attempt at rethinking the project of modernity as one continuous with Jewish modernity. An incessant interlocutor on the national and international scene, Buber situated his project as an alternative approach to the ongoing debate about re-imagining modernity. Confronting the problem of facing the tremendous tension between a fast-advancing process of industrial modernisation in Germany and a cultural uprooting that led to a compensatory need for the authenticity of inherited cultures, Buber felt the need to address this double alienation in a way that would resist the reification of both the "old" and the "new." His literary and philosophical work of the 1920s articulates a theory of modernity that is both critical and empowering.

While *I and Thou*, published in 1923, is often taken as a guidebook for authentic encounters, it is the book's articulation of a critique of alienation and instrumental reason that makes its particular phenomenological approach philosophically significant. To some degree a fortuitous variation of Simmel's approach, *I and Thou* distinguishes two ways to address the world, God, and self. Similar to Simmel's, Buber's account recognises the problems of modernity less in external conditions alone than primarily in the way we relate to them. If for Simmel this had remained a sociological concern, the diagnosis carried for Buber further reaching implications. The forms of relating to reality did not only share in substantial ways in creating it but also meant that if everybody's identity was always already divided according to the balance one struck between the two "basic words," *I-Thou* and *I-It*—that is, the two modes of relating to the world and others—there existed no originary identity that could be considered as primary. The dual origin of one's identity in this distinction of experiencing the world either "instrumentally" through an I-It relationship or "existentially" through an I-Thou relationship meant that the self itself was dynamically constituted navigating the two exclusive but equally necessary spheres of relationship. On this view, the challenge of modernity consisted in successfully negotiating the terms of the two kinds of relationships as neither one presented an exclusive option of primacy.

Buber's particular way to present Hasidism and its way of life to a modern audience by anthologising various collections of Hasidic tales suggests a helpful illustration of his philosophic concerns and more precisely his move to articulate a theory of modernity that would critically address the problems that so-called secularist accounts would eclipse. Gershom Scholem's criticism that Buber's account of Hasidism lacked the historic accuracy of a rigorous scholarly examination thus interestingly fails to touch on the central concerns of Buber's project, a project that was in the eyes of Buber primarily of a literary nature rather than simply an attempt at historical recovery. As Buber retold and occasionally rephrased Hasidic stories, his project exemplified the basic issue central to his dialogical thought.[14]

The critical moment in Buber's *Hasidic Tales* consists not just in the choice of material he introduces to the modern reader but more decisively in the way in which his texts do so. The *Hasidic Tales* are conceived as literary texts whose performative aspect points to a transformative purpose. Composed as modern texts, they seem to enchant the reader, take them to another, magical, and glorious world of the past. But upon closer attention, that world reveals itself as a world disenchantingly resonating with the present as its historic features become transparent to be just that: historical. Yet, these stories not only seem to take in and transport the readers to a place of fictional introspection but also conclude by returning the readers to their own world, thus releasing the transformative power of this particular mode of literary re-imagining of the present through the past. The gesture of return, of refusing to let the reader remain uncritically in the imaginary world of the past and of lore, signals the *Hasidic Tales'* particular edge. By retelling, the editor's work highlights the fact that staging stories as literary events is already once removed from the imaginary authentic world that the stories seem to invoke. The performative moment that informs the telling of these stories that are literally "out of this world" and no longer part of it underscores the stories' profound otherness with regard to a world that seems so tangibly realistic yet at the same time so elusively removed.

---

14 See Martina Urban, *Aesthetics of Renewal: Martin Buber's Early Representation of Hasidism as Kulturkritik* (Chicago and London: University of Chicago Press, 2008) for a thorough study of Buber's editorial practices of anthologising and editing the Hasidic Tales as part of his project of editing Jewish anthologies.

Presenting samples of authentic past the retelling seems to reinstate, the stories suggest, upon a closer look, a modernist countermove that complicates the readers' relationships to their own presents. Buber's retelling confronts the reader with experiencing the present as no less narratively constructed than the tales as they return the reader to the challenge of facing his own present as a construction of his own. As each and every one of the *Hasidic Tales* thus transports the reader back to the present, the tales' fictional impetus signals a phenomenological turn that confronts the reader at the end of each story with unassuming directness with themselves as each story returns them to their own hermeneutic challenge.

Many of the tales make this point more or less explicit, but one of the more compact ones brings the point home most directly. Its title is "The Ear That Is No Ear."

> Rabbi Pinhas said: "In the book *The Duties of the Heart*, we read that he who considers his life as he ought, should see with eyes that are no eyes, hear with ears that are no ears. And that is just how it is! For often, when someone comes to ask my advice, I hear him giving himself the answer to his question."[15]

The *Hasidic Tales* thus invoke what they artfully expose as the reader's problematic desire for authenticity, a desire the Hasidic narrative thematises as the obsessive reiteration of the ever elusive. Composed as artfully literary texts, they bring home modernity's predicament that the hermeneutic process cannot itself pose as the answer it seeks but at best sends the reader back to revisit the questions and expectations they bring to the text. With this hermeneutic turn, *the Hasidic Tales* offer some important elements towards a theory of modernity. Read in conjunction with Buber's early writings on dialogical thinking, *I and Thou* and *Dialogue*, there emerges a critique of instrumental reason that resonates with voices of the period such as Gustav Landauer, Walter Rathenau, and others. But Buber's critical contribution consists in the distinction of the relationality in which people relate to the world,

---

[15]   Martin Buber, *Tales of the Hasidim*, trans. Olga Marx (New York: Schocken, 1947 and 1975), vol. 1, 126.

themselves, and others. Rather than a defect in reason or rationality, Buber's diagnosis focuses on the way in which reason and rationality are brought into play. On his diagnosis, it is the split within the individual, the internalised experience of alienation, the loss of the ability to reconcile the two kinds of relationalities as I-Thou and I-It that defines the signature of modernity.

As Buber continued rewriting Hasidic tales, these narratives emerging at the point of transition to modernity took on a literary form that best suited Buber's own philosophic message. In the continuous rewriting of the Hasidic stories, Buber arrived at a literary medium that allowed him to couch his philosophic thought in the most convincing manner. *The Way of Man*, Buber's most succinct and accomplished companion of (Hasidic) wisdom, is the best example for how philosophy and literary form meet in Buber's unique style. Written as a breviary or guide, this later text illuminates the critical thrust of Buber's project with inspiring translucence. Buber introduces its concluding section "Hier wo man steht" (Here Where One Stands) with the following tale:

> Rabbi Bunam used to tell young men who came to him for the first time the story of Rabbi Eizik, son of Rabbi Yekel of Cracow. After many years of great poverty which had never shaken his faith in God, he dreamed someone bade him look for a treasure in Prague, under the bridge which leads to the king's palace. When the dream recurred a third time, Rabbi Eizik prepared for the journey and set out for Prague. But the bridge was guarded day and night and he did not dare to start digging. Nevertheless he went to the bridge every morning and kept walking around it until evening. Finally the captain of the guards, who had been watching him, asked in a kindly way whether he was looking for something or waiting for somebody. Rebbi Eizik told him of the dream which had brought him here from a faraway country. The captain laughed: "And so to please the dream, you poor fellow wore out your shoes to come here! As for having faith in dreams, if I had had it, I should have had to get going when a dream once told me to go to Cracow and dig for treasure under the stove in the room of a Jew—Eizik, son of Yekel, that was the name! Eizik, son of Yekel! I can just imagine what it would be like, how I should have to try every house over there, where one half of the Jews are named Eizik and the other Yekel!" And he laughed again. Rabbi Eizik bowed, traveled

home, dug up the treasure from under the stove, and built the House of Prayer which is called "Reb Eizik Reb Yekel's Shul."

"Take this story to heart," Rabbi Bunam used to add, "and make what it says your own: There is something you cannot find anywhere in the world, not even at the zaddik's, and there is nevertheless a place where you can find it."[16]

Rather than an intrinsic flaw, it is the very condition of modernity's openness that can be experienced as threatening. In a way, Buber theorises that the exclusion from the university of what matters most for a critical understanding of knowledge is the very crux of the problem of the university's limited scope. His thought underscores the necessity to look beyond the institutional confines for an approach that recognises what is shut out from the academic protocol. Buber's dialogical approach positions itself critically *extra muros* as it signals the imperative for thinking the complementary side of reason and rationality. For Buber, this is not an issue of irrationality but represents a crucial yet ignored critical aspect of reason itself, the shared source out of which both forms of relationships, I-Thou and I-It, that is, instrumental and non-instrumental reason, spring.

FRANZ ROSENZWEIG: OUTSIDE INSIDE

If Buber had sought to respond to the problem of the restricted and exclusionary stance of the German university by creating a public discourse outside and independent of the institutions, for Rosenzweig, the response became a self-consciously explicit challenge. Trained as historian by the eminent Friedrich Meinecke, who saw his brilliant student poised for a promising academic career, Rosenzweig, however, chose to forgo the institutional route, deciding instead to work outside the university in the context of the Jewish community. It was during World War I, while Rosenzweig served as a soldier and examined in a number of essays the larger strategic and political challenges that

---

16   Martin Buber, *The Way of Man According to the Teachings of Hasidism* (New York: The Citadel Press, 1966), 36–37.

the German state faced, that this change of mind took its dramatic turn as Rosenzweig plunged into an almost frantic writing experience, drafting *The Star of Redemption*. Initially jotting words down on a string of field service postcards, the only form of paper soldiers received in free supply, Rosenzweig set out to compose the first chapters. *The Star of Redemption* was early on recognised as a signal work of rethinking Jewish modernity. In the wake of Cohen's *Religion of Reason Out of the Sources of Judaism*, *The Star of Redemption* represented the next phase in the project of German Jewish affirmation and self-positioning in philosophy. If the philosophical ambition of *The Star* remained difficult to appreciate by the wider public, the book assumed a central place in the discussion among Jewish intellectuals.[17] But its critical significance became more palpable as *The Star* provided the philosophical framework for the Jewish House of Learning (Jüdisches Lehrhaus) that Rosenzweig was to direct in Frankfurt in the 1920s. It is through the daily practice of adult extra-university teaching and learning—a process Rosenzweig saw as intrinsically indivisible—that Rosenzweig's vision took hold as one that pits itself in creatively complementary manner over and against the university that provided formal training and "Bildung" of sorts, all the while excluding that aspect most crucial in the eyes of Rosenzweig and his Jewish contemporaries: the concerns of Jewish modernity. The book's final words signalled this in programmatic if enigmatic manner as they released the reader "Into Life."[18]

---

[17] An exception was Margarete Susman's review of *The Star* in *Der Jude* 6.4 (1921–1922), 259–264. See Franz Rosenzweig's letter of thanks from February 1922 in Franz Rosenzweig, *Der Mensch und sein Werk: Gesammelte Schriften*, vol. 1.2: *Briefe und Tagebücher*, 752. For early appreciations, see Nahum Glatzer, *Franz Rosenzweig: His Life and Thought* (New York: Schocken with Farrar, Straus, and Young, 1953) and the work of Hermann Levin Goldschmidt, especially his work on the Jewish House of Learning (1957) in Goldschmidt, *The Legacy of German Jewry*, trans. David Suchoff (New York: Fordham, 2007), 154–160, and the essay "Franz Rosenzweigs Existenzphilosophie aus den Quellen des Judentums," in Goldschmidt, *Aus den Quellen des Judentums: Aufsätze zur Philosophie, Werke* vol. 5 (Vienna: Passagen, 2000), 157–178. For a concise discussion that highlights the critically philosophic importance of Rosenzweig, see Robert Gibbs, *Correlations in Rosenzweig and Levinas* (Princeton: Princeton University Press, 1992).

[18] For a study of Rosenzweig's project in the context of this period, see Peter Eli Gordon, *Rosenzweig and Heidegger: Between Judaism and German Philosophy* (Berkeley: University of California Press, 2003).

Indeed, the Jewish House of Learning was according to Rosenzweig's vision a place where life as he re-imagined it could take root and find a home and a space for expression, a life that brought the advanced education of German Jews to fruition in dialogue with a rethinking of the Jewish tradition and vice versa. Rosenzweig's pedagogy of confronting academic experience with the everyday situation that the participants—students and teachers alike—would bring to the House of Study provided an open space for the new learning Rosenzweig envisioned. This "new learning"[19] took its lead from the "New Thinking" that Rosenzweig advocated in his companion essay to *The Star of Redemption*, which laid out the *Star's* project in programmatic manner. "The New Thinking" (1925) fleshed out the philosophic significance of the new thinking that informs the project of *The Star of Redemption*. Replacing the "thinking thinker" by the "language thinker" (*Sprachdenker*), Rosenzweig argues for grammatical rather than merely logical thinking, a thinking that "does not rest on loud versus quiet, but rather on needing the other and, what amounts to the same, on taking time seriously."[20] This dialogic move was self-consciously removed from the university whose very structure would ill accommodate this new kind of thinking:

> To think here means to think for no one and to speak to no one (for which one may substitute everyone, the famous "universality," if it sounds better to someone). But to speak means to speak to someone and to think for someone; and this Someone is always a quite definite Someone and has not only ears, like the universality, but also a mouth. (127)

Rosenzweig's "experiencing philosophy" (*erfahrende Philosophie*)[21] reopens the case of philosophy itself. The shift from logics to grammar

---

19   For the agenda of "New Learning," see Rosenzweig's address at the inauguration of the Frankfurt Jewish House of Learning, 1920, in Franz Rosenzweig, *Gesammelte Schriften, vol 3: Zweistromland*, 505–510. On the Jewish House of Learning see also Goldschmidt, *Die Botschaft des Judentums* (Vienna: Passagen, 1994), 157–179.
20   Franz Rosenzweig, *Philosophical and Theological Writings*, trans. Paul W. Franks and Michael L. Morgan (Hackett: Indianapolis, 2000), 109–139, 127.
21   The English translation gives "experiential philosophy" (117) but Rosenzweig's point is that philosophy itself is part of the experience as well, that is, a philosophy open to the necessary changes that the "New Thinking" calls for. Cf. Rosenzweig, *Gesammelte Schriften, vol. 3: Zweistromland*, 144.

attends to temporality as a central feature of Rosenzweig's approach that entails profound ramifications for both philosophic thought and pedagogy. As a matter of fact, "pedagogy," the guiding of pupils, is a problematic term for a project that recognises the adult student as interlocutor rather than merely recipient.

This learning "in the opposite direction" that starts from the everyday life experience in order to explore Jewish tradition transforms the conventional approach to knowledge.[22] As this new form of knowledge becomes part of lived life, it becomes dialogic in its substance. No longer detached from the subject, this new form of knowledge is eminently positional and perspectival, but also existentially constituted, that is, grounded "in life." Through the dialogical model of the House of Learning, Rosenzweig institutes a central insight at the heart of *The Star of Redemption*. The idea of the new thinking as a "philosophy of the standpoint" that no longer operates in an epistemological vacuum but in the context of a reality whose complexity exceeds the classic categorical grasp positions the philosopher in a radically new way.[23]

As the epistemological subject can no longer reflect the challenges that confront the philosopher, the philosopher's standpoint assumes constitutive significance for philosophy itself. Equally, the departure from universal ontological unity and the recognition of the tripartite nature of the universe's elements as man, world, and God, make the distinction between particular and universal obsolete. According to Rosenzweig, this distinction requires logical assumptions that, with the move to grammar and language thinking, have become problematic. Rosenzweig's philosophical line of argument moves thus deliberately on the margins of philosophy as the university conceives it. While Cohen argued from within such philosophy to attend to its internal problematic and Buber seeks to move outside to establish a new framework of public literary discourse on alternative philosophical grounds, Rosenzweig's project consists in rethinking philosophy from outside in. On Rosenzweig's account, a philosophy able to move past the impasse that defines the situation in the wake of Hegel and

---

22   "Neues Lernen," ibid. 507.
23   Rosenzweig, letter to Rudolf Stahl, June 2, 1927, vol. 1.2, 1154.

Nietzsche has to change its standing leg. Rosenzweig's critical push grounds in the very fact that he irreverently breaks with the tradition of thinking that he unforgivingly engages. Ironically, it is through the departure from the discipline of philosophy and by breaking it open that Rosenzweig gives his argument the philosophic rigor and force that philosophy claims but no longer commands. As he writes in a letter, "to philosophize is a human right, not a matter of a field of study."[24]

He thus feels no longer bound to commit or submit to a philosophic discourse he takes to task for its shortcomings. But at the same time and in principal manner, he rethinks the project of philosophy from the bottom up and in such a way that he recovers the liberating moment that informs philosophy but that had become buried and forgotten in the process of institutionalisation. As a consequence, Rosenzweig emerges as a philosopher of genuinely critical significance. A "postmodern" or rather postcontemporary philosopher, Rosenzweig insists on recovering a position of particularity that allows him to rethink the terms of an emancipatory vision of open thinking that the university's claim to universality would not permit.[25]

Certainly, Rosenzweig's complex argument and the literally provocative manner in which he presents it do not come without their own problematic. But part of Rosenzweig's genius consists precisely in articulating the issues and the problems that haunt philosophy as long as it is imagined as a self-contained system. Rosenzweig's bold step outside the disciplinary framework that defines the discourse of philosophy at the time enables him to re-imagine philosophy in the context of a vision of Jewish modernity that is no longer defined in terms of the deadlock of the distinction between particularity and

---

[24] Letter to Ernst Heinrich Seligsohn, October 29, 1925, Rosenzweig, *Gesammelte Schriften*, vol. 1.2, 1063.

[25] I would like to supplement Robert Gibb's insightful claim that Rosenzweig is no philosopher if considered in terms of the criteria of modern philosophy but certainly so if recognised as postmodern to the extent that this is the case if we consider Rosenzweig under the category under which he has posthumously begun to play the critical role he all along envisioned as postcontemporary philosopher, that is, a philosopher whose critical impetus poses the question of temporality in new fashion rather than submitting to a predefined notion of temporality imposed by "philosophy." Cf. Gibbs, *Correlations in Rosenzweig and Levinas*, 20–21.

universality. Addressing philosophy's own problematic, Rosenzweig pushes for its rethinking from the outside in. Against the discipline's unquestioned protocol to approach philosophy exclusively on its own terms as if it could be cordoned off from the theological-political implications that inform and define it in profound ways, Rosenzweig's shift to an outside-inside position situates him within and at the same time over and against "philosophy." This makes it possible to leverage his observer position in a way that re-imagines the role, place, and function of philosophy in a new way. In changing the observer position, Rosenzweig changes the frame of reference and brings philosophy's hidden assumptions to light.[26]

Nietzsche's reminder to heed the limits of philosophy and embrace the attitude of modesty as a genuinely philosophic one resonates along with other critical motives in Rosenzweig's approach. In *The Star of Redemption*, philosophy represents thus only one moment besides political, historical, and theological strands of thought. But these strands are interconnected in dialogical fashion. Rosenzweig's use of theology and of textual reasoning on various Biblical passages operates not simply as argument that—separate from philosophy—reframes the philosophic argument by complementing it but also enriches the agenda of philosophy. Similarly, historical and political concerns emerge as genuinely relevant for rethinking the task of philosophy in an alternative key. The particular fashion in which *The Star of Redemption* imports these concerns is critical: Rosenzweig makes a point not to confuse or mix the different kinds of discourses but secures their polyphonic otherness in pointed manner. As philosophy is no longer imagined in terms of a claim to totality, its particular accent represents a constituent but not all-determining thread in the weave of the argument. In other words, Rosenzweig takes the notion of relation philosophically to its logical conclusion as philosophy emerges in his account relationally reconfigured.

---

[26] For a discussion of the critical role of the change of position of the observer and the frame of reference, see Niklas Luhmann, *Theories of Distinction: Redescribing the Descriptions of Modernity*, ed., William Rasch (Stanford: Stanford University Press, 2002), 79–93.

The philosophic significance of *The Star of Redemption* consists in this move. Philosophy is no longer left on its own but emerges in its distinctive specificity with sharper precision only when considered in context of and in relation to other forms of reasoning. In other words, as Rosenzweig reframes philosophy in a larger context, it becomes possible to rethink the terms of philosophy in a principal manner. Rosenzweig's critical role in rethinking philosophy thus consists in his breaking out of the boundaries of the discipline. The attitude he recommends as dialogical principle for the Jewish House of Learning to engage in dialogue is thus one that also informs *The Star of Redemption*. Just like the dialogical relationship in the way Rosenzweig conceives it as a process of mutual constitution of the interlocutors through the relationship, philosophy emerges in *The Star of Redemption* as new thinking enriched by language thinking and the complementation of logic with grammar.

Rosenzweig's argument about the import of Jewish tradition in the context of modernity is thus in a remarkable way a genuinely philosophical argument. The discussion about Jewish tradition serves as more than just a departure point for buttressing Judaism's claim to modernity. Rosenzweig's account of Judaism is central to the philosophic argument his approach articulates. As a consequence, Jewish tradition assumes principal philosophic significance as it engages directly with the philosophical discourse it supplements.

Judaism is thus firmly grounded within a philosophical argument that in turn instantiates how they can both only be comprehended by attending the relation in which they stand. As a consequence, Rosenzweig relieves the burden of Jewish tradition from any kind of expectation philosophy might be tempted to impose. Judaism, on Rosenzweig's account, can just like any other historical phenomenon only be meaningfully understood if the approach used to explore it is itself grounded in reflecting the relation in which it stands. This requirement forestalls any assumption of inadequacy as it is exactly asymmetry that makes a dialogic relationship viable. In other words, precisely because besides continuity there is also some decisive discontinuity between philosophy and Jewish tradition, the latter assumes significance for the former. Not without some polemical undertones stands thus Rosenzweig's notion of the dialogical relationship between philosophy and Judaism as a rebuttal of any requirement that Jewish life submit to any perceived form of universal standards of philosophy. Instead, Rosenzweig's argument on Judaism suggests that it is exactly Judaism's tenacious resistance to universalisation that gives it its philosophic relevance as bulwark against any form of universalising or totalising thought.

If the proposition that the life of Judaism rests outside of history might appear curious coming from a trained historian such as Rosenzweig, it gains critical hold if seen as resistant to the attempt at assimilation to any concept of world history Hegel style. Reclaiming Judaism's place outside of history serves as a reminder that highlights the fact that the scheme of history rests on a kind of philosophical speculation that claims universal validity but that ultimately remains problematically particular. This move of dissimilation with regard to "universal" history serves not just to secure Judaism's particularity. With the Jewish tradition's assignment to an extrahistorical position, it becomes possible to engage the claim of philosophy to a vision of world history in philosophically critical terms. Just as Mendelssohn's critique of Lessing's commitment to an unexamined notion of progress begged to differ, Rosenzweig picks up where Mendelssohn left off as he highlights that the problem is not to be outside history but the idea that history is all-inclusive.[27]

If Rosenzweig's reinvention of the Jewish House of Learning may well have been the part of his legacy that became most successful in continuing to inspire generations of Jewish philosophers in breaking grounds for rethinking the tradition creatively, the impact of the theory and practice of this "New Learning" went well beyond a profound revitalisation of Jewish life. Rosenzweig's vision of the Jewish House of Learning also assumed wider importance in the larger context of rethinking the practice of learning and teaching as a form of emancipatory and self-empowering practice in general. Yet the project of the House of Learning's alternative approach to learning is grounded in the philosophical move "outside in" philosophy that Rosenzweig

---

27   Moses Mendelssohn, *Jerusalem or Religious Power and Judaism*, trans. Allan Arkash (Hanover: University Press of New England, 1983), 95–96.

deployed in *The Star of Redemption*. The book's concluding words "Into Life" signal the crucial "lifeline" that links philosophy with its praxis and vice versa. In other words, the House of Learning even in its most diluted variants thrives on the grounds of a strong reconceptualisation of the task and the function of philosophy that *The Star of Redemption* formulates.

One of the book's most remarkable interventions that highlights the German Jewish experience—and not just with regard to the project of philosophy—represents the way in which Rosenzweig addresses the relationship between "we" and "you" as a dialectically triangulated relationship that is constituted via God. The speech act of saying "we" performs at the same time both inclusion and exclusion. In other words, the logic of inclusion hinges on exclusion as its constitutive correlative. As a result, the dividing line between "we" and "you" informs the very speech act of saying "we." The "we" calls for a "you," but "we" at the same time presupposes "you" as its other. The possibility of the "we" hinges in a peculiar way on the double meaning of it being at the same time always both inclusive and exclusive. "We" is thus a speech act that marks the fine line of demarcation and difference that sets off inclusion against exclusion. It is itself the marker of the divide it sets up. As such, it functions like a symptom: it is the sign of the formation of a conflictual process and tension, a function of its forces rather than the self-contained entity it so desired to present.

The discussion of the "we" occurs at a particular junction in the *Star*.[28] It concludes the section "Grammar of Pathos (The Language of the Deed/Action)" that precedes the "Logic of Redemption" in book 3 of part 2 titled "Redemption or the Eternal Future of the Kingdom." As a result, the argument about the "we/you" stands at a particular conjunction in Rosenzweig's argument on redemption, one that cannot be separated from the way in which the "Grammar of Eros (The Language of Love)" addresses the I and you in the preceding book on revelation. For Rosenzweig, *we* is essentially a pronoun that is made possible only through its grounding in a redemptive perspective. But

---

[28]   Rosenzweig, *Gesammelte Schriften*, vol. 2: *Der Stern der Erlösung*, 263–265; Rosenzweig, *The Star of Redemption*, trans. William W. Hallo (New York: Holt, 1970), 236–238.

spoken, the word *we* lingers in a preredemptive and unredeemed space while it points forward to redemption. Through the grammar of redemption, through an eventual form of speech act, the "we" might transcend the limits of the human conditions of inclusion and exclusion that make the conception of a "we" possible in the first place. But such a standpoint of redemption can only be found in God, for Rosenzweig a pointedly dynamic notion that suggests Becoming or *Werden* rather than Being or *Sein*. Such a "we" marks the vanishing point on which the possibility of redemption rests and can thus never be claimed by any single or singular voice except at the moment of redemption. The pointedly theological and theological-political conception of this "we" resists therefore any appropriation by any particular instantiation of "we." Its theological nature highlights the theological implications of its claims as those that are and remain theological and, on the logic of theology, thus remain forever out of reach of any grasp by mundane and secular temporality. It is thus the very category of "redemption" that shields the "we" from a social or political appropriation.

The limit of the "we" represents all that what the "we" call "you." But this "you," or rather the pronouncing of it, Rosenzweig notes, is gruesome and harrowing: "*grauenhaft*." It is the result of passing judgment the "we" cannot prevent to pass. For, as Rosenzweig states, only in this passing of judgment (*Gericht*) does the "we" gain the determinate meaning (*bestimmten Inhalt*) of a universal totality, a determinate meaning which, however, Rosenzweig stresses, is not particular and does not limit the "we's" reach. This judgment does not exclude any particular meaning, except the nothing, so that the "we" gains whatever is not nothing for its meaning, all that is real, all that is actual.[29] As a consequence, Rosenzweig continues, the "we" is forced to say "you"; and the more force the "we" gains, the louder must it pronounce the "you." While it is forced to do so, it can only do so by way of anticipation prefiguring the kingdom to come. By doing so, Rosenzweig points out that the "we" subjects itself to the judgment of God. But for God, both the "we" and the "you" are "they." From the point of divine authority, the answer is no longer mere words but

---

[29]   *Der Stern der Erlösung*, 264f; *The Star of Redemption*, 237f.

redemption, a process that transcends language and words, a process in which both "we" and "you" become part of the moment of redemptive transformation. Language has reached here its limits at the "dawn of the day of the Lord." This at least is the conclusion of the section "Grammar of Pathos/Language of the Deed." Consequently, the book on redemption concludes with a discussion of "The Word of God,"[30] or, more precisely, with a reading of Psalm 115, whose grammatical construction highlights the grounding of the "we" in its relationship to God.

The "we" and "you" are thus in Rosenzweig's account constituted by triangulation via the relationship of God, that is, the vanishing point of redemption. While philosophy and theology are thus exposed as inseparably intertwined, the text argues through its explicit theological diction a pointedly philosophical reading.

"We," Rosenzweig reminds the reader, is not a plural that simply derives from the third person singular. Rather, "we" develops out of the dual that cannot be expanded but only limited. This means that the "we" is an all-inclusive pronoun of a dual construction that can only gain specificity by exclusion.[31] Any "we" of any community is therefore not originary or primary but always a derivative construction. Whereas community is built on the condition of anticipating and at the same time presuming redemption, the form of this expectation rests on a circular figure of constitution by way of performative anticipation. Its grounds are therefore always tentative, presumptive, and problematic. Their teleological nature underlines the fact that this "we" is a project, a work in progress. Any "you" it posits by exclusion is only a commentary about the "we" itself. Only from the perspective of a third, that is, God, can both become a simple plural of a "they." Otherwise "we" and "you" are mutually dependent pronouns, determined through reciprocal juxtaposition. As a result, "we" can never serve as grounds for determining oneself or another (nor can a "you"). As correlative categories, they represent the economy of redemption they cannot transcend. In other words, they are locked in the discourse they produce.

---

30   *Der Stern der Erlösung*, 278; *The Star of Redemption*, 250.
31   *Der Stern der Erlösung*, 264; *The Star of Redemption*, 236f.

As a consequence, Rosenzweig's phenomenology of the "we" liberates the claim of any "we" from the clutches of both a theological and philosophical hold. "We" remains immune to any such claim as an intrinsically unstable, dynamic, and open-ended, unfinished project that requires the notion of redemption as one that transcends it and remains forever deferred, only realisable at the moment of redemption. In the final analysis, Rosenzweig reminds us that there is no "we" and "you" but simply the next, the neighbour, the one we confront: "Anyone, the Other in general—the neighbor,"[32] as the penultimate paragraph of conclusion of the book on redemption puts it. As for the I and You and their critical function of correlation, the dialogic moment is no longer locked in an impossible theological deadlock of we/you and burdened with the expectation to present the other. Rather, the "we" can now be addressed from a post-theological perspective as an always already precarious pronominal signifier whose referent remains ever negotiable, continually reconstituted by the ever-new next it confronts.

CONCLUSION

The philosophical trajectories in Cohen, Buber, and Rosenzweig become legible in their critical function in confronting the German university politics of inclusion and exclusion from the 1860s to 1933. Their philosophical projects represent critical responses to the hegemonic discourse of philosophy whose secularised claims they expose as problematic traces of continuing theological commitments. In different ways, their projects are critical interventions in a philosophical discourse they attempt to reconstitute by rethinking philosophy's universal claims as inseparably linked to the problem of the conflicted way in which Jewish tradition has been (dis)figured, be it by repression or by partial acknowledgement and "integration." Remarkably, the critical impulse that informs their philosophic projects has become an integral part of the legacy of German and not just Jewish philosophy.

---

[32] *The Star of Redemption*, 252: "Irgendjemand, den andern schlechtweg, den—Nächsten," *Der Stern der Erlösung*, 281.

CHAPTER XI

CULTURAL TRANSFERS BETWEEN *OSTJUDEN* AND *WESTJUDEN*: GERMAN JEWISH INTELLECTUALS AND YIDDISH CULTURE, 1897–1930[*]

Delphine Bechtel

> The Western Jew first feared Eastern European Jews, then he pitied him. Now he is beginning to understand him, and soon, he will envy him.
> —Fabius Schach, "Jüdische Aphorismen"[1]

This aphorism, which appeared in a German Jewish *Volkskalender* in 1918, summarises the changing opinions of German Jews about their Eastern European brethren from the end of the nineteenth century and during the first third of the twentieth.

Inter-Ashkenazic cultural contacts had persisted throughout the centuries since the eastward migration of the majority of Jews from German-speaking countries and since the centre of gravity of Ashkenazic Jewry had moved from Western to Eastern Europe around 1500. During the seventeenth and eighteenth centuries, waves of Eastern European Jews remigrated westward, in particular after the Chmelnicki massacres.[2]

---

[*] The first draft of this paper was presented under the title "The Reception of Yiddish Literature among German Jewish Writers and Intellectuals," 1908–1933," at the Fourth International Conference for Research on Yiddish, held at the Hebrew University, Jerusalem, in May 1992. Support towards further research has been granted by the *Alexander von Humboldt-Stiftung*, the Memorial Foundation for Jewish Culture and the Franz Rosenzweig Centre at the Hebrew University. I am very indebted to Steven Uran for his invaluable help and constructive criticism of this paper.

[1] "Der Westjude hat den Ostjuden zuerst gefürchtet, dann bedauert. Nun fängt er an, ihn zu verstehen und er wird ihn bald beneiden." Fabius Schach, *Hickls Wiener Jüdischer Volkskalender für das Jahr* 5679 (1918–1919) (Brünn-Vienna: Hickel, 1918), 55.

[2] On the Jewish migrations during the early modern era, see Moses A. Shulvass, *From East to West: The Westward Migration of Jews from Eastern Europe during the Seventeenth and Eighteenth Centuries* (Detroit: Wayne State University Press, 1972).

During the Enlightenment, a breach developed between the two branches of Ashkenazic Jewry, and a few decades later the former unity of Ashkenaz had given way to a cultural gap between East and West. Through the process of emancipation, assimilation, and acculturation, the majority of German Jews had become part of the German middle class, identifying with a denationalised Judaism defined as *Glaubensgemeinschaft*. Eastern European Jews, in contrast, were still living in the *shtetlekh* under the influence of Orthodoxy or Hasidism, although they were increasingly confronted with modernity in the cities. Jews in Germany adhered to the German concepts of *Bildung* and *Kultur*, while Eastern European Jews had developed a cultural bilingualism,[3] combining Hebrew, the language of religious Orthodoxy as well as of Zionist-orientated cultural revival, and Yiddish, which completed its evolution into a modern literary language at the same time as Hebrew.

The negative attitude of German Jewry towards Eastern European Jews crystallised during the nineteenth century. For the philosophers of the Enlightenment and later the representatives of the *Wissenschaft des Judentums*, Hasidism was a synonym for obscurantism and corruption of the mind. The Yiddish language they had just cast off was seen as a reflection of this backwardness. For Moses Mendelssohn, the Yiddish language "had contributed not a little to the immorality of the common man"; the historian Heinrich Graetz called Yiddish "eine halb-tierische Sprache"; and Leopold Zunz described it as "eingeschlossenes, ausgeartetes Deutsch."[4] Polish Jews were reproached

---

[3]   Traditional Eastern European Jewish culture was characterised by a situation of diglossia, in which Hebrew was used as the language of high culture and Yiddish as the language of low culture. On this distinction, see Charles A. Ferguson, "Diglossia," *Word* 15 (1959), 325–340; Joshua A. Fishman, "Attracting a Following to High-Culture Functions for a Language of Everyday Life: The Role of the Tshernovits Language Conference in the Rise of Yiddish," in *Never Say Die! A Thousand Years of Yiddish in Jewish Life and Letters*, ed., Joshua A. Fishman (The Hague-New York: de Gruyter Mouton, 1981), 369–394. This diglossia progressively developed into bilingualism, so that at the turn of the century, most writers were writing in both languages and often published their work in two versions. See the essay of Bal Makhshoves (Israel Eliashev), "Tsvey shprakhn—eyneyntsike literature," idem, *Geklibene verk* (New York: L. M. Stein Folks Bibliotek of the Congress for Jewish Culture New York, 1953), 112–123.

[4]   *Moses Mendelssohn's Gesammelte Schriften*, ed., Georg B. Mendelssohn, 7 vols. (Leipzig: F. A. Brockhaus, 1843–1845), vol. 5, 505–506; Graetz is quoted by Emanuel S.

for their unattractive behaviour, such as wearing the traditional caftan and sidelocks, or for maintaining religious rituals that seemed undignified. The stereotype of the "Ghetto Jew" was epitomised in the title of a successful collection of short stories about Jewish and non-Jewish life in Galicia by Karl Emil Franzos (1848–1901), *Aus Halb-Asien* (1876). In fact, Franzos's stories did not simply portray Galician Jews as poor, dirty, superstitious, and ignorant.[5] On the contrary, a very characteristic story, "Schiller in Barnow," relates how a group of small-town would-be intellectuals, reflecting the diverse national backgrounds in Galicia, achieve *Bildung*, humanism, and brotherhood through reading a commonly owned copy of Schiller's works. But the actual title of Franzos's collection became synonymous with the world German Jews wanted to dissociate from, both geographically and chronologically.[6] By the end of the nineteenth century, the gap between *Westjuden* and *Ostjuden* seemed impossible to bridge.

The ups and downs of history soon provided a new opportunity for an encounter between East and West. The pogroms which erupted in Russia in 1881 triggered a huge wave of westward emigration. The number of Eastern European Jews in Germany swelled from 15,000

Goldsmith, *Architects of Yiddishism at the Beginning of the Twentieth Century: A Study in Jewish Cultural History* (Cranbury: Fairleigh Dickinson University Press, 1976), 38; Leopold Zunz, *Gesammelte Schriften* (Berlin: Duncker, 1878), vol. II, 110. The complete quotation reads: "Polen besorgte bekanntlich einige Jahrhunderte hindurch den größten Theil von Deutschland mit Jugendlehrern und Rabbinern, die ihr seit mehreren hundert Jahren in Polen und Litthalluen eingeschlossenes, ausgeartete Deutsch, mit ihrer Unwissenheit und dee Rohheir des Landes, das sie aussandte, verbreiteten, so daß bei Vernachlässigung aller Kenntnisse, selbst der hebräischen Grammatik und der Bibelkunde, Aberglauben und Finsternis um sich griffen."

[5]   See, for example, Ritchie Robertson, "Western Observers and Eastern Jews: Kafka, Buber, Franzos," *The Modern Language Review* 83 (January 1988), 87–105.

[6]   See Steven E. Aschheim, *Brothers and Strangers: The East European Jew in German and German Jewish Consciousness, 1800–1918* (Madison: University of Wisconsin Press, 1982); Sander L. Gilman, "The Rediscovery of the Eastern Jews. German Jews in the East, 1890–1918," in *Jews and Germans from 1860 to 1933: The Problematic Symbiosis*, ed. David Bronsen (Heidelberg: Winter, 1979); idem, *Jewish Self-Hatred: Anti-Semitism and the Hidden Language of the Jews* (Baltimore: Johns Hopkins University Press, 1986); Trude Maurer, *Ostjuden in Deutschland, 1918–1933* (Hamburg: H. Christians, 1986); Jack Wertheimer, *Unwelcome Strangers: East European Jews in Imperial Germany* (Oxford: Oxford University Press, 1987).

in 1880 to 78,000 in 1910. It reached 90,000 in 1914 and 107,000 in 1925. During the First World War, 70,000 workers were brought to German territory by force (although the majority returned to the East after the war).[7] As a result, German public opinion started to fear a veritable invasion of *Ostjuden*, as they came to be known at the turn of the century. In the press and in parliament there were fierce debates on the desirability of closing the border, a measure which was enforced in 1918. The same phenomenon could be observed in Vienna, where poor Galician Jews flocked to the capital of the then Habsburg Empire. During the war, the German occupation of Poland resulted in direct contact between Germans, among them German Jews, and the native Jewish population. Hundreds of *Feldpostbriefe* were published in the press, and the new literary genre of *Kriegsliteratur* featured a confrontation with a Polish-Jewish ghetto as an almost obligatory scene.

It is important to stress that while immigration and war made the face-to-face encounter between German and Eastern European Jews possible, assimilated Jews in the West had already been familiar with literature about their Eastern counterparts since the beginning of the century. The impact of antisemitism in Western Europe and the pogroms in the East had given a powerful impetus to Zionism, which was intimately linked with the Jewish intellectual renaissance. German Zionist ideology regarding Eastern European Jews evolved from a paternalistic and philanthropic condescension which was based on a feeling of cultural and social superiority. But German Jews increasingly recognised that Eastern European Jews could be regarded as a source of authenticity, and that they could be credited with intellectual and cultural pre-eminence because they had never broken the "golden chain" of Jewish tradition. A fruitful exchange could be envisaged to which German Jews would contribute economic and financial superiority, while Eastern European Jews were expected to bring fresh blood and vitality to German Jewish culture.[8] The concept of the

---

[7]   See S. Adler-Rudel, *Ostjuden in Deutschland 1880–1940: Zugleich eine Geschichte der Organisationen, die sie betreuten* (Tübingen: J. C. Mohr, 1959), 164 ff.

[8]   See also David N. Myers, "'Distant Relatives Happening onto the Same Inn': The Meeting of East and West as Literary Theme and Cultural Ideal," *Jewish Social Studies* 1 (1995), 75–100.

spiritual superiority of Eastern European Jewry stimulated an interest in Yiddish and Hebrew culture, literature, theatre, and art.

In Eastern Europe, Yiddish and Hebrew literature had gone beyond the founding phase of the *Haskalah*. Young writers, mostly disciples of Isaac Leybush Peretz (1851–1915), felt the need for a cultural renaissance and called for an introduction of Jewish culture to the West and to modernity. It is no surprise that from a cultural as well as ideological perspective, the year 1897 was a watershed for both East and West. It was the year of the First Zionist Congress in Basle and of the creation of the *Bund* in Vilna. In the East and the West, Jewish writers, folklorists, cultural activists, and politicians started a movement which sought to return to the *Volk*, to the past and tradition. But they also attempted to create something new, to encourage a development in Jewish culture which would correspond to modernist European aesthetics.

This essay attempts to illustrate some aspects of these inter-Ashkenazic cultural transfers by focusing on the reception and the interpretation of Yiddish literary culture by German and Austrian Jewish intellectuals. At first glance, these transfers appear to involve a linear movement from Yiddish writers as the source group to German-speaking Jewish writers and intellectuals as the target group. In fact, the process was far more complex, as it involved cultural mediators who translated and conveyed Yiddish culture to the German-speaking audience. Moreover, cultural transfers are always dynamic: they feed on a continuous chain of translations, book reviews, scholarly or popular works, interpretations, and essays which are generated by lectures or other forms of appreciation of Yiddish culture and mutually influence each other.

The reception of Yiddish literature in Germany and Austria was closely related to changing attitudes towards its medium, the Yiddish language. During the First World War, a new, positive view of Yiddish emerged which was unexpectedly linked with the defence of German cultural imperialism in the East. In 1914, the Zionist Max Bodenheimer created the *Komitee für den Osten* (KfdO) with the aim of linking the imperialist pursuits of Germany with the interests of the Jews of Eastern Europe. Because Yiddish appears to be a Germanic language, Eastern European Jews were virtually regarded as allies of

Germany against Tsarist Russia and as possible outposts of the policy of Germanisation in the East. A typical example of this propaganda is a pamphlet on Yiddish published on behalf of the KfdO by the Zionist Heinrich Loewe in 1915, which states:

> These Jews, who have now been settled in Poland for five hundred years, have preserved the German language in Lithuania, Volhynia, Bessarabia, and in deepest Asia, as well as in Galicia and Romania, just as they have preserved the German Middle Ages in its name …. With unparalleled faithfulness they have preserved the language they spoke in common with their persecutors. They preserved it as something sacred.[9]

This viewpoint became popular in wide circles during the war, mainly because it made Yiddish *salonfähig*, documenting as it did the Germanophilia of the Jews at a time of shrill political and cultural imperialism when they were constantly the target of antisemitic agitation. If Jews had preserved the German language better than the Germans themselves, in spite of distance, the passage of centuries, and the hostility of the Germans, their faithfulness needed no further demonstration. The theatre critic Alfred Kerr wrote a variation on the same motif:

> Yes, these Hebrews who now dwell far down the Volga or in Poland have held onto the German language for centuries. For "Yiddish" is *praeter-proper* medieval German. This is proof that Jews were already at home in Germany, already spoke German, when the ancestors of those Prussian swastika-beaked creatures were still squawking in obscure Slavic dialects.[10]

---

[9] "Die Juden, die jetzt schon fünf Jahrhunderte in Polen ansässig sind, haben dort in Litauen, Wolhynien, Bessarabien, jedoch auch im tiefen Asien, aber auch genauso in Galizien und Rumänien die deutsche Sprache bewahrt, wie sie auch in ihrem Namen das deutsche Mittelalter erhalten haben … Mit einer Treue ohne gleichen haben sie die Sprache erhalten, die sie gemeinsam mit ihren Verfolgern gesprochen haben. Wie ein Heiligthum bewahren sie sie." Heinrich Loewe, *Die jüdische Sprache der Ostjuden* (Berlin: Jüdischer Verlag, 1915), 2.

[10] "Ja diese Hebräer, die heute tief an der Wolga oder im Polenreich sitzen, Jahrhunderte durch hielten sie an der deutschen Spraehe fest. Das 'Yiddish' ist ja praeter-propter mittelalterliches Deutsch. Ein Beweis, daß in Deutschland Juden längst heimisch waren, längst Deutsch redeten, als die Ahnherrn preußischer Hakenkreuzschnabel noch dunkle Slawendialekte piepsten." Alfred Kerr, "S. Anski, 'Der' Dybuk', Jüdisches Künstler-Theater," *Berliner Tageblatt*, no. 495 (27th October 1921).

This shows how certain circles among German and Austrian Jews sought to reappropriate Yiddish not so much for the sake of Yiddish culture in itself but rather for political reasons—in the interest of the German fatherland and its military and cultural hegemony, or as a weapon against antisemitism.

A number of diverging opinions were put forward against this "official" theory. Anti-Yiddishist circles, whether Zionist or assimilationist, advocated the abandonment of Yiddish and its replacement with Hebrew or German. On the other hand, a minority of intellectuals tried to point out the singularity of the Yiddish language and culture and regarded the attempts made by German imperialists to utilise Yiddish for their own purposes with suspicion. In Martin Buber's journal *Der Jude*, for example, Moses Calvary published a precise comparison between poetry in *Plattdeutsch* and in Yiddish, and concluded that Yiddish possessed a "totally different character." In unison with Nathan Birnbaum, he declared that the "sprachgeistige Verwandtschaft" between German and Yiddish was insignificant.[11] Fritz Mordechai Kaufmann (1888–1921), another devotee of Yiddish culture, founded the journal *Die Freistatt* (1913–1914) to establish contact "between the Western periphery and the central parts of the *Volk*" (that is, the Eastern European Jews)[12] in order to allow the weary bourgeois and academic intelligentsia of the West "to experience the *Volk* as a powerful organism, brimming over with sap and life."[13] Kaufmann argued that only the "non-organic material," the "construction stones" of Yiddish, had their origin in medieval German, whereas the "organic functions" (rhythm, intonation, music, syntax) "receive their direction from a centre that is neither in Europe nor in Germany, but in the brain and the soul of the Jew." It was thus impossible, he claimed, to translate Yiddish into standard German since it was not possible to "de-Germanise this material once again" and to simultaneously "humanise and Judaise" it in order to obtain a form of High German that "could

---

[11] Moses Calvary, "Jiddisch," *Der Jude* 1 (1916–-1917), 30–-31.
[12] "... zwischen der westlichen Peripherie und den zentralen Volksteilen," Fritz Mordechai Kaufmann, "Zum Programm der Freistatt," *Die Freistatt* 1 (April 1913), 3.
[13] "... das Volk zu erleben, als gewaltigen, von Säften und Leben strotzenden Organismus," Fritz Mordrchai Kaufmann, "Die Erstarkung der westlichen Jüdischkeit," ibid., 5.

capture in a new manner the gestures and non-European movements of Yiddish."[14] Consequently, in his journal Kaufmann published Yiddish texts in transcription, later even in the original Hebrew type, with a complete apparatus of footnotes intended as a reading aid.

Kaufmann's very idiosyncratic mythology, according to which the organic and living Yiddish was opposed to a German which had become "herdenhaft und kadavergehorsam," was influenced by the vitalist and communitarian spirit ascribed to Eastern European Jews by Buber. The idea that Yiddish should be viewed as a non-European language was a variation on the official Zionist ideology which contrasted Yiddish, as the European language of exile, with Hebrew, the Semitic language corresponding to the essentially Asian nature of the Jewish people and culture. From yet another perspective, Gershom Scholem considered Yiddish to be "a reflection of the Hebrew language in German."[15]

These postulates about the vitality, mobility, and primitiveness attributed to Yiddish and Eastern European Jews by certain German Jewish intellectuals, including Buber, can be traced back to Johann Gottfried Herder's view of Hebrew as developed in his treatise "Abhandlung uber den Ursprung der Sprache" (1772).[16] According to Herder, the oriental languages and therefore Hebrew are characterised by their closeness to nature and their vitality. For him, verbs were primary elements in the evolution of language, as they denote action. In *Vom Geist der ebräischen Poesie*, Herder explains that a poetic language is distinguished by its verbs, as nouns tend to represent things only in stasis. Hebrew corresponds to his definition of a poetic language: "Now in Hebrew, almost everything is verb, that is, everything lives and

---

[14] All quotations from Fritz Mordechai Kaufmann, "Über Mendele und die Übersetzbarkeit seiner Dichtungen," idem, *Vier Essays über ostjüdische Dichtung und Kultur* (Berlin: Welt-Verlag, 1919), 13–14.

[15] Gershom Scholem, "Zum Problem der Übersetzung aus dem Jiddischen," *Jüdische Rundschau* (12 January 1917).

[16] On Herder's influence on Buber, sec Avraham Shapira, "Buber's attachment to Herder and German 'Volkism,'" *Studies in Zionism* 14 (1993), 1–30. See also the essay by Manuel Duarte de Oliveira, "Passion for Land and Volk: Martin Buber and Neo-Romanticism," *LBIYB* 41 (1996), 239–259.

acts."[17] Moreover, according to Herder, "The older and more primitive languages are, the more feelings cross each other in the roots of words." Feelings preceded reflective thought in the evolution of language since "the more primitive a language, the fewer the abstractions and the more the feelings"; and oriental languages, including Hebrew, reveal more feelings than Northern languages.

Finally, feelings and expressiveness are inversely proportional to the development of grammar: "the more primitive a language, therefore, the less grammar it has."[18]

Vitality, mobility, expressiveness of feeling, and lack of grammar—the same characteristics were ascribed to Yiddish by the German Jewish authors quoted above. Obviously they derived these characteristics not from an analysis of the inherent qualities of the Yiddish language, about which German-speaking Jews knew very little, but from the classical German culture adopted by German Jews, which, in this case, can be traced back to Herder's interpretation of the Hebrew language.

In his much-quoted "Rede uber die jiddische Sprache," Franz Kafka initiated a new approach to Yiddish which was based on a creative reinterpretation of widespread myths:

> *Jargon* is the youngest European language, only four hundred years old, and actually even younger than that. It has not yet developed linguistic forms of the clarity that we need. Its expression is short and quick. It has no grammar books .... Devotees try to write grammars, but *Jargon* is continuously spoken; it does not come to rest. The *Volk* does not leave it to the grammarians. It consists entirely of foreign words. Yet these words do not rest, they retain the haste and liveliness with which they were adopted. Great migrations run through *Jargon* from one end to the other.[19]

---

17 Johann Gottfried Herder, "Vom Geist der ebräisehen Poesie," *Sämmtliche Werke*, ed., Bernhard Suphan (repro Hildesheim: Olms, 1967), vol. 11, 227.

18 "Je älter und ursprünglicher die Sprachen sind, desto mehr durchkreuzen sieh auch die Gefühle in den Wurzeln der Wörter; "Je ursprünglicher die Sprache, desto weniger Abstraktionen, desto mehr Gefühl"; "so muß je ursprünglicher die Sprache, desto weniger Grammatik in ihr sein," Johann Gottfried Herder, *Ahhandlung über den Ursprung der Sprache*, idem, *Werke* (Darmstadt, 1917), vol. II, 304, 309, 313.

19 "Der Jargon ist die jüngste europäische Sprache, erst vierhundert Jahre alt, und eigentlich noch viel jünger. Er hat noch keine Sprachformen von solcher Deutlichkeit

Kafka makes a number of assumptions which he presents as historical truths. From a linguistic and historical point of view, however, almost all of them are erroneous, even considering the state of research at his time. By 1912, a number of scientific works on Yiddish were available, written by linguists and language sociologists.[20] Kafka's text reiterates some of the opinions about Yiddish which originated with Herder and were passed on by Buber, but with significant innovations.

The alleged youth of the language and the fact that it still seemed malleable put Yiddish at the opposite pole to the *Kanzleisprache* Kafka had to use in his work as an insurance official. The legend that Yiddish was created hastily, haphazardly, following the peregrinations and successive expulsions of the Jewish people, runs like a continuous thread through the commentaries of a number of other German and Austrian Jewish intellectuals. Thus, the Viennese journalist Alfred Polgar defined Yiddish as "a language which has not finished fermenting, taken in haste (like unleavened bread) on the flight through countries

---

ausgebildet, wie wir sie brachen. Sein Ausdruck ist kurz und rasch. Er hat keine Grammatiken .... Liebhaber versuchen Grammatiken zu schreiben, aber der Jargon wird immerfort gesprochen; er kommt nicht zur Ruhe. Das Volk läßt ihn den Grammatikern nicht. Er besteht nur aus Fremdwörtern. Diese ruehn aber nicht in ihm, sondern behalten die Eile und Lebhaftigkeit, mit der sie genommen wurden. Völkerwanderungen durchlaufen den Jargon von einem Ende bis zum anderen." Franz Kafka, "Rede über die jiddische Sprache," idem, *Hochzeitsvorbereitungen auf dem Lande und andere Prosa aus dem Nachlaß*, ed., Max Brod (Frankfurt a.M.: Suhrkamp, 1983), 306.

[20] See Max Weinreich, *History of the Yiddish Language*, trans. Shlomo Noble (Chicago: University of Chicago Press, 1980). Kafka ignored the writings of many "Western" linguists whose works on Yiddish would have been accessible to him. See, for example, Lazare Sainean, "Essai sur le Judéo-allemand et spécialement sur le Dialecte Parle en Valachie," *Mémoires dela de la Société Linguistique Paris* 12 (1901/1902), 90–138 and 176–196; Jakob Gerzon, *Die jüdisch-deutsche Sprache. Eine grammatische-lexikalische Untersuchung ihres deutschen Grundbestandes* (Frankfurt a.M.: Kauffmann, 1902), or the writings of Alfred Landau and Bernhard Wachstein, Mathias Mieses, Heinrich Loewe, and others. Later studies which appeared within the period under discussion include Solomon Birnbaum, *Praktische Grammatik der jiddischen Sprache* (Vienna-Leipzig: Hartleben, 1918); Mathias Mieses, *Die jiddische Sprache. Eine historische Grammatik des Idioms der integralen Juden Ost-Mitteleuropas* (Vienna: Hartleben, 1924). In the article "Di oyfgabes fun der yidisher filologye," in *Der Pinkes*, ed., Samuel Niger (Vilna: Kletzkin, 1913), Ber Borochov lists 500 works on Yiddish philology published between 1500 and 1912, the earliest being Johannes Boeschenstein's *Elementale introductorium in hebraeas literas teutonice et hebraice legendas* (Augsburg: 1514).

and through epochs. Traces of wanderings through many homelands adhere to it."[21]

It is interesting that both Kafka and Polgar associated the Yiddish language with the quintessential attribute of the Jewish people—exile. Polgar goes even further since his mentioning of unleavened bread recalls the Exodus out of Egypt, the founding event of Jewish history. This idea is expressed again in an anonymous article in the *Neue Freie Presse* of Vienna:

> Yiddish is a nervously flexible idiom with an extraordinary number of gutturals. At home anywhere in the world, spoken by millions but still homeless, it is strangely imbued with foreign elements. Traces of the road of suffering, which has led endless processions of Jews from East to West and from here over the sea, are easily discernible. It was probably invented by refugees, by people who could not linger in the same place for long, and who, forced to make themselves understood, took a little bit of each language with them on their restless wanderings. In Yiddish, therefore, there is animated haste, hurried whispering, fear. And this is its strongest dramatic strength. It lacks the soft, luxuriant melodiousness of the vowel, which resonates in sensual beauty. It is the language of light and was born in the shadow of life.[22]

Linguistic, historical, religious, and anthropomorphic planes are superimposed in this anonymous author's description of Yiddish, and

---

21 "... eine nicht ausgegorene Sprache, in Hast mitgenommen (wie das ungesäuerte Brot) auf der Flucht durch die Länder, durch die Zeiten. Spuren vieler Wanderschaft durch viele Heimaten kleben an ihr." Alfred Polgar, "Eine Woche Berlin," *Ja und Nein. Darstellungen von Darstellungen*, ed., Wolfgang Drews (Hamburg: Rowohlt, 1956), 223.

22 "Jiddisch [ist] ein nervös bewegliches Idiom außerordenlich viel Kehllauten. Überall in der Welt zu Hause, von Millionen gesprochen und dennoch heimatlos, ist sie seltsam durchwachsen von fremden Elementen. Man findet in ihr leicht die Spuren des Leidensweges, der endlich lange Züge von Juden aus dem Ost nach Westen und von hier übers Meer geführt hat. Sie wurde wahrscheinlich überhaupt von Flüchtlingen erfunden, von Leuten, die nicht lange auf einem Platz verweilen konnten und im Zwange, sich verständigen zu müssen, von überallher ein Stück Sprache mit sich nahmen auf ihre unrastvolle Wanderung. Darum ist im Jiddischen lebhafte Hast, eiliges Flüstern, Angst. Und das ist ihre stärkste dramatische Kraft. Der weiche üppige Wohllaut des Vokals, der in sinnlicher Schönheit ausschwingt, ist ihr versagt. Sie ist die Sprache der Flucht und wurde im Schatten des Lebens geboren." Anon., "Jiddisch. Die Sprache der Flucht," *Israelitsches Familienblatt* (14 July 1921).

his language reflects characteristics typically attributed to Jews—haste, flight, and fear. The subtext here oscillates between reference to the Exodus, constitutive of Jewish identity, and the image of the wandering Jew—in reality a Christian, not a Jewish, myth. This example clearly shows how Jews educated in German culture could be led to look at Yiddish from the point of view of Christian myths, including myths which figure prominently in antisemitic folklore.

The growing interest for Yiddish literature among German Jews was soon met by a plethora of translations, or rather adaptations. The first translations appeared as early as 1897 in the Zionist organ *Die Welt,* as well as in the journal *Die Jüdische Moderne.* From 1901 on, they were mainly published in *Ost und West* and the *Jüdische Rundschau.* The most frequently translated authors were Isaac Leybush Peretz, Sholem Aleichem (1859–1916), and Shalom Asch (1880–1957), followed by Mendele Moykher Seforim (Sholem Jacob Abramovitsh, 1836–1917), Hersh David Nomberg, Abraham Reyzen, David Pinski (1872–1959), Simon Samuel Frug, and Morris Rosenfeld. Interestingly, modernist authors from Warsaw, Łódź, or New York who made their debut before the First World War and became famous in the twenties, and even writers who emigrated from the Soviet Union to Berlin in the 1920s, such as David Bergelson, Der Nister (Pinkhas Kaganovitsh), Peretz Markish, and Moyshe Kulbak, were almost totally ignored.

When comparing the translations with the original Yiddish texts, the recurrence of certain problems is striking. One of the first Yiddish stories translated into German was Peretz's "Bontshe shvayg" (Bontshe the Silent). In this story, which has a fundamental importance for Yiddish and Jewish literature, Peretz portrays the Jewish anti-hero Bontshe, whose life amounts to an accumulation of misfortunes and ordeals, which he endures in total silence. Persecuted as an orphan by his stepmother, betrayed by his wife, and exploited by an employer who eventually runs him over and kills him, the dead Bontshe appears before the Heavenly Court and is invited to express a wish. In the Yiddish original, the story ends as follows: "'Well then'—Bontshe smiles—'I would like to have a hot roll with fresh butter every morning.' The judges and the angels bend their heads in shame, the prosecutor bursts out laughing."[23] With this story, Peretz intended to shake the traditional image of the God-fearing, passive, even submissive Jew, and pushed his contemporaries towards action, even political activism.[24] But the mediators who translated the story for the German Jewish audience imparted a totally different meaning to the text. In the first anonymous translation of 1897, as well as in a later translation by Theodor Zlocisti (1874–1943),[25] the last sentence is simply left out. This changes the thrust of the entire text: Bontshe has the last word and remains an unquestioned model of Jewish humility and martyrdom. Peretz's character is a simpleton; in the German translations he becomes a saint.

Another popular translator of the time, Alexander Eliasberg (1878–1924), was an Eastern European Jew born in Minsk, who came to Munich as a student and settled there. An untiring translator of Russian literature, he flooded the market with his biased renditions of Yiddish literature, of which his widely acclaimed translation of Sholem Aleichem's *Tevye der milkhiker* (Tevye the Milkman) is an example.[26]

---

23   "Nu, oyb azoy—shmeykhelt Botntshe—vil ikh take ale tog in der fri a heyse bulk emit frisher puter!" Yitskhok Leybush Perets, "Bontshe shvayg," idem, *Ale verk*, vol. 4, *Dersteylungen* (New York: Verlag Yiddish, 1920), 17. For an English translation, see *A Treasury of Yiddish Stories*, ed., Irving Howe and Eliezer Greenberg (New York: Viking Press, 1973). The translation here is by the present author.

24   The story, which appeared in *Literatur un lebn* in 1894, belongs to Peretz's early stories of social protest. See Ayzik Rozentsvayg, *Der radikaler period fun Peretses shafn (di' Yontev bletlekh')* (Kharkoy: Melukhe-Farlag far di Natsyonale Minderhaytn in USRR, 1934. For a reading of the story as expressive of "tensions between the radical and the conservative impulses," see Ruth R. Wisse, *I.L. Peretz and the Making of Modern Jewish Culture* (Seattle: University of Washington, Press 1991), 47. On the impact of Peretz's writing on workers' circles, see Samuel Niger, *Yitskhok Leybush Perets. Zayn lebn, zanh firndike perzenlekhkayt, zayne hebreishe un yiddishe shrftn, zany virkung* (Buenos Aires: Argentiner Opteil fun Alweltlechn Jidišn Kultur-Kongres, 1952), 232 -246.

25   The first anonymous translation appeared under the title "Bonze hat geschwiegcn," *Die jüdische Moderne* 2 (April 15, 1897). I wish to thank Itta Shedletzki for drawing my attention to this journal. Theodor Zlocisti's translation was published under the same title in *Ost und West* (January 1909), 35–39. There are only slight differences between these versions, which may allow us to consider Zlocisti as the translator of the first.

26   Scholem Alechem, *Die Geschichten Tewjes des Milchhändlers*, trans. Alexander Eliasberg (Berlin: Harz, 1922). The same translation was republished many times after the war in Germany. The quotations below are from the most recent edition, *Tewje der Milchman* (Leipzig: Reclam, 1995), 20, 39. On the problematic continuity which arises from republishing the same, faulty translations of Yiddish literature in Germany, see my review in *Etudes Germanique* 51/2 (April/June 1996), 418–419.

Sholem Aleichem's trilingual humour is certainly extremely complex to translate. But every page of Eliasberg's translation is marred by omissions and mistranslations, to say nothing of faults in the rhythm, register, and style. When Tevye quotes a biblical verse, he often distorts it and changes its meaning completely. Eliasberg, however, renders the original quotation without seeming to notice how Tevye transforms it. When Tevye says, for example, "Kol dikhfin yetei veyitzrakh" (Whoever is hungry, let him come and be needy), he misquotes and subverts the sentence from the Pesach *Haggadah:* "Whoever is hungry, let him come and eat, whoever is needy, let him come and celebrate Pesach." Eliasberg translates: "Wer da hungert, komme und esse," ignoring the social criticism underlying Sholem Aleichem's humour.[27] As for the Russian and Ukrainian proverbs which he often appends in a preposterous way to biblical verses coupled with incorrect Yiddish translations, Eliasberg frequently does away with them completely. Thus, Sholem Aleichem's sophisticated trilingual humour, with its self-criticism and subversion, is swamped by sentimental naivety and religious nostalgia.

Translations from Yiddish, in particular those by Eliasberg, were virulently criticised by the few contemporary specialists who had a real understanding of the original texts, such as Scholem and Kaufmann. Scholem, for instance, reproached Eliasberg for creating an "atmosphere of sentimentalism," which was absent from the original, and for "making concessions to the modern mind." Apart from his many errors, Scholem castigated Eliasberg for producing "adaptations" rather than translations, and for variously erasing details he deemed too Jewish or adding things according to whim. Above all, he criticised the "total lack of connection between the translator and his text."[28] In a review of Eliasberg's translation of Peretz's *Khsidish* (Hasidic Stories, 1904), another critic, A. Robinsohn, blamed Eliasberg for creating a "pretentious and bombastic style, while the original is deliberately kept

---

[27] Another example is Tevye's expression "be-Rahel bitkha ha·nakete" (about Rachel your daughter, the naked one), in which he misquotes Jacob's words to Laban, "be-Rahel bitkha ha-ketana" (about Rachel your younger daughter). Eliasberg translates "es geht um Rahel, deine jüngere Tochter", thus eliding the saucy humour of the author.

[28] Scholem, "Zum Problem der Übersetzung aus dem Jiddischen," 16–17; Kaufmann, "Über Mendele."

simple," and for "translating Yiddish into *Jargon*."[29] This criticism is, of course, ironic since the word *Jargon*, so often used by the belittlers of the Yiddish language, is here turned against those who mistranslate it and distort its original meaning. Translation is never neutral or simple. Whether of Eastern European or of German descent, cultural mediators had to respond to specific pressures. They had to "sell," and thus had to produce a text which would match the prejudices and tastes of their intended audience. Moreover, they may have wanted to impart a certain meaning to the text according to their own personal or political priorities.

The debate was carried on in the interpretations which accompanied Yiddish literature in German translation. One of the very first translators and mediators of Yiddish literature was the above-mentioned Zlocisti, a convinced German Zionist who wrote a biography of Moses Hess (1905) and edited his works. In his preface to *Aus einer stillen Welt* (1910), the first anthology of modern Yiddish literature in German translation (published by Leo Winz's Verlag Ost und West; Zlocisti was also a regular contributor to the journal *Ost und West*), Zlocisti adhered to Herder's idea of language as "kristallisierte Volksseele." Consequently, he regarded Yiddish literature and, in particular, the work of the classic writer Sholem Jacob Abramovitsh, who wrote under the pseudonym of Mendele Moykher Seforim, as an expression of the world of the ghetto, a world that, from a Zionist perspective, was doomed to disappear:

> This ghetto world has been destroyed. It has lost its unity. But the works of Mendele are a reflection of its entirety .... [They] rescue what time has destroyed .... [He gave us] ethnology in Bastian's sense, i.e., that the customs, traditions, life and language of a people reveal its soul.[30]

---

[29] A. Robinsohn, "I.L. Perez, Chassidische Geschichtcn," *Jüdische Rundschau* (September 7, 1917), 2–3.

[30] "Diese Ghettowelt ist zerbrochen. Sie hat ihre Einheit verloren. Aber das Spiegelbild ihrer Ganzheit sind die Werke Mendeles .... [Seine Werke] retten, was die Zeit zerstören konnte .... [Er gab uns] Ethnologie im Sinne Bastians, also daß Sitte, Brauch, Leben und Sprache eines Volkes die Volkssele enthüllen." Theodor Zlocisti, "Einleitung," *Aus einer stillen Welt. Erzählungen aus der modernen jüdischen Literatur*, trans. by Theodor Zlocisti (Berlin: Winz & Co., 1910), vol. 1, xxvii.

Bearing in mind that Abramovitsh was an adherent of the *Haskalah* and a fierce critic of the backwardness and passivity of the *shletl* world, it is surprising that Zlocisti manages to regard his work as an ethnographic museum dedicated to a world supposedly perceived by the author as a harmonious whole. Abramovitsh was only too aware of the social conflicts in the *shtetl* and revealed them satirically in works such as *Dos kleyne mentshele* (The Homonculus, 1864) and *Di takse* (The Meat Tax, 1869). Seeking to fight poverty and ignorance, he even evolved from a standard *Haskalah* outlook, advocating education, to a more political one, addressing the question of empowerment. Zlocisti did, in fact, notice that the heroes of Abramovitsh's works, often powerless and destitute beggars, seem tormented by hunger, poverty, and antisemitism. But he explained their predicament away, so that his image of the *shtetl* remained unaffected: "The Ghetto Jew feels nothing of this bitterness. Abramovitsh's characters moan and complain by inclination and profession. But they are very satisfied with 'God's little world.'"[31] Zlocisti here reiterates another stereotype of Eastern European Jews, who were perceived to be constantly sighing and whining while at the same time remaining joyful even in the darkest misery. Zlocisti summarises this under the motto "Brethren, let's be merry," which clearly indicates the connection he establishes between faith, brotherhood, and happiness. The "whining" and the "joking" *Ostjude* merge, and their fundamental satisfaction with this world comes from the one thing the German Jew feels deprived of—a sense of community.

Every interpretation of literature is inevitably coloured by the experience and commitments of the critic. While Zlocisti's views reflected the attitudes of German Zionists, other critics had different backgrounds and agendas. Israel (Isidor) Eliashev (1873–1924), for example, a Lithuanian-born Jew, moved to Berlin in 1901 to complete his studies. He belonged to a circle of young Jewish intellectuals who wanted to develop a modern Yiddish literature and criticism and became famous in Yiddish letters under the pseudonym Bal Makhshoves (the master of thoughts). Eliashev strove to introduce German Jews

---

31 "Diese Bitterkeit fühlt der Ghettojude nicht. Abramowitsch's Gestalten stöhnen und klagen aus Neigung und Beruf. Und sind mit 'Gottes Welten' sehr zufrieden." Ibid., xxvi.

to contemporary Yiddish literature and contributed to a number of German Jewish journals, including *Ost und West*. In contrast to Zlocisti, Eliashev saw Abramovitsh as expressing "the disdain for the patriarchal popular Jewish masses" and "the disgust for the half-dead past, which is a burden for the Jewish popular masses." Unlike Zlocisti, who "idealises" Abramovitsh's heroes as joking whiners, Eliashev unmasks them as "half-corpses ... who are in a state close to death." He was also writing from a different historical perspective. While for Zlocisti, the Jewish world of the 1860s to 1880s described by Abramovitsh seemed still viable, Eliashev compared the writer to the "keeper of a cemetery who cannot leave the place of burial."[32] At Abramovitsh's time, Eastern European Jewish society was not yet in a state of decay, threatened by assimilation and modernity—the premises under which Zlocisti wrote in Germany at the beginning of the twentieth century. For Eliashev, the atmosphere of morbidity came from the economic and political backwardness in which the Jews were kept by the anti-Jewish policy of the Tsarist regime. Zlocisti retrospectively idealised the *shtetl* from the outside, from a distance in time and space, while Eliashev described its crisis from within.

If therefore certain Yiddish writers, such as Abramovitsh and Sholem Aleichem, were misunderstood while others were praised, this was because the outlook of the latter corresponded to the aspirations of German Jewish intellectuals. Asch's novel *A shtetl* (1905) is a case in point. It conjures up a neo-Romantic, sentimental, and idealised vision of Eastern European Jewry. This trend appeared in Yiddish literature in the first decade of this century as Yiddish writers realised that the world which *maskilim* such as Abramovitsh had fought against was about to vanish. Zlocisti therefore prized Asch's novel highly:

> Asch ... gives us happy expectations, the reassurance of a pleasant future ... In overcoming the ghetto, he directed Jewish literature back into the

---

[32] "Die Verachtung für die altväterliche Volksmasse"; "der Ekel vor der halbtoten Vergangenheit, mit der sich die jüdische Volksmasse herumschleppt"; "Halbleichen ... die sich in einem todähnlichen Zustande befinden"; "[ein] Friedhofswachter, der die Begräbnisstalte nicht verlassen darf." All quotations from Dr. [Isidor] Eliaschoff, "S. L. Abramowitz," *Ost und West* (October 1907), 637–638.

flow of European art. He transcended the ghetto by discovering its eternal
beauty, its inner freedom, its chaste love of nature. He transcended it,
but has not destroyed it. Rather, he has rescued it for a renaissance of
Jewish art and perhaps of the Jewish soul.[33]

Zlocisti was fascinated with this novel because it transcends the
problems and the realities of the actual ghetto (significantly, he uses the
word "ghetto" while Asch used *shtetl*). But it also transforms the *shtetl*
world into something it never was for those who lived and toiled in
it; beauty, freedom, and nature were precisely the elements they most
lacked.[34] Zlocisti was not interested in realism but in a "renaissance of
Jewish of art," which he wanted to rejoin the current of European art
and to concur with its aesthetic and social imperatives. This renaissance
could therefore only be built on the ruins of the *shtetl*, or rather on its
idealised image. Thus the *shtetl*, embalmed and aestheticised, became
hypostatised as a Jewish national symbol.

Zlocisti's theories echoed Buber's programmatic article "Jewish
Renaissance," published in the first issue of *Ost und West* in 1901,
where he appealed for the emergence of a new Jewish art, after its
"redemption from ghetto and Golus." For Buber, the Jewish renaissance
would reestablish the Jews' feeling for life: "It will shake the dust and
cobwebs of the inner ghetto from the soul of our people and provide
the Jews with an awareness of nature." The combination of an emergent
national identity and reconciliation with nature would, Buber held,
develop a new Jewish aesthetics: "The national movement is the form
in which a new aesthetic culture is dawning for our people."[35]

---

[33] "Asch … gibt und sie frohe Erwartung, gibt die Gewissheit einer schönen Zukunft
…. Ein Ghettoüberwinder, hat er die jüdische Literatuar wieder in das Strombett
europäischer Kunst geleitet. Er hat das Ghetto überwunden, in dem er seine
unvergängliche Schönheit, seine innere Freiheit, seine keusche Naturliebe entdeckt
hat. Er hat es übenwunden, aber nicht vernichtet. Sondern für die Neugeburt der
jüdischen Kunst und vielleicht der jüdischen Seele gerettet." Zlocisti, "Einleitung," ixiv.

[34] See, for example, Sholem Aleichem, "Di shtot fun di kleyne mentshelekh," the first text
in the cycle *Kasrilevke*.

[35] "Sie wird Staub und Spinnweb des inneren Ghetto von unserer Volksseele abkehren
und dem Juden den Blick in der Natur verleihen"; "Die nationale Bewegung ist die
Form, in der sich die neue Schönheitskultur ankündigt." Martin Buber, "Jüdische
Renaissance," *Ost und* West (January 1901), 7–10.

The Eastern European writer and journalist Shemarya Gorelik (1877–1942) also contributed to this debate. Born in Ukraine, he founded the first modern Yiddish literary journal, *Literarishe monatsshriftn*, in Vilna in 1908, together with the Yiddish writers and critics Samuel Niger and A. Vayter. A pacifist, he lived in Switzerland during the First World War and eventually moved to Berlin. Here, he became one of the major mediators between Yiddish and German Jewish culture, publishing works on European literature in Yiddish and works on Yiddish literature in German. For Gorelik, the fascination of Asch's *A shtetl* for Western European readers is in the novel's projection of "a world of perfect harmony [which] reveals itself before the eyes of the jaded European":

> Instead of the barbaric alienation of human beings—a patriarchal community; instead of forced individualism ... warm, brotherly social relations; no trace of inner turmoil, of the European reflexes, of the doubts and hellish distress which set the soul of the modern European intellectual on fire and make it scream heavenwards.[36]

Gorelik held that Asch's novel fascinated the European intellectual because "this is what he longs for, what his soul thirsts for, here he finds his way back to his mother's bosom." Following the trauma of the war, more and more people wanted to "find a refuge in far-away and unexplored countries." In short, echoing Zlocisti, Gorelik concluded that "art has wrested the *shtetl* from the past."[37]

It is a striking irony that German Jews sought and found a past of mythical harmony in the ultrarealistic and satirical works produced by Yiddish literature during the nineteenth century. It is not surprising that they had little interest in the revolutionary and avant-garde

---

[36] "Statt der barbarischen Entfremdung der Menschen—patriarchalische Gemeinschaft; statt des erzwungenen Individualismus ... —ein warmes brüderlich-soziales Verhältnis; keine Spur von innerer Zerrissenheit, von europäischen Reflexen, von Zweifel und höllischen Bedrängnissen, von denen die Seele des modernen europäischen Intellektuellen in Brand gerät und gen Himmd schreit." Sch[emarya] Gorelik, "Schalom Asch 'Das Städtchen,'" *Jüdische Köpfe* (Berlin: F. Gurlitt, 1920, 84 and 90. The same article first appeared in Yiddish in *Literarische monatsschrift* 2 (March 1908), 114–126.

[37] Ibid.

works of contemporary Yiddish literature: German Jews recoiled at the depiction of poverty and social struggle in Eastern Europe, and at modernist trends from the East. They wanted neither the present nor the future. What attracted them to the East was a transfigured version of the past.

Beside Asch, Peretz was the second writer who fulfilled the expectations of the young generation of German Jewish intellectuals. In the course of his long literary career, Peretz participated in a variety of different movements, including Realism, Socialism, Populism, and Expressionism, but German Jews were attracted above all to his Symbolist works. Ludwig Geiger (1848–1920), the editor of the *Allgemeine Zeitung des Judentums*, a defender of assimilationism and unsympathetic to Yiddish literature, nevertheless hailed Peretz as a writer who "leaves out what is too blatantly horrible and pitiful and attempts at least occasionally to fill our soul with lovely pictures," quite unlike the early, "Realist" Asch, who "intentionally uncovers defects and ... feels justice demands that the depiction of things should be as stark and disgusting as they are in reality."[38]

The reception and translation of Peretz's work can be exemplified paradigmatically through the reception of the central scene from his drama *Di goldene keyt* (The Golden Chain, 1907–1914). At the end of the first act, Rabbi Shloyme, the head of a Hasidic dynasty, refuses to conclude the Sabbath by performing the traditional ceremony of *Havdalah*. The Sabbath, the day of rest and prefiguration of the world to come, thus stretches over the beginning of the new week, while the return to daily activity is postponed indefinitely. As Gorelik noted, Shloyme wanted to realise the ideal of the "eternal Sabbath and the perfect man and Jew."[39] The identification of Eastern European Jews,

---

[38] "Unsere Sympathie neigt sich im höherem Grade Perez zu,] der ... der ... doch das allzu Grausige und Bejammernswerte beiseite läßt und wenigstens machmal bestrebt ist, unsere Seele mit lieblichen Bildern zu erfüllen ... [hat man bei Asch den Eindruck, daß er] mit einer gewissen Absichtlichkeit die Schäden aufdeckt und ... es als ein Gebot der Gerechtikeit empfindet, die Dinge so kraß und abscheulich zu schildern, wie sie sind." Ludwig Geiger, "Jüdische Denker und Dichter. Schalom Asch und J.L. Perez," *Allgemeine Zeitung des Judentums* (September 13, 1918). Geiger refers to the works by Asch which preceded his romantic novel *A shtetl*.

[39] Sch[emarya] Gorelik, "Jüdisches Theater. Die Nacht auf dem alten Markt. Granowski

as models of Jewish authenticity, with the Sabbath, the symbol of harmony and completeness, runs like a leitmotif through German Jewish literature. The way the Sabbath was variously interpreted by German Jews illustrates the way a concept can be the object of a cultural transfer from one text to another. The first examples of war literature overwhelmingly emphasised the experience of the Sabbath in Eastern Europe. Sammy Gronemann (1875–1952), who was sent as an army translator to the Bialystok region, contrasted the misery and poverty in the city during the week, which he described as "merely appearance and delusion," with a higher reality:

> ...The Jewish city and its inhabitants reveal themselves in their true distinctiveness only during the Sabbath, when all weekday activities have vanished without a trace. For on the Sabbath, only on the Sabbath, does the Jew actually live in accordance with his nature.

Gronemann establishes a distinction between the misery of everyday life and the spiritual elevation which is felt on the Sabbath, since "in those holy hours humans live only in the transcendental."[40] This quotation again indicates the longing for harmony, truth, and a higher level of reality which was common among so many Western Jews.

The distinction between Sabbath and weekday is represented in a diametrically opposed way in the review of Gronemann's book written by Max Naumann, editor of the extreme assimilationist journal *Der nationaldeutsche Jude*:

> Those who sympathise, with these Eastern Jews, who remain stuck in Jewish *Volkstum* and roam the world as eternal anachronisms, see only the Sabbath Jew, the festive man purified through the holiness of the

---

im Theater des Westens," *Jüdische Rundschau* (October 12, 1928).

40 "... Die Judenstadt und ihre Bewohner aber offenbaren in ihrer ganzen Eigenart nur am Sabbat, in der Zeit, da alles Werktagtreiben spurlos verschwunden ... Denn am Sabbat, nur am Sabbat lebt der Jude recht eigentlich so, wie es in seinem Wesen entspricht." Sammy Gronemann, *Hawdalaha und Zapfenstreich. Erinnerungen an ostjüdische Etappe, 1916–1918* (repr. Königstein im Taunus: Jüdischer Verl. Athenäum, 1984), 84–85.

Seventh Day, elevated above the earthly dirt. For such an observer, the six days of "*Kötern*" are only a secondary phenomenon. But we ... fight against the moral and spiritual *Asiatentum* which [the Eastern Jew] brings into our European world, which is alien to him, during the six weekdays.[41]

The word *kötern*, meaning to scavenge, as dogs do, is a direct reference to one of Heinrich Heine's most famous Jewish poems, "Prinzessin Sabbath," which is contained in the cycle *Romanzero* (1851).[42] However, while Naumann appears to be quoting Heine, he in fact inverts his meaning. Heine compares the people of Israel to a prince who has been changed into a dog by a witch's curse. Only on the Sabbath is he able to regain his human form. Naumann, on the other hand, presents the essential Eastern European Jew not as a prince, but as a dog, an "ordinary person with whom we must come into frequently very embarrassing contact during the remaining six days of the week." He concludes: "The sympathy for the Sabbath Jew should not prevent us from putting an end to the stream of everyday Jews from the East in the German interest."[43] Thus Naumann's article ends on a note of xenophobia.

This digression shows in how many different ways the Sabbath motif was used in the West. The same motif received yet another different interpretation in the East. The figure of Rabbi Shloyme from Peretz's

---

[41] "Wer gefühlsmäßig Sympathien mit diesen Ostjuden, die im jüdischen Volkstum Stecken geblieben sind und als ewige Anachronismen über die Erde wandeln, der sieht nur den Sabbatjuden, den durch die Heiligkeit des siebenten Tages geläuterten, aus dem Schmutz des Irdischen herausgehobenen Feiertagsmensehen. Die sechs Tage des 'Köterns' sind für diesen Betrachter nur unwichtige Nebenerscheinung. Wir aber ... wehren uns gegen das moralische und geistige Asiatentum, das [der Ostjude] während der sechs Tage seines Werktagslebens in unsere, die ihm wesensfremde europäische Welt hereinträgt." Max Naumann, "Bücherschau. Hawdoloh und Zapfenstreich von Sammy Gronemann," *Mitteilungen des Vereins Natianaldeutscher Juden* (November 1924), 9.

[42] "Hund mit hündischen Gedanken,/Kötert die ganze Woche/Durch des Lebens Kot une Kehricht,/Gassenbuben zum Gespötte./Aber jeden Freitag Abend,/In der Dämmrungstunde, plötzlich/Weicht der Zauber, und der Hund/Wird aufs Neu ein menschlich Wesen." Heinrich Heine, *Sämtliche Werke* (Leipzig: Hesse & Becker, 1910–1914), vol. II, 135.

[43] "... Alltagsmensch, mit dem wir die ubrigen sechs Tage der Woche in oft sehr pcinliche Berührung treten mussen ... daß uns keine Sympathie für den Sabbathjuden abhalten darf, dem Zustrom der ostjüdischen Alltagsjuden im deutschen Interesse eincn Riegel vorzuschieben." Max Naumann, "Bücherschau," 9.

drama *Di goldene keyt* had in the past been interpreted as an extreme, Promethean character, perhaps even tinged with Nietzscheanism, as a rebel whose Messianism was inspired not so much by Hasidism as by Expressionism. Young Yiddish writers, who regarded Peretz as their mentor and as the pioneer of modernism in Yiddish literature, reacted strongly against what they considered a gross misinterpretation of his work. The Soviet Yiddish writer David Bergelson (1884–1952), for example, who lived in Berlin in the 1920s, voiced his outrage at this interpretation. He spoke out in the actual forum of his opponents, the German Jewish Zionist periodical *Jüdische Rundschau*:

> Peretz's main topic was Earth, earthliness and earthly happiness, not Heaven, Heaven's light, and Paradise .... Generally speaking, all the people who consider Peretz to be the poet of Hasidic-heavenly cosiness are wrong .... While reproducing them, Peretz secularised the old Hasidic motifs in order to undermine them and to trigger revolt.[44]

Bergelson was interested in a totally different aspect of Peretz's work, namely, his defence of the oppressed, a motif that Peretz seductively clothed in the form of the Hasidic tale so he could reach his intended audience more easily. According to Bergelson, it was not possible to interpret Peretz's drama "as if Peretz did not know that the Seventh Day is the Sabbath only when preceded by six hard days of labour."[45] In contrast to German Jewish intellectuals, Bergelson claimed that Peretz's work was filled with "Empörerwucht." A year later, in 1926, he advocated that the group of exiled Yiddish writers in Berlin should return to the Soviet Union, the only country that, in his opinion, could guarantee the survival of Yiddish literature. Thus Bergelson's ideological commitments led him, in turn, to stress the social, even proletarian, side of Yiddish

---

[44] "... Erdhaftigkeit und irdisches Glück im Gegensatz zu Himmel, Himmelshelligkeit und Paradies - das war Perez' Hauptthema... Im allgemeinen befinden sich alle im Irrtum, welche Perez für den Dichter da chassidisch·himmlichcn Traulichkeit halten ... Perez hat vielmehr bei der Wiedergabe der alten chassidischen Bilder diese verweltlicht, um sic dadurch zu untergraben und Empörung hervorzurufen." David Bergelson, "J.L.Perez und die chassidische Ideologie. Anläßlich der zehnten Wiederkehr (sic) von Perez Todestag," in *Jüdische Rundschau* (April 8, 1925), 26. The article appeared simultaneously in Yiddish, "Y L. Perets un di khsidishe ideologye," *Literarische bleter* (April 1925), 3.

[45] Ibid., 267.

literature and culture and to tone down its religious aspects.

Facing one another across a cultural divide, German Jewish and Eastern Jewish intellectuals were at odds over the reading and interpretation of Yiddish texts. When translated into German, a new meaning was forced upon Yiddish literature. Indeed, it began a second career, a new life with a new agenda. As Michael Werner and Michel Espagne have argued in a noteworthy contribution to the study of cultural transfers, it is obvious that "the appropriation of a foreign cultural good is never only a cumulative process, but also a creative one" since "the selection and integration of foreign cultural goods is determined by parameters immanent to the 'host-culture.'"[46] Their original meaning notwithstanding, these texts were modified, reinterpreted, distorted, recast, and diverted to serve new purposes. A cultural gulf separated the Jewish West and the Jewish East, and despite the dialogue between German and Eastern European Jewish intellectuals, writers, and critics, they were able neither to bridge it nor to find a common tongue. In this sense, any attempt at interpretation must remain a creative betrayal, but a betrayal that is necessary as the founding stone of a new "invented tradition."[47]

---

[46]   Michael Espagne and Michael Werner, "Deutsch-französischer Kulturtransfer als Forschungsgegenstand. Eine Problemskizze," in *Transferts. Les relatians interculturelles dans l'espace france-allemande* (Paris: Editions Recherche sur les civilizations, 1988), 21–22.

[47]   The notion of creative betrayal has been used very convincingly by David Roskies, see, for example, *A Bridge of Longing: The Lost Art of Yiddish Storytelleing* (Cambridge, MA: Havard University Press, 1995). On the notion of "invented tradition," see Eric Hobsbawm and Terence Ranger, *The Invention of Tradition* (Cambridge: Cambridge University Press, 1983); Shulamit Volkov, "Die Erfindung einer Tradition. Zur Entstehung des modcrnen Judentums in Deutschland," *Historische Zeitschrift* 253 (December 1991), 603–628.

CHAPTER XII

A JEWISH *HEIMAT* ON BORROWED TIME

Nils Roemer

The Weimar Republic is rightly associated with the prestigious accomplishments of German Jews in the arts and sciences at a time when the size of the Berlin community dwarfed all other German Jewish congregations. Yet the fast-paced life of the metropolis, associated with rapid change and historical amnesia, also gave a new importance to the small-town communities that prided themselves on being the last vestiges of a world that had otherwise vanished.[1] The prolific novelist Georg Hermann's article "Grossstadt oder Kleinstadt" prompted a flood of responses concerning the differences between Berlin's Jews and those in the rural villages and small towns.[2] Jews of the larger urban centres appeared to be stuck in a self-selected isolation, in contrast to Jews of the small-town communities, who were represented as thoroughly enmeshed in the local and regional lives of Germans. Those metropolitan Jews, therefore, lived vicariously through the memories of the older rural communities.[3] Partly marred by antisemitic stereotypes, the debates nevertheless reflected the accelerated urbanisation and centralisation of an increasing number of Jews in Berlin, a trend that had separated many of them from their older communities and heritages.

---

[1] Peter Fritzsche, "Cities Forget, Nations Remember: Berlin and Germany and the Shock of Modernity," in *Pain and Prosperity: Reconsidering Twentieth-Century German History*, ed. Paul Betts and Greg Eghigian (Stanford: Stanford University Press, 2003), 35–60 and 227–32.

[2] Georg Hermann, "Grossstadt oder Kleinstadt," *CV-Zeitung*, no. 22 (June 3, 1927), 309–10; Ludwig Basnitzki, "Der Dorfjude," *CV-Zeitung*, no. 24 (June 17, 1927), 338; and "Grossstadt oder Kleinstadt," *CV-Zeitung*, no. 6 (July 1, 1927), 369–70 (July 22, 1927), 413–14, and (October 7, 1927), 566–67.

[3] "Großstadt ssoder Kleinstadt," *CV-Zeitung*, no. 6 (July 1, 1927), 369.

The dichotomy between rural, small-town communities and those in larger urban centres also turned on the question of Jewish identity. During the Weimar Republic, when the process of urbanisation had peaked, Leo Baeck considered it to be responsible for the shift from what he called *Milieufrömmigkeit* (piety of the milieu) to *Individualfrömmigheit* (piety of the individual). Within this binary opposition, Baeck viewed urbanisation as a rite of passage from a location in which Judaism had governed every aspect of life to a location dominated by non-Jewish customs.[4]

Urban German Jews became infatuated with rural communities at the same time as Jews in Germany were increasingly being viewed as foreign elements among the German people, so the commitment to one's local *Heimat* signified ownership and belonging. *Heimat* allowed German Jews to mediate among different Jewish identities and conceptualise the interactions between Jews and other Germans. Indeed, in the context of the Weimar Republic—and even after the erosion of democratic structures with the establishment of the Nazi state—Jews negotiated and debated their affiliation and cultural heritages within overlapping German, Jewish, local, urban, and metropolitan communities by seizing the language of local *Heimaten*. Precisely because these concepts were subject to interpretation and contestation, Jews promoted their local heritages to define their place in the national community of the Weimar Republic. For many Worms Jews, pride in the community's past and a profound German nationalism went hand in hand. Their "resistant nostalgia," to use Svetlana Boym's formulation, coincided with the community's efforts to honour its fallen soldiers of the First World War with monuments and memorials which Weimar-era tourist guides described.[5]

The complexities of German Jewish identity formation as they were repeatedly invoked in contemporary scholarly discussion remained unstable, contingent, and culturally constructed. Again during the Weimar Republic, the harnessing of a larger German Jewish tradition remained significantly tied to the history of individual communities.

---

4   Leo Baeck, "Gemeinde in der Grossßstadt," in *Wege im Judentums. Aufsätze und Reden*, ed., Werner Licharz (Gütersloh: Gütersloher Verlagshaus, 1997), 218–25.

5   Svetlana Boym, *The Future of Nostalgia* (New York: Basic Books, 2001), xiii.

Reviewing the current scholarship in 1929, the German Jewish historian Adolf Kober observed that no history of German Jewry in fact existed, although the history of individual communities had been "enthusiastically looked after."[6] This provincialised grounding of Jewish traditions made concepts of a German Jewish identity more tangible and local histories more relevant.

During the Weimar Republic era, Worms's plans to open a Jewish museum finally came to fruition under the guidance of Isidor Kiefer, a tin manufacturer and chairman of the Jewish community of Worms who had been born there in 1871. The museum was officially opened on the synagogue's 300th anniversary in November 1924 to link it with another famous restoration project: the rebuilding of the synagogue. The museum, which was promptly featured on illustrated postcards, displayed medieval privileges, bindings, prayer books, a *Memorbuch*, Juspa Shammes's collection of legends, circumcision chairs, and torah ornaments.[7] Photographs of the interior of the museum indicate that religious objects and historical documents were placed alongside each other to demonstrate their integration in the community's past. Kiefer attached explanatory plates to some of the items and guided tourists through the museum (fig. 25).[8]

The display of Jewish artefacts in Worms had an impact well beyond the perimeters of the city. Worms became one of the formidable icons by which the German Jewish past—and culture—came to be represented in the Weimar Republic. The Jews of Worms and the Rhineland also had a significant part in the 1925 Cologne installation entitled *Thousand-Year*

---

[6]   Adolf Kober, "Die Geschichte der deutschen Juden in der historischen Forschung der letzten 35 Jahre," *ZGJD* 1 (1929), 19.

[7]   Isidor Kiefer, "Das Museum der israelitischen Gemeinde Worms," *ZGJD* 5 (1934), 182–86; Samson Rothschild, "Das jüdische Museum in Worms," *Israelitisches Familienblatt* 25 (June 21, 1925), 172–73; and Rothschild, *Führer durch Worms und Umgebung (mit Plan) mit ausführlichen Beschreibungen des Lutherdenkmals, Domes, Paulusmuseums u.s.f. Mit 70 Abbildungen und Plan von Worms*, 6th ed. (Worms: Christian Herbst, 1925), 82–83. Kiefer himself gives November 12, 1924, as the opening date. See his "Das Museum der Israelitischen Gemeinde Worms am Rhein (1938)," Stadtarchiv Worms, Abt. 203/10b, p. 16.

[8]   Stadtarchiv Worms, F2776/71 and 73; Stadtarchiv Worms, CH 267–268; and Isidor Kiefer's letter to Friedrich Illert, January 13, 1949, Stadtarchiv Worms, Abt. 20, Nr. 71.

Exhibition of the Rhineland, part of a year of wide-ranging festivities to celebrate the region's German cultural heritage.[9] Introduced by Cologne's mayor, Konrad Adenauer, this public display of age-old German history fulfilled obvious political ends at a time when France still occupied parts of the Rhineland. The exhibition's section on the Jews presented their traditions as the foundation of contemporary German Jewish culture. The display of Constantine's privilege from 321 CE functioned as a "discrete propaganda tool," as the co-curator of the Jewish section, Elisabeth Moses, described it because it situated Jews in the Rhineland already in late antiquity.[10] Moreover, the presentation showcased documents, models of Jewish baths, images of synagogues, a map with Jewish settlements in the region prior to 1349, *Memorbücher*, letters of protection, medieval *mahzorim*, bibles and *mohel* books, replica tombstones, and a seder room.[11] It also exhibited copies of important documents from Worms, Herbst's photographs of the synagogue, and a model of Worms's *mikvah*.[12]

The major periodicals of this period, such as the *C.V.-Zeitung* and *Israelitische Familienblatt*, extensively reviewed the exhibition's section about the Jews' rich history in the Rhineland. For the CV, the exhibition succeeded in its mission by demonstrating that the "synthesis of *Deutschtum* and *Judentum*" was more than the mere construction of great and intemperate Jewish German scholars. The Rhineland, the papers opined, was the first place where Jews had settled on German soil; therefore, its culture remained as evidence of the German Jews' longstanding attachment to Germany.[13]

---

9   Rüdiger Haude, "'*Kaiseridee*' 'oder' "*Schicksalsgemeinschaft.*" 'Geschichtspolitik beim Projekt "Aachener Krönungsausstellung 1915"' und bei der Jahrtausendausstellung Aachen 1925 (Aachen: Aachener Geschichtsverein, 2000), 121–31.

10   Elisabeth Moses, "Jahrtausend-Ausstellung, Köln," *Soncino-Blätter* 1 (1925), 87. On the exhibition, see Katharina Rauschenberger, *Jüdische Tradition im Kaiserreich und in der Weimarer Republik. Zur Geschichte des jüdischen Museumswesens in Deutschland* (Hannover: Hahnsche Buchhandlung, 2002), 205–14.

11   Adolf Kober, "Von der Jahrtausendausstellung der Rheinlande im Köln," *C.V.-Zeitung* 4 (June 26, 1925), 448, and Kober, "Die jüdische Abteilung auf der Kölner Jahrtausendausstellung," *Israelitisches Familienblatt* (July 23, 1925), 194–96.

12   W. Ewald and B. Kuske, ed., *Führer durch die Jahrtausend-Ausstellung der Rheinlande in Köln 1925* (Cologne: M. Dumont Schauberg, 1925), 133–42.

13   Artur Schweriner, "Köln—ein Markstein in der Geschichte des C. V. Glänzender Verlauf der Kundgebung und Verbandstagung," *C.V.-Zeitung* 4 (July 3, 1925), 469.

Travelling to Cologne to visit the exhibition was one way Germans could express their solidarity with the occupied areas, and their trips helped to prop up the local economy as well. To this end, in the summer of 1925, German newspapers outside the Rhineland urged their readers to travel to Cologne. Likewise, *Die jüdische Frau* wrote: "German women, Jewish mothers and men, come to us to the Rhine."[14] Along with German Jewish associations of rabbis, cantors, and teachers, the West German branches of the Central Union of the German Citizens of the Jewish Faith responded to the exhibition by moving one of their meetings to Cologne.[15] "Who wants to miss this celebration?" the CV newspaper asked its readers.[16] The meeting commenced with a special concert in the Cologne opera house performed by the city orchestra and also included a talk from Kober, who with the assistance of Elisabeth Moses, had created the exhibition. Ludwig Holländer, chairman of the CV, greeted the 250 delegates with his hope that the convention in Cologne would express "the intimate attachment of German Jews with the German *Heimat*."[17] Under the title *The German Jew on Rhineland Soil*, his newspaper emphasised that Jews in the Rhineland had contributed to the creation of its particular regional culture and had therefore acquired a right "to this soil and to this people."[18] Similarly, the *Reichsbund jüdischer Frontsoldaten* (Reich Federation of Jewish Front Soldiers) held its general assembly in the Rhineland to underscore German Jewry's age-old association with that region. For Leo Löwenstein, the founder of the *Reichsbund* and a retired captain in 1919, the Rhineland was "the cradle of German Jewry."[19]

Worms certainly seized the opportunity offered by the Cologne exhibition. Its newspaper celebrated the recognition of the city's

---

14   Betty Stern, "Die jüdische Abteilung in der Jahrtausend-Feier zu Köln," *Die jüdische Frau* 1 (1925), 1–2.
15   "Der 8. Lehrerverbandstag in Köln," *C.V.-Zeitung* 4 (June 12, 1925), 416.
16   "Auf nach Köln," *C.V.-Zeitung* 4 (June 12, 1925), 414.
17   Ludwig Holländer, "Der westdeutschen Tagung zum Gruss!" *C.V.-Zeitung* 4 (June 26, 1925), 447.
18   Bernhard Falk, "Der deutsche Jude auf rheinischer Erde," *C.V.-Zeitung* 4 (June 26, 1925), 445.
19   Leo Löwenstein, "Die deutschen Juden und der deutsche Rhein," *Der Schild* 4 (September 3, 1925), 317.

past, including that of the Jewish community.[20] Within weeks of the special meetings of the CV and the *Reichsbund* in Cologne, Rothschild contributed to the series "Aus jüdischen Gassen" by writing about the Jewish sites of Worms.[21] Rothschild presented Worms as a popular destination for Jewish travellers, observing that the city had many more historical documents, artefacts, and monuments on view than nearby Speyer did.[22]

Heeding the calls to travel that deemed it a national duty, the *Reichsbund jüdischer Frontsoldaten* brought hundreds of delegates to Worms. To the members of the *Reichsbund*, after all, the synagogue there represented a memorial to the "right of the Jewish community to celebrate with the German people the thousand-year anniversary of the German Rhineland."[23] With Isidor Kiefer; Friedrich Illert, the director of the city library; and Erich Grill, the director of the city collection, the delegates toured Jewish attractions in Worms as well as the special exhibition in Cologne. In addition to the delegates, many individual visitors came to Worms, within a few weeks, 1,000 people had seen the special exhibition, as Rothschild proudly noted. In comparison, a local exhibition by Worms's Protestant community attracted only 500 visitors over the span of a few months.[24]

The close affinity between German and Jewish historical traditions that was evident from the Cologne exhibition influenced other Weimar-era artistic refutations of the Zionist interpretation of the Diaspora. One prominent example was the *Haggadah*, published in 1927, by Siegfried Guggenheim, a lawyer living in Offenbach on the Rhine.

---

[20] "Worms auf der Kölner Jahrtausendaustellung," *Wormser Zeitung* (June 30, 1925).

[21] Samson Rothschild, "Aus jüdischen Gassen," *Israelitisches Familienblatt* (March 19, 1925), 113–14; Rothschild, "Der jüdische Friedhof," *Israelitisches Familienblatt* (May 28, 1925), 164; and Rothschild, "Das jüdische Museum in Worms," *Israelitisches Familienblatt* (June 11, 1925), 172–73.

[22] Samson Rothschild, "Jüdische Altertümer in Worms und Speyer," *C.V.-Zeitung* 4 (June 26, 1925), 460.

[23] "Die Rheinlandtagung des Reichsbundes jüdischer Frontsoldaten," *Der Schild* 4 (September 11, 1925), 341.

[24] Samson Rothschild, "Ausstellung jüdischer Altertümer in der Wormser Stadtbibliothek anläßlich der Rheinlandtagung des Reichsbundes jüdischer Frontsoldaten," *Israelitisches Familienblatt* (September 24, 1925), 236.

According to Guggenheim, the traditional conclusion of the *Haggadah* prayer, *le-shanah ha-ba'ah bi-yerushalayim* (Next Year in Jerusalem), referred to Jews' hope for a time when all men walk in the light of God and when the *Wahn* (insanity) is ended and all weapons are destroyed. He noted, however, that a Moravian author of one 15th-century *Haggadah*, with which he was familiar, had added the words "or in Brünn" to the conclusion. He then added that his own family in Worms replaced the conclusion altogether with the sentence, "Next year in Worms-on-the-Rhine, our *Heimat*."[25]

Guggenheim's carefully crafted *Haggadah*, of which only 300 were printed, on handmade paper in a Bible-esque Gothic type, recorded his family's tradition of observance in order to authenticate his version: "The Seders, which I had experienced in my father's house under the eyes of my grandparents and parents, led me to hold on in my own family to the custom of the private (*häuslichen*) Seder celebrations."[26] The title page underscored the family's association with the city by featuring the Guggenheim coat of arms (*Hauswappen*). The Worms newspapers viewed Guggenheim's at once personal and political *Haggadah* as having "come forth" from the soil of Worms, announcing that it "breathe[d] the spirit of the Rhineland's depth of feeling and cheer."[27] The journal of the *B'nai B'rith* agreed that the work's characteristic cheerfulness constituted part of its particular religious virtue.[28] Its pronounced regional flair inspired the celebrated writer Stefan Zweig to conclude that this *Haggadah* merited a place "at any German exhibition on the art of the book"; Guggenheim had artfully implanted "Jewish tradition into German soil," he tellingly exclaimed.[29] For the *C.V.-Zeitung*, the *Haggadah* was further evidence of the proximity between German Jewish and German cultures. Herman Meyer, secretary of the Soncino

---

25 Siegfried Guggenheim, *Offenbacher Haggadah* (Offenbach am Main: Guggenheim, 1927), 77 and 79, and Brenner, *The Renaissance of Jewish Culture in Weimar Germany*, 171–72.

26 Guggenheim, *Offenbacher Haggadah*, 1.

27 "Die Haggadah eines Wormser," *Wormser Zeitung* (June 19, 1928).

28 *Der Orden Bne Briss. Mitteilungen der Grossloge für Deutschland. U. O. B. B.* (February 1928), 31.

29 Siegfried Guggenheim Collection, Leo Baeck Institute, New York, AR 180, D/C 8.

Society for the Friends of the Jewish Book, heralded it in his review as "the dawn of the revival of Jewish religiosity, which draws the elements of its piety—as does your book—from Jewish heritage and the reality of life in Germany."[30] Like no other *Haggadah*, the book brought out the close relationship between German Jews and German culture, noted the periodical.[31]

Guggenheim's *Haggadah*, like the Cologne exhibition, illustrates the complex interaction between German nationalism and various forms of Jewish self-understanding. The exhibition had a particularly lasting impact. For Adolf Kober, it helped further the study of Jewish local history in general and even spurred the creation of several local Jewish museums in later years.[32] Various communities in addition to Worms, including nearby Mainz, either created small exhibits of Jewish artefacts or displayed their collections within local German museums, localising their Jewish institutions of remembrance. But the question persisted: should this be a central Jewish museum, local Jewish museums, or dedicated sections in existing regional and national museums? Erich Toeplitz, the director of the Jewish museum in Frankfurt, proposed the creation of a new Jewish museum in the mid-1920s, inspired by Eugen Täubler's central archives. He was, however, keenly aware that Jewish communities would be reluctant to part with their treasured items. To counter this opposition, he picked up where Täubler had left off, arguing that limited resources, lack of knowledge, and vandalism in the local communities would endanger their historical treasures, which would be safer somewhere else.[33]

In the ensuing debate, Jakob Seifensieder, a teacher from Nuremberg, famously furthered the notion of German Jews' obligation to contribute to the Jewish collection in the national museum in Nuremberg. His article was immediately countered by voices from Breslau, Berlin, and Mainz, who favoured a more broadly

---

[30] "Die neue Offenbacher Haggadah," *C.V.-Zeitung* 6 (December 16, 1927), 702–3, and Siegfried Guggenheim Collection, Leo Baeck Institute, New York, AR 180, D/C 8.

[31] "Die neue Offenbacher Haggadah," *C.V.-Zeitung* 6 (December 16, 1927), 703.

[32] Adolf Kober, "Die Geschichte der deutschen Juden in der historischen Forschung der letzten 35 Jahre," *ZGJD* 1 (1929), 23.

[33] Erich Toeplitz, "Jüdische Museum," *Der Jude* 8 (1924), 339–46.

conceived Jewish museum that might encompass Jewish artefacts in their original locations.[34] Using the longstanding Jewish traditions of Frankfurt and Mainz as examples, these opponents argued that such a museum could only be created in these cities.[35] In his rejoinder, Seifensieder clarified his position and argued that the inclusion of a Jewish exhibition in the Nuremberg national museum need not be at the expense of other local museums. While he did oppose the creation of museums in small cities, he conceded that a central museum could be constructed in Berlin, Frankfurt, Mainz, or even Worms. That Seifensieder included Worms on this list reflects the high visibility of the community's past, a credit to its effort to preserve and display its heritage.[36]

The tension between the ideas of a centralised museum and local museums eventually also raised the question of original artefacts versus replicas as new capabilities in mass distribution led to the commodification of images, for one, that then circulated via newspapers, travel guides, and illustrated postcards. Worms, of course, rated very well in this new hierarchy of authenticity. The city centre had not been radically altered, so Worms appeared to travellers as still free of the forces of modernity; its long-time economic disadvantage now became a major asset, as its more modest modernization enabled visitors to "recapture the permanent spirit of the Rhineland."[37] The Jews of Worms publicised their historical sites as places that offered visitors a "shuddering and deep reverence as with the bliss of mental uplifting," as Isaak Holzer, the rabbi of the community, put it. This authentic cognitive and spiritual experience was facilitated by the presence of the physical remnants of the past where, he contended, the "stones talk."[38]

---

[34]   Jakob Seifensieder, "Wohin mit den deutsch-jüdischen Altertümern," *C.V.-Zeitung* 6 (June 24, 1927), 359.

[35]   "Wohin mit den jüdischen Altertümern?" *C.V.-Zeitung* 6 (September 9, 1927), 515.

[36]   Jakob Seifensieder, "Sammelt die jüdischen Altertümer!" *C.V.-Zeitung* 6 (September 16, 1927), 526.

[37]   Hilaire Belloc, *Many Cities* (London: Constable, 1928), 210.

[38]   Isaak Holzer, "Das jüdische Worms und seine Sehenswürdigkeiten," *Der Jugendbund* 18 (December 1932), 2–3. See also Rudy Koshar, *From Monuments to Traces: Artifacts of German Memory, 1870–1990* (Berkeley: University of California Press, 2000), 80–83.

The veneration for historical patina contributed greatly to Worms's popularity as tourism continued to grow. In the aftermath of World War I, the upper class gave up their extended visits to spa towns and joined the middle class on more limited ventures with overnight stays in economical accommodations, such as youth hostels. Package holidays were popular during this period, and were even a common feature of newly negotiated worker contracts. Reflecting the diversification of the travel industry, the traditional dominance of the Baedeker guides gave way to a plethora of new tour books targeted to specific audiences.[39] Alerted to the rich legacies of the various German cities, serialised articles in the *Israelitische Familienblatt* also invited Jews to places like Worms.[40] New brochures about Worms featured even more detailed descriptions of its Jewish sites, including new images of the *Judengasse*, the synagogue, and the cemetery, with its tombstones covered in supplications.

Along with its allure for individual travellers, the city also attracted organised Jewish tours. The synagogue's guest book of this period reveals that journalists, politicians, rabbis, and scholars like David Sasson and his family from Calcutta and London, the banker Otto Schiff and his brother Arthur, Jewish artists from the university in Moscow, and the scholar and Sephardic rabbi Moses Gastner all found their way to the synagogue. The precursor to Franz Rosenzweig's famous *Lehrhaus*, the Frankfurt *Gesellschaft für jüdische Volksbildung*, founded in 1919 by the liberal rabbi Georg Salzberger, enhanced its program of adult education with excursions to historical sites like Worms in 1922.[41]

As the city increasingly engrossed Jewish visitors from afar, Rothschild, Kiefer, and the community's rabbi, Isaak Holzer, tirelessly promoted Worms in the German Jewish periodicals. Their close

<hr/>

[39] Christine Keitz, *Reisen als Leitbild: Die Entstehung des modernen Massentourismus in Deutschland* (Munich: Deutscher Taschenbuchverlag, 1997), 30–53, and Rudy Koshar, *German Travel Cultures* (Oxford: Berg, 2000), 65–114.

[40] Samson Rothschild, "Aus jüdischen Gassen," *Israelitisches Familienblatt* (March 19, 1925), 113–14.

[41] Arnsberg, *Die jüdischen Gemeinden in Hessen*, 427–28; Georg Salzberger, "Zwischen zwei Weltkriegen. Die Gesellschaft für jüdische Volksbildung und das Jüdische Lehrhaus," in *George Salzberger, Leben und Lehre*, ed. Albert H. Friedländer (Frankfurt a.M.: Waldemar Kramer, 1982), 100–101.

cooperation with Illert suggests that city officials endorsed their work. Rising antisemitism, however, was already beginning to complicate things. In their propaganda, right-wing parties targeted and exploited the presence of Eastern European Jews in Worms, eventually compelling Karl Guggenheim, the chairman of the local branch of the CV, to attack antisemitism in his confessional speech in Worms on the fusion of Germaness and Jewishness.[42] When Holzer gave a dedicatory speech in 1932 at the monument to the city's fallen soldiers of World War I, he expressed the hope that the commemoration would enhance the spirit of solidarity and unity for the benefit of their *Heimat* and for the blessing of the fatherland and the German people. For Holzer, the monument was to be a testament to Germany's transcendence of its social and religious divisions.[43]

And certainly all was not yet lost. Confidence and dedication motivated Kiefer in 1932 to reorganise the museum's holdings in a year when he also enlarged the collection through the acquisition of a painting of the interior of the synagogue. The revamped museum's entrance hall showcased tombstones that had, over the centuries, been stolen from the cemetery and used for buildings around the city. Upon the museum's reopening, Worms's mayor joined the director of the museum and the city archivist to pay tribute there; the local newspaper likewise noted that the Jewish museum had contributed greatly to Worms's international reputation.[44]

Ironically, the intensification of antisemitism in German spa towns during the early 1930s probably further contributed to the popularity of small towns like Worms on the vacation itineraries of German Jews. During these years, the CV kept these travellers informed through

---

[42] Karl Guggenheim, "Deutschtum und Judentum. Vortrag gehalten in der Freimauerloge Worms am 25. Januar 1930," Karl Guggenheim Collection, Leo Baeck Institute, New York, AR 179.

[43] "Grundsteinlegung zum 118er Denkmal in Worms," *Wormser Zeitung* (May 9, 1932), and "Die Denkmalsweihe der 118er in Worms," *Wormser Zeitung. Morgenblatt* (August 22, 1932).

[44] "Das innere des neuen jüdischen Museums in Worms," *Wormser Zeitung* (October 22, 1932); "Wiedereröffnung des jüdischen Museums in Worms," *Wormser Zeitung* (October 26, 1932); and Isidor Kiefer, "Das Museum der israelitischen Gemeinde Worms," *ZGJD* 5 (1935), 182–86.

an increasingly elaborate system of information gathering and classification regarding specifically antisemitic spas and hotels. At the same time, German Jewish periodicals promoted German Jewish travel destinations, and from 1930 onward, the *Israelitische Familienblatt* published serialised articles on Jewish travel in Germany as well.[45]

Manfred Lehmann, who became a scholar on Worms's Jewish history after World War II, recalled that in 1931, his parents took him to the city, likely in response to such advertising. He wrote that his "late father wisely realised that such a visit would make a lasting impression on us." From the cemetery, the family went to the Rashi chapel, and Lehmann remembered "clearly the awe we felt when we visited the ancient synagogue of Worms, with 'Rashi's chair' where, according to tradition, Rashi had sat while he wrote his monumental commentaries on the Tanach and Talmud." Next to the synagogue, the Lehmanns "saw with our own eyes the vestige of a miracle that took place there," referring to the wall's indentation. Contrary to the caption on the illustrated postcards for sale at the site, but in line with many other visitors and commentators, Lehmann believed that it was Rashi's mother who had been miraculously saved there, not the mother of Yehuda he-Hasid.[46]

One of the most famous and frequent visitors to Worms during this period was Martin Buber. As he engaged in his musings on Christianity and Judaism in 1933, he related at the Stuttgart *Jüdisches Lehrhaus* that he occasionally visited Worms, whose old Jewish cemetery provided him with a telling perspective on the cathedral as well. For Buber, the cathedral consisted of individual elements crafted into a harmonious whole, while the Jewish cemetery contained only formless and directionless stones.[47] Buber contrasted the aesthetically appealing

---

[45] Frank Bajohr, *"Unser Hotel ist judenfrei": Bäder-Antisemitismus im 19. und 20. Jahrhundert* (Frankfurt a.M.: Fischer Verlag, 2003), 53–115, and Saul Lilienthal, *Jüdische Wanderungen in Frankfurt am Main, Hessen, Hessen-Nassau* (Frankfurt a.M.: J. Kauffmann, 1938), introduction.

[46] Manfred Lehmann, "Worms—One of Our 'Mother Cities,'" http://www.manfredlehmann.com/sieg278.html (accessed June 2004).

[47] Martin Buber, *Die Stunde und die Erkenntnis. Reden und Aufsätze* (Berlin: Schocken, 1936), 164.

order and grandeur of the church with the remnants of the Jewish past: "One only has the stones and the ashes beneath the stones. One has the ashes no matter how much they have disappeared .... I have them as a physical presence of my memory reaching far back in history, back to Sinai." The historical site thus functions for Buber as a pathway to the entirety of Jewish history. The cathedral does not. Seen from a distance, the silhouette of the cathedral converts historical differences into what Buber ultimately finds is a misleading sense of harmony, from his position in the cemetery: "I have stood there, connected with the ashes and, through them, the ancestors (*Urväter*). This is the memory of God's acts that is given to all Jews."[48] Whatever the splendour of the cathedral, it is the concreteness of the cemetery that is reassuring. Buber illustrated the point in his published dialogue with an often-reproduced view of the cathedral that could be found in tour guides and on illustrated postcards.[49]

Notwithstanding the ongoing popularity of Worms, the raging political clashes and increased anti-Jewish hostility in Germany by the Nazis and their accomplices affected local communities. Jews who might hitherto have had very little contact with the congregation now became forcibly part of it. The promulgation of the "Law Against Overcrowding in German Schools and Universities," passed on April 25, 1933, forced the children of the Russian-born Jew Illi Kagan, for example, to attend lessons at the school in a community building adjacent to the synagogue. For one of them, the young Vladimir, this coercion entailed an even bigger change, as he "until then had spent more time in Worms's famous cathedral than in the synagogue, and had never even attended synagogue services," he later recalled.[50]

In response to these changes, the Jewish community soon developed an autonomous and diversified cultural life beyond the previously dominant religious sphere. Educational activities, lecture series

---

[48] Ibid., 164–65.

[49] See the postcard "Worms—Der aelteste israelitische Friedhof Deutschlands—Blick auf den Dom (1016)" (Worms: Christian Herbst, 1914).

[50] Vladimir Kagan, *The Complete Vladmir Kagan: A Lifetime of Avant-Garde Design* (New York: Pointed Leaf Press, 2004), 23; see also Tanya Josefowitz, *I Remember* (London: Published by the author, 1999), 37.

sponsored by the Zionist association, local sporting events organised by the Jewish War Veterans, and chess clubs all emerged. Members of the Worms community in 1935 conducted a memorial service for Theodor Herzl; they commemorated those who died during World War I; later, they celebrated the memory of Hindenburg in August 1938.[51] It was within this emerging, segregated Jewish landscape of local associations that the Jews in Worms memorialised the 900th anniversary of their synagogue on June 3, 1934. Commemorating the German Jewish past was not limited to Worms but indicative of the CV's attempts to utilise history to assert German Jewish identity.[52] In Worms, the event's press release noted that it was hardly the time to celebrate but that the anniversary could not be passed over. Nevertheless, designated ushers, wearing white buttonhole rosettes, welcomed guests at the train station on the day of the event and led them to the decorated synagogue, which was filled with members of the community dressed in festive attire. Long before the ceremony began, guests had filled the old synagogue, so organisers broadcast the service simultaneously over loudspeakers in the adjacent Levy synagogue. Among the guests were numerous community representatives from around the country as well as Leo Baeck, the chair of the *Reichsvertretung der deutschen Juden* (national representation of German Jews).[53]

The celebration did more than summarise the synagogue's by now well-established historical traditions; it also brought together various strands of earlier constructions of the local heritage, now linking it to the merits of the ancestors. Isaak Holzer, the rabbi of the community, equated the synagogue with the burning bush in his opening speech. Citing "Put off thy shoes, for the place is holy ground" (Ex. 3:5), he

---

[51] Henry Huttenbach, "The Reconstruction and Evaluation of a Social Calendar as a Primary Source for the History of the Jewish Community of Worms (1933–1938)," *Proceedings of the Sixth World Congress of Jewish Studies* (Jerusalem: 1975), 2:367–97.

[52] Jacob Boas, "Germany or Diaspora: German Jewry's Shifting Perception in the Nazi Era (1933–1938)," Leo Baeck Institute YearBook 27 (1986), 109–26.

[53] "Die 900-Jahr-Feier in Worms. Ein Bericht und eine Betrachtung von unserem nach Worms entsandten Spezialberichterstatter Dr. M. Spitzer," *Jüdische Rundschau* 39 (June 8, 1934), 3, and "Bericht des Pressedienste der israelitschen Religionsgemeinde Worms über die Weihe-Stunde aus Anlass des 900 jährigen Bestehens der Synagoge in Worms," Stadtarchiv Worms: Abt. 203, Nr. 8.

presented the building as a sacred site that illuminated the path for other communities. In his review of Worms's Jewish past, Holzer portrayed a devout Jewish community from which God's teaching emanated; it had long served as a model and leader for others. He became almost defiant as he elaborated upon the religious devotion that had enabled the Jews of Worms to endure many challenges and even die as martyrs when necessary.[54]

It was left to Leo Baeck to transform this local anniversary into a commemoration of German Jewish history. German Jews had the desire to "commemorate in a worthy manner the past generation by looking back reverently at the century-long Jewish history in Germany," he announced. Like Holzer, Baeck wanted to draw lessons from the community's past because certainly, the site that had existed for 900 years "speaks about our German Jewish nobility." German Jewry now had to "remain noble" and overcome its disunity, which contradicted "the old spirit of Worms." Baeck then concluded that 900 years signified *Heimat* in Worms's convergence of Jewish spirit and German soil.[55]

Central to the celebration of the synagogue was the idea that the Jewish past had again taken hold among the Jews of Germany in light of the Nazis' rise to power: "We take hold of our past from a [perspective] of familiarity, which is not lectured, not deduced, but immediately verified by our experience," wrote one newspaper.[56] Along these lines, Max Grünewald of Mannheim explained in a special table talk that nothing obstructs historical memory more than history itself. As time passed and the Jews invested their hopes in a better future, the past became increasingly distant. But faith in progress and advancement, however admirable, had rendered historical documents, stones, and artefacts more and more impenetrable. The German Jews' radically

---

54 See Isaak Holzer's speech in Stadtarchiv Worms: Abt. 203, Nr. 8.
55 Leo Baeck, "Rede des Rabbiners Dr Baeck," Stadtarchiv Worms: Abt. 203, Nr. 8, and "Der Geist von Worms. Die 900-Jahrfeier der Synagoge—Eine erhebenden Weihestunde—Dr. Baecks Ansprache," *Jüdisch-liberale Zeitung* (June 8, 1934), Stadtarchiv Worms: Abt. 203, Nr. 8.
56 "Die 900-Jahr-Feier in Worms," *Israelitisches Gemeindeblatt. Offizielles Organ der Isr. Gemeinden Mannheim u. Ludwigshafen* (June 14, 1934); see also Stadtarchiv Worms: Abt. 203, Nr. 8; and "Schabbath in Worms," *Jüdische Rundschau* (September 28, 1934), 1–5.

altered situation in 1930s Germany, however, suggested new pathways to the understanding of the past and encouraged Jews to redeem their heritage. The contemporary experience of harassment and persecution made the examples of the Worms community's martyrdom much more immediate and profound, for example, stirring faith in the Jews' ability to endure: "That which we experience, they too experienced." Whereas the legends of the *Nibelungen* perhaps evoked death and downfall, Jewish legends demonstrated above all that the Jewish soul was ultimately "invulnerable and unassailable."[57]

All of the major German Jewish periodicals carried extensive articles. Through a tightly organised management of the press, Karl Guggenheim, the president of the Jewish veteran association in Worms, who acted as the press liaison, provided news agencies and periodicals with news releases that formed the base of their articles.[58] Therefore, the depiction of the celebration in newspapers was fairly uniform, even when the papers had special correspondents of their own in Worms. Most of them cited Leo Baeck's speech extensively, along with his notions of *Heimat* and German Jewish nobility.[59] Many newspapers also used the occasion as an opportunity to commission separate articles about the history of Worms's Jewish community. The CV published a special issue adorned with newly made sketches of the synagogue and the cemetery, accompanying them with a retelling of the legend of Rothenburg's Torah scroll by Henriette Mannheimer.[60] The *Zeitschrift für die Geschichte der Juden in Deutschland* published a special commemorative volume. Its authors praised the community as a "mother in Israel" from the perspective of its significance to Jews in general and German Jewry in particular. The synagogue symbolised

---

[57] Excerpts of Max Grünewald's table talk appear in his letter dated July 8, 1934, to the board of the Jewish community of Worms, Stadtarchiv Worms: Abt. 203, Nr. 8.

[58] A letter from the Centralverein to Karl Guggenheim, May 15, 1934, Stadtarchiv Worms: Abt. 203, Nr. 8 lists the various action points.

[59] "Baeck über den Geist von Worms," *Gemeindeblatt für die jüdischen Gemeinden in Rheinland und Westfalen* (June 8, 1934); "900 Jahre Synagoge Worms," *Frankfurter Israelitsches Gemeindeblatt* (June 1934); "Die 900-Jahr-Feier in Worms," *Bayerische Israelitische Gemeindezeitung* (June 15, 1934); Stadtarchiv Worms: Abt. 203, Nr. 8.

[60] "900 Jahre Synagoge Worms, 1034–1934," *C.V.-Zeitung* 13 (May 31, 1934), and "900 Jahre Wormser Synagoge," *Israelitisches Familienblatt* (May 31, 1934).

German Jews' constant presence in Germany as well as their devotion to their religion and culture, and this "great past" placed an obligation upon present-day Jews for the future.[61]

Despite the general unanimity, of course, slight differences in tone emerged in the Zionist press. The *Jüdische Rundschau* reminded its readers that the history of the Jews in Worms was full of both suffering and learning and even hinted that the community had silenced those accusers who believed that the Jews had always remained homeless. The paper then, however, went on to stress that current events were forcing German Jews to distance themselves from German society, whatever their history in that country, pointing out that the Jews of Worms would likely have disappeared if they had not remained so devoted to Judaism and its culture.[62] The neo-Orthodox press ridiculed the presence of an organ and choir in the synagogue but was impressed with Leo Baeck's speech.[63]

Beyond the extensive newspaper coverage, the celebrations garnered telegrams and other greetings from Germany and around the world. Many German Jewish communities noted that all of German Jewry shared in this celebration and took solace and pride in Worms's legacy.[64] In its congratulatory letter, the *Reichsvertretung der deutschen Juden* also emphasised that Worms's legacy implied an obligation for the future: "This celebration tells of a historical place and a historical task … that leads from an important past through the present to the future."[65] The letter also echoed the by now familiar observation that the history of the Jews in Worms proved how deeply rooted Jews were in the German lands and culture: "This building testifies to the history of Jews in

---

61 "Zum Geleit," *Zum 900jährigen Bestehen der Synagoge zu Worms. Eine Erinnerungsausgabe des Vorstandes der Israelitischen Religionsgemeinde Worms. Sonderheft der Zeitschrift für die Geschichte der Juden in Deutschland* 5 (1934), 85.

62 "Das Judengespenst. Vor 900 Jahren—und heute", *Jüdische Rundschau* 39 (June 1, 1934), 1, and "Die 900-Jahr-Feier in Worms. Ein Bericht und eine Betrachtung von unserem nach Worms entstandten Spezialberichterstatter Dr. M. Spitzer," *Jüdische Rundschau* 39 (June 8, 1934), 3.

63 "Die 900-Jahrfeier in Worms," *Der Israelit* (June 7, 1934), 11.

64 See the folder "Glückwünsche," Stadtarchiv Worms: Abt. 203, Nr. 8.

65 See the letter by the *Reichsvertretung der deutschen Juden*, May 28, 1934, to the board of the Jewish community of Worms, Stadtarchiv Worms: Abt. 203, Nr. 8.

Germany more than scrolls and books. The attachment of German Jewry to the German *Heimat* finds a symbolic expression [here]."[66]

Yet despite the recurrent invocation of belonging, the celebrations had been undeniably affected by the Nazis' seizure of power and policy of intimidation and harassment, social isolation, and economic exploitation of German Jews, including the Worms community, which numbered around 1,000 members in 1933. In their correspondence with Leo Baeck, community members feared that the celebration would bring numerous international guests to the city and thus too much attention to the community. In light of these concerns, it was decided to celebrate the occasion rather locally and only with guests from Germany proper.[67]

Already in March 1933, Isidor Kiefer had terminated his membership in the antiquity society, as had other Jewish members such as Leopold Nickelsburg, Siegfried Guggenheim, and Max Levy. One year later, Kiefer informed the Jewish community from Brussels that he had decided not to return from a trip abroad.[68]

Kiefer was not alone; in 1933, over 160 Jews left Worms, which was the highest number to depart in a single year. This figure was roughly halved in 1934 and declined to as low as 32 in 1935.[69] Isaac Holzer left that year, eventually arriving in the United States. Cognizant of the slowly diminishing community, Herta Mansbacher, who had been a teacher in the city in the early 1900s, began to record the names and dates of those who migrated abroad between 1933 and 1941. Quoting

---

[66] See the letter by the chair of the C.V. from June 2, 1934, to the council of the *Religionsgemeinschaft Württenbergs* and the letter by the chair of the Jewish community of Braunschweig from June 1, 1934, to the board of the Jewish community of Worms, Stadtarchiv Worms: Abt. 203, Nr. 8.

[67] See the letters by Karl Guggenheim to the Jewish community of Worms, February 22, 1934, to Leo Baeck, *Reichsvertretung der deutschen Juden*, from March 2, 1933, and to the *Centralverein deutschen Staatsburgers jüdisches Glaubens*, May 3, 1934, Stadtarchiv Worms: Abt. 203, Nr. 8.

[68] See the letter from Isidor Kiefer from March 20, 1933, to the *Altertumsverein* in Stadtarchiv Worms, Abt. 75/1, and Stadtarchiv Worms, Abt. 75, Anhang 1, which includes a list of the members and their resignations, and the letter from Isidor Kiefer to the *Vorstand der israel. Religionsgemeinde Worms,* September 22, 1934, Isidor Kiefer Collection at the Leo Baeck Institute, New York, AR 1894–1903, box 1.

[69] Brodhaecker, *Menschen zwischen Hoffnung und Verzweiflung,* 367.

Heinrich Heine's famous lines, penned in Paris about his German fatherland, Mansbacher wrote in the introduction to her "emigration book" that she expected these Jews to experience a nostalgic yearning for their former *Heimat*. Hopefully an awareness of their origins would help them to adjust in their new homelands.[70]

During *Kristallnacht* in November 1938, the old synagogue was set ablaze in two consecutive attacks, while many shops owned by Jews were demolished. Anti-Jewish measures and acts of violence intensified many German Jews' search to secure their migration. Despite the mounting difficulties in procuring the financial resources and entry documents to enable them to emigrate to other countries, around 170 Worms Jews emigrated between 1938 and 1939. Under the impact of the accelerating migration of Jews from Worms, Herta Mansbacher in 1937 radically changed her understanding of the process. Now she saw the migrants not as leaving their home but searching for a new *Heimat*.[71] Those who had remained were in October 1940, together with Jews from Baden, Pfalz, and Saarland, deported to Gurs.[72]

---

[70]   See Henry R. Huttenbach, *The Emigration Book of Worms: The Character and Dimension of the Jewish Exodus from a Small German Jewish Community, 1933–1941* (Koblenz: Landesarchivverwaltung Rheinland-Pfalz, 1974), 5–6.

[71]   Huttenbach, *The Emigration Book of Worms*, 6–9.

[72]   Richarz, *Jewish Life in Germany*, 424–429, and for the historical background to the deportation, see Peter Longerich, *Krieg der Vernichtung: Eine Gesamtdarstellung der nationalsozialistischen Judenverfolgung* (Munich: Piper, 1998), 282–283.

INDEX

Pincus, Lily, 88
Pinkus, Sally, 130
Pinski, David, 123, 137, 320
Pinthus, Kurt, 136
Plato, 288
Plessner, Helmuth, 197
Polgar, Alfred, 318-319
Posener, Julius, 101
Preuß, Hugo, 23, 41-42
Prussian Association of Jewish
    Communities (PLV), 260
Pucks, Stefan, 158-160
Pulzer, Peter, 18, 45

R
Rabinbach, Anson, 114
Rahden, Till van, 17, 108n196
Rathenau, Emil, 18-19, 34, 143-145, 147-156,
    165
Rathenau, Erich, 147
Rathenau, Walther, 33, 38, 55, 57, 143-144,
    146, 148-149, 156-165, 178, 192, 295
Reform, 26
Reichmann, Eva, 14, 261n6
Reichmann, Hans, 261n6
Reichstag, 36, 39, 61, 194, 212, 262
Reinhardt, Max, 132, 133
    Kammerspiele, 132
Reyzen, Abraham, 137, 320
Rieger, Paul, 209
Riesenfeld, Adolf, 87
Riesser, Gabriel, 23-25, 27-28, 30, 167
Riesser, Jakob, 34
Rilke, Rainer Maria, 168
Robinsohn, A., 322
Rosenberg, Curt, 81
Rosenfeld, Morris, 320
Rosenthal, Nora, 102
Rosenzweig, Franz, 12, 19, 200-201, 205,
    215, 220, 230, 236, 240, 242-247, 249-
    255, 280, 286, 290, 297-308, 342
    Lehrhaus, 342
    "New Thinking, The," 299
    Star of Redemption, 200-201, 240,
    255n101, 298-300, 302-303, 305-307
Rothschild, Carl Meyer, 172, 338, 342
Ruppin, Arthur, 9

S
Sallis, Margarete, 84, 101, 105
Salomon, Alice, 88
Salzberger, Georg, 342

Samter, Nathan, 55
Sasson, David, 342
Sassoon, Siegfried, 185-186
Schach, Fabius, 122, 126, 134
Scheffler, Karl, 145
Schiefler, Gustav, 144
Schiff, Arthur, 342
Schiff, Otto, 342
Schiller, Friedrich, 94
Schine, Robert S., 204
Schleiermacher, Friedrich, 200
Schmitt, Carl, 42, 183
Schnitzler, Arthur, 117
Schoenlank, Bruno, 37
Schoeps, Hans-Joachim, 272
Scholem, Gershom, 15, 19, 76, 100, 109, 111,
    117, 139, 201, 205, 206, 219, 220, 236,
    242, 245-247, 250-253, 255, 294, 316, 322
Schopenhauer, 84
Schumann, Robert, 94
Schwaner, 57
Schwartz, Frederic J., 154
Schwechten, Franz, 150
Schweitzer, Albert, 200
    Quest for the Historical Jesus, The, 200
Seeger, Karl von, 187
Segel, Binjamin, 179
Seifensieder, Jakob, 340-341
Seldte, Franz, 184
    Vor und hinter den Kulissen, 184
Seligmann, Caesar, 199, 273-275
Shammes, Juspa, 335
Shapira, Elana, 18
Sherston, George, 185
Simmel, Georg, 73, 280, 288-289, 293
Simon, Ernst, 242
Simson, Eduard, 27
Singer, Paul, 36
Social Democratic Party (SPD), 35-41, 194
Sombart, Werner, 187
Sonnemann, Leopold, 30
Sorkin, David, 45, 46, 53, 233
Spector, Mordechai, 137
Spengler, Oswald, 185, 208, 209, 240, 244,
    251
    Decline of the West, 208, 240
Spinoza, Baruch (Benedict), 84, 285, 292
Sprengel, Peter, 129, 132-133
Stahl, Friedrich Julius, 23, 28-29
Stahl, Heinrich, 277
Stampfer, Friedrich, 37
Stein, Edith, 81